Of Kith and Kin

Of Kith and Kin

A History of Families in Canada

MAGDA FAHRNI

OXFORD
UNIVERSITY PRESS

OXFORD
UNIVERSITY PRESS

Oxford University Press is a department of the University of Oxford.
It furthers the University's objective of excellence in research, scholarship,
and education by publishing worldwide. Oxford is a registered trade mark of
Oxford University Press in the UK and in certain other countries.

Published in Canada by
Oxford University Press
8 Sampson Mews, Suite 204,
Don Mills, Ontario M3C 0H5 Canada

www.oupcanada.com

Copyright © Oxford University Press Canada 2022

The moral rights of the author have been asserted

Database right Oxford University Press (maker)

All rights reserved. No part of this publication may be reproduced, stored in
a retrieval system, or transmitted, in any form or by any means, without the
prior permission in writing of Oxford University Press, or as expressly permitted
by law, by licence, or under terms agreed with the appropriate reprographics
rights organization. Enquiries concerning reproduction outside the scope of the
above should be sent to the Permissions Department at the address above
or through the following url: www.oupcanada.com/permission/permission_request.php

Every effort has been made to determine and contact copyright holders.
In the case of any omissions, the publisher will be pleased to make
suitable acknowledgement in future editions.

Library and Archives Canada Cataloguing in Publication

Title: Of kith and kin : a history of families in Canada / Magda Fahrni.
Names: Fahrni, Magda, 1970- author.
Description: Includes bibliographical references and index.
Identifiers: Canadiana (print) 20200334972 | Canadiana (ebook) 20200335057 |
ISBN 9780199012169 (softcover) | ISBN 9780190161934 (ebook)
Subjects: LCSH: Families—Canada—History.
Classification: LCC HQ559 .F34 2021 | DDC 306.850971—dc23

Cover image: Fred Taylor, "Looking Up St. Cecile Street, Montreal, 1957."
Reproduced with permission of Alan Klinkhoff Gallery, for the Estate of Frederick B. Taylor.
Photo courtesy of Cowley Abbott.

Oxford University Press is committed to our environment.
Wherever possible, our books are printed on paper which comes from responsible sources.

Printed and bound in Canada
1 2 3 4 — 24 23 22 21

*For Jake
and
for Beatrice,
with love and gratitude*

Contents

Acknowledgements ix

Introduction: The Writing of Family History in Canada 1

1. Indigenous Families and French Settler Families, 1500–1750 15

2. Families in British North America, 1750–1840 43

3. The Industrial Revolution in Canada, 1840–1889 73

4. Families and the State, 1840–1914 95

5. Two World Wars, the Great Depression, and a Mixed Social Economy of Welfare, 1914–1945 123

6. Thirty Glorious Years? Families and the Postwar Settlement, 1945–1975 157

7. Metamorphosis and Persistence: Challenging the Nuclear Family, 1975–2005 187

Conclusion: Twenty-First-Century Families 207

Notes 227

Selected Works 301

Index 331

Acknowledgements

I CONSIDER MYSELF TRULY fortunate to have been able to work with Susan Ferber of Oxford University Press: her professionalism, efficiency, and intelligent common sense make her a model editor. I thank the anonymous readers of this manuscript for their detailed comments and for the very useful suggestions that have improved this book considerably. Thanks to historian Matthew Hayday for initiating this project and to production coordinators Michelle Welsh and Lisa Ball and copy editor Jennifer McIntyre for their careful work.

I am blessed with brilliant and generous colleagues. Four of them in particular took time out of their own busy schedules to read and comment upon different chapters of this book: immense thanks go to Christopher Goscha, Andrée Lévesque, Martin Petitclerc, and Carolyn Podruchny. It goes without saying that they bear no responsibility for any limitations or shortcomings that remain.

Students at the Université du Québec à Montréal who have taken my undergraduate family history courses or who have written theses or dissertations under my supervision have stimulated my thinking about many of the topics analyzed in this book. I thank them for their curiosity and their enthusiasm. Special thanks go to Sophie Doucet, a family historian in her own right, who prepared bibliographies for me at the very beginning of this project.

For almost twenty years now, fellow members of the Montreal History Group/Groupe d'histoire de Montréal have shaped my thinking on history, politics, collegiality, and mentorship, for which I thank them. Jonathan Crago, a loyal friend of the Montreal History Group, is always a much-appreciated source of good advice.

In closing, I would like to acknowledge my own family. My parents, siblings, in-laws, nieces, and nephews are constant sources of support and encouragement. The people with whom I am lucky enough to share my home—Jake Estok and our daughter, Beatrice—make every day a delight.

Introduction
The Writing of Family History in Canada

> *"The family structure is the source of psychological, economic, and political oppression."*
> —SHULAMITH FIRESTONE, *The Dialectic of Sex: The Case for Feminist Revolution* (1970)

> *"Who is society? There is no such thing! There are individual men and women and there are families."*
> —MARGARET THATCHER, Interview for *Woman's Own* (1987)

REVILED BY SOME RADICALS and progressives, a reassuring touchstone for most conservatives, the family is, and always has been, both an institution and an idea. A concept about which some Canadians are deeply ambivalent, it is nonetheless a structure within which most of us live our lives, or at least a good part of them. Often a source of emotional sustenance and material support, families can also be sites of conflict and abuse. Families have also been, for most of Canada's history, a basic institution of society, and an institution that had formal and informal links with other institutions, among them the state, schools, churches, and professions.

This book traces the changing forms and meanings of family in the territory that now comprises Canada, from the first contacts between Indigenous peoples and French explorers, traders, missionaries, and settlers in northeastern North America in the sixteenth and seventeenth centuries to the present. It draws on the rich historiography of the family in Canada and elsewhere to provide an overview of the many, and sometimes radical, shifts in the composition and significance of family over these five centuries. These works can also help us to understand why family remains important—to individuals, certainly, but also as one of the organizing principles of twenty-first-century society. Debates about family—who is allowed to marry and for what reasons, who shall bear children and at what moment in their life, who shall adopt and what child they might adopt, who shall inherit family property—regularly make the headlines. A vehicle for the most intimate sentiments and senses of belonging, the family—or, better, families—are also eminently political, in all senses of the word. Too often, misconceptions about families in the past are used to fuel current policy and societal debates—debates about "working mothers," for instance, or about divorce, daycare, juvenile delinquency, or same-sex marriage. Understanding the variety of family forms and experiences throughout our history can help to better put the present into perspective.

While this book documents and explains these changes over time, it also explores the diversity of experiences of family within Canada in numerous historical periods. The Industrial Revolution, for instance, meant very different things to the coal-mining families of Cape Breton, the French-Canadian families heading south to the textile mills of New Hampshire, the English-Canadian families deciding which of their adolescent boys to send out to work in the furnace and stove factories of Hamilton, Ontario, or the Indigenous women, Chinese-Canadian men, and Japanese-Canadian women who worked in British Columbia's turn-of-the-twentieth-century canneries. Region, ethnicity, and race shaped families' experiences in Canada, as did social class. Age and gender made a difference *within* families. The Industrial Revolution, for example, meant different things to married men, married women, adolescent sons, unmarried daughters, and young children.[1]

This book explores the histories of Indigenous and settler families in both Quebec and English Canada—experiences too often treated in isolation—and draws on both French-language and English-language historiographies. French civil law, the social and political importance of the Catholic Church, and a marked preference for the institutionalization of family members deemed burdensome or problematic (babies born outside of marriage, orphaned or semi-orphaned children, the delinquent, the physically and mentally ill, the elderly) from the mid-nineteenth to the mid-twentieth century meant that the experiences of families in Quebec were in some ways different from those of families living in the English-Canadian provinces. This book covers a considerable sweep of time, from the sixteenth century to the present. To be sure, in a context where the human presence in North America can be traced back thousands of years, five centuries are but a drop in the bucket.[2] Yet for readers intrigued by the meanings and purposes attributed to families, a study of their evolution in northern North America from the sixteenth century to the present day provides a relatively long-term perspective on the transformations experienced by both Indigenous and settler families. Finally, in every chapter of this book, families are situated in relationship to the evolution of the state and the various nations to be found within this country. In this book, as in life, the private and the public are intertwined. Indeed, the borders between what constitutes "family history" and what constitutes social or political history more generally are porous and frequently artificial. Families have always evolved within the larger world and have always been affected, sometimes tragically or irrevocably, by decisions made by local and national governments or in boardrooms on Bay Street or Wall Street. Newspaper headlines and the Internet remind us that a worldwide refugee crisis is tearing apart families around the globe; here in North America, migrant children separated from their parents are being interned along the border that separates the United States from Mexico. All history includes family histories; conversely, families provide us with a fascinating lens through which to view and understand the collective choices made by the state and by civil society.

Most people, if asked, would have no difficulty coming up with a definition of the family. Chances are that that definition would be both basic and relatively traditional: some variation on the theme of a mother and a father, probably legally married, and their biological children. Yet in the past, as today, families are far more complex than this simple definition. Throughout Canada's history, there have been families large and small; parents legally married and not; families reconstituted after death, divorce, or separation; children born to couples or single persons, sometimes with medical assistance, or adopted, legally or informally; parents of different sexes and, more recently, of the same sex. Some families have been happy, sources of tangible support and emotional nourishment. Others have been deeply unhappy, the locus of physical and emotional abuse.

This book takes as its most basic starting point the Canadian Census's current definition of a "census family," that is:

> . . . a married couple and the children, if any, of either and/or both spouses; a couple living common law and the children, if any, of either and/or both partners; or a lone parent of any marital status with at least one child living in the same dwelling and that child or those

children. All members of a particular census family live in the same dwelling. A couple may be of opposite or same sex. Children may be children by birth, marriage, common-law union or adoption regardless of their age or marital status as long as they live in the dwelling and do not have their own married spouse, common-law partner or child living in the dwelling. Grandchildren living with their grandparent(s) but with no parents present also constitute a census family.[3]

This relatively expansive definition acknowledges the variety and complexity of families living in Canada today. However, its focus on the residential unit obscures the important material and emotional roles often played by extended family and kinship networks, or even by immediate family members living outside the household. This book is intended to expose readers to the diversity of families in the past and to explore the different forms that these families took, as well as the different meanings they had for those who lived within their confines. While the Canadian state has frequently tried to shape families through legislation and judicial decisions, it has also been obliged to recognize and adapt to the multiple kinds of families that have been formed by those living within its borders.

Family history, as a field of research and teaching, has flourished internationally since the 1960s, and in Canada since the 1970s. Initial research into the history of the family was inspired in large part by questions of a demographic nature. At what age did people marry? Was this age different for men and for women? Was it different for members of the aristocracy, those belonging to the bourgeoisie, or members of the popular classes? Did people have sex outside of marriage? Did most women survive childbirth? How many babies lived past their first birthday? How big were families in the past? Did couples practise some form of birth control in the past? Precisely how did they control the size of their families and, more importantly perhaps, why? How long did people live? Did the poor live as long as the rich? Did men live as long as women?

The work of historian Peter Laslett, who used statistical analysis in order to understand some basic facts of life among ordinary people in preindustrial England, served as a model for a number of pioneering historians of Canadian families.[4] The influence of the European *Annales* school of history, which focused on social history and on long-term structural change, combined with the availability of computers that made possible the elaboration of statistical databases, also spurred on research in Canadian family history in the 1970s. The important work of Hubert Charbonneau and other demographers over the past fifty years in putting together the *Programme de recherche en démographie historique* at the Université de Montréal has made available huge sets of data regarding the population of New France and early Quebec, drawn from the colony's meticulously kept and preserved parish records.[5]

Other early historians of the family were more interested in what scholars called family "sentiments." Did husbands and wives love one another in the past? What did love mean in the past? Did parents love their children? Or were they reserved and distant? Was the authority of parents absolute? In a context where families were large and infant mortality rates were catastrophic, did parents mourn children who died young, or were they resigned and fatalistic in the face of this very real possibility?[6]

Beginning in the early 1980s, historians influenced by Marxist theory tried to understand the impact of the Industrial Revolution on the family. Were families uprooted by the Industrial Revolution, removed from familiar life ways and rural traditions and plunged into the isolated, atomistic, alienated world of industrialized cities, struggling to survive without the help of kin networks and preindustrial institutions, such as churches, town hall meetings, or communal work "bees" undertaken to carry out tasks such as barn-raising and quilt-making? Or did family and kin survive in the working-class neighbourhoods of these industrial cities, continuing to provide material and emotional support amid changing economic circumstances and transformed relations to the means of production?[7] Studies of families in western metropolises have generally concluded that families were not torn apart by industrialization, but remained important economic units, as well as important sources of help that was more difficult to quantify, such as emotional support and unpaid care.[8]

Historians have asked similar questions about the impact of migration upon families. Both immigration and emigration have been key processes in the structuring of Canada, a settler society that regularly received new influxes of population, but that also lost people, especially to the neighbouring United States. Internal migrations—movements of population within the country—have also been important in Canada, whether migrations from the countryside to the city or from cities to newly opened regions of colonization. Depending on the time and place, much of this migration was familial. In nineteenth- and early twentieth-century Quebec, many rural families left for

New England, where almost all members of the family (married men, married women, and adolescents of both sexes) could secure jobs in the region's booming textile mills and shoe and boot factories. In the wake of the Second World War, families, or what remained of them, left the war-ravaged countries and Displaced Persons camps of Europe for reasons that were both political and economic, in order to begin new lives in Canada. Even when migration appears at first glance to concern only individuals (male "sojourners" or female domestic servants, for instance), closer study reveals that these individuals left families behind them and often intended either to return to them or to bring them to Canada. Many fascinating studies of migration have thus explored the links between the people who migrated to Canada and the family members they left in their country of origin, links that were both reinforced and made tangible by family correspondence.[9] Early works in American migration history often emphasized the "uprooted" nature of immigrant families, torn from familiar places and customs and unaccustomed to North American ways of life. In response, a subsequent generation of historians insisted on the "transplanted" nature of these same families, emphasizing their ability to exercise agency and the ways in which they actively adapted to life in their new society.[10] Recent work has examined the ties maintained between these newcomers and the worlds that they had left behind (and might one day return to), ties that took the form of letters, parcels, and cash remittances, and that were manifested in visits and in recurrent departures and returns.[11]

Studies of migrant families focus on the practice of chain migration, whether from rural Molise, in Italy, to downtown Toronto, from South China's Guangdong Province to Vancouver's Chinatown(s), or from the Canadian countryside to the city.[12] Studies also reveal how, despite the changes wrought by migration, family ties from "back home" remain important. Researchers have discovered that, among nineteenth-century rural migrants, for instance, kin from the same village acted as godfathers or godmothers to new babies born in the city.[13] While family life in the city could be very different from family life on the farm, rural habits and practices often persisted in urban areas.[14] Some recent studies adopt a transnational perspective, analyzing family migration on scales much larger than that of the single nation-state.[15]

A significant branch of Canadian family history, influenced by feminist analyses of the family honed in the women's liberation movements of the 1960s and 1970s, has focused on the paid and unpaid work of mothers, alongside the prescriptions to which they were subjected. Advice for mothers came from the state, from charitable associations, from doctors and those who belonged to what are sometimes called the "helping professions" (nurses, social workers, psychologists), and, of course, from other mothers. Was this advice imposed upon mothers, or did they seek it out? Did they always follow this counsel or did they sometimes defy doctors, nurses, and social workers? When was and when wasn't motherhood considered something that was "natural"?[16] Far less is known about expectations held of fathers in the past or about how fathers acted as fathers, concretely, in the Canadian past. Recent studies, however, have gone some way to helping readers to uncover particular aspects of fatherhood in the nineteenth and twentieth centuries, notably the ways in which fathers confronted the financial and psychological challenges posed by the Great Depression, along with the roles of fathers as family breadwinners and consumers in the decades following the Second World War.[17]

For the past few decades, but especially since the end of the twentieth century, children have also been the objects of particular attention on the part of historians. Scholars have sought to understand whether all children worked in the past and if so, what kind of work they did. They have tried to determine the ways in which their lives on the farm differed from lives in the city. When did children begin going to school in large numbers? Did they attend regularly? Did boys and girls have equal access to instruction? Did children have formal rights in the past? Where was the boundary between childhood and adolescence, and did this boundary shift over time? When was the notion of the "teenager" invented? How should we understand formal, often live-in institutions that were created for children, such as orphanages, crèches, day cares, boarding schools, reform schools, and industrial and residential schools for Indigenous children? Were they institutions that protected children and adolescents, or that sought to control or punish them?[18] And what about associations that targeted youth, such as 4-H Clubs, Girl Guides, Boy Scouts, the Canadian Girls-in-Training, Catholic youth movements, summer camps, or sports teams?[19] How did girls learn to become women and boys to become men?[20] How did adolescents strive to conform to, or else defy, gendered norms of body image and attractiveness?[21] How did they understand and negotiate sexuality, whether consensual or coercive?[22] It is clear that in all regions of Canada, children's work, both paid and unpaid, remained important for rural families, as it did for working-class families in cities and towns, well into the twentieth century.[23] It is also clear that, as children acquired more social rights over the course of the late nineteenth and twentieth centuries (compulsory schooling, restrictions on child labour, and family allowances, for example), a new vision of childhood gradually developed that insisted upon children as people to be protected and dependent—upon their parents, but also upon the state.[24] Over the same period, children, and then teenagers, became increasingly perceived as small consumers—markets to be exploited by department stores, cinemas, fast food chains, and purveyors of toys, clothing, comic books, and records.[25]

Studies of family violence in its various forms (wife battering, the corporal punishment of children, neglect, incest) serve as forcible reminders of the power imbalances within every family, inequities shaped in large part by gender and by age. While historians have uncovered remarkable instances of agency exercised by those who suffered such violence, their work also serves as a reminder of just how vulnerable children, especially, were and are in most societies. They also reveal the roles played by neighbours, churches, and private associations such as the Montreal Society for the Protection of Women and Children in denouncing domestic violence and providing some assistance to its victims.[26] Recently, in a context where the Canadian population is aging, scholars have turned their attention to the phenomenon known as "elder abuse," that is, the physical mistreatment or neglect of older people.[27]

Indeed, historians of Canada have begun to study the stage of the life cycle typically called "old age." How old did one have to be to be considered "old" in the past? How did people too old to work earn their keep in the days before old-age pensions existed? When did the federal and provincial governments decide to establish old-age pensions and why? What did it mean to be an elderly widow or widower in the past?[28] Recent work on "singleness" has underscored the fact that unmarried adults have often been key sources of both financial support and unwaged labour for their elderly parents.[29] The elderly without children of their own—or whose children were unable or unwilling to care for them—have frequently been housed in charitable institutions, in public long-term care, or in commercial, for-profit "old folks' homes."[30] Recent studies have made clear, however, the extent to which retired and elderly people continued to exercise agency well into old age, writing to their governments to demand better pensions, for example.[31]

Much of the work in family history in Canada has analyzed interactions between families and other institutions, notably the state, churches, and schools. How did the state—whether government or judiciary—conceive of families? At what moments did the state consider the needs of families? When did the federal and provincial levels of the state begin to provide for families, or at least some kinds of families, or at least some of their members? Did families resent this state intervention? Did they see it as intrusive and nosy? Or did they welcome state aid, even actively seek it out?[32] Did parents want to send their children to school and agree with compulsory schooling legislation? Did they do so regularly? If not, why not? Did children feel torn between their own desire to be in school and their awareness of their parents' need for their paid or unpaid labour?[33] To whom did the courts attribute children in the case of the divorce or legal separation of their parents?[34] Family historians have also studied the creation and influence of so-called family experts, especially public health doctors, nurses, social workers, psychologists, and psychiatrists. Often of genuine help to families in need or in distress, most of these experts nonetheless had clear and sometimes rigid ideas of what constituted "normal" families, and much of their work involved doling out encouragement, and sometimes exercising coercion, so that men, women, and children would conform to dominant gendered roles and ideas of proper motherhood and responsible fatherhood and would act as dutiful daughters and stalwart sons.[35]

Among the families who most frequently experienced the coercive dimensions of the Canadian state and its allied experts were Indigenous (First Nations, Inuit, and Métis) families.[36] Colonialism has profoundly shaped the lives of Indigenous families. Historians, archaeologists, and ethnographers have studied the ways in which Catholic missionaries, such as the Jesuits, the Recollects, and the Ursulines, deeply destabilized by the gendered and family relations they encountered in seventeenth-century North America, sought to modify familial practices and contain the sexuality of women, in particular, among the Indigenous peoples of the northeastern part of the continent. They have also explored Indigenous resistance to these "civilising" campaigns.[37] Scholars have examined attempts by Catholic and Protestant clergy to instill European morals and values in Indigenous children, through boarding schools, day schools and, from the late nineteenth century onward, residential schools across Canada.[38] And they have brought to light state practices that constrained Indigenous families' ability to earn a living through the nineteenth and twentieth centuries and that forcibly encouraged particular kinds of familial and sexual relationships.[39] Historians and other scholars have also studied the Métis, the "new nation" that grew out of the Northwest fur trade and the Plains buffalo-hunting economy, and have highlighted the roles played by Indigenous women and Métis families in eighteenth- and nineteenth-century fur trade economies.[40] Much recent work has examined the centrality of kinship networks and what historian Nicole St-Onge calls "kinscapes" among Métis families and communities in the Red River Settlement and across the northern Great Plains. Historian Brenda Macdougall argues, in fact, that family "is the organizing principle of aboriginal societies."[41] Furthermore, a number of important studies explore the history of the multi-ethnic (French-Anishinaabe, in particular) fur-trade families rooted in the Great Lakes basin.[42]

Recent scholarship also scrutinizes the role played by Canadian governments in intervening in Indigenous families. Historians have examined what has come to be known as the "Sixties Scoop"—that is, the adoption of Indigenous children by non-Indigenous Canadians in the 1960s, 1970s, and early 1980s.[43] In the early twenty-first century, testimony before the Truth and Reconciliation Commission of Canada forced many non-Indigenous Canadians to confront some of the consequences of settler colonialism, in particular the long shadow of residential schooling, an institution that tore Indigenous children away from their families and whose legacy continues to have an impact upon Indigenous families a half-century after most were closed.[44] This testimony also underlined the fact that, in many Canadian provinces in the early twenty-first century, Indigenous children are disproportionately likely to be removed from their families and taken into state care.[45]

Innovative studies in the history of sexuality have also contributed immensely to understandings of Canadian family history. Heterosexuality, of course, was always an implicit object of study in works that examined courtship and marriage, but more recent scholarship has explicitly interrogated the meanings of heterosexuality and their transformations over time.[46] Historians have demonstrated the ways in which, for both the state and members of certain professions (educators, psychologists, psychiatrists, criminologists), heterosexuality was a project to be encouraged, achieved, and enforced. They have also uncovered efforts by these same historical actors to marginalize and discipline same-sex practices and communities.[47] Histories of LGBTQ+ communities and Two-Spirit people across twentieth-century Canada prove that attempts at marginalization and suppression always encountered resistance and were markedly less successful from the late 1960s on.[48] Indeed, the famous Omnibus Bill introduced by the federal Liberals in late 1967, which partially decriminalized same-sex relations between consenting adults, was an acknowledgment of the fact that the law was out of step with lived experiences in Canada.

The concept of "chosen families," popularized by American anthropologist Kath Weston, was first used to describe the kinship networks of close friends created by members of LGBTQ+ communities, networks maintained in addition to relationships sustained with biological family and sometimes more durable than the latter, particularly in cases where relations with biological family members were strained or disrupted. The idea of chosen families thus goes beyond ties of either blood or marriage and stresses the constructed nature of kinship.[49] Influenced by campaigns to legalize same-sex marriage in various North American and European jurisdictions, including Canada, scholars have also explored early debates within gay and lesbian communities around the interest or necessity of marriage. While some members of LGBTQ+ communities criticized the late-twentieth-century marriage equality movement as a conservative quest for acceptability, rooted in domesticity, consumption, and the privatization of sexuality, historians have uncovered examples of gay or lesbian couples who, in the decades following the Second World War, sought to marry as an expression of what scholars have called "love-politics," namely, "a radical assertion of self-love and queer dignity."[50]

Finally, some of the most exciting family history written in Canada in recent years has adopted a transnational lens. Some of this work compares particular dimensions of family life in Canada to those in other countries such as the United States.[51] Other studies examine phenomena and people that spanned national boundaries.[52] Cross-border adoption is one such phenomenon; it calls into question what makes any family history "Canadian" as such. Adoption in general serves as an explicit reminder that families are complex and that biology is only one part of the story. Adoption has a long history in Canada, but until the early twentieth century, adoptions were informal and usually relatively local affairs, sorted out among kin and neighbours, sometimes administered by churches or private charities. By the end of the 1920s, most Canadian provinces had passed legislation setting out formal conditions for the adoption of children. Quite often, these laws severed all ties between the child's birth family and his or her adoptive family, erasing the past and creating, in a sense, an instant "second" family.[53] Transnational adoptions laid bare, even more explicitly than local adoptions, the political economy of such exchanges, poorer countries and regions sending "their" children to wealthier ones.[54] Yet the phenomenon known as the "Sixties Scoop" makes painfully obvious the relationships of power inherent in many adoptions that took place within Canadian borders.

It is not always easy to define what makes a particular history "family" history. As historian Cynthia Comacchio writes, "There is, ultimately, very little historical space that 'family' does not impinge upon."[55] Much very good history is family history without explicitly naming itself as such.[56] Family history, however, must absolutely be distinguished from genealogy. Rather than looking for their own ancestors (preferably illustrious ones) in an attempt to give themselves "roots," most academic historians of the family are concerned with thinking critically about families in the past, in the sense of interrogating their forms and their purposes, along with their habits, their practices, and what they passed down through the generations.[57] Family historians have, however, often borrowed the tools and, especially, the rich databases of genealogists in order to reconstruct and flesh out the histories that they write.[58]

※ ※ ※

Historians remain, at least to a certain extent, at the mercy of their sources. Traces of family life in the past have been bequeathed by the winds of fortune, helped along by happenstance, historically conscious grandchildren, conscientious archivists, and local history societies.

Records that lend themselves to demographic analysis remain crucial for practising historians, notably parish records of births, baptisms, marriages, and deaths—especially rich sources for Catholic families—and statistical records such as censuses, established and taken with some regularity by an expanding state from the mid-nineteenth century on. Censuses allow historians to put together demographic snapshots, roughly every ten years, to trace specific individuals or families over time, and to compare Canadian locales at particular moments in time. What historians of France call "les écrits du for privé" are also of critical interest to family historians: correspondence and diaries, especially, but also photograph albums, baby books, scrapbooks, and cookbooks. The diaries and correspondence to which historians have access tend to be those of elite families, or at least of literate families with the means and leisure in which to write.[59] In a white settler society such as Canada, those who considered themselves to be—or were considered by others to be—"pioneers" are also overrepresented among those whose diaries have been preserved.[60] Yet even the diaries of ordinary people, preoccupied with daily routines, have much to say about family life.[61] This is also the case for correspondence among family members. Extensive correspondence was evidently the preserve of those who were literate, but also of those who were separated from family members for long periods of time: the correspondence of migrant Canadians has provided glimpses of the intimate lives of non-elite members of society.[62] Written retrospectively, life writings such as memoirs and autobiographies are sources that can also be very useful for historians of the family.[63]

Seemingly less intimate sources also have much to reveal about family life. Many historians of the family have used notarial records in order to understand family structure, inheritance practices, wives' rights within marriages, or the arrangements taken by families to protect themselves against embarrassing family members who might run down family fortunes or tarnish the family name through drunkenness, bankruptcy, and other habits judged disreputable.[64] Prescriptive literature, such as etiquette manuals, advice columns, or counsel published in popular media by psychologists and other professionals, can give some sense of the expectations that were placed upon wives, husbands, mothers, fathers, and children. Advertisements, whether in print media such as newspapers or magazines or on the radio or television, convey a sense of the norms governing family roles in any given period. The advice literature produced by the state—often by ministries concerned with health and welfare—gave explicit instructions to parents (usually mothers) and often provided clear counsel as to how funds originating from the state ought to be spent.[65] State-endorsed school textbooks likewise provided models of good girls and boys, and of mothers and fathers.[66] Iconographic sources and material culture—such as portraits, photographs, architectural plans of houses, textiles, and clothing patterns—give some sense of idealized notions of family, but can also provide real insight into daily life in the past.[67]

Ever since Neil Sutherland first wrote, in the 1990s, about the benefits of listening to "the winds of childhood," many historians of youth have chosen to engage in oral history, resulting in rich histories of Canadian childhood.[68] Historians interested in the lives of ordinary women, both married and single, who have left few written records to posterity, have also opted for oral history.[69] Like all other historical methods and primary sources, oral history must of course be practised critically.[70] But social historians, including historians of the family, are accustomed to reading sources "against the grain," that is, reading official documents in theory only marginally concerned with family life for what they might reveal about the experiences and expectations of families or of some of their members. While historians often experience starts of recognition when reading historical documents, they cannot assume that the emotions and sentiments felt by individuals in the past necessarily resemble those of the twenty-first century.[71]

Although social historians "listen" carefully to their sources, they also read them through twenty-first century lenses. And they bring to bear upon these sources questions and concepts anchored in the historical discipline. Among the most frequent concepts employed as categories of analysis by historians of Canadian families are gender, age, class, religion, race, ethnicity, language, and region. As this book demonstrates, such factors made a difference to the ways in which people experienced their own families and perceived the families of others.

There is still much unknown about families in Canada. Topics that have begun to awaken interest in other national contexts have barely been touched in the Canadian context: relations among siblings, for instance, or the role played by grandparents, especially as life expectancy has increased and mandatory retirement policies and old-age pensions have been implemented.[72] Relatively little is known about families in rural Canada over the course of the twentieth century and about the daily lives of migrant families who settled in Canada from the 1960s on. Moreover, although the Canadian historiography of the family is clearly well developed, there are few syntheses such as this book, which draws on the wealth of published material by historians and those working in related disciplines to offer a comprehensive analysis of the evolution of families living in the territory that is now Canada over the course of some five centuries.[73]

I

Indigenous Families and French Settler Families, 1500–1750

INDIGENOUS PEOPLES LIVED in the territory that now comprises Canada for thousands of years before Europeans arrived in the northeastern part of North America in any significant numbers. An Indigenous presence along the Saint Lawrence River—the principal waterway of northeastern North America—can be traced back some 9,000 years.[1] Contact between the Indigenous peoples of North America and the people who arrived from Europe (explorers, fur traders, missionaries, and settlers) was a prolonged and uneven process that took place at various moments and in different ways across the continent. On the northern Great Plains, for example, the first contacts between Indigenous peoples and Europeans happened over the course of the seventeenth and eighteenth centuries. In the Pacific Northwest, these first encounters took place as late as the eighteenth century.[2] As historian Michael Witgen argues, "the reality of European conquest varied."[3] Some Indigenous peoples experienced the impact of the Europeans' arrival through the acquisition of trade goods such as brass kettles and knives, or through the spread of communicable disease, before even meeting the newcomers.[4]

This chapter explores what is known about Indigenous families in northeastern North America during the era in which they first encountered European migrants, that is, the sixteenth and seventeenth centuries. Written sources that purported to describe Indigenous families multiplied during these years. In addition to learning from Indigenous oral tradition, iconography, and archaeological evidence, historians can study the impressions noted, preserved, and transmitted by European explorers and Catholic missionaries,

FIGURE 1.1 Brass kettles used by the Indigenous peoples of the Eastern Woodlands, especially women, in the seventeenth century. Likely secured through trade with Europeans. McCord Museum, Montreal. M10942.

groups of people motivated, as Mohawk scholar Audra Simpson remarks, by "a need to describe the difference that was found in new places."[5] European descriptions of Indigenous families must be examined critically: the observations made by the authors of these texts were conditioned by their particular reasons for finding themselves on North American soil and, more often than not, lacked the knowledge of the larger context necessary to understand that which they thought they were observing.

Indigenous Families in Northeastern North America

Recent work on Indigenous peoples in sixteenth- and seventeenth-century North America insists upon the importance of kinship networks as the linchpin that connected Indigenous peoples over vast expanses of space. Kinship was absolutely central in Indigenous societies: kinship networks and clans structured marriage networks and political alliances, settlement patterns, the occupation of land, and access to local resources. The existence of family networks also made travelling over long distances much easier.[6] North American Indigenous peoples were highly mobile in this period: this mobility could take the form of seasonal movements, but also of periodic relocations, expansion, aggregations, dispersals, or displacements. Both the Haudenosaunee and the Wendat, for instance, moved their villages every 10 to 30 years in search of more fertile agricultural land.[7] Among agricultural peoples like the Haudenosaunee and the Wendat, villages were organized around extended families, or what some have called "clan segments."[8] Among Anishinaabe peoples, hunter-gatherers who practised seasonal movements, "real and socially constructed kinship established through trade, ritual, language, and intermarriage crisscrossed over a vast space connecting peoples to one another, but not in such a way that territory could be considered a bounded space."[9] The ties between kinship and land were made clear through the regular integration of new members into Indigenous family networks through adoption or capture during warfare.[10] As historian Susan M. Hill demonstrates, the integration of refugees or captives into the clan often meant the expansion of Haudenosaunee territory. In the seventeenth century, Hill notes, "territorial gains were important factors in the Haudenosaunee adoption of Mahicans, Hurons, Eries, Tobacco, and Neutrals, to name but a few." These gains were significant because land and territory, Hill argues, were "the prime determinants of Haudenosaunee identity."[11]

Among the first Indigenous groups to encounter new European arrivals in the sixteenth and seventeenth centuries were the Mi'kmaq who lived near the Baie des Chaleurs in the Gulf of Saint Lawrence, on the Atlantic coast, and the Innu residing on the north shore of the Saint Lawrence River. The Mi'kmaq and Innu had probably been meeting fishing peoples and whalers for generations, as Europeans (from Brittany, Normandy, the Basque country, Spain, and Portugal) in search of cod and whales sojourned on the Atlantic coast of North America seasonally for short periods of time. Although European boats were moored in the coves of Newfoundland during the summer fishing season, migratory cod fishermen had little contact with the Indigenous peoples of Newfoundland, the Algonquian-speaking Beothuk.[12] In the Saint Lawrence Valley and the lower Great Lakes region, the Laurentian Iroquoians, the Wendat, and the Anishinaabeg all came into contact with European explorers, fur traders, missionaries, and, eventually, French soldiers and settlers. The Haudenosaunee peoples, who lived south of Lake Ontario and in what is now the Mohawk Valley region in New York State, along with their members who migrated to the northernmost part of their hunting grounds in the seventeenth century, near what became the communities of Kahnawà:ke, Kanehsatà:ke and Ahkwesáhsne, also had frequent and prolonged contact with European migrants.[13] As the fur trade developed over the course of the seventeenth and eighteenth centuries, fuelled by the European desire for beaver pelts in order to make the hats then fashionable in elite European circles, Anishinaabe families in the upper Great Lakes region and the western interior—what French fur traders called the *Pays d'en haut*—regularly interacted with newly or recently arrived Europeans, both French and British.

Scholars who have drawn on Indigenous oral traditions, iconography, and material culture have been able to paint more complex portraits of Indigenous families than those recorded by European observers.[14] The French explorers who arrived in northeastern North America in the sixteenth and seventeenth centuries in order to claim territory for their sovereign were keen to establish trading relationships with Indigenous peoples, but were also alert to the possibility of converting their trading partners to Christianity. Their descriptions of Indigenous peoples, written for a European readership, reflect their twin preoccupations: trade and religious conversion. When explorer Jacques Cartier, a navigator from Saint-Malo, on the coast of Brittany, made his famous first trip to what would become Canada at the behest of the French Crown, in 1534, he encountered members of the Mi'kmaq nation near the Baie des Chaleurs and then Laurentian Iroquoians, probably from Stadacona (the site of today's Quebec City), fishing for mackerel on the Gaspé Peninsula. Of his encounter with the Mi'kmaq, Cartier wrote:

> And so much at ease did [they] feel in our presence, that at length we bartered with them, hand to hand, for everything they possessed, so that nothing was left to them but their naked bodies; for they offered us everything they owned, which was, all told, of little value. We perceived that they are people who would be easy to convert, who go from place to place maintaining themselves and catching fish in the fishing season for food.[15]

While descriptions such as this one sometimes include useful details (what people ate, how they procured and prepared food), they must be interpreted cautiously. As anthropologist Audra Simpson makes clear, Europeans newly arrived in North America were fascinated by what they perceived to be the fundamental strangeness of Indigenous peoples. Yet they were also eager to point out what they viewed as similarities with European habits, or parallels with customs that explorers and adventurers had noted in other parts of the world. This "form of knowledge production sought to make the indigenous people of North America legible to the peoples of Europe," notes historian Michael Witgen.[16] Of the Laurentian Iroquoians that

Cartier and his crew encountered on the Gaspé Peninsula, the French explorer wrote, for example:

> We saw a large quantity of mackerel which they had caught near the shore with the nets they use for fishing, which are made of hemp thread, that grows in the country where they ordinarily reside; for they only come down to the sea in the fishing-season, as I have been given to understand. Here likewise grows Indian corn like pease, the same as in Brazil, which they eat in place of bread, and of this they had a large quantity with them.... Furthermore they have plums which they dry for the winter as we do, and these they call, *honnesta*; also figs, nuts, pears, apples and other fruits, and beans which they call, *sahé*.[17]

The Catholic missionaries, male and female, who landed in North America after the turn of the seventeenth century were particularly concerned with Indigenous family forms and practices. Many of these missionaries lived out their entire lives in the French colony that came to be known as New France. Inspired by the mysticism and zeal of Europe's Counter-Reformation, missionaries such as the Jesuits, the Recollects, and the Ursulines were profoundly devout and prepared to withstand the three-month-long ocean voyage and the physical hardships of life in seventeenth-century Canada in the hope of convincing Indigenous peoples to adhere to the word of God.[18] As Carolyn Podruchny and Kathryn Magee Labelle argue, Jesuit priests such as Jean de Brébeuf, erudite, polyglot, and highly educated, were possessed of a "double vision": that of ethnographers, eager to document all that they observed, but also that of men of the cloth, quick to denounce practices that they saw as contravening Christian teachings.[19] The *Jesuit Relations*, long, exhaustive accounts of the Catholic mission in the part of the world that Europeans would come to call "New France," thus insist upon the aspects of Indigenous family life that these male Catholic missionaries, all of whom had taken a vow of chastity, found profoundly destabilizing. These aspects included overt expressions of sexuality, or the autonomy of women and children within the family, in defiance of the authority of the husband and father considered normal by most Europeans.[20] Like the Jesuits, Recollect friar Gabriel Sagard insisted upon Wendat women's sexual autonomy, claiming, in words that need to be parsed and carefully pondered, that "after nightfall the young women and girls run about from one lodge to another, as do the young men for their part on the same quest, possessing them wherever it seems good to them, yet without any violence, leaving all to the wishes of the woman."[21]

Missionaries also contended that a form of divorce was a common practice. Brother Sagard declared that among the Wendat in the seventeenth century, "if in course of time husband and wife like to separate for any reason whatever, or have no children, they are free to part."[22] Father Paul Le Jeune, Superior of the Jesuit Mission at Quebec for many years, likewise wrote, "The young people do not think that they can persevere in the state of matrimony with a bad wife or a bad husband. They wish to be free and to be able to divorce the consort if they do not love each other."[23]

Jesuit attempts at religious conversion were accompanied by efforts to implement masculine authority, feminine sexual fidelity, and family structures that resembled those prevailing in the European communities with which these elite and celibate men were familiar.[24] Missionaries were thus quick to pounce upon examples of what they perceived to be their beneficial influence upon Indigenous families, such as female chastity, or wifely obedience. Hence, they celebrated the young Mohawk woman, Kateri Tekakwitha, converted to Christianity by the Jesuits. That Tekakwitha chose to eschew sexual relations was seen as proof of her own virtue, but especially of the Jesuits' success in proselytizing.[25]

European commentators, both male missionaries and religious sisters such as the Ursulines who arrived in New France in the 1630s, remarked upon what they saw as the permissive nature of Indigenous parenting, in contrast to what they believed to be European forms of parenting in the same era. Recollect friar Gabriel Sagard insisted upon the love and affection shown by Wendat parents to their children.[26] Father Paul Le Jeune, writing of the Innu, commented upon what he perceived to be "the excessive love [they] bear their children."[27] The physical punishment of children appears to have been largely unknown in these Indigenous communities; children who misbehaved were reprimanded by shaming techniques and by exclusion from group activities. Indigenous mothers reportedly perceived French mothers as cold and distant from their children, allegedly likening them to "porcupines."[28] Indigenous children, in contrast, were never far from their families, accompanying them on fishing expeditions and on trips to the forest, helping with tasks such as gathering nuts and berries. According to Wendat historian Georges Sioui, "children were taught good behaviour by having their attention called to exemplary actions, as they were taught the consequences of unacceptable behaviour. They acquired the ability to hunt, fish, plant gardens, and master other vital skills by direct participation."[29]

Some of what historians know about Indigenous children in New France in this period comes from sources created by the Jesuits who taught

Indigenous boys at their Quebec seminary or from the Ursuline nuns who were in contact with Indigenous girls. Over the second third of the seventeenth century, the Ursuline sisters instructed Indigenous girls ranging from the age of five to the age of twelve in reading, writing, catechism, prayers, and Catholic teachings more generally. They also taught them domestic skills that would have been useful to European peasant girls, such as sewing and embroidery. The religious, moral, and domestic instruction of young Indigenous girls and boys was undertaken in the hope that the children—disciplined, fixed in one place, Europeanized, and converted to Catholicism—would then influence their parents and other adults in their communities.[30] The Ursulines taught Indigenous girls separately from the daughters of French settlers, in part for linguistic reasons: Ursuline sisters learned Anishinaabe, Wendat, Innu, and Haudenosaunee languages and attempted to teach Indigenous girls in these languages rather than in French, so as to more effectively transmit their messages. They also relied a great deal on the use of images, particularly for religious instruction. Some Indigenous pupils boarded at the Ursuline convent; the sisters fed these girls and replaced their clothes with red serge dresses sewn by the nuns and by friends of the community. Some of these girls had been brought to the Ursuline convent by their parents out of a hunger-induced desperation, in the hope that their daughters would at least be well fed by the sisters.[31] Other Indigenous girls were day-pupils ("externes") who returned to their families every evening. The separations imposed by the practice of boarding young Indigenous children at the Jesuit seminary or the Ursuline convent in Quebec City were clearly extremely difficult for both Indigenous children and their parents. Some children were reported to be melancholy or ill; many died in these institutions. Parents often removed their children from these institutions when they could; others refused to hand their children over to these religious communities in the first place. Some children, boarders at the Ursuline convent, took the initiative to jump the fence and run away "like squirrels," Ursuline Mother Marie de l'Incarnation wrote in 1668.[32] The tragedy of these separations can be glimpsed in the *Jesuit Relations* of the 1640s, in between glowing accounts of the successful Ursuline schooling—and conversion—of young Wendat and Anishinaabe girls.[33]

The active resistance of many Indigenous pupils and their parents to the Ursuline sisters' colonizing project is clearly visible in these sources. The thousands of letters written by Marie de l'Incarnation, mother superior of the Ursuline convent at Quebec, are particularly revealing. Widowed at the age of twenty, Marie de l'Incarnation (Marie Guyart) left her young son behind in Tours, France, in order to pursue the Catholic mission in Canada. By 1668, almost thirty years after arriving in New France, she seemed convinced that, although efforts at conversion might prove successful, attempts to Europeanize Indigenous children were fraught with difficulties, perhaps even futile. "It is a very difficult thing, not to say impossible," the Ursuline mother superior wrote to her son,

> ... to make the little [girls] French or civilized. We have more experience of this than anyone else, and we have observed that of a hundred that have passed through our hands we have scarcely civilized one. We find docility and intelligence in these girls but, when we are least expecting it, they clamber over our wall and go off to run with their kinsmen in the woods, finding more to please them there than in all the amenities of our French houses.
>
> Such is the[ir] nature ...; they cannot be restrained and, if they are, they become melancholy and their melancholy makes them sick. Moreover, the [parents] are extraordinarily fond of their children and, when they know they are sad, they leave no stone unturned to get them back and we have to give them up.
>
> We have had Hurons, Algonkins, and Iroquois; these last are the prettiest and the most docile of all. I do not know whether they will be more capable of being civilized than the others or whether they will keep the French elegance in which we are rearing them. I do not expect it of them, for they are [Indigenous] and that is sufficient reason not to hope.[34]

Recent scholarship on Wendat boys who attended the Jesuit seminary at Québec, however, interprets "failed" conversion and Europeanization attempts differently, contending that, in the 1630s, Wendat boys were sent to the Jesuit seminary by their families as "diplomats," in an effort to consolidate Wendat–French friendship and thus their political alliance against the Haudenosaunee. From a Wendat perspective, sojourns at the seminary in the care of the Jesuit fathers were akin to adoptions: the boys were baptized, given a new name, fed, clothed, housed, and taught European ways. The objective, for these Wendat families, was not a durable conversion to Christianity, but rather the creation of "a fictive kinship bond" and the political alliance that that entailed.[35]

The accounts of Indigenous families written down by European adventurers and by male and female missionaries—sometimes highly detailed, often anecdotal—had an enduring impact upon the writing of the history of Indigenous peoples in northeastern North America. Twentieth-century anthropologists and ethnographers, for example, used these sources, alongside archaeological findings that revealed the location of longhouses and villages, the tools and utensils employed by men and by women, and the toys with which Indigenous children played, to address the questions about family life that they found interesting: the sexual division of labour; family rites and rituals related to menstruation and adolescence; hunting and fishing patterns; hierarchy and authority within the family.[36] Anthropologists' concern with classification and order in turn influenced historians' accounts of Indigenous societies in northeastern North America.[37] Historians of what are now Ontario and Quebec, for example, have long emphasized the differences between Iroquoian and Algonquian linguistic groupings, including the matrilineal nature of the former.[38]

Many Iroquoian-speaking peoples, such as the Haudenosaunee and the Wendat, were in fact matrilineal and matrilocal, that is, clans and thus settlement patterns were determined through the mother's family line.[39] European observers believed that this conferred considerable autonomy upon women. The Catholic nuns labouring in New France were struck, for instance, by the decision-making powers held by some Wendat women—called "Capitanesses" by the nuns—within their councils.[40] Yet Haudenosaunee scholar Susan M. Hill argues that both seventeenth-century missionaries and later anthropologists exaggerated women's authority within these communities. That Wendat and Haudenosaunee peoples were matrilineal and matrilocal should not be taken to mean that these were matriarchal societies. Men and women held power together, Hill contends, and the labour was divided between that which was considered to be part of the "clearing" (generally women's work) and that viewed as part of the "forest" (generally men's work). The clearing included the village, made up of longhouses "organized through the matrilineal clan families," and the surrounding fields and gardens. Responsibility for "the forest" meant that men's work included hunting and fishing, but also diplomacy and warfare.[41]

In Iroquoian-speaking societies, such as those of the Haudenosaunee and the Wendat, men were responsible for clearing the land, growing tobacco, commercial trading, fishing and hunting expeditions away from home, making weapons and fishing equipment, making tools out of wood, stone, and bone, chopping firewood, and building canoes, toboggans, and fishing nets. Warfare was also part of their sphere of labour. Women were responsible for managing adoptions and the integration of new family members (such as captives) into the maternal lineage, planting crops such as corn, beans, squash, and pumpkins, maintaining the fields, allocating and distributing food crops, collecting plants, butchering, preparing food, preparing skins, sewing and decorating clothing, making containers out of clay or bark, sewing leather bags, weaving baskets, spinning hemp, weaving snowshoes, sewing canoes, and distributing firewood.[42] In Algonquian-speaking societies such as that of the Anishinaabeg, which were patrilineal and patrilocal, it was expected that men would be hunters; women were responsible for cultivating the soil, chopping firewood, drying fish, and harvesting wild rice.[43] Although these gendered divisions of labour were not absolute, they appear to have been generally observed. The Wendat, for instance, were said to laugh at Jesuit missionaries who gathered their own firewood, as this was a woman's job; in carrying out this task themselves, the Jesuits were clearly feminized in the eyes of Wendat observers.[44]

What historians know about Indigenous families in the northeastern part of North America in the sixteenth and seventeenth centuries is partial and incomplete; the fragmentary bits of evidence and claims to knowledge left by explorers seeking to claim Indigenous territory for European sovereigns and by male and female missionaries attempting to convert Indigenous peoples to Christianity must be weighed carefully. It is clear, though, that contact with European arrivals (a prolonged moment that Georges Sioui argues should be called "The Accident") had devastating consequences for many Indigenous families over the course of the seventeenth century, as members were lost to communicable diseases and as the military alliances and warfare in which Indigenous peoples had always participated were intensified by the fur trade and European geopolitics and made more deadly by European firearms.[45] Numerous scholars have noted that Jesuit conversion efforts, particularly among the Wendat, became more successful from the 1640s onward, as Wendat social, economic, and political structures were dealt significant blows by the spread of European diseases such as smallpox, influenza, and measles, and by Haudenosaunee military victories. In the context of the tangible threats posed to the Wendat by disease, famine, and warfare, the Jesuits promised food, shelter, guns, and preferential treatment in the fur trade in exchange for religious conversion.[46]

Sioui describes the arrival of Europeans in North America in the following manner: "We saw a poor, unhealthy set of angry, suspicious, intolerant and violent men, already behaving themselves as the owners and the lords of our land, planting their crosses, shooting their firearms and hiding themselves in their forts from the ones who brought them food and cured them from their diseases, which immediately began to take a disastrous toll on our people."[47] The Wendat, like other Indigenous peoples living near the waterways that led to the Atlantic coast, were on the front lines of European conquest in this period. The Jesuits, for example, were a constant presence in Wendake, the Wendat homeland that stretched west of Montreal to Lake Simcoe, and north to the Georgian Bay, from the 1630s onward. A series of epidemics in the 1630s killed up to 60 per cent of the Wendat population, devastating entire families.[48] The impact of disease was compounded by a period of intense warfare in the 1640s with the Haudenosaunee, who were seeking captives to replenish their own population; the combined impact of disease and warfare led to the abandonment of Wendake by the survivors in 1649. A few thousand Wendat, accompanied by Jesuit missionaries, moved to Gahoendoe Island. Most of these migrants later moved again, many to Kamiskouaouangachit (Sillery) or Lorette, in the Quebec City region. Some Wendat people went west to live alongside Anishinaabe neighbours near Michilimackinac; others moved southeast to settle alongside Haudenosaunee groups.

This dispersal and relocation of the Wendat people was the product of a series of choices that built upon previous, well-established alliances with the Anishinaabeg and the French. It resulted in the creation of a Wendat diaspora that stretched from the Quebec City region west to Michilimackinac. Family networks were thus key to surviving the impact of disease and war with the Haudenosaunee.[49] Marriages between Eastern Wendat and Western Wendat reinforced the kinship ties within the diaspora. By marrying a Western Wendat woman, for example, Eastern Wendat Jacques Otratenkoui "created familial ties at Michilimackinac, and his daughter consequently possessed ancestral bonds to both her community in the west and her father's homeland of Lorette." In the Quebec City region, marriages between Eastern Wendat women and French men, although not numerous, reinforced the decades-old Wendat–French alliance. The Wendat woman Marie Félix Arontio, for instance, married French settler Laurent du Bocq in September 1662; the couple had seven children.[50]

By contrast, the Anishinaabeg of the upper Great Lakes region and the northwest interior were far less affected in this period by "the European accident"[51] than the Wendat, the Anishinaabe peoples living in the Laurentian Valley, or the Haudenosaunee.[52] Even after "the arrival of European explorers and settlers in inhabited lands," Michael Witgen insists, "Native peoples nonetheless remained in control of the vast majority of the North American continent. They were not conquered and dispossessed."[53] Clearly, the Indigenous peoples of the *Pays d'en haut* remained autonomous in this period;

the authority enjoyed by French fur traders, soldiers, and imperial authorities in the region was limited. This vast region, termed the "Middle Ground" by historian Richard White, was a space of intercultural (Indigenous–European) interaction and accommodation. The numerous forms of contact between Indigenous peoples and European interlopers in the *Pays d'en haut* between 1660 and 1715 were facilitated by the proximity between Indigenous villages and fur-trading posts.[54] Among these forms of interaction were the intimate (sexual and romantic) relationships that developed between Anishinaabe women and French *voyageurs* (employees of the fur trade) or French soldiers stationed at the Great Lakes forts or fortified trading posts. Some of these relationships were of short duration, or seasonal; others were lengthy relationships, often celebrated according to Anishinaabe customs, sometimes formalized as Christian marriages by Catholic priests. Many of these couples had children, who were raised among their Anishinaabe kin.[55]

Despite the coexistence and mutual adaptation to be found in the "Middle Ground," it is likely that the "germs of [European] domination" were already present in the *Pays d'en haut* by the turn of the eighteenth century.[56] In the Saint Lawrence Valley, settler colonialism—and thus the dispossession of Indigenous peoples—was clearly well underway by then, as families from France began settling in northeastern North America in the seventeenth century.[57] Even though the written record of French colonization is relatively complete, there are fundamental questions that remain difficult to answer. What did these French peasant families, integral to seventeenth-century settler colonialism, know of the Indigenous families already present in northeastern North America? How did they understand their participation in settler colonialism and their existence alongside Indigenous families? How were the families of artisans, merchants, soldiers, and peasants from *Ancien Régime* France, like their compatriots belonging to the colonial elite, transformed by the transatlantic migration process and life in this North American colony? As historian Leslie Choquette asks, how were "French men" (and French women) transformed into "peasants"?[58]

French Settler Families, from Europe to North America

Few European fishers, explorers, fur traders, or missionaries—men, for the most part—were permanent settlers in North America. The arrival of significant numbers of French settlers in the seventeenth and eighteenth centuries would pose new and durable challenges to Indigenous communities, as the new European settlements encroached upon Indigenous lands and as

European administrators sought to delineate their territorial claims through maps and borders.

In the early seventeenth century, the French Crown gave to the *Compagnie des Cent-Associés* (Company of the One Hundred Associates) the monopoly of the fur trade in Canada, in return for a promise to settle the colony with Europeans. From a French perspective, the colonization project was slow to evolve. In the early 1660s, there were still only 3,000 Europeans in the Saint Lawrence Valley, and some 300 European settlers in Acadia, the territory on the Atlantic coast that included the islands that the French called Île Royale (present-day Cape Breton) and Île Saint-Jean (present-day Prince Edward Island).[59] In 1663, Louis XIV of France, determined to secure a permanent foothold in North America, took over the responsibility for the colonization of New France. His Minister of the Interior, Jean-Baptiste Colbert, implemented concrete policies designed to encourage French migration to, and settlement in, the colony, and immigration increased significantly from the 1660s onward, although it never came close to rivalling the population growth in the neighbouring Thirteen Colonies that belonged to Great Britain.[60]

Gross migration from France to New France might have been as high as 67,000 individuals. This estimate includes the many migrants who ultimately returned to France, but does not include the migration of seasonal workers or those who immigrated to Acadia. French emigrants to the colony were mobile and outward looking, integrated into the Atlantic world and economy: for many of them, migration to New France was but one move in a series of migrations. For some, this overseas migration would prove temporary. Around two-thirds of indentured servants, known as *engagés* or "thirty-six-monthers" for their three-year terms of servitude, eventually returned to France. Anywhere between one-third and three-quarters of French soldiers (including the Carignan-Salières Regiment, sent to New France in 1665 to wage war upon the Haudenosaunee and thus protect the French colony and its fur trade interests) also returned to Europe after serving in the colony.[61] Future generations of French Canadians and francophone Quebecers could all trace their ancestry back to "some 10,000 original immigrants" who stayed in the colony and founded families.[62]

These migrants came principally from Paris and its surrounding region (Île-de-France) and from the northern and western provinces of France, such as Normandy, Poitou, Aunis, and Brittany, that bordered the Atlantic Ocean and were integrated into the Atlantic economy. Up to two-thirds of these migrants—and three-quarters of female migrants—came from urban areas: villages, towns, and cities. Thus, the European colonization of New France involved a "double paradox of a profoundly rural nation replicating itself overseas by means of its least rural elements."[63]

The Filles du Roi

Marriage and family were central to the French settler project. Among the first initiatives taken by Colbert and his monarch was the campaign to recruit marriageable (single or widowed) women of childbearing age in France and to sponsor their migration to Canada. This campaign, designed to rectify the gender imbalance among New France's European population (six single men to one single woman in the early 1660s; fourteen single men to one single woman after the arrival of the Carignan-Salières Regiment in 1665), resulted in the arrival of approximately 800 French women in the colony between 1663 and 1673. The *Filles du Roi* must be seen as the raw material for colony-building, a settler project intended to rely heavily on immigration, but also on natural increase, in a context where, by the 1660s, the French state was beginning to prefer the marriage of two Europeans to relationships between European men and Indigenous women.[64] For most of the seventeenth century, French authorities encouraged the conversion and "Frenchification" of Indigenous peoples and counted upon marriages between Indigenous women and French men to lead to the eventual assimilation of Indigenous peoples. By the end of the century, however, the French state was opting for the segregation of Indigenous peoples.[65] Between 1644 and 1760, only 54 Indigenous–French marriages were recorded in the Catholic parish registers of the Saint Lawrence Valley.[66]

Long a source of fascination and myth-making for popular historians, variously celebrated as Quebec's founding mothers or denigrated as prostitutes (*Filles de joie*), the *Filles du Roi* (the King's daughters) have left concrete traces in the archives.[67] Although the Intendant of New France, Jean Talon, expressed a desire for healthy young women from the countryside for this populationist project, the vast majority of the *Filles* arrived from Paris or other towns and villages of northern and western France. One-third of these women (250 of 770) arrived directly from the *Hôpital Général de Paris*, a massive Parisian institution that sheltered a varied clientele including the poor and the homeless, orphans, the mentally and physically ill, the disabled, prostitutes, unmarried mothers, and those convicted of petty crimes such as theft and vagrancy.[68] Almost all of childbearing age—the average age of the almost eight hundred women sent to the colony was twenty-four—the majority of these women had never been married. One-fifth of them, however, were widows. Almost a quarter of the women—23 per cent—signed the marriage register and are thus assumed to have been literate. The Ursuline Marie de l'Incarnation reported to her son that some of the *Filles* were "very coarse and very difficult to manage," while others were apparently "of higher birth" and "more seemly."[69] Some 12 per cent of the *Filles du Roi* were "drawn from the bourgeoisie and the minor nobility."[70] Why did these 800 women choose to leave France? This decision is most easily understood in the case of the women housed in the *Hôpital Général de Paris*, who faced particularly important material challenges. More generally, however, life in seventeenth-century France was difficult for most people and characterized by poverty, shortages of food, and land that was not always productive. Some French regions had seen the countryside drained of its men by European wars, and so there were few opportunities for marriage for many women living in rural areas and small villages.

Once they arrived in New France, the *Filles du Roi* quickly found partners, most of them within mere weeks. A full 11 per cent of these young women met a man shortly after arriving in the colony and agreed to marry him, then broke off their engagement in order to become engaged to a new partner—a testament to the large numbers of unmarried men in Canada seeking European wives.[71] These eager bachelors apparently descended on the colonial capital of Quebec to meet the boats from France; so many marriages were contracted in such a short space of time, wrote Marie de l'Incarnation, that "couples are married by thirties." At the end of October 1665, this Ursuline nun commented in a letter to her son:

> The hundred girls that the King sent this year have just arrived and already almost all of them are married. He will send two hundred more next year and still others in proportion in the years to come. He is also sending men to supply the needs of the marriages, and this year fully five hundred have come, not to speak of the men that make up the army. In consequence, it is an astonishing thing to see how the country becomes peopled and multiplies.[72]

Marie de l'Incarnation regularly noted in her correspondence the number of French "girls" who arrived in the colony each year, alongside the number of "horses, mares, goats, and sheep." For their part, the newly arrived "girls" apparently made sure to ask prospective suitors if they had already built a house; the ones who had were clearly favoured in this highly competitive marriage market.[73]

Marriage and Childbirth

Whom did the *Filles du Roi* marry? Their husbands were drawn from among the European men present in the colony in the 1660s and 1670s: men who had been peasant farmers in France; former *engagés* or contract labourers; artisans; merchants; and soldiers in the military regiment known as the Carignan-Salières, sent to New France in 1665 to conduct raids upon Haudenosaunee villages and protect French interests in the fur trade. Writing of the Carignan-Salières Regiment in 1667, Marie de l'Incarnation remarked to her son, "It is said that the troops will go back to France next year, but there are indications that the greatest part of them will stay here as habitants, being able to find farms here that they would perhaps not be able to obtain in their own country." For some men, then, the availability of land served as a draw to keep them permanently in the colony.[74] Louis XIV paid the transportation costs of some male immigrants to the colony and apparently provided new male arrivals with bacon and a cask of flour.[75] *Engagés*, or indentured servants, were contracted to work for thirty-six months in New France, performing the heavy labour of land clearing and of construction. They were not allowed to marry during their three-year contract, but many of them did so at the end of their term and stayed in the colony rather than returning to France.[76]

Some 82 per cent of the *Filles du Roi* settled in rural areas once married.[77] This corresponds with the rural-urban distribution of the population of the Saint Lawrence Valley as a whole, which was roughly four-fifths rural for most of the French regime.[78] Unlike the *Filles du Roi*, who arrived with dowries provided by the French Crown, most other brides in New France did not have dowries. Instead, their marriage contracts often included promises by their parents to provide help to the new couple in setting up its own home — help that could be monetary or could be in kind or in services. Such promises of material assistance, called an *avance d'hoirie*, were essentially advances, or down payments, on the daughter's inheritance. The mean ages at marriage of women and men living in New France and born before 1739 were 22 years and 26 years, respectively. Eldest daughters were more likely to marry and tended to do so at younger ages than their younger sisters. Eldest sons also had "modest yet consistently higher chances of marriage" than their younger brothers.[79] In seventeenth-century New France, almost a third of marriages were remarriages, a fact that attests to the high rates of mortality among young adults, due to disease, the frequency of accidents in the course of men's work, and the risks that women faced during childbirth.

Statistics suggest that the *Filles du Roi* were more fertile than women in France in the same era, perhaps owing to a colonial diet high in protein and iron. On average, the *Filles* gave birth to 7.4 children each, a figure consistent with fertility rates for the colony more generally, and considerably higher than both those of Indigenous women in northeastern North America and those prevailing in Western Europe at the time.[80] In 1669, Marie de l'Incarnation claimed that couples already married for some years "have so many children that it is marvellous, and everything is flourishing."[81] In 1671 alone, between 600 and 700 babies were born in the colony.[82] In most years, the birth rate in New France was over fifty per thousand people; the colony's population doubled every twenty-seven years or so.[83] Between 1700 and 1830, a long period spanning the British Conquest, the French-speaking population of the colony alone multiplied by twenty. For most married women, this meant a new baby every two years or so. Births took place at home, with the husband present, and under the supervision of a midwife, who was usually an older married woman from the community, with children of her own and considerable experience in assisting with the labours of other women. The practice of wet-nursing—sending infants out to the countryside to be breast-fed by a woman, usually married, who was not their mother—was much less common in New France than in *Ancien Régime* France. However, in New France, wet-nursing became a more frequent practice over the course of the eighteenth century, particularly among families of the colonial elite, or sometimes in cases where the mother had died giving birth.[84]

Childbirth could often be a time of apprehension and anguish for women. Death in childbirth was common, although rates of maternal mortality appear to have been lower in New France than in France. Nonetheless, women between the ages of thirty and forty-five were statistically associated with an abnormally high death rate, one attributable to deaths in childbirth. Rates of infant mortality were also high, although perhaps somewhat lower than in France. It is estimated that one child in five born in the colony in the seventeenth century did not live to see its first birthday; by the eighteenth century, this had risen to one child in four.[85]

Relatively few babies were born—or even conceived—out of wedlock in New France. Only 6.1 per cent of births in New France from 1621 to 1724 were conceived before their parents' marriage, a percentage quite similar to that for France during the same period. Premarital conceptions were often the result of the sexual activity of a young couple already intending to marry. This sexual activity in anticipation of marriage appears not to have been particularly taboo, provided that the couple married before the arrival of the baby. Of course, some couples not initially intending to marry might also have been spurred on to action by an unplanned conception, thus conforming to the Catholic Church's insistence that procreation take place within the confines of marriage.[86]

Settlement

Marie de l'Incarnation noted in the 1660s that some newly married soldiers and labourers were given "a habitation and food for eight months so they can clear fields to maintain themselves."[87] The Ursuline nun acknowledged the heavy labour involved in clearing and settling land covered in pines, maples, and oaks. Although she expressed optimism about life in the colony for settlers, she was also reasonably prudent. The "bounteousness" of the colony's natural resources, she argued in 1665,

> does not prevent there being a great many poor folk here; the reason is that, when a family commences to make a habitation, it needs two or three years before it has enough to feed itself, not to speak of clothing, furniture, and an infinite number of little things necessary for the maintenance of a house; but when these first difficulties are past, they begin to live comfortably and, if they have guidance, they become rich with time—or as much so as is possible in a new country such as this. In the beginning they live on their cereals and vegetables and on wild game, which is plentiful in winter. To obtain clothing and other household utensils, they make roofing planks and cut timber, which they sell at a high price. When they have thus obtained all their necessities, they begin to trade and in this way advance little by little…[88]

Yet even she perhaps underestimated the time needed to become self-sufficient in New France; scholars have suggested that it could take up to ten years, not just two or three, to clear enough land to feed one's family.[89] During the intervening years, husbands might also take on seasonal or occasional waged work as day labourers, or in the fur trade, or in fishing or sealing, until such time as their families were able to live off what their farms produced.[90]

Like all other *Ancien Régime* societies, New France was built upon a gendered division of labour. Jean Talon was not the only member of the colonial elite to express a preference for female migrants accustomed to the heavy labour associated with rural and agricultural regions; Marie de l'Incarnation also commented in 1668 that "it is intended to ask henceforth for only village girls that are as fitted for work as men; experience shows that those not thus reared are not fitted for this country, since they are in a wretchedness from which they cannot raise themselves."[91] In addition to seventeenth-century domestic labour, arduous in the best of circumstances, women were involved with the heavy work involved in clearing land, planting it, and sometimes (especially in the absence of their husbands) tending to crops.

The relatively high life expectancy of European settlers in New France suggests the general state of good health that prevailed in the colony, which owed much to the varied and relatively abundant sources of food. Food shortages did occur in New France, notably in 1629 and in the winter of 1757–1758, but famines were not recurrent.[92] Unlike peasants in Europe or Indigenous peoples in Canada, French colonists were generally spared the impact of prolonged epidemics, although smallpox raged in the colony in 1733 and again during the later 1750s and 1760s.[93] In an era during which the average life expectancy at birth in France was between 25 and 30 years of age, the average age of death of the Filles du Roi (who had of course survived the risks associated with infancy and childhood) was 62. Those *Filles* who survived their childbearing years lived, on average, until the age of seventy.[94]

How did urban men and women, from large cities, small towns, or villages in France, become peasant farmers and settle into the long seigneuries of New France fronting the Saint Lawrence River? Far from extended kin and the familiar institutions of their French home, they were obliged to adapt to their new physical environment in rough settler conditions. The embryonic nature of institutions in New France and thus their lack of regulatory capacity might have meant a greater degree of liberty and personal autonomy for some French settlers. What is clear is that in the seventeenth century, at least, the family was one of the few institutions in New France that enjoyed a significant degree of power and influence.

Colonization and the Politics of Population

Over the course of the eighteenth century, various institutions imported from France—the Roman Catholic Church, the seigneurial regime, the state, and the system of French civil law known as the *Coutume de Paris* (Custom of Paris)—took root in northeastern North America. Initially administered by colonial officials and religious personnel who had themselves emigrated from France, these men and women were gradually replaced by Canadian-born state officials, lawyers and notaries, nuns, and priests and teaching brothers. The institutions themselves became "Canadianized," to a certain

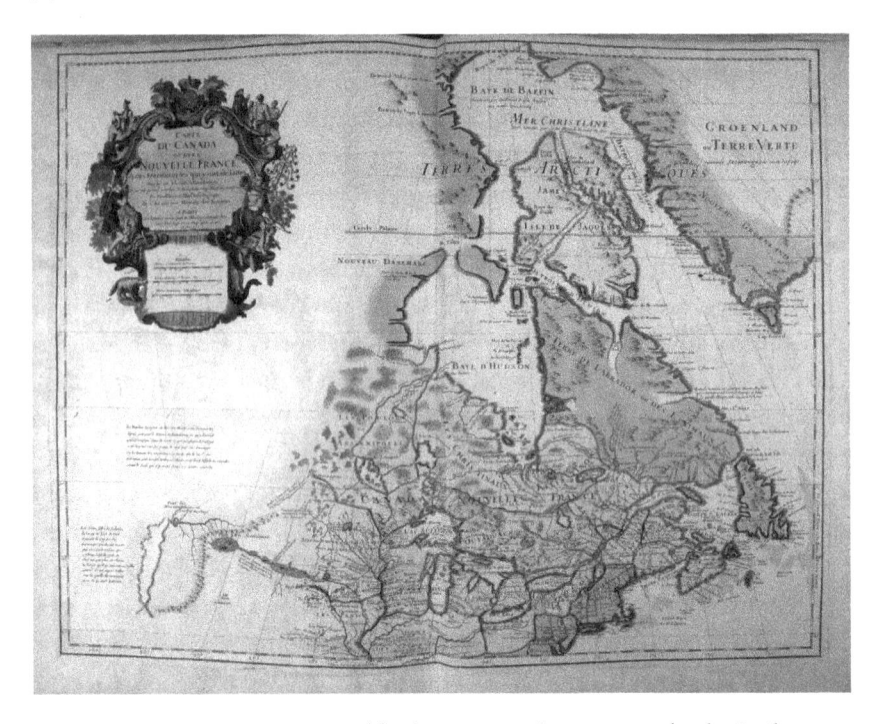

FIGURE 1.2 New France, 1703. Bibliothèque et Archives nationales du Québec.

extent—that is, influenced by their North American setting. The family itself, probably the most important institution of all in New France, adapted to the new geographical, physical, and political environment.

In the context of relatively sparse immigration and a small European population scattered across vast distances and expanses of territory, the Roman Catholic Church had its limits. This was still a missionary Church in the seventeenth century, preoccupied with the work of colonization, not yet institutionalized. Some have argued that the colonization objectives directed by the clergy towards the Indigenous population were similar to those directed at French settlers. The Jesuit seminary at Quebec City was established for both Indigenous boys and the sons of French settlers; the Ursuline convent took in both Indigenous girls and the daughters of Europeans. Yet, of these four groups of children, only European boys were judged worthy of extensive education; neither European girls nor Indigenous children of either sex were encouraged to pursue their instruction to any great length.

Hospitals were also established soon after arrival: in Quebec City, the Hospitalières de Dieppe founded l'Hôtel-Dieu de Québec in 1639; four years later, in 1643, lay nurse Jeanne Mance, from Langres, France, and the

Hospitalières de la Flèche founded l'Hôtel-Dieu de Montréal. In addition to responding to the most basic needs of the colonists, institutions such as schools and hospitals were designed in order to maintain the religious faith of the French settlers and to establish a Catholic culture in the colony. If the educational work of the Ursulines, cloistered nuns, was hidden behind the high convent walls, it was, as Marie de l'Incarnation observed, "quite otherwise with the Hospitalière Mothers; the hospital being open and the good done there seen by everyone, their exemplary charities can be rightly praised."[95] The charitable works of missionary women in New France were intimately linked to their efforts to convert Indigenous people to Catholicism, but also to the instilling or reinforcing of the faith among French settlers.[96] Between 1650 and 1762, 841 Canadians, 630 of them women, chose to enter into the religious life. At the time of the British Conquest in 1760, the female religious communities in the colony were entirely "Canadianized," that is, composed of women born in the colony, and not in France.

In 1674, Monseigneur Laval was named the first Bishop of Quebec. Among his many other accomplishments was the creation of a series of parishes; a century later, there were over a hundred parishes in the colony. Each parish had its *curé* (parish priest), its church, and its cemetery. A parish created a web of solidarity—and also the possibility of exclusion—among parishioners. It provided a framework for the usual Catholic rituals of life: baptisms, marriages, and funerals. It was a religious institution but also a social one. The *curé* was in some ways, for good and for ill, the symbolic father of his parishioners. Through confessions, he was privy to the intimate details of their lives.[97]

The cartography of parishes overlaid the division of land into seigneuries, a division that began in the 1620s. Inspired by the feudalism of *Ancien Régime* France, the seigneurial regime was a form of land tenure that parcelled the Saint Lawrence Valley into lots (*seigneuries*) conceded by the Crown to the *seigneur* (or lord) and then by the seigneur to the *censitaires* or *habitants* (peasants). In addition to working the land, the censitaires were required to pay annual rents and dues (*cens et rentes*) to the seigneur, including the gristmill *banalité* (one-fourteenth of the grain ground each year). Habitants were also required to pay a tithe equal to one twenty-sixth of their grain harvest to the Church. Finally, the adult men of the colony were expected to serve in the militia and were required to provide the state with their participation in regular work parties, known as *corvées*, for roadwork and military construction.

Most of these seigneuries, established in the seventeenth and early eighteenth centuries, were long rectangular parcels of land that fronted on the

Saint Lawrence River or other waterways such as the Richelieu and Chaudière Rivers. The family's house tended to be located at the river end of the lot, with the barn and other outbuildings directly behind it. A kitchen garden came next, followed by the cleared part of the farm, which stretched back to the forest at the end of the lot furthest from the river. The strips of houses along the river, at the end of their respective lots, came to be known as *côtes*.[98] The "framework of settlement" that was the seigneurial regime ensured that the farm family was the typical family unit in New France. These families grew wheat and sometimes peas, oats, and barley. They usually kept a few animals, such as pigs, cows, sheep, hens, and, by the later eighteenth century, horses. For the most part, this was subsistence farming: farm families produced enough to meet their basic needs and to pay their seigneurial dues; most families produced little in the way of surplus or profits. The labour of all family members was mobilized and was occasionally supplemented by the labour of hired men, particularly as the eighteenth century advanced and in the case of larger than average land holdings.[99] As long as they respected their seigneurial obligations and the customary rights attached to the *Coutume de Paris*, habitants could sell their land or pass it along to their children.[100]

Debates have flourished among historians over the precise nature of the seigneurial land-holding regime in New France. Was it as onerous, from the habitants' point of view, as the feudalism in France? Or did the colonial context mean that the obligations linked to the seigneurial regime weighed less heavily on the *censitaires* of New France than on the peasants of France—except, perhaps, in times of economic crisis? Did the seigneurial regime contribute significantly to the European settlement of New France, or was it a hindrance to the colony's development?[101] What is clear is that the seigneurial regime was not simply a way of parcelling up land into territorial units; it also structured hierarchical social relations in the colony.[102] Moreover, it ensured that the dominant family model among the European population of New France was that of the peasant farm family tied to the seigneurie and, to a certain degree, to its seigneur. For the French Crown, colonization and settlement were inseparable from agriculture and the sedentary lifestyle that it imposed.[103]

Seigneurial land tenure was also implemented in parts of Acadia. However, the extent to which seigneurs were present on their Acadian seigneuries, the degree to which they collected seigneurial dues, and the impact of this system of land tenure on the daily lives of Acadian families is the subject of much debate.[104] In seventeenth-century Acadia, peasant families, many of them originally from the French provinces of Poitou and Touraine, cleared the lands around the Bay of Fundy, dug ditches, built dikes, and drained marshlands in order to establish their farms. Marshlands were sources of food such as fish and waterfowl and also provided pasture for livestock. French settlers in Acadia established themselves in small hamlets of three to five families linked by kinship ties. They grew wheat, peas, hay, oats, and barley, and raised livestock such as cattle, sheep, and pigs, probably purchased in New England. As in the Saint Lawrence Valley, this was mixed family farming and, in most cases, subsistence farming, with few important surpluses to speak of. It is estimated that "at least a third of Acadian households in 1707 did not grow enough food to meet their family's needs and instead seemed to rely on trade or artisanal activity."[105] Very different from the practice of freehold tenure (or outright land ownership) in place in many of the neighbouring Thirteen Colonies, seigneurial land tenure would not always find favour among the British Loyalists who arrived in the 1770s and 1780s.

Most habitants probably had relatively little direct contact with the state. As in other *Ancien Régime* societies, people did not vote for their political representatives. Militia captains were probably the state representatives with the most regular contact with the population. Otherwise, state institutions and representatives were most present and visible in the small towns of the colony. In Canada, these were Quebec City (established in 1608), Montreal (established in 1642), and Trois-Rivières (founded in 1617 and still just a village when New France was conquered by the British). In Acadia, the principal towns were Port Royal and, after 1713, Louisbourg. The French Crown, represented in New France by colonial officials, took an interest in family formation. Officials developed a constellation of incentives, encouragements, and punishments in order to reward marriages and the birth of children and to punish celibacy. For instance, bonuses were promised to the fathers of large families (those with ten or more living children). Single men were threatened with fines. Those who married young (under the age of twenty in the case of men; below the age of sixteen in the case of women) were promised gifts from the state.[106] However, it is unclear to what extent and with what frequency these rewards and fines were actually meted out and, thus, to what degree they actually influenced the behaviour of the colony's inhabitants. Only two per cent of New France's population, for example, had ten children or more.

That said, the *Coutume de Paris* (Custom of Paris), adopted in the colony in 1664, undeniably played an important role in family life by establishing a legal framework within which families could act. French civil law offered a certain degree of protection to wives and to widows—considerably more, historians agree, than the British common law. The *Coutume de Paris* allowed couples to marry in community of property or in separation of property. Under the community of property regime, all property acquired by the couple during the course of the marriage became part of the community of goods. When one spouse died, the community was split, with half of the property going to the surviving spouse and the other half to the deceased's children. Under the separation of property regime, each spouse was the sole owner of the property that he or she acquired during the marriage. In cases where no marriage contract had been signed, community of property prevailed. Almost all couples wed in New France—even those with marriage contracts—married in community of property.[107] Husbands controlled and administered the community of goods, but if at the time of their death the community of goods was encumbered with debt, widows could choose to simply walk away from it. Widows' dower rights allowed them the use of half of their husband's personal property (acquired before the marriage or obtained through inheritance) for as long as they lived, plus half of the community of goods. Dower took precedence over any debts incurred by the husband during his life and thus could not be used to sponge up these debts. Widows also recovered their judicial capacity—a capacity denied to all women under the age of twenty-five and to all married women, who were represented in all legal affairs by their fathers or their husbands. In theory, according to the *Coutume de Paris*, all children—male and female—inherited equally. This was a system of partible inheritance, not the British system of primogeniture that favoured first-born sons. In practice, however, the land usually went to one of the sons, who compensated his siblings in money or goods. This prevented the continual subdivision of the land into smaller and smaller parcels. In general, sons tended to inherit land and buildings; daughters received furniture and other household goods and, sometimes, farm animals.[108] In the eighteenth century, as settled agricultural lands became saturated, the adult children who did not inherit the land were at a considerable disadvantage, often waiting years to be compensated, in cash or otherwise, by the sibling who had retained the land. Daughters in particular were the principal losers in these arrangements.[109]

The protection offered to families by the *Coutume de Paris*, and the fact that it gave married women and widows certain advantages not found in the British common law, have contributed to what has come to be known as the "femmes favorisées" debate. Were women in New France "favoured," that is privileged or advantaged, compared to women in France, women in other colonial societies (such as New England), or Quebec women of later generations?[110] Were women in New France favoured demographically? Were they favoured with regard to work opportunities? Did they enjoy particular advantages as a result of the *Coutume de Paris*?

Historians convinced that New France offered extraordinary opportunities to women tend to point to a few exceptional women who contributed to the development of the colony, such as the nun Marie de l'Incarnation (Marie Guyart), widowed in France at the age of twenty, who directed the Ursuline convent in Quebec; Marie Madeleine Chauvigny de la Peltrie, widowed in France at the age of twenty-two, who joined Marie Guyart to become the lay co-founder of the Ursuline convent in Quebec; lay nurse (and co-founder of Ville-Marie, later Montreal) Jeanne Mance; uncloistered teaching sister Marguerite Bourgeoys; or businesswoman Marie-Anne Barbel, the widow Fornel.[111] Seventeenth-century missionary women were among the most extraordinary of these women. Both the Ursulines and the *Hospitalières de Dieppe* put down roots in New France in 1639. These female religious communities provided a teaching convent, a hospital, and charitable assistance to the poor, all of which constituted different ways of ensuring the transmission of the Catholic faith.[112] In some ways, these "founding mothers" of New France were the symbolic mothers of the whole European community in this part of North America, providing material aid and sustenance, but also spiritual guidance and surveillance.

If women in New France did enjoy unusual opportunities, this situation seems only to have lasted until the early eighteenth century. In 1710, women lost their demographic advantage; after that date, the numbers of European women and European men in the colony were roughly equal, so the women no longer enjoyed an advantage in the marriage market. By the eighteenth century, in both Quebec City and Louisbourg, for example, widows were much less likely than widowers to remarry, and this was particularly the case if they were over forty (and thus assumed to be beyond childbearing age) or if they already had children. Younger widows and wealthy widows generally had an easier time finding a new marriage partner.[113] By the early eighteenth century, moreover, women in New France, both European and Indigenous, were more closely regulated by the colony's institutions, such as the Catholic Church. Despite the relative advantages provided by the *Coutume de Paris*, patriarchy continued to structure European families in New France, as elsewhere.

The institution of slavery, present in New France since the seventeenth century, also ensured that some women in the colony were in no way "favoured," although slaves were fewer in number—and fewer proportionately—in New France than in the neighbouring Thirteen Colonies.[114] The majority of slaves in the Saint Lawrence Valley were Indigenous people, of both sexes and of various nations, including Foxes, Sioux, Apaches, and Pawnees. The name "Pawnees," translated as "Panis," gradually became the usual designation for most Indigenous slaves in New France. Some slaves were of African origin; they arrived with settlers from the neighbouring British colonies or were bought by masters from New France travelling in the French West Indies (Guadeloupe or Martinique). An estimated 4,000 slaves lived in the Saint Lawrence Valley between 1627 and 1760, 1,200 of them Black and 2,400 Indigenous.[115] Some Indigenous slaves, offered by France's Indigenous allies "as symbolic gifts to French merchants associated with the fur trade," were employed in the fur trade or in agricultural work on seigneuries in the Saint Lawrence Valley, compensating in part for the shortage of European labour in the colony. The majority of Indigenous and African slaves, both men and women, worked principally as house servants in elite households in Montreal or Quebec City. "About 13 or 14 percent of Montreal's households claimed an Indian slave by 1709."[116]

Over two hundred slaves are known to have lived in Île Royale between 1713 and 1760, most of them in the fortress town of Louisbourg. In contrast to the Saint Lawrence Valley, over 90 per cent of the slaves in Île Royale were of African descent, not Indigenous. This reflected the integration of Louisbourg into the Atlantic economy and its close trading ties with the French West Indies. As in the Saint Lawrence Valley, female slaves worked as house servants. Male slaves worked in household gardens, tended to domestic animals, and chopped wood for their employers. Most of the slaves in Louisbourg knew one another and probably attended events such as weddings and baptisms within the colony's slave community. Only six of these 216 slaves were ever freed in Île Royale.[117]

The debate surrounding Marie-Josèphe-Angélique, a Montreal slave who belonged to Thérèse de Couagne, the widow of a wealthy merchant named François Poulin de Francheville, gives the lie to the idea that all women in New France were "favoured." Of African descent, Marie-Josèphe-Angélique was born in Portugal and was enslaved to a master in the Thirteen Colonies before being sold to de Francheville in 1725. During her years in Montreal, Marie-Josèphe-Angélique gave birth to three children, none of whom survived infancy. In April 1734, the day after Thérèse de Couagne threatened to sell her, de Couagne's house burned down, along with 40 other homes and the Hôtel-Dieu hospital. Arrested, imprisoned, interrogated, and tried, Marie-Josèphe-Angélique, still in her twenties, was found guilty of arson, although she maintained her innocence. Tortured, then hanged in the empty lot where the burned-down houses had once stood, Marie-Josèphe-Angélique's corpse was burned and her ashes left to scatter in the wind. Some researchers suggest that Marie-Josèphe-Angélique might well have been innocent of the crime of which she was accused, and that her judicial conviction reflects the racist and sexist nature of life in New France. Other scholars maintain that Marie-Josèphe-Angélique probably did set fire to her mistress's house as a form of vengeance and that her crime thus represents an example of the broader phenomenon of slave resistance.[118]

In all likelihood, neither the women who stepped off the boats sent from France in the 1660s, nor the European men who awaited them on the wharves in Quebec City, would have recognized the established French settlement that existed in the Saint Lawrence Valley and Acadia a century later, on the eve of the British Conquest. Nor could the Mi'kmaq who had traded goods with navigator Jacques Cartier in the 1530s or the Wendat who had allowed Jesuit missionaries to live alongside them in Wendake in the 1630s have predicted the long-term consequences of European colonization. Among these consequences were the absolute devastation wrought among some Indigenous peoples, including the Mi'kmaq and the Wendat, by European diseases and by warfare made deadlier by the firearms brought by European fur traders and soldiers.[119]

By 1750, New France was a small outpost of the far-flung French empire. It consisted of tens of thousands of peasant families engaged largely in subsistence farming and of colonial officials, merchants, artisans, day labourers, Indigenous and African slaves, and members of religious communities living and working in a few small, but bustling, towns. It also consisted of Indigenous communities—some, such as Lorette, Kahnawà:ke, and Kanehsatà:ke, quite close to the small towns that were Quebec and Montreal. Montreal was also the gateway to the world beyond the Saint Lawrence Valley, namely the Great Lakes basin and the western interior, known as the *Pays d'en haut*, where thousands of Indigenous families, particularly the Anishinaabeg, participated in the fur trade alongside French voyageurs, soldiers, and missionaries. In the colony of New France, families of European descent, whether rural or urban, interacted with each other and dealt with the representatives and obligations of institutions that bore the imprint of their French heritage. Four or five generations after their arrival in northern North America, however, they were no longer simply a "fragment" of *Ancien Régime* France.

2

Families in British North America, 1750–1840

IN 1766, 68-YEAR-OLD Madeleine Bouat, the widow of military officer Paul-Louis Dazemard de Lusignan, Chevalier de Saint-Louis, was newly arrived in France, ill and destitute. After the capitulation of the French troops to the British in 1760, Bouat and her husband were expected to board one of the ships leaving their home in Canada for Europe. Since Paul-Louis Dazemard de Lusignan was ill, he was ordered by his military general to stay behind until he was healthy enough to make the journey. A few years later, fully recovered and ready to join his regiment in France, Dazemard de Lusignan died suddenly of an unnamed illness. Madeleine Bouat, alone in Canada, having watched all of the family's money disappear during the Seven Years' War and its aftermath, left for France. Once there, she petitioned the French Minister of the Navy and the Colonies for a pension befitting the widow of a military officer with a long history of distinguished service to the French navy.[1]

This chapter examines the consequences of the British Conquest for families in the colony, notably the French-speaking settlers and the Indigenous families living in New France, before turning to the mostly English-speaking families who would begin to arrive after the colony was transferred from Louis XV to George III as a result of the Seven Years' War. It ends some ninety years later, in the aftermath of the Rebellions that took place in the Canadas, Upper and Lower, in 1837 and 1838. The Rebellions had a significant, often dramatic, impact on the families living in these British colonies in the 1830s, regardless of their political affiliations. The suppression of these Rebellions, alongside the political changes that accompanied this suppression, signalled in some ways the end of an era. The 1840s ushered in a series of important political, legal, and economic transformations that would help to determine family structures—and the possibilities for individual family members living within them—over the remainder of the nineteenth century.

In between these moments of dramatic social and political upheaval—the Conquest of 1760 and the Rebellions of 1837–1838—lay other momentous events and processes, linked to new waves of migration and the arrival in Canada of new kinds of families. They included Yankee Planters, who settled in Nova Scotia in the 1750s and 1760s; the American colonists (or refugees) known as Loyalists, who arrived in the 1770s and 1780s and settled in the Maritime colonies and in the vast Province of Quebec; and the various migrants who left the British Isles in the 1810s and 1820s after the end of the Napoleonic Wars. Most of this migration was familial; these families brought with them practices and customs from their country of origin and, to varying degrees, maintained or adapted them once established in these newly British colonies. This European colonization and settlement meant increasing encroachment upon Indigenous lands, especially along the Atlantic coast and around the Great Lakes. New and heightened competition for wildlife, natural resources, and especially for land had a major impact upon the lives and livelihoods of the Indigenous families who inhabited these regions.

The British Conquest of New France

For the families of France's military officers and colonial administrators, and for the merchant families who had earned their livelihood by trade with the French metropole or by provisioning the French military troops in the colony, the British Conquest was a decisive, often disastrous, event that caused them to pull up roots, leave the North American colony, and "return" to France, a country many of them had never known. In all, some 4,000 people, most of them born in the colony, went "back" to France, most of them in 1759 or 1760.[2] This return was not easy, even for the most privileged refugees. Many of them had no firsthand experience of life in Europe. The friendships, connections, and patronage positions that they had cultivated over generations in New France were worth little in the mother country. Many had lost their homes and material goods over the course of the Seven Years' War and, after the capitulation of New France, had difficulty being reimbursed by the French Crown for the Canadian paper money they possessed. Those men who had been part of the military elite in New France found that in France, they were simply colonial officers among many others. Many families were separated during the years of upheaval following the Conquest; in many cases, the relatives who had stayed behind in Canada remained there permanently. *Canadiens* exiled to France missed the family members who had stayed in North America and found themselves lonely and uprooted in France.[3] Not all of those who left the colony at the Conquest belonged to the elite; some of those families who returned to Europe were dependent upon the charity of the French state, at least for a time. Some of these emigrants had lost spouses, children, their homes, livestock, and all of their possessions in the war; among them were widows who had fled the colony with small children in tow.[4]

The vast majority of *Canadiens*, however, remained in North America, no doubt with some trepidation, faced with the potentially momentous changes heralded by the British takeover of this territory. These included some members of New France's military and seigneurial elite, such as the Tarieu de Lanaudière family. This prosperous, well-connected family showed proof of adaptability, pragmatism, or opportunism—depending on one's point of view—and, rather than going into exile in France, it sought to cultivate ties with the new British leaders and forge a new place for itself under the British regime. Its efforts were highly successful, and the Tarieu de Lanaudière family remained important seigneurs and landholders, administrators and politicians, into the nineteenth century.[5] The families rooted in New France for generations were joined by almost a thousand French soldiers who came to North America in the context of the Seven Years' War, married *Canadiennes*, and decided to remain in the colony, despite the military defeat. Almost 2,000 French-speaking Acadian refugees also settled in Canada in the wake of the Acadian deportation and dispersion and the Conquest of New France.[6]

Some historians of Quebec have argued that the word "cession" better captures the political and juridical complexities of the 1760s than the military term "conquest," since it underlines France's ceding of the colony to Great Britain in 1763.[7] While just about all historians of Quebec recognize the dramatic political changes occasioned by the military and political defeat of the French in North America, many insist upon the profound social and economic continuities in the colony, despite the replacement of Versailles and La Rochelle by London as the new European metropole.[8] Catholic, French-speaking families no doubt worried, with some reason, that their religion and language would come under attack. Indeed, the Royal Proclamation of 1763, which turned New France into the Province of Quebec, the fourteenth British colony in North America, did threaten some of the key components of *Canadien* society by attempting to impose British law and the Anglican Church upon the colony. But the Quebec Act, adopted in 1774, restored some guarantees to the *Canadien* people—soon known as French Canadians—notably by maintaining the privileges of the Catholic Church and by allowing the use of the French language relatively unhindered. From 1775 on, Catholics were permitted to hold political office. While British criminal law was imposed in the colony, French civil law was preserved. These were, in large part, attempts to gain the loyalty of the conquered population, not least because the British were worried by the possibility of the revolt of the Thirteen (American) Colonies.[9] Furthermore, for most of the colony's inhabitants, daily life and their means of earning a livelihood did not change profoundly, or at least not immediately. Most *Canadiens* lived in the countryside, far from the colonial officials newly installed in Quebec towns and from the new ruling institutions. Initially, too, British immigration was relatively sparse. British officials soon realized that attempts to convert the *Canadiens* to Protestantism were largely in vain, resisted by both local Catholic clergy and ordinary *habitants*. Instead, the hierarchy of the Catholic Church made concerted efforts to forge links with the new governing powers.

Most *Canadien* families had been established in the Saint Lawrence Valley for four or five generations by the time of the British Conquest. For these families, the Conquest signified a number of major political changes in a short space of time; in 1791, a scant thirty years after its creation, the new Province of Quebec was divided into the separate colonies of Upper and Lower Canada. Yet the socioeconomic foundations of the colony were transformed less rapidly. This remained a fragile colonial economy, dependent upon exports to Europe (furs, until the early nineteenth century, then timber). The growth of the timber industry in Lower Canada provided work for men in the woods, in the sawmills of Quebec City especially, and in the ports of both Quebec City and Montreal. Male inhabitants of rural parishes often worked in the forestry industry during the winter; in the spring, summer, and fall, they cleared the fields, planted, and harvested crops. The timber industry thus provided an additional source of seasonal revenue for the family. For women, it meant long stretches of time (three or four months a year) managing the household and children alone, while husbands worked in the woods.

After the Conquest, as before, the majority of French-speaking Catholics lived in rural areas. The largely self-sufficient peasant household, dependent upon the production of wheat and livestock, remained the principal unit of society for most settlers in Lower Canada between the mid-eighteenth and

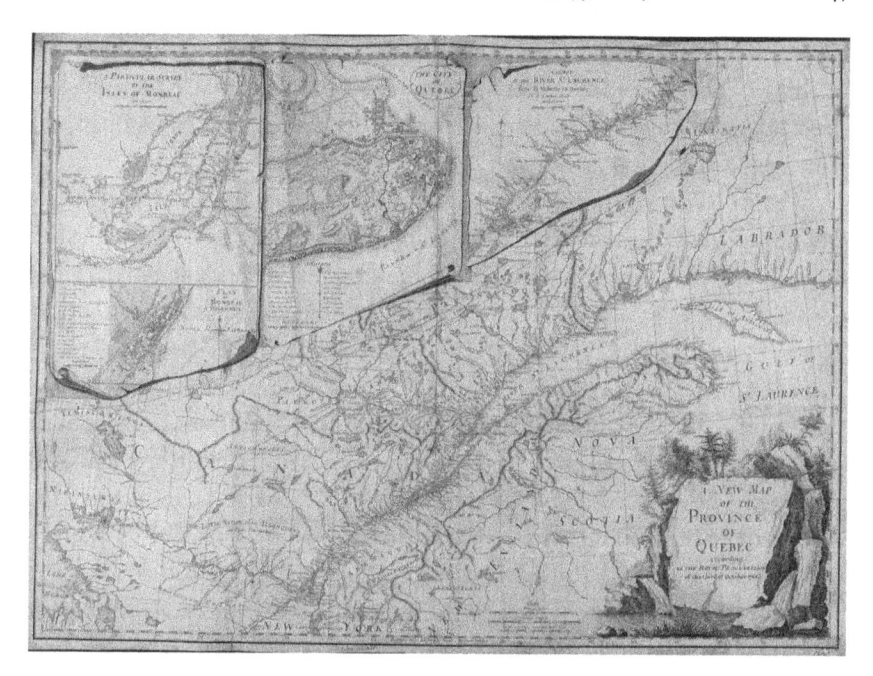

FIGURE 2.1 Province of Quebec after the British Conquest, 1763. Bibliothèque et Archives nationales du Québec.

the mid-nineteenth century. The family economy, dependent upon the waged and unwaged labour of all family members save the very youngest and the very oldest, remained crucial; within families, the nature of this labour varied according to sex and to age. Young girls helped their mothers with tasks in the house and in the yard, and supervised younger children. The seigneurial regime continued to shape, to a certain degree, settlement patterns, social structure, and the possibilities for agricultural families of earning a living. However, seigneurial land tenure was not always adopted by later arrivals to the colony, whether refugees from the newly independent United States or migrants from the British Isles. Because of the rapid population growth among French-speaking Catholics, the established seigneuries became more and more crowded and arable land more difficult to procure. Younger families found themselves obliged to move to lands further away from the Saint Lawrence River. Families subdivided their lands, up to a point, in order to establish several children on land of their own.[10] When parcels of land were in danger of becoming too small to be productive, parents opted to leave the land to one of their children, usually a son, who was required to compensate his siblings, in cash or otherwise. Girls tended to lose out in these decisions, generally receiving property such as furniture while their brothers got land.

Such practices also point to the discrepancies between the letter of the law—in this case, the Custom of Paris—and actual practice, that is, the adaptations made by Lower Canadians to their evolving circumstances in North America.[11]

Within *Canadien* families, Catholic rituals and values maintained a certain importance. Indeed, many commentators argued at the time that, in the context of the Conquest and British immigration, French-Canadian families needed to act as a bulwark against efforts at anglicization and attempts at Protestant conversion; mothers, in particular, were exhorted to be the guardians of both the language and the faith. For many families, the parish was an important institution of daily life. It had religious significance, giving both rural and urban residents of Lower Canada their own church, their own graveyard, and their own *curé* (parish priest), and providing a framework for the rituals of life for practising Catholics: baptisms, weddings, and funerals. But Lower Canadian parishes were also built through local solidarities, and they helped to attenuate geographical isolation by providing families with neighbours and with friends. In the early nineteenth century, after the new British rulers forbade the Jesuits and the Sulpicians from recruiting in the colony, parish priests were in short supply. In this context, local communities would sometimes draft petitions requesting the creation of new parishes and the appointment of a parish priest. Such petitions contributed, in the process, to the forging of local solidarities.[12] Of course, the parish also provided a framework for monitoring individual behaviour and the establishment of a set of community norms against which to measure such behaviour. The parish priest was the symbolic "father" of his community, well aware of the behaviour of his parishioners through knowledge acquired at home visits, through the ritual of confession, and through local gossip, and he was usually quick to reprimand behaviour considered inappropriate. The *curé* visited the ill and administered the sacraments, including the last rites. He was present at baptisms, weddings, confessions, communions, and deathbeds.

Birth rates were high among *Canadien* families after the Conquest. Some have termed this the "revenge of the cradle" ("la revanche des berceaux"). At the end of the French Regime, there were some 55,000 people of European descent in Canada, and almost 65,000 with European background living in the larger colony of New France, which included Acadia and the *Pays d'en haut*.[13] The Catholic, French-speaking population grew rapidly after the Conquest, perhaps in part because men were no longer taken away from their homes by war. In 1791, when Lower Canada was officially created, it housed 160,000 residents, 90 per cent of whom were French-speaking Catholics.

This significant population increase was almost entirely attributable to natural increase, as the new British rulers prohibited new immigration from France. This interdiction would remain in place until 1831.[14]

Most of the Indigenous peoples present in the Saint Lawrence Valley in the 1750s were allied with the French. The Wendat of Lorette, for instance, were heavily involved in the defence of Quebec City in 1759 and fought alongside French soldiers on the Plains of Abraham in an attempt to resist the British invasion. By 1760, the Wendat were being pressured by the British to abandon their alliance with the French. Aware that the British conquest of New France was imminent, they signed treaties of alliance with the British in September.[15] Most Haudenosaunee peoples fought alongside the British from the very beginning of the Seven Years' War, although in many cases they did so "reluctantly."[16]

Despite their long history of alliance with the defeated French forces, Indigenous peoples such as the Wendat did not consider themselves to have been conquered by the British. Rather, as treaties concluded by British officials with the Indigenous peoples of the Saint Lawrence Valley and with the Mi'kmaq in the Maritime colonies suggest, Indigenous nations negotiated the terms of this political transition with the new metropolitan power. Moreover, the Royal Proclamation of 1763 appeared to confirm Indigenous understandings of themselves as sovereign nations. The British conquerors were well aware of the fact that they needed the military support of Indigenous peoples. The Indigenous nations of the Saint Lawrence Valley, for their part, hemmed in as they now were by the British to the west and thus physically separated from potential Anishinaabe allies in the Great Lakes region and the interior of the continent, knew that it was in their interests to respect these treaties of neutrality and of alliance.[17] In the short term, daily life remained essentially unchanged for most of the Indigenous peoples living in the Saint Lawrence Valley. The Wendat, for instance, continued to structure their family economies around agriculture, supplemented by hunting, fishing, and craft production.[18] Other Indigenous peoples were affected more dramatically by the British Conquest: the encroachment of what historian Michael Witgen calls "a land-ravenous British settler population" upon Anishinaabe and Haudenosaunee territories was one major consequence of the Seven Years' War.[19] In many cases, these land encroachments disrupted family and kin networks, forced Indigenous peoples to move their homes and villages, and interfered with their ability to remain economically self-sufficient.

Over the decades following the British conquest of New France, Indigenous peoples would be increasingly integrated into the British logic of "protection," where they would be treated as dependents, not military allies. Indigenous nations, including the former allies of the French, accepted British protection in exchange for certain rights guaranteed by the treaties signed at the Conquest. This, however, meant accepting a much more contractual relationship with the European rulers, one in which the terms—including the nature of these new legal rights—were set by the British.[20]

In the Maritime colonies, the British Conquest happened in stages, beginning with the military conquest of 1710 and the Treaty of Utrecht of 1713, when Acadian communities in Nova Scotia passed definitively into the hands of the British. Despite the official change in the metropole, daily life for most Acadian families was not dramatically transformed in the first half of the eighteenth century. French-speaking families established in small hamlets linked by kin networks in the marshlands of the Bay of Fundy continued to make livings from subsistence farming, raising livestock, fishing, and trade. Indeed, the thirty years following the Treaty of Utrecht have been dubbed Acadia's "Golden Age," a prolonged period of peace that allowed for prosperity, the expansion of cultivated land, and considerable population growth among the French-speaking colonists.[21]

Well into the eighteenth century, the Europeans in Acadia remained outnumbered by the Mi'kmaq and by other Indigenous peoples such as the Maliseet, the Passamaquoddy, and the Abenaki. During the summer months, Indigenous families settled in villages along the coastline, where their days were spent fishing salmon, harvesting eels, and trading furs. During the winter, small groups of extended Indigenous families lived together in their hunting grounds, hunting moose and caribou for meat and trapping animals for their furs. Acadian farming families had little sustained contact with their Indigenous neighbours in this period. Marriages between Indigenous women and Acadian men were not unknown, but were never numerous and became less frequent over time.[22]

In 1755, in the early stages of what came to be known as the Seven Years' War, British colonial officials in Nova Scotia decided that the neutral political stance of these Catholic and French-speaking British subjects was both unsatisfactory and worrisome. Close to seven thousand Acadians were thus rounded up by troops from New England and shipped to the Thirteen Colonies, England, and France. Thousands of other Acadians fled their homes and took refuge in the woods or with friends and supporters, many of them making their way to Canada, that is, the part of New France centred on the Saint Lawrence Valley. In what has become known as the Deportation or the *Grand Dérangement*, Acadian communities were devastated, and over the next several years Acadians found themselves dispersed to Canada, to English colonies up and down the North American coast (Massachusetts, Connecticut, Maryland, Georgia, South Carolina, Louisiana), to the Île Saint-Jean (today's Prince Edward Island), to England and to France. Many of the Acadians transported to France had difficulty adapting to life in Europe and returned to the Americas, settling in Louisiana or the French Antilles. Extended families were torn apart during the dispersal of the Acadians; their farms were pillaged and burned and their livestock and crops appropriated by the British. *Canadiens* in the Saint Lawrence Valley who heard about the Acadian Conquest of 1713 and the subsequent Deportation might well have had forebodings about what lay ahead for them.[23]

In some sense, a "new Acadia" was born after 1763, with the return to the Maritime colonies of some Acadians dispersed in the *Grand Dérangement*.[24] Henceforth, Acadian families and communities would co-exist with New England Yankee families who settled in the Maritimes in the 1750s and 1760s, and then with the American colonists known as Loyalists, who began arriving from the newly independent United States in the 1770s and continued coming through the 1780s.

Migration, Dispossession, and Settlement

After the expulsion of the Acadians, Yankee families known as New England Planters, largely from Connecticut, Massachusetts, and Rhode Island, moved into western Nova Scotia, in search of land and access to the fisheries. These families were often evangelical Protestants (Baptists, Methodists, Congregationalists), and their particular brand of Yankee Protestantism would inflect the culture of the Maritime colony for decades to come. These new arrivals—more than 8,000 people—came as entire families. There was thus no striking gender imbalance in Nova Scotia in the eighteenth century, and by the mid-nineteenth century the colony's European population was made up of men and of women in roughly equal numbers.[25]

In the 1770s and 1780s, Loyalist refugees from the American War of Independence (1775–1783) arrived in Nova Scotia and Quebec. The first wave of migrants to arrive, in the 1770s and early 1780s, were considered refugees who fled the Thirteen Colonies for ideological reasons. Preferring to remain under British rule rather than to live in the newly independent United States, these American colonists migrated north to Quebec or northeast to Nova Scotia, seeking familiar political institutions. Those migrants who left in the later 1780s and the 1790s, referred to as "late" Loyalists, frequently had economic motivations rather than ideological ones and they moved to Quebec with the intention of acquiring inexpensive land from British officials. Although American colonists invaded Quebec in 1775, hoping to mobilize the *Canadiens* to join the revolt against the British, this invasion bore little fruit. Most *habitants* remained neutral in the conflict, and the Catholic clergy—and some seigneurs—actively supported the British rulers of the former French colony.

Accounts of Loyalist migrations highlight the difficult conditions in which many of these refugees escaped the Thirteen Colonies and made their way to what remained of British North America. Diaries and correspondence tell of political harassment, even persecution, by Patriot neighbours in the Thirteen Colonies, of separated and estranged family members, of middle-of-the-night clandestine departures, wagon rides through the mud and the woods, and makeshift camps on the shores of the Saint Lawrence River. In the late 1770s, a Vermont woman, Mary Munro, wrote to her Loyalist husband John Munro, already exiled to Quebec,

> I hope when you receive these few lines they may find you in good health. Your Dear Children are all well. As for myself, I am in a poor state of health and very much distresst [sic]. I must leave my house in a very short time and God knows where I shall get a place to put my

FIGURE 2.2 Encampment of the Loyalists at Johnstown. Toronto Public Library.

head in, for my own relations are my greatest enemies, the mills they have had a long time in their possession—likewise all their tenants' houses and lands. They have distresst [sic] me beyond expression. I have scarcely a mouthful of bread for myself or [the] children.[26]

These refugee families left behind neighbours, friends, extended family, and often, almost all of their worldly possessions: houses, furniture, and personal effects.[27] Many Loyalist families—men, women, and children—spent months, even several years, in the British refugee camps, awaiting shelter, land, money, and resettlement. Some of these families would eventually settle the area of Quebec known as the Eastern Townships, an intermediate zone between Quebec's seigneuries and the freehold properties of the newly independent United States of America. Others settled the western edges of the vast Province of Quebec, in what would become, in 1791, Upper Canada (later Ontario). In response to the massive arrival of Loyalist settlers, Nova Scotia was divided into three distinct colonies in 1784: Nova Scotia, New Brunswick, and Cape Breton.

Not all Loyalists were of European background. Ten per cent of the 30,000 Loyalists who migrated to Nova Scotia, for instance, were African-American—some of them former slaves.[28] Some Loyalists, such as the Haudenosaunee Konwatsi'tsiaiénni (Mary or "Molly" Brant), the long-term partner of British official Sir William Johnson and mother of their eight children, and her brother Thayendanegea (Joseph Brant) and his wife Adonwentishon (Catharine Brant), were Indigenous. The Brant siblings and their families constitute a striking example of the ways in which family and kinship networks were intertwined with political and military alliances during the War of Independence. Konwatsi'tsiaiénni and Thayendanegea were both staunch supporters of the British during the war and worked hard to convince Haudenosaunee kin of the importance of the Covenant Chain of Friendship between the Haudenosaunee and the British, an alliance going back to the 1670s.[29] The migration and resettlement of Indigenous Loyalists was thus determined by military alliances, but also by these extensive family and kin networks. In the 1783 Treaty of Paris that put a formal end to the American War of Independence, the British failed to make any provisions for the Haudenosaunee peoples who had fought alongside them. Indeed, the British relinquished some Haudenosaunee lands to the new American republic. By way of compensation, British military leader and Governor of Quebec Sir Frederick Haldimand negotiated with some Haudenosaunee people, notably the Mohawk, to resettle them in their western hunting grounds along the banks of the Grand River, on the western edges of the Province of Quebec. Other Mohawk families decided to settle on the Bay of Quinte, on the north shore of Lake Ontario; this settlement would become known as Tyendinaga.

For the Haudenosaunee, this migration involved leaving behind their homes, villages, and the burial grounds of their ancestors in the Mohawk River Valley in what is now New York State. The migration process also meant long periods of time waiting, often hungry and ill, in refugee camps established at Lachine and Fort Niagara, before beginning the lengthy and arduous process of clearing land and building new homes and villages.[30] This massive resettlement also weakened familial bonds and kinship networks already rendered fragile by the political divisions among the Haudenosaunee occasioned by participation on one side or the other of the American War of Independence. The children of Konwatsi'tsiaiénni and Sir William Johnson, particularly their six daughters, married into elite Upper Canadian families and apparently moved in these colonial circles with ease. The same was true of two of the children of Adonwentishon and Thayendanegea, John and Elizabeth. However, one of Konwatsi'tsiaiénni's children, and five of Adonwentishon's

FIGURE 2.3 African Nova Scotian Wood Cutter, by Captain William Booth, 1788. Nova Scotia Archives.

seven children, decided to settle permanently in the Mohawk community established at Grand River and took Mohawk spouses.[31]

Among the white Loyalist migrants, there existed a diversity of ethnic backgrounds, notably Scots, English, Irish, German, and Dutch. This was an overwhelmingly Protestant migration, including minority Protestant sects such as the Quakers. Socially, as well, this was a diverse group of migrants: the Loyalists included members of wealthy, socially prominent families, but also small farmers, including tenant farmers, of much more modest backgrounds. Generally speaking, they were ideologically conservative, proponents of British institutions and of a hierarchical social order, and opposed to the radicalism and the republicanism of the American War of Independence.[32] Their ideas of loyalty would colour the political ideology of Upper Canada and, to some degree, of Nova Scotia, through the first decades of the nineteenth century.[33] The letters of Rebecca Byles, a young woman from Boston, Massachusetts whose Loyalist family escaped to Halifax, Nova Scotia, testify to some of the difficulties of political uncertainty and estrangement from family members. In November 1777, 15-year-old Rebecca wrote to her Boston aunts:

> I received your agreable [sic] Letter very safe. It gives me great pleasure to hear that you are alive, and well, which is all I can know in the present state of affairs; we are impatient to get Letters from our Friends, and when we do, we know very little more than we did before. I hope with you that the unhappy Barrier will soon be removed, and we shall meet again, but we must not Repine. I know it will give you pleasure to hear how happily we are situated in this Time of Universal Confusion. We enjoy a large share of the Comforts of Life, and the greatest uneasiness is the Situation of our Country.[34]

Rebecca Byles's adaptation to life in Nova Scotia is interesting, for surely she had little say in her family's decision to flee Massachusetts. In times of upheaval such as that wrought by the American War of Independence, what are often characterized as family decisions were in fact choices made by the adults in the family, and sometimes by the husband and father, as head of the household.[35] How children or adolescents felt about leaving their home was probably a question rarely asked, even by their own parents.

The decades following Loyalist settlement in the Canadas and the Maritime colonies (Nova Scotia, New Brunswick, and Prince Edward Island) witnessed the arrival of further waves of English-speaking migrants. Leaving behind the social and economic upheaval of post-Napoleonic Britain,

English, Scots, and Irish families hoped to better their conditions in North America. Some of them took advantage of organized emigration schemes and assisted passage. Some were the families of army and navy officers who sold their commissions for land in the Canadas. Once they arrived in British North America, many of these migrant families would move several times. Was staying in one place a guarantee of eventual upward mobility, or was it in fact a sign that one had already done well?[36] Most of the Scots who migrated to Glengarry County, in Upper Canada, between 1784 and 1815 were families, often families with young children. Moreover, extended families often moved together from the Scottish Highlands to Upper Canada. Opposed to the commercialization of landholding and the introduction of large-scale sheep farming in the Highlands, these families hoped to recreate their communities of kin and friends in North America. These were relatively prosperous farmers compared to those who had stayed behind in the Highlands.[37]

Historian Peter Russell has characterized the period from 1822 to 1827 as one of "low but rising immigration into Upper Canada." Rates of immigration to the colony were consistently high between 1827 and 1835; these rates dropped dramatically from 1835 to 1839.[38] Some of the English immigrants who settled in Upper Canada in the 1830s benefited from the assisted passage provided by emigration schemes such as that organized by the Petworth Emigration Committee. William Phillips, for instance, was a shoemaker from Sussex who settled in Ancaster. In August 1832, he wrote to a Mrs. Newell in England this decidedly mixed review of life in Upper Canada:

> ... I am in very good health at present, thanks be to God for it, and have been ever since I left England. Here is a great deal of sickness in the country, the cholera morbus is raging very much in some places.
>
> I promised I would send the best account of the country that I could: so I intend to do. It is a fine country, but it is not half like England, every thing being very mean, when compared to that. Yet a person may get a very good living by working hard; for there is a great many hardships in coming out here. So I would advise them that can get a comfortable living at home, to bide there, but they as cannot, why they cannot change for the worst. Here is plenty of work, but it is very different for what it is at home. They here all work by the month: so much for a month and their board. They have not much money; so that you are obliged to take part in money, and part in goods, here being a great deal of barter amongst them. If you work a month, and can get all your wages in cash, it is thought much of. You can

sometimes, and that is best for single men. But they that have families, why it is not much difference, as they must buy for them, if they did not so, as it is almost always in provisions.[39]

Catharine Parr Traill and her sister Susanna Moodie have become probably the best-known English emigrants to Upper Canada in the 1830s. Two of the nine children of a well-connected and well-educated English gentry family based in Suffolk, Catharine and Susanna Strickland, like almost all of their siblings, were published authors. Catharine Parr Traill's *The Backwoods of Canada* was a series of letters written between 1832 and 1835 and first published in 1836. Traill's letters recount her settlement experience in Douro, near Peterborough, Ontario, on land that her husband, Thomas Traill, a retired officer of the Royal Scottish Fusiliers, had secured as a military grant. A detailed description of daily life in the Upper Canadian "backwoods," Traill's letters were also intended to inform future English emigrants, particularly gentlewomen like herself, of the life that awaited them in Canada.[40] Susanna Moodie's *Roughing it in the Bush*, first published in 1852, was considerably less optimistic than her sister's *Backwoods*. Moodie and her husband, Officer J.W. Dunbar Moodie, eventually settled, after stints near Port Hope and Cobourg, Ontario, near the Traills and their brother Samuel Strickland in Douro. Moodie explicitly intended her account of daily life in Upper Canada to dissuade English emigrants unsuited to the rigours of life in the "bush." She was categorical, writing that "To the poor, industrious working man [life in the backwoods of Canada] presents many advantages; to the poor gentleman, *none*!" While the poor, industrious working man might reasonably hope to achieve financial independence by settling the backwoods, the gentleman, with no experience of hard manual labour, "expends his little means in hiring labour, which his bush-farm can never repay. Difficulties increase, debts grow upon him, he struggles in vain to extricate himself, and finally sees his family sink into hopeless ruin."[41]

Although the great waves of "Famine Migration" in the mid-1840s are probably the best-known of the migratory movements from Ireland to North America, Irish immigrants to Upper and Lower Canada and to the Maritime colonies were numerous well before the famine. Ireland was a largely agricultural society at the beginning of the nineteenth century. Its high birth rates meant that there was too little land to feed its population. The solution for many was emigration. Between 1815 and 1845, many of these emigrants set their sights on North America. The majority of those who settled in the Canadas and the Maritime colonies were Protestant. Like most Canadians of the period, they became rural-dwellers. Large parts of eastern Upper Canada such as Lanark County, for instance, were settled by Irish immigrants.[42] In Lower Canada, even before the Famine Migration, the Irish-born were the most numerous group of people born abroad.[43] Ulster Irish also settled in Nova Scotia in the later decades of the eighteenth century; they were joined in the 1840s by Irish fleeing the Great Famine.[44]

This period saw the effective end to forced migration in the British North American colonies: slaves in most parts of the British Empire were emancipated in 1834. Upper Canada passed legislation in 1793 prohibiting the further importation of slaves; this legislation did not, however, emancipate the slaves already living in the colony. In Lower Canada, the last known sale of a slave took place in 1799. During the four decades between the British Conquest and the turn of the nineteenth century, signs that the practice of slavery was still alive and well could be found in the newly British colony's press, which advertised slaves for sale and published notices of runaway slaves and offers of rewards should they be captured. Readers of the *Quebec Gazette* in February 1778, for instance, might have seen the following notice proposing the sale of a young Black woman:

TO BE SOLD
... 28 years old, healthy and strong; has had the small-pox and meazles [sic]; understands cooking, also to keep a house in order; can work at her needle, and is remarkably careful of young children.

Any family wanting a servant, may be informed of further particulars by applying to Mr Samuel Morin in the Upper-town.

The price will be fixed at a word.

Clearly, many wealthy settler households in the British North American colonies, especially in urban areas, continued to include enslaved men and women until at least the turn of the nineteenth century.[45]

Sexuality, Marriage, and Parenthood

It is difficult to gain a thorough knowledge of the private lives of married couples in preindustrial Canada, particularly of those couples that did not belong to the educated elites and did not leave behind diaries and letters. Insight into intimate topics such as sexuality frequently comes from ecclesiastical, judicial, and notarial sources, and sometimes from diaries and letters.

In Lower Canada, as elsewhere in the British North American colonies, the norms governing sexuality and marriage were Christian.[46] For most Lower Canadians, they were, more precisely, Catholic. In theory, sexuality was to be expressed only within the confines of Church-recognized marriage. Married couples were told that they needed to be sexually faithful to one another and that marriage's principal purpose was reproduction. Forms of sexuality not intended to favour reproduction—masturbation, common-law unions, homosexuality, incest, and prostitution—were denounced as illegitimate and taboo. That the Catholic Church and other social actors bothered to denounce these practices suggests that they did in fact exist in the colony, although the practices were often clandestine and thus difficult to quantify.[47]

Marriage offered huge advantages to both men and women. In addition to being a socially approved site for the expression of sexuality, marriage gave men a partner without whom running a household and a farm and raising a family would have been exceedingly difficult. Financial autonomy was a state unknown to most unmarried women in early-nineteenth-century Canada; without significant family money, they were forced to rely upon the charity of relatives, friends, or their community in order to survive. Although it offered no guarantees, marriage assured them a better chance at financial security.

Marriage in the early nineteenth century was a social institution, in the sense that it involved far more people than just the couple in question. The wishes of individuals were less important than the needs and norms of their families, their community, and their parish. As the nineteenth century progressed, love-matches appear to have become more frequent, as the idea of companionate marriage became more widely accepted in the British colonies.[48] Nonetheless, for both the couple hoping to marry and their respective families, love was never the only consideration.

In Lower Canada, churches, and especially the Catholic Church, had a monopoly on marriage. The Catholic Church and the Anglican Church both required the publication of the banns: that is, a potential marriage needed to be announced at mass in church on three consecutive Sundays. Parishioners, including the families of the prospective couple, were invited to lodge objections to the marriage for legitimate reasons, which included bigamy and incest. Bigamy was a real possibility in this North American colony; communities worried that a soldier or a recent male immigrant might have left a wife behind in Britain or continental Europe. Incest was defined broadly to include cousins and also the siblings of a deceased spouse. The clergy could occasionally be convinced (usually by a financial donation) to dispense with one or more of the banns if the future couple was in a hurry—if the fiancée were pregnant, for example, and her family wished to protect its reputation, or if the fiancé needed a wife to help with the upcoming harvest.[49]

The Catholic Church also regulated the wedding itself. Couples were required to be married by the parish priest of at least one of the parties, before witnesses. A wedding could not take place on a Friday, which according to the religious calendar was a day of abstinence, or fasting. Saturday weddings were also discouraged, as it was feared that several-day-long festivities might spill over into Sunday, a day of rest. As in *Ancien Régime* France, weddings usually took place on Tuesdays, and occasionally on Mondays. Morning weddings were preferred, so that the new couple might attend mass together. Weddings were adamantly discouraged during Advent and Lent.

The state also had its say in regulating the institution of marriage. Marriages took place within a clearly defined legal framework. The Quebec Act of 1774 preserved French civil law in the new British colony. In Lower Canada, most couples—even couples with few material possessions—had a notary draw up a marriage contract. Couples who married under what was known as the regime of community of property pooled the worldly goods acquired during the course of their marriage. A husband was the official manager of the community of property, but could not dispose of the property without his wife's consent. A married woman—like all women under the age of 25— was not considered a legal actor and required her husband's or, if single and under the age of 25, her father's signature in legal matters. Most women thus went directly from the legal supervision of their father to that of their husband. Widows recovered their legal capacity, acquiring the same legal rights as unmarried women over the age of majority. If a widow remarried, however, she forfeited once again her legal capacity. Of course, there was often some distance between the letter of the law and daily practice.[50] Married women, for instance, found various ways of participating in legal matters. Active participants in family businesses, they sometimes stood in for absent husbands. Widows managed the inheritances of their children and acted as "tutors," making decisions, for instance, about their children's schooling.

Families, alongside churches and the state, also regulated the institution of marriage. Their opinion was particularly important when it came to young adults under the age of majority (25 until 1782, when the Legislative Council of the Province of Quebec ruled that it would be 21), who required parental consent to marry. The social contacts of these young adults, particularly of young women, were closely supervised. Parents could encourage courtships that they considered desirable and frustrate courtships about which they were less than enthusiastic.[51] Families wanted their children to make a "good match," since much was at stake, notably family property and family reputation. This was particularly the case among wealthy families. Money and social status were taken into consideration, as were religious and ethnic homogeneity. Social and ethnic endogamy—that is, marrying within a group or a local community—was perceived as a guarantee that family sociability would be maintained. In some cases, members of the elite—particularly the seigneurial elite—deliberately favoured intercultural (*Canadien* and British) marriages as a way of cementing political and economic alliances in the context of post-Conquest Quebec. Among bourgeois and aristocratic families in Lower Canada, husbands were often older than their wives, sometimes by a good ten to fifteen years. Couples of more modest economic backgrounds were generally more closely matched in age.[52]

Finally, the community also had its say in regulating marriage. Community members attended weddings, which often occasioned festivities lasting for days, despite the opposition of parish priests to such merry-making. They often felt free to pronounce judgment upon what they considered to be unsuitable weddings; their vehicle of choice was the charivari. Charivaris took place in both Lower and Upper Canada: the couples targeted were those where one of the parties was rapidly remarrying after the death of their husband or wife, or where the partners were considered to be mismatched in terms of age, status, or fortune. Generally, a crowd gathered outside the newlyweds' home and taunted them with jeers and yells until the couple acknowledged their social transgression and bought the peace with a payment in money to those carrying out the charivari. Despite the opposition of the clergy, who considered charivaris to be disruptive, even pagan, such expressions of community disapproval continued throughout this period.

Not all marriages in these late-eighteenth- and early-nineteenth-century colonies were happy, of course. Sources of marital discord included jealousy, sexual incompatibility, conjugal violence, alcoholism, and quarrels regarding family finances. In theory, wives were expected to obey their husbands; the reality, however, was often quite different. Only the death of one's spouse could put an end to an unhappy marriage. For all intents and purposes, divorce did not exist in Lower Canada. The Custom of Paris allowed for the "separation of bed and board" under certain circumstances, including male sexual incapacity, a wife's adultery, or excessive cruelty (that is, conjugal violence) inflicted upon a woman by her husband. Although the Catholic Church considered adultery to be a very grave sin—adultery that had come to the attention of the community was a sin pardonable only by the bishop, not by the parish priest—adultery committed by the husband was not considered sufficient reason to obtain a legal separation. Separation of bed and board allowed married couples to live apart and to manage their finances separately, but it did not allow for remarriage. Nor did the abandonment of one's spouse allow for remarriage. Widows and especially widowers tended to remarry, but remarriages were subject to restrictions. A widower could not marry his deceased wife's sister, for instance.

While French civil law and the importance of the Catholic Church shaped Lower Canadian family life in particular ways, there were also experiences common to both the French-Canadian families established in North America since the seventeenth century and those families more recently arrived from the United States and Britain who settled in Lower Canada, Upper Canada, and parts of the Maritimes in the late eighteenth and early nineteenth centuries. In all of these colonies, extended family provided important material and emotional support in the form of frequent and sometimes prolonged visits among family members and regular and sometimes lengthy correspondence between parents and children or between siblings. Such support was invaluable in times of political crisis such as the Rebellions of 1837–1838, when families were separated or forced into exile. But it was also crucial in more ordinary times, for example during childbirth.

In the period between the British Conquest and the Rebellions, births tended to follow closely upon the heels of marriages. Relatively primitive forms of contraception existed, such as periodic abstinence, prolonged breastfeeding, and the male partner's withdrawal before ejaculation (*coitus interruptus*), but it is difficult to estimate the frequency with which couples used these methods. Births took place at home and were attended by midwives and occasionally, in the case of wealthier families, by nurses or doctors. Husbands were sometimes present at the birth of their children: as the English half-pay officer Edmund Peel noted in 1833 shortly after his wife Lucy gave birth in Lower Canada's Eastern Townships,

> I was present all the time to support Lucy and I was much distressed to witness her agonies, I thought it the proper place for a husband at such a moment, considering it nothing less than false delicacy which would make a man absent himself at a time when his presence and support are most required, it is a fearful thing to see a woman in her pain.[53]

Female kin (mothers, mothers-in-law, sisters, sisters-in-law) were almost always in attendance at births, helping with the labour itself and with all of the attendant housework—caring for the other children in the household, cooking, and cleaning. In a period when illness and death were very real possibilities at any stage of life, female kin were also called upon to assist relatives on sadder occasions.

Inhabitants of these British colonies in the early decades of the nineteenth century lived with the constant presence of illness and the nagging fear of death, emotions that are regularly expressed in diaries and in correspondence with family members.[54] In an era before vaccination or antibiotics, infants and young children were at particular risk of both illness and death from endemic contagious diseases such as tuberculosis, epidemic diseases such as cholera or typhus, or diseases that particularly affected children, such as whooping cough, croup, diphtheria, scarlet fever, measles, and mumps. The letter-diary of Lucy Peel testifies to the immense suffering that she and her husband endured when their daughter, not yet a year old, died suddenly in 1834. Theirs was a sorrow shared by thousands of women and men in preindustrial Canada, including many with far fewer resources, material and otherwise, than the Peels, who belonged to the English gentry.[55] Throughout this period, infant mortality rates remained high in both Upper and Lower Canada, beginning to decline only after the turn of the twentieth century.[56]

Family Labours

The seigneurial land-tenure regime implanted in New France in the early seventeenth century was dependent upon the labour of individual farm families who turned over a certain proportion of the agricultural yield to their seigneurs and owed certain other obligations to the Catholic Church and to the community. Disparities in size among seigneuries and thus inequalities existed within the Lower Canadian seigneurial regime.[57] In the Eastern Townships, unlike other parts of Lower Canada, land was held in freehold tenure. This was a result of the determined lobbying of the Loyalists who had settled the southern parts of the Townships in the 1790s.[58]

In Upper Canada, too, initial European colonization and settlement took place along the waterways: south of the Ottawa River, along the north shore of the Saint Lawrence River, along the north shores of Lake Ontario and Lake Erie, and west as far as the St. Clair River. Subsequent generations of immigrants from Great Britain and the United States, alongside the children of earlier generations of arrivals, settled the backwoods. By the 1850s, the era of inexpensive and productive land available for European settlement was drawing to a close.[59] It was in this context that competition between European and Indigenous peoples over wildlife resources and land became more fierce and European encroachments upon Indigenous lands ever more extensive. The Haudenosaunee who had moved to the banks of the Grand River after losing their homelands in the Mohawk River Valley during the American War of Independence had spent decades rebuilding their cabins and villages. They had managed to ensure their livelihoods through hunting, fishing, and farming. From the 1820s onward, Haudenosaunee spokesmen such as John Brant (Ahyouwaeghs) and Robert Kerr regularly protested the refusal of the colonial government to protect their lands near the Grand River from Euro-Canadian squatters. Moreover, infrastructural projects such as the building of a dam by the Welland Canal Company in the 1820s flooded the agricultural lands of the Haudenosaunee and made economic activities such as hunting, farming, and fishing increasingly difficult. In the 1840s, the Haudenosaunee faced a second move in the space of some sixty years, to a reduced parcel of land on the banks of the Grand River.[60]

European settler families lived first in a rough log cabin, or shanty, while they built a more solid framed house. After a few years, these more permanent houses would be surrounded by barns, outbuildings, gardens, and some livestock. Some families could become "settled," even prosperous, within a generation.[61] Yet such financial security required great effort. Historians, like Upper Canadian diarists and letter-writers, have justly emphasized the rough nature of pioneering working and living conditions. British immigrants often had difficulty adjusting to the climate, the weather, the landscape, the insects—especially the mosquitoes—and the absence or poor condition of the roads, which hindered communication and the transportation of goods. All of this was in addition to the principal challenge, that of clearing enough land to eventually feed one's family. A successful move to the bush, or the backwoods, required children old enough to contribute to the family economy, particularly sons able to help with the physical labour of clearing the bush.[62] The labour involved in turning "forest into farmland" and clearing land for settlement was immense. Whether settlers opted for "girdling" or "ringing" trees (cutting a ring of bark from the lower part of the trunk, which eventually killed the tree) or for the outright chopping method, clearing forests was a slow, arduous process, particularly for men working alone or with only a son or two to help them. In the absence of sons, more prosperous settlers might opt to hire seasonal male labour, but this was costly.[63] In communities that were sufficiently settled to provide an adequate number of adult men, settlers without sons or the means to hire paid help turned to logging bees, where the men of the community worked together to clear forests. The emigrant gentlewoman Susanna Moodie was quick to dispel the romantic visions of community solidarity associated with the logging bee, as she insisted upon the labour required of women to feed the men of the community involved in the bee. She also declared that logging bees were sites of excessive drinking, violence, and occasionally serious accidents. "[T]o me," Moodie wrote, logging bees

> present the most disgusting picture of a bush life. They are noisy, riotous, drunken meetings, often terminating in violent quarrels, sometimes even in bloodshed. Accidents of the most serious nature often occur, and very little work is done when we consider the number of hands employed, and the great consumption of food and liquor.
>
> I am certain, in our case, had we hired with the money expended in providing for the bee, two or three industrious, hard-working men, we should have got through twice as much work, and have had it done well, and have been the gainers in the end.[64]

The actual rates of land clearing were a fair bit slower than the rates vaunted in the numerous recruitment talks aimed at potential British emigrants. While a male colonist engaged full-time in land clearing in his first few years in Upper Canada might hope to clear between four and seven acres per year, by his third or fourth year in the colony, when other work (plowing, planting, harvesting, house-building) required his attention, the rate of land clearance could slow to an acre or two per year. Thus, while settlement in Upper Canada offered British tenant farmers the opportunity to become land-owners, land ownership did not necessarily signify prosperity, or at least not right away. Indeed, in periods of high immigration to Upper Canada, some immigrant men worked first as labourers on other people's farms before acquiring land of their own.[65]

Throughout this period, this was an overwhelmingly rural society; the Upper Canadian economy was largely dependent on farming and agriculture. After the intensive labour of clearing land for farming came the work of "planting, tending, harvesting, and marketing their crops."[66] Much depended upon the success of the annual wheat crop; a significant portion of the year's income could be wiped out by excessive rainfall or the ravages of insects.[67] Upper Canadian farm families also produced other crops, including barley, rye, hay, and tobacco; and they repaid debts at the local general store with other kinds of goods, including pork, lumber, and ashes.[68] In some cases, agriculture was combined with other forms of paid work. In Lanark County in eastern Upper Canada, for instance, Irish immigrants who had settled on relatively poor land offset their meagre crop yields by working on the construction of the nearby Rideau Canal and in the timber trade.[69]

Small urban settlements could be found in Upper Canada by the 1790s, notably Kingston, Niagara, and Detroit (Detroit became part of the recently independent United States in 1794). By the early nineteenth century, the principal Upper Canadian towns were Kingston, Niagara, and York (later Toronto); these remained the colony's most important towns through the mid-nineteenth century. Each of these towns had inns and taverns, a school, an Anglican church, a weekly market, and some small shops.[70] In rural Upper Canada, a tavern could be found every six to eight miles; in towns, they were to be found on busy street corners, but also interspersed among houses on smaller and quieter streets. While often perceived as sites of masculine sociability, women were in fact present in inns and taverns; indeed, women (both mothers and daughters) played an integral role in running these establishments and in providing food and lodging. Drinking establishments could also be socially, ethnically, and racially heterogeneous, although Indigenous and African-Canadian clients often met with hostility, even violence, on the part of white clients.[71] General stores provided Upper Canadian farming families with the commercial credit necessary to purchase goods for both house and farm.[72]

By the early nineteenth century, these Upper Canadian farming households were already integrating the commercial economy and the marketplace. Agricultural surpluses or cash crops were sold in town.[73] The situation in Lower Canada's Eastern Townships appears to have been somewhat different, however. In 1834, Lucy Peel wrote to her family back in England, "This is not a country for grain, and supposing it were, there is no one to buy it, each petty farmer growing enough for his own consumption, and we are too far from the market towns to make it answer to send it there." The region would only really be integrated into the market from the later 1830s and the 1840s on, following the establishment of mills and factories in Sherbrooke and the arrival of the railway.[74] By the mid-nineteenth century in Upper Canada and the Maritimes, some household items such as factory-made cloth, molasses, tools, and sewing needles were bought at town stores: it is clear that agricultural families were not completely self-sufficient.[75] Particularly in the early stages of settlement, families relied upon supplies from the closest stores. Catharine Parr Traill wrote in the 1830s, "Till we raise our own grain and fatten our own hogs, sheep, and poultry, we must be dependent upon the stores for food of every kind. These supplies have to be brought up at considerable expense and loss of time, through our *beautiful bush-roads* . . . ."[76]

The gendered division of labour in the Upper Canadian and Maritime colonies would probably have looked familiar to colonists in the United States and to peasant families in Western Europe. Men worked in the fields, did much of the heavy outdoor work such as logging and land clearing, and sometimes hunted and fished. Adult women of all social classes took care of the household, the housework, and the children, including providing all members of the household with food and clothing. Among the upper classes, of course, wives and mothers benefited considerably from the labour of other women, namely general servants, milliners, laundresses, and cooks. Some women made cloth at home, for their own use or for exchange; some farmwomen sold or exchanged eggs and butter in the marketplace.[77] In August 1815, eighteen-year-old Nova Scotian Louisa Collins described her work and the work of the women around her on a typical summer Tuesday:

> The dairy as ushal thakes [sic] up most of my morning on Tuesdays and after finishing there I picked a baskit [sic] of black currents [sic] for Miss Beamish – in the afternoon I sowed [sic] a littel [sic] while and then went out and raked hay, I wrote a note to my friend Harriet this evening – Aunt Cliffords girl and her sister have bin [sic] over all day picking Currents – Mama is know [sic] tying up her readishes [sic] and turnips for market to morrow morning; as that don't belong to my part of the work I have left her to her self – we have had a fine day to day, I shall retire early to night for I feel quite tired after my days work....[78]

Clearly women's work in early-nineteenth-century rural communities extended beyond the four walls of the house to include a great deal of outdoor labour. Collins's 1815 diary entries reveal her constant worry that poor weather would destroy that year's crop of hay.[79] The diary entries of New Brunswick woman Jacobina Campbell in April and May 1830 likewise shed light on the outdoor work necessary in springtime, which included making cabbage beds, boiling sap, planting potatoes and peas, sewing beets and carrots, and shearing sheep.[80] Work bees, including logging bees, remained popular in Upper Canada until the 1830s.[81] Catherine Parr Traill appears to have held a more favourable view of bees than her sister Susanna Moodie, writing in the 1830s that the word "bee" signified

> those friendly meetings of neighbours who assemble at your summons to raise the walls of your house, shanty, barn, or any other building:

this is termed a "raising bee." Then there are logging-bees, husking-bees, chopping-bees, and quilting-bees. The nature of the work to be done gives the name to the bee. In the more populous and long-settled districts this practice is much discontinued, but it is highly useful, and almost indispensable to new settlers in the remote townships, where the price of labour is proportionately high, and workmen difficult to be procured...."[82]

In towns and villages, men's labour took place in their workshops, if they were artisans such as shoemakers or tailors. Some men worked in the world of small commerce, for instance, running a general store. Some women worked in family businesses such as shops, inns, and taverns; many of them maintained, or even increased, this participation in family businesses when widowed.[83] Some married women of the labouring classes took in boarders to help make ends meet; other labouring women, single and sometimes married, worked as servants, prostitutes, or brothel-keepers. Montreal's Elisabeth Deganne, "a married woman and the mother of eight children," in 1822 "set up a brothel in her home on Dorchester Street. Adapting her household to the requirements of prostitution allowed Deganne to earn an income without leaving her home, which permitted her to nurse her dying husband, care for the youngest of her children, and ensure that essential domestic tasks were completed."[84]

Differences in social status existed among both Upper Canadian and Lower Canadian families.[85] In Lower Canada's Eastern Townships, for example, English gentry settlers socialized among themselves and looked down upon their Yankee colonist neighbours, whom they deemed to be "vulgar," lacking in respect for social hierarchy, and less cultured than the English. Patronage positions in the Townships also tended to be awarded to British settlers, as colonial officials were suspicious of Yankee political leanings, despite having encouraged these same American migrants to settle the region in the 1790s. Ironically, in the context of the Lower Canadian countryside, these Yankee settlers often did much better financially than the English gentry settlers.[86]

In Upper Canada, Loyalism had political purchase and signified financial, social, and cultural capital. The provincial oligarchy known as the Family Compact (an elite group closely associated with the members of Upper Canada's Executive and Legislative councils) was notorious for its conservative political ideology.[87] Yet outside the fashionable and restricted circles of these political and social elites there existed a great many settler families living in much more difficult material conditions. Many Upper Canadians lived without land or families of their own, assisting the families and households of others as hired men, seasonal labour, or general servants.[88] Upper

Canada had no formal Poor Law system as Great Britain did at the time. But its political rulers did share much of what might be called Poor Law ideology, such as the principle of less eligibility—that is, giving charity to only the most desperate and destitute, for fear that the existence of charity might dissuade able-bodied individuals from working. In the early nineteenth century, some of the poorest and sickest Upper Canadians went from being the responsibility of private voluntary associations, otherwise known as charities, to being taken under the more formal, institutional wing of the House of Industry.[89]

Even within the wealthiest and most prestigious colonial families, gender and age imposed significant constraints. Women born to families of wealth and social stature lived within narrow strictures of what was possible and tolerated according to the gendered norms and laws of the day. The daughters of Anne Murray Powell and Judge William Dummer Powell, a Loyalist couple who, after much moving about, settled in York (Toronto) in 1798, Anne, Elizabeth, and Mary grew up in Upper Canada's most elite political and social circles. Yet, to their mother's everlasting regret, they were never given much formal education, unlike their brothers. According to historian Katherine M.J. McKenna, the three sisters embody the "three 'types' of Upper Canadian womanhood: Mary the wife and mother, Elizabeth the self-sacrificing spinster, and Anne the nonconformist, whose inability to transcend the restrictions of her sex and social class reveals the strength of those social sanctions."[90]

Family life could be affected, sometimes dramatically, by larger political events. The impact of the War of 1812 on families in Upper Canada, for instance, appears to have been two-fold. First, loyal Upper Canadian men were expected to act both honourably and manfully in order to defend their "helpless" wives and children from American invaders. Conversely, loyal patriots were presumed to be male (and masculine): women's overt manifestations of political loyalty during the war were largely ignored or minimized.[91] Even Laura Secord, the famed Upper Canadian woman of Loyalist background who walked nineteen miles through the woods of the Niagara Peninsula in June 1813 in order to relay crucial information about a possible American attack to British troops, was portrayed over subsequent decades in typically feminine terms that emphasized her roles and identity as wife and mother.[92]

Second, after the War of 1812 and the end of the Napoleonic Wars in Europe, British immigrants poured into Upper Canada in search of land, desirous of settling the "expanding Upper Canadian frontier."[93] In addition to diversifying the kinds of families to be found in Upper Canada, these new waves of migration and settlement constrained the possibilities open to Indigenous families, pushing them further into the interior of the continent. As British and American settlers moved into Upper Canada in search of agricultural land, the Anishinaabeg and the Haudenosaunee were under increasing pressure to cede their land and to move to reserves. Once the War of 1812 was over, Indigenous peoples were no longer as militarily useful to British officials or to white settlers. Military alliances thus faded, despite the fact that the Anishinaabeg who had fought alongside the British to repel American incursions regularly reminded Euro-Canadian officials of their loyalty and the key role that they had played in 1812–1814.[94] During this period, Indigenous peoples, once imperial allies, were increasingly viewed through the lens of "colonial paternalism," as "wards of a settler state."[95] The Haudenosaunee, some of whom actively supported the British during the War of 1812, went from being considered "brethren" to being considered "children" by the imperial government in the wake of the war.[96] Indigenous self-government was increasingly challenged, at the same moment that Christian missionaries—Catholics, but also Protestants such as Anglicans and Presbyterians—were increasingly present in the Canadas and the Maritimes, where they called into question Indigenous belief systems and family structures.[97]

The Rebellions of 1837–1838 also had an impact on families in Upper and Lower Canada. Families who supported the colonial officials in place were often subject to political charivaris and harassment by the rebels (known as *Patriotes* in Lower Canada and reformers in Upper Canada). Rebel families, in contrast, faced retaliation from colonial officials and the local militia. In both Canadas, *Patriotes* and reform leaders were forced to flee their homes; some were imprisoned, banished from the colony, or transported to Australia, and over a dozen were hanged for treason. Reine Harnois and her husband Ludger Duvernay, a well-known newspaper editor, printer, and *Patriote*, spent years apart during and in the wake of the Lower Canadian Rebellions. Duvernay fled to the United States in 1837 and remained in exile until 1842. During his absence, Reine Harnois left Montreal with their five children and sought refuge with her own family in Rivière-du-Loup, where her sister, Marguerite Harnois, provided essential material and emotional support to all of the family members.[98] The letters exchanged between *Patriote* leader Louis-Joseph Papineau and his wife, Julie Bruneau, likewise testify to the extreme difficulties imposed upon their marriage and their several children by political harassment and exile. Here, too, various members of the extended Papineau and Bruneau families stepped into the breach during and after the Rebellions, transmitting messages and letters and providing shelter and sustenance.[99]

Liberal Capitalism and a New Gendered Order: Towards a Separation of "Spheres"?

Lower Canadian *Patriotes*, including Louis-Joseph Papineau, espoused republican ideologies that affirmed that the public sphere, including politics, was men's domain. Women who wished to remain virtuous were expected to eschew the corrupt, immoral, masculine world of politics and confine themselves to a so-called private sphere, composed of home, hearth, and family. In this, Lower Canadian *Patriotes* were no different than their political allies and brethren in revolutionary France or in the newly independent United States. This explains, for instance, why the *Patriotes* appear to have fully endorsed the political measures that took away women's right to vote in Lower Canada. The Constitutional Act of 1791 had given the right to vote to all persons of property, without specifying whether this right applied to both men and women. In 1834, *Patriote* representatives in the Lower Canadian Assembly voted to exclude women from this measure; this loss of suffrage rights, alongside that of the women of Upper Canada, was confirmed in 1849.[100]

The ideology of "separate spheres" would colour prescriptions, and sometimes lived experience, in Canada through the second half of the nineteenth century. This helps to explain why in 1851 Nova Scotia, too, would see the beginnings of a move to explicitly prevent women from voting.[101] Idealized visions of separate spheres accompanied the spread of liberal capitalism throughout the British North American colonies. In Lower Canada, widows' dower rights were chipped away at in the 1840s, and the seigneurial land-tenure regime was—officially, at least—abolished in 1854: these two new measures were intended to favour the sale of land on the market and the circulation of capital. Both of these measures, however, signified the loss of customary family protections that had been inscribed in the French civil law.[102] In Upper Canada and the Maritime colonies, too, the popularity of ideas variously referred to as the "Cult of True Womanhood" or the "Angel in the House"—where women were expected to take care of home and family and men permitted to rule the worlds of work and politics—spread and increased after 1840.

In 1840, however, these were still largely rural and resource-based societies, where the borders between public and private spheres were permeable. The ideas about men's and women's respective "spheres" of action that had begun to circulate in the 1830s seemed to have made headway only in elite settler circles. Lower Canada, with a population of some 650,000 people in 1841, was made up of agricultural lands and at least three significant towns

(Montreal, Quebec City, and Trois-Rivières), important sites of commerce and government. Upper Canada, with a population of roughly 430,000 in 1840, consisted of farming communities and well-established towns and villages linked by networks of roads.[103] New Brunswick could count some 156,000 people in 1841 and Prince Edward Island some 47,000 people that same year; in 1838, the population of Nova Scotia was over 202,000.[104] While farm families were important in all of these British North American colonies, forestry, fishing, and hunting also enabled many families to achieve some form of economic self-sufficiency and structured the roles, forms, and rhythms of work undertaken by different family members. There were as yet few hints, at the dawn of the 1840s, of the dramatic economic developments that would fundamentally transform family life in all of these colonies in the second half of the nineteenth century.

In northwestern North America and on the northern Great Plains, Indigenous peoples structured their family lives around economic activities such as hunting, fishing, and gathering. The fur trade shaped the domestic lives of many Indigenous peoples in the Pacific Northwest, in the Plateau region of what would later become British Columbia, and on the northern Great Plains.[105] At the end of the eighteenth century and in the early nineteenth century, numerous Indigenous women entered into sustained, often long-term, romantic or domestic relationships with British or Euro-Canadian men who had travelled long distances to trade for beaver, muskrat, and buffalo or to search for water routes that would enable furs to be transported from the interior of the continent to the Pacific coast. The unpaid labour undertaken by these women, such as preparing food and clothing, or establishing links between their British or Euro-Canadian partner and Indigenous trappers, was a crucial source of assistance to their partners and to the fur trade. On the northern Plains, many Ojibwa, Cree, and Chipewyan women partnered with Scots, Orcadian, and French-Canadian men employed in the fur trade.[106] Numerous French-Canadian men active in the Pacific Northwest fur trade also founded families with Indigenous women. Toussaint Charbonneau, for example, was born in Montreal in 1767 and worked as an interpreter alongside his Shoshone partner, Sacagawea. Their son, Jean-Baptiste, was born on the Pacific coast in the winter of 1805–1806. Pierre Charles, an Abenaki man born near Yamaska around 1799, worked in the Pacific Northwest fur trade through the 1820s and 1830s. After the death of his Clallam wife, Louise, he married a Sassette woman, Marguerite.[107] In the 1840s, the non-Indigenous population of these regions would increase considerably, as British women arrived in western Canadian fur-trade communities and as American settlers and missionaries established themselves in the future British Columbia.

3

The Industrial Revolution in Canada, 1840–1889

IN THE MIDDLE of the nineteenth century, economic structures in the British North American colonies underwent the slow but profound transformations dubbed the Industrial Revolution. In particular pockets of the colonies, the landscape, already dotted with villages and towns, began to change shape as the larger of these towns were transformed from places of commerce or government into sites of industrial production. Popular wisdom often associates the Industrial Revolution with technological change (notably the introduction of steam power) and large, mechanized factories looming over the surrounding countryside, and this portrait is not entirely wrong. Nonetheless, the Industrial Revolution involved much more than a technological revolution; it brought about fundamental changes in economic structures and in the organization of work, and it had an enormous impact on both the physical landscape and the people who inhabited it. This phenomenon was both drawn out over decades and uneven, affecting different regions of British North America and of early post-Confederation Canada at different moments and in different ways.

This chapter examines the impact of the Industrial Revolution on families. It pays particular attention to the question of work, both paid and unpaid. It also details the migratory movements undertaken by families in response to industrialization, notably migrations from the countryside to the city (a phenomenon present in virtually all of the British North American colonies), but also the vast transnational movement of people living in Canada, especially Maritimers and French-Canadians, to the United States.

It concentrates on the Maritime and Central Canadian provinces, those that were the most thoroughly industrialized during this period, while also providing glimpses of industrial work in the western provinces, particularly British Columbia. What did urbanization and industrialization mean for families in the Canadian colonies and, after 1867, in Canada? To what extent was family life actually transformed by these large processes? Who came to the assistance of those families whose lives were fundamentally disrupted or impoverished by the Industrial Revolution?

The Industrial Revolution in Canada

Industrialization in the British North American colonies and then in early post-Confederation Canada was, like almost everything that happened in these colonies, highly dependent upon regional specificities. Nonetheless, industrialization in early Canada shared certain essential elements with industrialization elsewhere in the western world. Beginning in the 1850s, the phenomenon of urbanization was solidly implanted in parts of the colonies. Growing cities dotted the landscape, especially in Canada East (soon to be Quebec) and Canada West (soon to be Ontario). In 1851, only 15 per cent of Canada East's population was considered "urban"; four decades later, 34 per cent of Quebec's population was considered to be "urban" (generally defined as inhabiting a town of more than 1,000 people). In Canada West, 14 per cent of the population was urban in 1851; forty years later, this was the case for 39 per cent of Ontario's population. The proportions of urban dwellers were less important in the Maritimes. In Nova Scotia, a mere 7 per cent of the population was urban in 1851; this percentage had climbed to 17 per cent by 1891. And in New Brunswick, there was little change over these forty years: 14 per cent of the population was already considered urban in 1851; that figure was 15 per cent four decades later.[1] The colonies' towns and cities grew because of developments in transportation and communications (canals, roads, steamboats, railways, the telegraph), because of developments in the financial sector and in commerce, and because of the implantation in these sites of new industries, workshops, and factories.

Industrialization as such began in these colonies at mid-century, near the end of the 1840s. By the 1870s and 1880s, certain Canadian cities, notably Saint John, Montreal, Quebec City, Hamilton, and Toronto, could be considered "industrial cities." The Industrial Revolution, a term first used to describe the dramatic economic and social changes that took place in Great Britain between 1760 and 1850, involved a variety of phenomena: technological innovation, urbanization, the restructuring and consolidation of capital, migration (the general rule being that labour followed capital), and the development of a sharper distinction between social classes, notably between the bourgeoisie—those who owned capital—and the members of an emergent working class, who exchanged their labour for wages.

One of the most important consequences of industrialization was a change in the nature of work. In the first half of the nineteenth century, agricultural labour and domestic labour, paid or unpaid, occupied most British North Americans. Some men combined farming with other kinds of seasonal work, while household-based commodity production—the preparation of food, cloth, and clothes—was an important part of the work performed by girls and women.[2] Many adolescent boys entered into apprenticeships in order to learn a craft such as blacksmithing, carpentry, shoemaking, masonry, or barrel making, eventually rising to the position of journeymen and then to that of master artisans. Apprentices were housed by their masters and fed and clothed by the master's wife. One apprenticeship contract signed in 1821 by Abel Thompson, a Montreal baker, and the family of his apprentice, Gabriel Edouard Mailloux, read, in part, as follows:

> Thompson promises to provide boarding, lodging and wearing apparel suitable to the employment of him the said apprentice, to teach and instruct Gabriel Edouard Mailloux in the art and trade of a baker, allow him to follow the Roman Catholic religion, send him to evening school during the first two winters, with his father to pay expenses and it is further agreed that once a year Mailloux will be allowed to go visit his family in Ste Thérèse.[3]

Some girls also undertook formal apprenticeships. In 1840s Montreal, thirteen-year-old Hannah Crotty was "apprenticed to learn straw bonnet making, received board but no pay, and [her] father cancelled the contract when he found her 'doing servant's work' and enduring beatings by the wife [of the master artisan]."[4] In addition to formal apprenticeships, many young men (and some young women) learned a craft within their own families.[5]

As the Industrial Revolution took hold in Canada, the primacy of farm labour and cottage industries was challenged by industrial work, concentrated in workshops, but also in new kinds of workplaces known as manufactories, then factories, usually found in urban areas. For those who worked in the new industrial workshops or in the manufactories—boys and adult men, girls and unmarried adult women—work became a place distinct from home.

No longer did they work in their own dwelling or in a workshop attached to their living quarters. The separation of home and workplace for many residents of the British North American colonies meant that people began to think in terms of distinct "hours of work," rather than in terms of specific tasks to be accomplished. Within the new manufactories, the labour process became fragmented, that is, divided into distinct parts. Rather than making an entire shoe, as a master artisan would have done, employees in a shoe factory might work on the heel, or the sole, or the laces, before handing off their part to a co-worker in another department who would concentrate on another element of the product.[6] These tasks became routinized and often mechanized. In this context, since it was no longer necessary to be a master shoemaker in order to produce a shoe, factory owners could hire women or adolescents without any particular training or skills to do these routinized tasks, and they could pay them much less than a skilled artisan who had completed an apprenticeship and years as a journeyman. Yet some historians caution against overly linear interpretations of the Industrial Revolution. As studies of the baking and confectionery industry in Halifax, Nova Scotia, and the cabinet and furniture industry in late nineteenth-century Ontario demonstrate, some sectors of production were the site of an "uneasy coexistence of the handicraft, manufactory and the factory."[7]

Montreal was Canada's industrial metropolis in the nineteenth century. According to historian Robert Sweeny, it was "the first colonial town in the world to industrialize."[8] Much early industrial production took place along the Lachine Canal (built in the 1820s and widened in the 1840s), in industrial workshops and manufactories ranging in size from 5 to 1100 employees. The availability of hydraulic energy made the canal an attractive site for entrepreneurs, and between 600 and 1000 industrial workplaces were opened there between 1840 and 1940.[9] Saint John, New Brunswick, was home to shipbuilding, but also to nail and brass production. In Quebec City, shoemaking was key; in Hull, Quebec, the lumber industry dominated the local economy. Toronto was home to various forms of "light" industry (for example, clothing and boot and shoe production), but also to heavier industry such as the agricultural implements, notably threshers, produced by the Massey Manufacturing Company. In Hamilton, Ontario, factories housed industries ranging from tobacco to iron moulding to locomotive construction. London, Ontario was home to the baking, brewing, tobacco, and garment industries, but also to wood processing and metalworking factories. In smaller industrial towns such as Sherbrooke (Quebec), Cornwall (Ontario), and Paris (Ontario), the production of textiles such as woollens, knit goods, and cotton predominated.[10]

Towards the late nineteenth century, the Prairies and British Columbia, whose economies were based largely on agriculture or resource extraction, were also touched by the impact of industrialization. The completion of the Canadian Pacific Railway in 1885 contributed to some of these social and economic changes by bringing new Euro-Canadian settlers to the West and by helping to create new markets for processed goods in the western provinces, even if their own economies did not diversify into manufacturing.[11] The arrival of the railway also had a dramatic impact on the lives of Indigenous families living in the Red River settlement and in the territory that later became Saskatchewan.

The colonies of Vancouver Island and British Columbia (after 1871, the province of British Columbia) were driven by resource extraction: furs until the end of the 1840s, then mining (notably gold and coal) and lumber. On Vancouver Island, the Hudson's Bay Company recruited coal miners and their families from England to settle in Nanaimo. Indigenous men and women were also involved in mining and transporting surface coal in Nanaimo. Other coal miners, and many of those mining for gold along the Fraser River, were men on their own, both Chinese and Euro-Canadian. The typical non-Indigenous figure in the province was the "transient male labourer," far from his family.[12] A small number of Chinese gold miners partnered with Indigenous women. In 1870, for instance, 25-year-old Chin Lum Kee, known as Ah Lum, settled down with 16-year-old Lucy, a Stó:lo woman from the eastern Fraser Valley; the couple would have seven children.[13] A very small proportion of B.C.'s population earned its living through agriculture, and at the end of the nineteenth century, only seven per cent of "the total value of goods and services generated in British Columbia ... emanated from secondary manufacturing."[14]

Sawmills and salmon canneries processed two of B.C.'s important resources. From the 1860s onward, Indigenous and Euro-Canadian men

FIGURE 3.1 A 14-year-old coal miner, 1912. Library and Archives Canada/C-030945.

worked in the sawmills of the Alberni Inlet, the Burrard Inlet, and Puget Sound.[15] Squamish men were also central to the longshoring industry on Burrard Inlet.[16] Lekwammen families living on Vancouver Island took advantage of new opportunities in the salmon-canning industry, which sent tinned B.C. salmon to Great Britain from the late 1870s onward. This industry reproduced, to some extent, existing gendered divisions of labour in Lekwammen communities: men fished for salmon, while women worked mending the fishing nets and processing the fish. Even "young children had work cleaning cans."[17]

During the same period, Lekwammen families began to undertake seasonal migrations to the Fraser Valley and to Puget Sound in order to work for cash wages in the hop fields, where the labour of women and children was in particularly high demand. Older children helped with the hop picking, while younger children played nearby as their mothers and other female relatives filled baskets and boxes with hops. Indigenous women also earned money in the tourist industry during their annual migration to Puget Sound, by selling baskets that they had woven during the winter months and posing for tourists'

FIGURE 3.2 The cedar baskets woven by Stó:lō women in British Columbia were exchanged for other trade goods and, later, for cash. Royal British Columbia Museum - PN996.

photographs.[18] Opportunities for industrial labour eventually contributed to a decrease in the average size of Lekwammen families and to a loss in status for elderly members of the community, whose work was devalued in a context where cash wages were increasingly central.[19]

By the end of the nineteenth century, new strategies had been developed in many parts of Canada by which some family members—usually adult men, and often adolescents of both sexes—sought jobs in these industrial workplaces in order to bring home cash wages with which to buy factory-made items that had once been produced at home. In this "family wage economy," cash played an increasingly important role and the work of family members was determined "by the household's need for money to pay for food and to meet other expenses, such as rent."[20]

Migration

The mid-nineteenth century saw the arrival in the British North American colonies of new immigrants who would come to furnish a good part of the industrial workforce, initially building essential infrastructure such as canals and roads. Irish immigrants were already central to certain labour sectors in the Ottawa Valley in the 1830s, most notably the timber trade.[21] In the 1840s, unskilled migrant labourers, especially Irish, constituted the core of the substantial workforce needed to expand the Lachine Canal and to build a new network of canals in the newly United Canada, notably the Welland, Beauharnois, Williamsburg and Cornwall canals.[22]

Most of the Irish immigrants who arrived in the British North American colonies before the 1840s were Protestant. Between 1845 and 1849, great waves of new migrants arrived, fleeing the devastation wrought by the Great Famine. The arrival of these tens of thousands of migrants, most of whom were Catholic, would profoundly reshape the composition of the population of the Canadas and the Maritime provinces. Moreover, these migrants would constitute a central part of the labour force essential to Canada's Industrial Revolution. Many of these immigrants settled in the towns of the British North American colonies: Halifax, Quebec City, Montreal, and Kingston. In 1847 alone, close to 98,000 immigrants, 78,700 of them apparently Irish, came through Quebec City. Many of these migrants eventually moved on to the United States. Some of them were in truly dire straits; their health and their financial situation, already precarious when they left Ireland, were exacerbated by the long transatlantic voyage. Typhus, caused by the body louse, was rampant on their ships. Many ill Irish immigrants were removed at the quarantine station of Grosse-Île, near Quebec City; others were sheltered in the makeshift hospitals known as "sheds" in Montreal's Griffintown and Pointe-Saint-Charles neighbourhoods, where religious sisters such as the Grey Nuns attempted to nurse them back to health. More than 17,000 people died of typhus in the United Canada in 1847.[23] Anti-immigrant sentiment—and anti-Irish sentiment more particularly—was strong in these colonial cities, whose inhabitants feared this influx of poor migrants spreading typhus. Yet those who made it to North America were not the poorest of the poor, but those who possessed the connections and financial resources to undertake the trip.

One of the first consequences of the Industrial Revolution for families was that it encouraged many of them—especially their younger members—to move in search of work. Thus, the Maritime colonies, where industrial production was relatively limited outside Saint John and Halifax, experienced significant outmigration in the second half of the nineteenth century. Many young men left to find work in other parts of Canada or in the United States. Young women also left, most of them to work in the "Boston States," as many Maritimers called New England. In the 1870s and 1880s, these young women tended to work as domestic servants or in the textile and shoe industries. These young women workers sent a good part of their wages back to their parents in the Maritimes, which helped their families participate in an economy increasingly reliant on cash. In times of slowdown at the New England factories, these young women returned temporarily to their homes in the Maritimes.[24] After 1850, such outmigration from the Maritime colonies increased, and there was little in-migration to compensate for this population loss.[25]

In Quebec, families moved from rural areas to industrial towns such as Quebec City, Montreal, or Hull so that various members of the family could work in industries such as leather tanneries, boot and shoemaking, or the fabrication of matches. Often, entire families left overcrowded seigneurial lands and settled in towns and cities. Among the French-Canadian families who left the countryside to relocate in cities, the phenomenon of chain migration was very important. Migrants followed in the tracks of family members who had already left and settled in the same neighbourhoods as those family members, creating a situation where neighbours in the city's industrial quarters were also extended family members. These family members helped their rural relatives adapt to urban life, sometimes providing living quarters and helping them secure industrial jobs. Migrants often married someone from their home parish or their region of origin; extended family members acted as witnesses at these marriages and as godparents when these migrants' children were baptized. Finally, the male members of these extended families often shared a craft such as leather working. Rather than being torn apart by the Industrial Revolution, nineteenth-century families were essential to the transition made by individuals from rural to urban life.[26]

Sometimes, however, only the daughters left the countryside, seeing few prospects for themselves on the family farm and greater possibilities in the city, where they tended to become domestic servants for wealthy families or work in industrial workshops and factories. Men, on the other hand, could often count on inheriting land in rural areas or on paid work in regions dependent upon resource extraction (fishing, forestry, and mining). This meant that nineteenth-century cities such as Montreal and Toronto were home to more women than men, a gender imbalance that was the norm in most western cities in the nineteenth century.[27] It also meant that not all women living in the city could count on finding a husband, making paid labour a lifelong occupation for some.

Both Quebecers and Ontarians, like Maritimers, left in large numbers for New England, the American Midwest, and occasionally the American west coast.[28] The northeastern United States industrialized earlier and more intensively than most parts of Canada, and their factories needed an abundant industrial workforce. Moreover, wages were generally higher in the United States than in Quebec, at least. Between 1840 and 1930, around 900,000 Quebecers settled in the United States, two-thirds of them in New England. In 1840, 60 per cent of the French-Canadians in New England lived in Vermont and 30 per cent of them in Maine. Between 1840 and 1860, the arrival of the railway enabled French-Canadian migrants to travel further and settle in Massachusetts, Rhode Island, Connecticut, and New Hampshire, where they found work in the cotton, wool, and shoemaking industries. As with most other groups of migrants, chain migration was the norm. In 1850, for instance, 70 per cent of the French-Canadians in Southbridge, Massachusetts were from the small town of Saint-Ours, Quebec.[29]

Before the American Civil War, this migration was often temporary, even seasonal. After earning cash wages in the factories of New England, migrants frequently returned to Quebec. The family members who stayed in Quebec facilitated the frequent cross-border movement.[30] After 1865, what had been a phenomenon of temporary migration often became permanent. Increasingly, too, this was a familial migration, as almost all family members could find jobs in these New England factories. The labour of women and that of teenagers of both sexes was highly sought after. Sometimes a factory would hire an entire family. Some employers offered housing to families, a form of industrial paternalism designed to secure workers' loyalty to their employer. The most important factor in the decision about where to settle was the presence of extended family already in the town. Family networks advised new arrivals of the presence of jobs in particular regions and the range of wages offered. Extended family members met new arrivals at the train station, introduced them to employers, helped to find them somewhere to live and even secured them credit with the local grocer, butcher, and baker.[31] Family relations were also crucial inside the factory. In what was then the world's largest textile mill, the Amoskeag Manufacturing Company in Manchester, New Hampshire, kin were expected to "bring their relatives to the factory, assist in their placement, and socialize them into industrial work."[32] While this cushioned the transition to industrial work for many migrants, it also meant that family hierarchies and, sometimes, conflicts, were reproduced within the workplace.

In New England, unlike most parts of Canada at the time, waged work could be a lifelong experience for women. Young girls in their teens secured a factory job, kept working after their marriage and until the birth of their first child, withdrew from the workplace while their children were very young, then returned once the children were a little older. Other women—extended family members and neighbours—in the French-Canadian neighbourhoods that became known as Little Canadas watched the children while their mothers worked at the factory. In many ways, these informal networks of shared childcare, housework, and lodging resembled those in Paris, Ontario, a textile town where women had access to lifelong work in the knitting mills belonging to the Penman Manufacturing Company, and in Lynn, Massachusetts, where Maritime women worked in the shoe industry.[33]

In some New England cities, the French-speaking population was as numerous as in many mid-sized Quebec cities. In 1900, 40 per cent of the population of Manchester, New Hampshire, and 60 per cent of Woonsocket, Rhode Island, residents, for instance, were French-Canadian.[34] The Little Canadas in cities such as Manchester and Woonsocket housed institutions and services catering to French-speaking workers and their children: Catholic churches, parishes, and priests; French-language schools and newspapers; mutual aid societies and credit unions. These institutions knit together communities and offered familiar services in what was then a largely Anglo-Protestant country. They were also a way for French-Canadian elites (priests, teachers, doctors, lawyers, merchants) to supervise the members of these families and, perhaps, to prevent them from becoming too rapidly or too thoroughly "Americanized."

Working in the Factory

For many men, unmarried women, and adolescents, the new manufactories in Canadian cities offered new ways of earning a living. These jobs implied a radical shift in ways of thinking about work, fragmenting the labour process and creating relatively rigid divisions of labour. Workdays in factories were between 10 and 13 hours long, six days a week. Little in the way of protective legislation existed, so adolescents and older children worked days as long as those of adults. Factories were often poorly lit and poorly ventilated; some were insufficiently heated, others overheated. When cooper Richard Somerville was asked in the 1880s if the barrel-making factory in which he worked in Windsor, Ontario was clean and well ventilated, he answered, "Well, there is lots of ventilation, because you can see the snow drifting in."[35] The machinery in these factories was often primitive and dangerous. Workplace accidents were frequent—workers lost limbs and eyes, and female workers were sometimes scalped when their long hair was "caught in the machinery."[36] Children and teenagers, lacking experience, were particularly susceptible to workplace accidents. In Halifax, Nova Scotia, for example, eleven-year-old biscuit maker Joseph Larkins lost a finger when his hand was caught in the rollers of the cracker machine. James Purcell, a fourteen-year-old employee of the same biscuit company, also seriously injured his hand when it was caught in the cogwheels of the cutter.[37]

Children and Youth

Working-class adolescents—and sometimes children as young as 11 or 12—were employed in large numbers in industrial workplaces. In Montreal in 1871, for instance, a full 25 per cent of boys aged 11 to 14 earned a salary. Their chances of finding employment were particularly good in "light" industry, sectors such as textile production (cotton, silk), shoemaking, the rubber industry, and the clothing industry. These children and teenagers tended to give most, if not all, of their salary to their parents; the weekly pay packet was usually handed over to their mother, who would put it towards family expenses. The wages of these children made a significant difference to the family economy. When Daniel Burgess, an employee of the Mayflower Tobacco Factory in Halifax, was asked in the 1880s whether he could live comfortably on wages of $6 per week, he replied by saying, "Well, I have two children working." One of his teenage children worked in the same tobacco factory as his father, the other in a cotton factory.[38] For boys, an industrial job could represent the beginning of lifelong work. For a girl or a young woman, it was usually the beginning of a life-stage that would last for a decade or so, until she married and withdrew from the paid labour force. Most women employed in factories were under the age of 30, even under the age of 25. They typically earned half of what a man their age might earn, the assumption being that they lived at home with their parents and thus could be paid as secondary workers. Children under the age of fifteen earned much less than adults. Older teenage boys could earn almost as much as adult men, and considerably more than older teenage girls.[39]

The workdays of children and teens were just as long as those of adults—typically from 7 a.m. to 6 p.m., which in the winter months meant that these young people barely saw daylight. In one rope-manufacturing factory in Saint John, boys and girls as young as thirteen often worked fourteen-hour days and sometimes worked nights.[40] Employers and foremen sometimes used corporal punishment on children in the workplace, particularly on boys. The Royal Commission on the Relations of Labor and Capital in Canada, which investigated working conditions under industrial capitalism between 1886 and 1889, discovered that children working in Montreal's tobacco industry were beaten for badly cutting tobacco leaves or placed in what was known as the "black hole" (the factory's coal cellar). Children working in the cigar industry were likewise beaten, sometimes with a broomstick or a cigar mould (made of wood or, occasionally, of cast iron). In one notorious case, a seventeen-year-old apprentice named Georgiana Loiselle was beaten with a cigar mould by her employer, J.M. Fortier, a well-known Montreal cigar manufacturer. Fortier's detailed testimony before the Royal Commission on the Relations of Labor and Capital reveals the ways in which corporal punishment was sometimes administered to young employees as a way of teaching them about hierarchy, obedience, and workplace norms under industrial capitalism. Speaking of Loiselle, Fortier stated:

> I cannot contradict what she said, for she told the truth, that I asked her to make one hundred cigars. It was in the afternoon or in the morning before the quitting hour, and she said she was not going to do it; and she spoke in a very impertinent manner. I had had several troubles with the same young lady previous to that, and I had seen her mother, and her mother had prayed me to do the best I could and to correct her the best way I could. So after receiving those instructions, and as I had three or four of her brothers working for me at the time, I took a great interest in the girl—the mother being alone and

supported by her children—to see that the children were properly attended to. I took this young lady by the arm to have her sit down. She would not, so I turned her around and tried to sit her down. She would not. I took the cover of a mould and tried to sit her on my knee, but she was too heavy and fell on the floor. I held her on the floor and smacked her on the backside with the mould. I asked her if she would do it, and after a couple of strikes she said "I will." She got up and sat down at her table and made her one hundred bunches and went off quietly. She never lost one hour, and I think she is very glad to-day to have received the lesson she did, for she has been an obedient girl ever since then.[41]

Children and adolescents also paid fines if they were late for work, if they missed a day of work, or if they broke machinery or other workplace materials. These young workers risked incurring the wrath of their parents, for whom fines took a significant bite out of weekly pay packets.

In the 1880s, different Canadian provinces began adopting factory acts and protective legislation, designed to regulate industrial workplaces and to protect those perceived to be the most vulnerable of workers—principally women and children—from the most extreme consequences of industrial capitalism. Ontario's Factory Act was adopted in 1884 and Quebec's *Acte des manufactures* the following year. Nova Scotia followed suit with similar legislation in 1901. These different pieces of protective legislation limited working hours for women and children and often proscribed night work for them. They also established minimum ages for factory work, in an effort to ensure that children were at school or under the care of their parents rather than in an industrial workplace. Factory and social reformers worried that young women's capacity to conceive and bear children might be compromised by their factory labour; their worries for women's health were often intermingled with concerns about the morality of industrial workplaces and the fact that women sometimes worked in close proximity with men. In fact, however, factories, like other workplaces, were often sex-segregated, with different departments coded "masculine" or "feminine." The enforcement of these factory acts was another story. Not all employers followed the rules. Moreover, many working-class parents sent their underage children out to work because they needed the meagre wages that their children could earn. Some of them lied to factory foremen about their children's ages, or pleaded with them to take on their children despite the fact that they were underage.

Working at Home

Just as in preindustrial Canada, the contributions of all family members to the family economy remained crucial in industrial Canada. These contributions varied, of course, by sex and by age. The republican ideology espoused in Lower Canada by the *Patriotes* hinted at the ideology of "separate spheres." The public sphere—the world of politics, commerce, and work—was increasingly seen to belong to men, while the so-called private sphere—the world of home, family, and domesticity—was seen to be the natural place for women. With industrialization, separate-spheres ideology was reinforced and had an increasingly powerful impact upon societal prescriptions. It nourished and accompanied another influential nineteenth-century ideology, that of the male breadwinner. Adult men were expected to be able to financially support their families; married adult women were expected to be homemakers and nurturers. This set of prescriptions was quite different from those that prevailed in preindustrial Canada, when the boundaries between home and work had been much more fluid and porous. Adult men were now expected to go out to work, leaving the family home—at least during the day—to their wives and the younger children, especially daughters. Working-class men left their homes to work as day labourers or in the new factories; men of the bourgeoisie worked in the liberal professions, as doctors, notaries, or lawyers, or as merchants in the world of trade. The breadwinner ideology remained influential in Canada, as elsewhere in the western world, through the end of the nineteenth century and well into the twentieth, and it shaped institutions and practices ranging from union politics to state policy.

In contrast to life in many parts of preindustrial Canada, the role played by cash in the family economy became much more important in the second half of the nineteenth century. In cities, particularly, families needed cash in order to purchase goods that they might once have produced themselves on the farm—bread, butter, cheese, tobacco, and fuel, for example. Cash wages were thus central to family economies. It was increasingly assumed that the adult men in the household—and notably the husband and father—would, as the family breadwinner, earn this cash wage. If his wage was insufficient to provide for a family—as was frequently the case in the late nineteenth century—it was expected that he would be helped by secondary earners such as older children, both sons and daughters. In all parts of Canada, married Euro-Canadian women, however, were actively discouraged from working outside the home.

For many women (most married women and most very young girls), industrialization thus rooted their work more firmly in the private home. The home clearly remained a site of productive labour through and well beyond the Industrial Revolution, although this work was not always valued as such in official records such as the decennial census. Given the inadequacy of the male breadwinner wage, particularly for working-class jobs, married women were faced with the challenge of finding ways to supplement the male wage—and the meagre wages of their older children—in order to make ends meet. Married working-class women stretched the wages of their husband and children by eating less, so as to reserve scarce quantities of meat for those members of the family who had to go "out" to work. They also found other ways of earning cash—taking in boarders, taking in laundry, and raising chickens, pigs, and even cows in their urban backyards. Elizabeth Martin, for example, lived in Montreal's Sainte-Anne ward. The 1861 census taker found that 50-year-old Madame Martin, the wife of a day labourer and the mother of four children, kept seven pigs and four cows in her tiny urban courtyard so as to have a source of pure milk and fresh meat for her family.[42] Housework—cleaning, cooking, feeding and clothing children—was clearly seen as women's work. In this period, moreover, the technological advances associated with the Industrial Revolution had scarcely any impact on women's domestic labour. The iceboxes and early washing machines that became available in Canada towards the very end of the nineteenth century were not affordable for most families.

Some married women also took in sewing, part of what is called the "putting-out" system. Industrial employers would frequently contract out piecework to individual women, who would complete these sewing tasks in their own homes, often with the help of older daughters. This allowed women to earn extra cash while keeping an eye on their children and undertaking other domestic tasks. Despite its flexible nature, this work had its disadvantages. Women were required to provide their own equipment (sewing machines, needles). They worked in their homes, which were usually poorly lit and poorly ventilated; this situation contributed to problems of eyesight and health. The work was also clearly exploitative. Women earned very little for piecework, and because they worked in isolation, they had little idea what other women doing similar work earned. Evidently, the unionization of this fragmented and isolated female labour force was virtually impossible.

Young girls who did not go out to work helped their mothers with piecework and with domestic chores such as cleaning, cooking, and childcare. Quite frequently, they did not attend school or attended only irregularly, as their unpaid labour was indispensable to the well-being of their families. Whether young girls wanted to undertake domestic labour or paid piecework, or whether they wanted to miss school, were questions that might not even be asked in this period. Although Ontario first passed compulsory schooling legislation in 1871, authorities had difficulty enforcing this legislation and were forced to recognize working-class parents' obvious need for their children's labour. Even children as young as six or seven could be useful "hidden workers" and were often put to work scavenging—gathering coal cinders or wood chips in city streets, alleyways, and lumber yards. Boys and adolescents also worked selling newspapers and shining shoes: newsboys and bootblacks were among the favourite causes of nineteenth-century social reformers, in Canada and elsewhere.[43]

Working in Someone Else's Home

Adolescent girls and young women had a long history of working as domestic servants. Indeed, this was often the first step for a young woman newly arrived in the city from the countryside, or newly arrived in Canada from the United Kingdom or Europe. Service offered the security of a place to live and food on the table and, in very wealthy households, the company of other servants. These advantages were not negligible, but service was also hard work. Since servants lived with their employers, they were always on call, even beyond their workdays of 16 to 18 hours a day. They were required to undertake housework: cleaning, childcare, and sometimes cooking. Occasionally, they were also required to look after the garden and any animals that the employing family might keep. In most households in Canada, there was only one domestic, known as a "general servant," which meant that she did everything. Since bed and board were provided, salaries were low. Often, young women sent a considerable proportion of their salary to their own parents in the countryside or overseas; going out to work as a servant was thus one family strategy in the context of an industrialized society.

In addition to the discrete tasks shouldered by servants, there were other, sometimes less tangible, requirements for the job. Servants were expected to be single and "respectable" (a somewhat vague term that included being clean, polite, honest, and discreet).[44] Most servants came from working-class or rural backgrounds; many were immigrants, largely from the United Kingdom. In Quebec cities, servants were often French-Canadian girls or young women from the countryside. Thus, there were often considerable differences in class, age, and sometimes ethnicity between servants and their employers. These differences could exacerbate everyday tensions, in a context where employer and employee lived in close quarters. Servants had little time off and little freedom. If they were fired, they also lost their home. Moreover, although private homes were often seen as secure sites of employment—rural and working-class parents often preferred to see their daughters working as servants in private homes, rather than as employees in a factory—these settings could be sites of violence and abuse. Numerous instances were recorded of servants being victims of sexual assaults by their employer or a member or guest of the employing household.[45]

As Canada industrialized and jobs for women in new industrial workplaces became more numerous, domestic service became a less popular option for many young women. At least the hours of factory work were clearly defined. The relationship between the factory worker and her foreman or boss was not as personal (some would say as stifling) as between a servant and her mistress. Finally, service was indelibly tainted with the stigma of inferiority. In the 1890s, Prince Edward Islander Lucy Maud Montgomery, who would later become famous for her *Anne of Green Gables* books, noted in her diary:

> Clara C., by the way, is in Boston now, working out as a domestic servant. It is absurd. Clara herself never had any lofty ideals or ambitions but I simply cannot understand her parents, especially Aunt Annie, permitting such a thing. If she wanted to earn her living they were quite able to afford to educate or train her to some occupation which would not have involved a loss of social caste. The idea of Clara Campbell "working out." It would be laughable if it were not so tragic.[46]

By the end of the nineteenth century, service had clearly become an occupation for the most newly arrived women in a city and often an occupation of last resort, for women without the skills, resources, or contacts to find other work.[47] That said, across Canada, service remained the largest single employment sector for women through the end of the century. According to the 1891 *Census of Canada*, over 40 per cent of Canadian women over the age of ten listed as having an occupation worked as domestic servants. By 1901, this percentage had dropped, but remained significant at 34 per cent.[48] Domestic service as an institution was thus central both for working-class women and their families and for the bourgeois households and families that they helped to maintain.

Living in an Industrial City

What did an industrial city look, smell, and sound like? Historian Nicolas Kenny writes of city-dwellers experiencing industrialization through their senses:

> The large factories, warehouses and transport infrastructures that confronted the eye, the noise and rumblings, the vast plumes of black smoke that thickened and fouled the air, as well as the increasing population density that resulted in a new level of physical proximity among individuals, often in crowded and unsanitary conditions, made urban dwellers acutely aware of their bodily contact with the environment, and were denounced by hygienists as the "evils" common to the "prosperous" cities of Europe and North America.[49]

As urbanization and industrialization took root in Canada, living conditions as well as working conditions were transformed. Working-class families often chose to live near their workplaces; thus, entire working-class residential neighbourhoods grew up in the shadow of factories. Older housing in these neighbourhoods tended to be shabby and sometimes dilapidated; newer constructions were often thrown up in a hurry and cheaply built. Old or new, this housing was often overcrowded. Families lived without electricity or electrical appliances. Until the 1860s in Montreal, and later in many other cities and small towns, they lived without running water in their house or flat. Proper secondary sewer systems came even later, so most nineteenth-century working-class families relied upon outdoor privies, and not the indoor water closets that had begun to be installed in wealthier homes in the last decades of the century.[50] A reporter writing in the Montreal *Star* in the 1880s described a row of outdoor privies in Montreal's working-class Griffintown neighbourhood:

> In front of the house twelve closets are ranged, and at one side separated by a board fence, is a stable. From the occupants of this house it was learned, that there have been some fifteen cases of diphtheria and typhoid fever recently in that locality. The twelve closets are used by the inmates of this row of houses, and by those of a row on McCord Street, or twelve families in all. Under the houses about fourteen loads of rubbish from cellars of grocery stores on McCord Street, consisting, so it is said, of old fish and other foul smelling matters, were recently dumped. When it rains the smell from this stuff is overpowering.[51]

Toronto health inspectors likewise complained of the stench emanating from outdoor privies and from industrial slaughterhouses, especially during the summer.[52] Even in Canada's largest cities, animals such as chickens, cows, pigs, and of course horses, were everywhere. City streets were thus covered in animal droppings; the noises made by animals were also a part of the everyday soundscape.

Historian Bettina Bradbury has described the ways in which city streets filled up at particular hours of the day, as men and teenagers left for industrial worksites and then returned at the end of the day:

> Most workers walked to their jobs, seeking housing that made the journey to work and home again possible. As a result the streets filled up well before six each morning with men, boys, and young women, the proportions of each depending on the work available in the neighbourhood. Six days a week, from homes throughout the city, thousands of workers took to rickety, rat-eaten, wooden sidewalks, brick pavements, or dilapidated flagstone footpaths, spilling over into the streets and converging on the major thoroughfares that led to the city's largest factories. Ten, eleven, or even twelve hours later, at dusk and at times well after dark, hundreds of work-weary men, women, and children, released in waves, again trudged the streets, now heading for home. This filling up of streets at predictable and increasingly standardized times ... was a new phenomenon, a product both of the growing spatial separation of home and work and of the formalization of work hours that accompanied the spread of waged labour in large workplaces.[53]

Urban streets also filled up at other hours, as married women set out to do their daily errands at the market or at the small businesses that dotted their neighbourhood. During the working day, homes and residential neighbourhoods became, to some extent, feminized, that is, populated largely by women and girls. In working-class neighbourhoods during the day, women could be found in their homes, but also on their doorsteps and balconies and in the streets, talking, borrowing and lending goods, trading services, and sometimes arguing, with their neighbours.[54]

At the same time, the more dramatic differentiation of social classes that resulted from industrialization was visible in the urban landscape. Cities also made room for wealthy bourgeois neighbourhoods, where capitalists and members of the liberal professions lived with their families. These neighbourhoods were usually geographically and topographically favoured, sheltered from the prevailing winds that transmitted industrial odours and high up from the flood plains, whereas poorer neighbourhoods were inundated during rainstorms or with the melting of the snow in the spring. Houses were much larger in these neighbourhoods, more solidly built, and surrounded by green space in the form of gardens, trees, and soon, city parks.[55]

The rapid expansion and industrialization of Canadian cities were accompanied by the development of new public health problems. Drinking water, although filtered, was often polluted; in most Canadian cities, municipal water supplies were not treated until the beginning of the twentieth century. Cow's milk was often contaminated; pasteurization would not be widespread until the early twentieth century. Uncontaminated meat was also difficult to procure in urban areas. Dirt roads were paved over the course of the nineteenth century, which made it somewhat easier to keep houses and residential neighbourhoods cleaner. In most Canadian cities, however, municipal garbage collection was unheard of before the later decades of the nineteenth century. Many residents of nineteenth-century cities suffered from contagious diseases such as tuberculosis, or from diseases of privation or malnutrition such as anemia and rickets. Infant mortality rates were scandalous by today's standards, particularly in Montreal, which was notorious for having infant mortality rates comparable to those of Calcutta. As late as 1900, the infant mortality rate in Montreal was 190 deaths per 1000 births; this meant that almost 1 child in 5 did not live to see his or her first birthday. These babies died of gastrointestinal diseases related to contaminated water and cow's milk. By 1921, rates of infant mortality had decreased to 6 per cent in wealthier neighbourhoods such as Westmount and Outremont, but remained close to 20 per cent in the city's working-class districts. These residential and class differences were overlaid by religious and linguistic differences. Infant mortality rates in Montreal were worst among French-speaking Catholic families, slightly better among English-speaking Catholic families, and better still (although still very high by today's standards) among English-speaking Protestant families. The variation in these rates owed a great deal to differing levels of income and wealth. It also owed something to the fact that French-Canadian mothers tended to wean their infants sooner than did Irish-Catholic or Anglo-Protestant mothers; their babies were thus exposed to the contaminants in cow's milk and municipal water supplies earlier than were other babies. Some French-Canadian physicians were willing to classify stillbirths as live births, so that these babies might be baptized and thus, in the eyes of their parents, avoid purgatory; this had the effect of making the rates of infant mortality in Quebec higher than those in other Canadian provinces.[56] Maternal mortality rates were also very high across Canada.[57] While rural areas were by no means exempt from infant and maternal mortality or from contagious disease, the sheer density of industrial cities, alongside poverty and inadequate living and working conditions for many, and the absence of effective state services, meant that city-dwellers were particularly badly affected by these public health problems.

Charity and Social Assistance

Families in need of assistance relied on charity from churches and religious organizations (Catholic, Protestant, and Jewish), from private associations often managed by bourgeois women (known colloquially as "Ladies Bountiful"), and from philanthropists. Few residents of British North America or early Canada expected the state to step in to assist the poor or the needy, although the state did provide small subsidies to private institutions. Moreover, Nova Scotia and New Brunswick had their own versions of the English poor law, and poorhouses established in Halifax and Saint John took in the most destitute individuals without families of their own to care for them. Those in need of tangible assistance also relied upon institutions such as the Jost Mission, a city mission established in Halifax in 1868 by a local businessman and administered first by the Young Men's Christian Association, and then by the Methodist Church.[58] In Canada West, later Ontario, larger towns and cities such as Kingston and Toronto had established asylums and Houses of Industry by the second half of the nineteenth century; voluntary societies and denominational charities were also key providers of charity in these towns. The need for poor relief in nineteenth-century British North America was particularly acute during the winter. Winter meant a slowdown in many trades and industries, lower wages, and much larger portions of the family budget allocated to the costs of fuel such as coal and firewood.[59]

In Canada East, later Quebec, the vast majority of assistance to the poor, the ill, and those without families came from the Catholic Church, and more particularly from female religious orders such as the Grey Nuns (Sisters of Charity), the Sisters of Providence, or the Sisters of Mercy. Female religious orders were already active in charity work in New France. Beginning in the 1840s, however, as part of the phenomenon that has come to be known as the "renouveau religieux" (religious renewal), Montreal Archbishop Ignace Bourget recruited a large number of religious communities, both male and female, from France and encouraged the creation of new orders in Canada.[60] The implantation in Quebec of all of these new religious communities helped to increase the strength and institutionalize the presence of the Catholic Church in Quebec through the 1850s and 1860s. While some of the female orders were devoted to teaching, many others made nursing and charitable work their vocations. These religious communities provided essential services to the poor and the ill. They set up orphanages, for instance, for children without parents, or sometimes for children with only one living parent, or with parents who were both alive, but unable to look after their children. The

Grey Nuns, for example, administered a hospital for abandoned children, most of them considered "illegitimate" because their biological parents were not married. Records for the year 1867 show that, of the 652 children admitted that year, only 33 survived. Such devastating numbers speak to the poor health of many working people in this period, but also suggest that the mothers of these children, who were in many cases unmarried, were particularly reluctant to seek medical assistance for fear of revealing their pregnancy—considered a sin for unmarried women in this society. Those children who did survive infancy were housed by the Grey Nuns until the age of eighteen. They were made available for adoption to families seeking a child. Older boys were often placed in apprenticeships in order to learn a trade.[61]

Female religious communities such as the Grey Nuns and the Sisters of Providence also managed "salles d'asile," where parents could place their children temporarily, by the day. Religious orders ran hospices for the elderly—and particularly for elderly women—without families to take care of them. They administered schools for children who suffered from visual impairment or who were hard of hearing. Like lay reformers or Ladies Bountiful, they conducted home visits. Ostensibly carried out in order to survey the material needs of poor families and provide them with tangible aid, they were also opportunities for the nuns to observe the living conditions of these families and to dispense advice, often unsolicited.

The *Report of the Royal Commission on the Relations of Labor and Capital in Canada*, published in 1889, took stock of many of the consequences for Canadians of the first several decades of the Industrial Revolution. It shows that the Industrial Revolution had an enormous, albeit uneven, impact on Canadian families. It provided new paid work opportunities to some of them, encouraged many of them to move from the countryside to the city, or from one geographic region to another, and altered, often considerably, both their working and their living conditions. It also imposed serious limits on the choices open to members of these families—choices that varied by social class, by gender, and by age, as well as by religion, language, and race. It had an impact on such key family decisions as "how long to stay in school, when to move into or out of wage work, when to leave home, and when to marry."[62] During the second half of the nineteenth century, as the next chapter details, the state, politics, legislation, and the legal system too shaped—or attempted to shape—the Indigenous and Euro-Canadian families living in the territory that became Canada.

4

Families and the State, 1840–1914

ALONGSIDE MAJOR ECONOMIC transformations, developments in state formation and new legal regimes had a significant impact on families in Canada over the second half of the nineteenth century. Among these political and legal developments were a series of measures designed to tie married women more closely to their homes and to limit their participation in the public sphere. Towards the end of the nineteenth century and at the turn of the twentieth century, women—particularly married women—fought back, demanding judicial reforms and new civil and political rights around crucial issues such as property and suffrage. In the same period, legislation designed to see that children were both educated and protected—compulsory schooling, alongside laws limiting children's paid work—was adopted in many (but not all) Canadian provinces. Measures designed to be protective, but sometimes also punitive, such as the establishment of industrial and reform schools in the nineteenth century and, in the first decades of the twentieth century, the adoption of a federal juvenile delinquency law and the creation of juvenile courts, also took place. Finally, various laws adopted by the new federal government targeted Indigenous families, constraining, often severely, the choices and opportunities open to men, women, and children in these communities. All of these legislative measures were implemented against a new political and judicial backdrop, created by the adoption of the Lower Canadian Civil Code in 1866, the passage of the British North America Act by the British Parliament in 1867, which enabled the Canadian Confederation and the creation of a Canadian state, and the adoption of the Canadian

Criminal Code in 1892. To a significant and increasing extent, then, aspects of the lives of both Indigenous and settler families were shaped by the Canadian state taking form in these decades.

Marriage, the State, and the Law

The 1840s and 1850s witnessed what many historians consider to have been the masculinization of the public sphere. In Canada East (Quebec), for instance, widows' dower rights were gradually chipped away, becoming, for many widows, little more than a legal fiction. The formal abolition of the seigneurial land-tenure regime in 1854 likewise favoured a system of property holding conducive to capitalism and land speculation and less concerned with the protection of customary familial rights. In 1849, women's right to vote in Canada East—a right that had been indirectly accorded with the Constitutional Act of 1791, but that had been voted away by the Lower Canadian assembly in 1834—was officially abolished. Prince Edward Island had decided to prohibit women from voting in 1832.[1] In Nova Scotia, the 1850s saw the beginnings of a "movement to explicitly exclude women from the vote."[2]

The Civil Code adopted in Canada East in 1866 constituted an attempt to modernize the Custom of Paris brought to North America in the seventeenth century with the first French settlers and the French imperial government. Modelled in part upon the French Napoleonic Code of 1804, it adapted French civil law to the North American setting. Like the Custom of Paris, the Civil Code was designed to offer a certain amount of protection to family property (what was known as the *communauté des biens*, created by the pooling of property accumulated by the husband and the wife respectively over the course of their marriage). But it was little—if at all—better than the Custom of Paris in recognizing the autonomy of married women. According to the Civil Code, married women in Quebec were, like minors and the intellectually disabled, judicially "incapable," that is, unable to represent themselves in court or to sign legal documents, including, for example, rental leases. Husbands were the sole managers of the family property (*communauté des biens*), which included all of the property acquired by either spouse after their marriage. The Civil Code was designed to protect what were seen to be "family interests," assumed to be equivalent to the interests of the husband and father, and only to a lesser degree the interests of other members of the family. Men and women under the age of 21, for instance, were not allowed to marry without parental consent.[3]

Marriage and Divorce

The British North America Act and the Canadian Confederation of 1867 set out a constitutional and political framework for aspects of family life. Marriage was deemed to fall under federal jurisdiction.[4] Legal historian Constance Backhouse's characterization of nineteenth-century Canadian marriage as "pure patriarchy" seems relatively accurate given contemporary statutes and, especially, the workings of the courts.[5] The common-law provinces (all provinces but Quebec) inherited from the English common law the principle of "marital unity"; as the famed English jurist William Blackstone declared in 1765, "By marriage, the husband and wife are one person in law." For all intents and purposes, this meant that the wife's legal personhood was subsumed in that of the husband; marriage meant "civil death" for women.[6] In the common-law provinces, then, as in Quebec, married women could not contract or sue in their own names. In the English-Canadian provinces, however, where the concept of a *communauté des biens* did not exist, married women's personal property belonged to their husbands. They retained ownership of any real estate acquired before marriage, but it was their husbands' prerogative to manage this property.[7]

The 1867 Confederation made the federal government responsible for the regulation of divorce, but it would be a century before Ottawa passed divorce legislation.[8] In practice, then, the provinces continued to manage divorce as they had done before Confederation. Prior to the twentieth century, divorce was an extremely rare phenomenon in Canada: in most communities, it was both socially unacceptable and difficult to procure. For most couples, the possibility of divorce was so remote that it would not have even sprung to mind as a solution to an unhappy marriage. A handful of petitions for divorce, based on English legal tradition, were submitted to the legislature of Upper Canada/the United Province of Canada between 1839 and 1867; five of these were granted. The English tradition allowed for the granting of a divorce to a husband who could prove his wife's adultery; wives, however, had to prove that their husbands were adulterous and, in addition, "that they had been guilty of some other serious crime such as incest or bigamy."[9] New Brunswick and Nova Scotia appear to have been more lenient. Nova Scotia, for instance, passed a series of laws permitting divorce under certain circumstances as early as 1758, New Brunswick did the same as early as 1791, and Prince Edward Island passed a divorce law in 1833.[10] These Maritime colonies, later provinces, established matrimonial courts designed to hear petitions for divorce. In New Brunswick, legally admissible reasons when seeking a divorce were sexual impotence, frigidity, consanguinity, and adultery. In Nova Scotia, marital cruelty (physical and mental) was also an admissible reason for applying for a divorce. Yet, what lawyers and judges considered "ordinary" domestic violence was not seen to warrant divorce. One Nova Scotia judge, Justice R.H. Graham, argued that cruelty "must in order to be ground for divorce establish bodily hurt, or injury to health, or a reasonable apprehension of one or the other. Danger to life or limb or health is the foundation of the doctrine."[11] In Quebec, the Civil Code made no provision for divorce, stating clearly that "Marriage can only be dissolved by the natural death of one of the parties; while both live it is indissoluble."[12] After Confederation, the federal government did assume the responsibility for married couples across the country seeking a divorce through a special statute, but a Parliamentary divorce was an option that was not only costly, but also extremely public. In British Columbia, which entered Confederation in 1871, the courts decided that they would issue divorces, as was then the practice in England.[13] In all of these provinces, however, as at the federal level of government, prevailing morals discouraged divorce whenever possible. Even the most brutal forms of conjugal violence—beatings with heavy objects, strangling, scalding with boiling water—could be deemed an insufficient justification for women to seek and obtain a divorce.[14]

In the absence of a realistic chance of securing a divorce, a wife who wished to live apart from her husband could sue (or could have her father or another male relative sue) her partner in the civil courts for alimony. While such an action did not put a legal end to the marriage and thus did not allow for remarriage, it did provide some financial support to a woman who saw no other option than to live apart from her husband. These civil suits for alimony, when successful, provided comparable results to the "separation of bed and board" (*séparation de corps* and *séparation de biens*) requested by some married women in Quebec, who were thus permitted to live apart from their legal husbands and to manage their own finances—but who, evidently, could not remarry. Obtaining a *séparation de corps* in Quebec was easier for a husband than for a wife: while the former had to prove a wife's infidelity, the latter had to prove not only that her husband had been unfaithful, but that he had moved his mistress into the family home![15]

In the nineteenth century, fathers almost invariably received custody of their children in the event of divorce or legal separation.[16] This changed, however, at least in Quebec, around the turn of the twentieth century, as judges began increasingly giving custody to mothers in the event of a *séparation de corps*, citing what was seen to be women's "maternal instinct" and their natural superiority in the field of child-rearing. Although paternal authority was enshrined in Quebec's Civil Code, adopted in 1866, the fact that the breadwinning role assigned to fathers physically removed them from the home during the day and, indeed, often for long stretches of time, increasingly made them, in judges' eyes, less than suitable caregivers.[17]

By the later decades of the nineteenth century, married women were seeking new rights, including married women's property acts, laws restraining and punishing domestic violence, and the right to vote. Late-nineteenth-century female activists sought not so much to make divorce easier to obtain, but to make life within the confines of legal marriage better. In all of the common-law provinces, as in the United States, women campaigned for married women's property acts over the second half of the nineteenth century. Such laws, adopted in Ontario in 1872, in British Columbia in 1873, and in Nova Scotia in 1884, gave married women property rights similar to those enjoyed by single and widowed women. By the beginning of the twentieth century, laws protecting the property of married women had been passed in all Canadian provinces except Quebec.[18] Married Women's Property Acts allowed married women to maintain property that they had brought to the marriage, or that they inherited after their wedding, or wages that they had earned, separate from that of their husbands and gave them the right to manage this property. In practice, such laws sometimes had little impact since few nineteenth-century women owned property of their own; this was particularly the case in rural areas, where farmland tended to be inherited by sons and where women were more likely to bring to their marriages household goods and sometimes small sums of cash.[19] In contrast, in urban areas such as Hamilton, Ontario or Victoria, British Columbia, Married Women's Property Laws did allow some women, and sometimes even those possessing only modest amounts of property, to exercise considerable financial independence.[20]

In the same period, other kinds of protection for family property were adopted in some of the western provinces. Social and political reformer Emily Murphy, for instance, was instrumental in the passage of Alberta's Dower Act in 1911. Dower gave widows the right to use one-third of their deceased husband's property, including the family home, for the remainder of their life; in England, this common-law right (abolished in the 1830s) had long been known as the "widow's third." Within the framework of its Homestead Act, the colony of British Columbia had introduced "homestead dower"—a measure that gave widows the right to continued use of family homesteads as long as they were raising their children—as early as 1867. Moreover, the Pacific Northwest colony of Vancouver Island had already adopted a

Deserted Wives Act in 1862. The 1862 legislation "provided a deserted woman, at the courts' discretion, with financial independence and contractual autonomy and protected her property and earnings from seizure by her husband or his creditors." Legislation providing some financial protection to deserted wives was especially useful in a settler colony where adult men were particularly mobile. Both deserted wives legislation and homestead dower "insulat[ed] family property from the volatility of the capitalist marketplace"—protection that appeared increasingly essential to some legislators and reformers.[21]

Daughters (and their reputations) constituted another kind of family property, and civil law offered some protection of this property through what was known as "the tort of seduction." Fathers of unmarried women who had become pregnant could use seduction law in order to extract financial compensation from their daughter's lover, arguing that the daughter's pregnancy and childbirth deprived the father of a significant source of domestic labour and also brought shame to the family name. It is no accident that these legal proceedings were required to be undertaken by the woman's father, whose interests were seen to be paramount.[22]

Family Matters in the Criminal Code of 1892

The BNA Act and Confederation made criminal law the responsibility of the federal government, and the existing body of criminal law in what had been the British North American colonies was codified in 1892. The Criminal Code adopted in 1892 confirmed the criminalization of infanticide, abortion, and all forms of contraception or what later generations would call "family planning." Its Section 179c (replaced by Section 207 in 1900) stated the following:

> Everyone is guilty of an indictable offense and liable to two years' imprisonment who knowingly, without lawful excuse or justification, offers to sell, advertises, publishes an advertisement of or has for sale or disposal any medicine, drug or article intended or represented as a means of preventing conception or causing abortion.[23]

The advertising, sale, and distribution of contraceptives such as condoms and pessaries (diaphragms) were thus outlawed. The criminalization of contraceptive devices was a major reason—although not the only reason—that *coitus interruptus*, or the withdrawal method, remained the most popular form of contraception in Canada right through the 1930s.[24]

The 1892 Criminal Code likewise consolidated the various statutory rulings against abortion that had been passed by the different British North American colonies over the course of the nineteenth century. Public opinion opposing abortion, including abortions practised early on in the pregnancy, before what was termed "quickening" (when the woman first felt the fetus's movements) hardened over the last decades of the nineteenth century.[25] Yet in a society where existing birth control methods were unreliable or difficult to procure, women and couples sometimes resorted to abortion when contraception failed them. Some women hoping to terminate a pregnancy relied upon abortifacients. These included herbal remedies such as tansy or commercial remedies such as "Friar's French Female Regulator," the latter advertised in Canadian daily newspapers. Others sought the assistance of abortionists—occasionally bona fide physicians, but also unlicensed practitioners who over time came to be known as "back-alley" abortionists. All acts leading to abortion were considered criminal. Historians and demographers have only an imperfect idea of the numbers of women in Canada who resorted to abortion during this period, however, since the cases that came to the attention of the public or the courts were generally those that ended with the death of the mother, deaths usually caused by infection, blood poisoning, or hemorrhage.[26]

Infanticide—the killing of an infant—was a crime generally committed by young, poor, unmarried women with limited material and familial resources, for whom the prospect of raising a child alone seemed virtually impossible. The 1892 Criminal Code included both "concealment of a birth" and "failing to obtain reasonable assistance during childbirth" as offences of lesser judicial weight than murder or manslaughter. Across Canada, judges were notoriously lenient with women suspected of having committed infanticide. These men of the law appear to have opted for mercy, frequently acquitting women charged with an infanticide-related offence because they recognized the social costs and consequences of unwed motherhood. Furthermore, these members of the legal elite were fundamentally little concerned with the fate of babies born to poor mothers. These babies were often "illegitimate" to boot, in the sense that their parents were unmarried. Researchers have noted a remarkable stability in the judicial treatment of infanticide: whether studying the eighteenth or the twentieth century, Nanaimo, British Columbia or Montreal, Quebec, they all come to relatively similar conclusions about the decisions made by judges and the reasoning behind these decisions.[27] That said, not all women benefited from the mercy of the courts: in 1905, Maggie McCarthy, 21 years old, was sentenced to three years in Kingston Penitentiary for "neglecting to obtain assistance in childbirth." Lucy Nadgwan, a sixteen-year-old Indigenous woman from Walkerton, Ontario who was, like Maggie McCarthy, a domestic servant, was sentenced to two years in Kingston Penitentiary for the same crime.[28]

Family Violence

Issues related to marriage and family could come before the criminal courts in other ways, notably when a woman charged a violent husband with assault and battery. Family violence, of course, has a long history, but most cases of such violence were spoken of only within the immediate circles of family and neighbourhood. Family violence could be motivated by psychological factors, but it could also have social causes such as poverty, unemployment, migration, isolation, illness, or alcoholism. Such violence is a reminder that families in the nineteenth century, like families today, were not always harmonious entities and that power, authority, and resources were unequally distributed within families, depending on age, generation, and gender. A longstanding unwillingness to interfere with the right of the husband and father to manage "his" family meant that outsiders were reluctant to intervene even if they suspected abuse. It was in working-class neighbourhoods, where homes were smaller and closer together, walls were often paper-thin, and boarders were sometimes present, that neighbours and others not part of the immediate family could least easily turn a blind eye or a deaf ear to domestic violence and where, if this violence reached limits considered unacceptable, they might intervene.

From the 1870s onward, under the influence of the temperance movement, the movement for the prevention of cruelty to animals, and the activism of "first-wave" feminists, what was perceived to be excessive family violence increasingly became construed as a social problem.[29] Yet the cases that appeared before the courts were just the tip of the iceberg, as taking a violent husband to court was costly and the chance of winning one's case slim. Furthermore, a wife who saw her husband successfully convicted of domestic violence was a woman forced to make do without her husband's wages if he was imprisoned. In the event that he was fined, this was money taken away from the household budget. Small wonder, then, that most women sought other solutions, including leaving, seeking help from neighbours, extended family, or local policemen, or staying and putting up with the physical abuse. The fact that a number of women who decided to have their husband charged with wife-beating subsequently neglected to show up for the hearing suggests that they hoped that the charge itself might have an impact on their husband's behaviour. Yet when the situation was intolerable, some women went through with their recourse to the law: as a Mrs. Irvine declared before the judge in 1879, "I can live better without him, your Honor, I only stand in dread of my life day after day." Just under half of the husbands charged with domestic violence in historian Kathryn Harvey's sample from 1870s Montreal were actually convicted: 154 of the 331 verdicts that she uncovered were guilty convictions. The violence of husbands was attributed to drinking, to conflict over money, to jealousy, and to questions of authority over children. Harvey has found that roughly 15 per cent of domestic violence cases in this decade involved violent wives: in working-class Montreal, as in other cities around the western world, physical violence (between spouses, between parents and children, among neighbours, even directed at grocers or bailiffs) was a much greater part of everyday life for both women and men than it would come to be in the twentieth century.[30]

Women's Suffrage

Visions of marriage and the family were imbricated even with laws that appeared outwardly to have little to do with familial matters, such as the securing of the federal vote for many Canadian women in 1918. Family considerations dictated which women would first obtain the federal vote in 1917: in a political ploy designed to secure the re-election of Robert Borden's Union (pro-conscription) government in Ottawa, military nurses and the immediate female relatives (mothers, sisters, wives) of men in the armed services were granted the vote in federal elections. The following year, the federal suffrage was extended to all adult women, with the significant exception of Indigenous women and women originally from China or Japan, who would not be permitted to vote in federal elections until the middle decades of the twentieth century. Questions of ethnicity and race were crucial to suffrage battles: educated white women, both Protestant and Catholic, asked why they should be denied the vote when men that they considered their social inferiors—immigrants from southern and eastern Europe, presumed to be poorly educated—should be allowed this privilege by sole virtue of their sex. In debates around the federal suffrage, as in the discussions of provincial suffrage that took place in all of the provinces, women's right to vote was seen as a potential point of tension, even overt conflict, within the family and notably within married couples. How would the married couple, the cornerstone of the heterosexual family, survive should women choose to vote differently than their husbands? Supporters of women's right to vote chose to emphasize the "social housekeeping" that women armed with the vote would be able to undertake, using their political citizenship to carry out the social and municipal reforms for which they were best "suited" as wives and mothers.[31]

Legislating and Regulating Childhood

Education and charity—two realms of social life that were crucial for families—were deemed provincial responsibilities in the 1867 British North America Act, which meant that there would continue to be a certain degree of variation among the provinces through the nineteenth and twentieth centuries. In the nineteenth century, informal schooling took place within private homes and in the context of apprenticeships; more formal forms of education were dispensed by the private schools—many of them religiously based—that flourished in the nineteenth-century Canadian colonies. From the mid-nineteenth century onward, most Canadian provinces funded common schools through provincial grants and, increasingly, municipal property taxes. Attendance at these state-funded schools was highly irregular, however. In rural and agricultural areas, many children attended only in late fall and winter, once the harvest was over. Within individual families, not all children attended school; some were kept at home to help with unpaid domestic labour or with the work of the farm. Most children who did attend school did so for a relatively short period of their life, gradually abandoning formal learning somewhere between late childhood and early adolescence, when their families could no longer make do without their salary or their unwaged work. Even the most willing parents and children had to confront logistical obstacles to school attendance: an 1851 report on schooling in rural Clarence Township, in eastern Canada West (later Ontario), noted that "the inhabitants of this county are widely scattered; many of them are commencing to clear the bush, roads in many parts bad, schools few and far between, good teachers fewer, and difficulty experienced in paying such as are employed."[32]

Increasingly, sporadic and short-lived school attendance was seen to be a problem by "school promoters" (teachers, school superintendents, school and factory inspectors, union representatives, politicians) who believed that public schools could contribute to the making of good citizens and to the creation of an educated workforce in a society that was gradually industrializing.[33] State intervention was seen by many school promoters to be necessary in order to convince parents to send their children to school. Indeed, some argued that the state needed to take over certain tasks, such as education, religious instruction, and discipline, traditionally left to parents. Reverend Egerton Ryerson, superintendent of schools in Canada West, then Ontario, from 1844 to 1876, went so far as to declare in 1858 that "the State, ... so far from having nothing to do with the children, constitutes their collective parent, and is bound to protect them against any unnatural neglect or cruel treatment, on the part of the individual parent, and to secure them all that will qualify them to become useful citizens to the state."[34]

In all provinces but one, then, state schooling was made free, and minimal attendance obligatory, for certain children (aged 12 and under, or 14 and under) over the last decades of the nineteenth century and the first decades of the twentieth. Ontario was the first province to legislate, in 1871, followed by British Columbia in 1873, then Prince Edward Island in 1877. By the end of the First World War, only Quebec had not adopted compulsory schooling legislation: this would happen in 1943. (Newfoundland, which would remain outside the Canadian Confederation until 1949, adopted compulsory schooling in 1942.) As rates of school attendance gradually increased in Canada, it became characteristic for children to spend a period of their lives in the company of their peers.[35] In most provinces, compulsory schooling laws were coupled with legislation limiting child labour, as teachers and truancy officers alike came to understand that in cities and manufacturing centres, at least, one of the principal sources of competition for the school was the factory. Yet significant loopholes to this legislation existed in all Canadian provinces, as civil servants and politicians were forced to acknowledge that some working-class families simply could not survive without their children's paid or unpaid work. Moreover, while free public schooling meant that families no longer had to foot the bill for tuition or textbooks, parents still needed to be able to find the money necessary to purchase shoes and decent clothing for their children to wear to school.[36]

In addition to compulsory schooling laws, aimed at all children, the state began intervening at the turn of the twentieth century to protect children seen as particularly in need of help and to regulate the behaviour of children considered delinquent. In both of these cases, state intervention was also a way of regulating the behaviour of these children's parents, judged inadequate or misguided. Ontario, for instance, adopted a Children's Protection Act in 1893. The province's first Superintendent of Neglected and Dependent Children was social reformer John Joseph Kelso, one of the best-known nineteenth-century Canadian "child-savers." [37] Kelso developed a longstanding working relationship with Ontario's network of Children's Aid Societies, and he in fact constituted one of many bridges between the world of private charity, or philanthropy, and the growing involvement of the state in social life. Children's Aid Societies, regulated and financed in part by the government, took an interest in children abandoned or severely neglected by their own families. Eschewing the institutional model of orphanages so important in mid-nineteenth-century Ontario and which would remain prevalent in neighbouring Quebec through the mid-twentieth century, CAS employees worked to locate foster families for those children deemed neglected.

In the last decades of the nineteenth century and at the turn of the twentieth, "delinquent" children were increasingly of concern to social reformers and to legislators. Exactly what was considered to constitute juvenile delinquency could vary. Loitering in the streets, petty theft, smoking, and insubordination to adults (swearing, for instance) were all forms of behaviour considered unacceptable by turn-of-the-century social and political elites. Historian Susan Houston notes that in late nineteenth-century Toronto, "youngsters who drank, swore, pilfered orchards, played with catapults, harassed Salvation Army cadets, lit bonfires, stole newspapers, or broke into letter boxes were routinely disciplined."[38] Some of the "street urchins" deemed suspect because they loitered in public thoroughfares were in fact working-class children contributing to the family economy through wages legally earned—as bootblacks, newsboys, messengers, or delivery boys, for example—or through less acceptable activities such as gleaning or pilfering.

During the second half of the nineteenth century, Canadian provinces established a variety of institutions designed to shelter and perhaps "improve" or rehabilitate juvenile delinquents, such as reform schools and industrial schools. It became increasingly important both to state authorities and to social reformers that delinquent children be removed from prisons and other carceral institutions that housed adults perceived to be hardened criminals; children were seen to require protection from potentially damaging adult influences. In Quebec, for instance, legislation allowing for the creation of reform schools and industrial schools for children under the age of 16 was adopted in 1869, due to the combined pressure of civil servants, municipal authorities, and religious authorities. The reform schools set up in that province over the following decades, although regulated and, to a significant degree, financed by the provincial government, were administered by Catholic religious communities and, as in other provinces, were segregated by sex. The Sœurs du Bon Pasteur took under their wing delinquent girls and adolescents from Catholic families beginning in 1862. From the 1860s on, the Société Saint-Vincent-de-Paul and the Frères de la Charité administered the Hospice Saint-Antoine, for Catholic boys judged delinquent. Social reformers in Quebec created separate charitable institutions for delinquent children from Protestant or Jewish families, such as the Protestant Home and School of Industry, created in 1847, or the Protestant Boys Home, established in the 1860s.[39] These institutions, designed to house large numbers of children and adolescents, would remain important in Quebec through the 1950s. Elsewhere in Canada, similar institutions were largely replaced over the course of the twentieth century by strategies such as probation, designed to allow delinquent children and adolescents to remain within their families and to circulate within the larger society. Exceptions to this rule existed, however. For example, the Ontario Training School for Girls was established near Galt, Ontario, in 1933 to house "delinquent" girls aged 12 to 18.[40]

At the turn of the twentieth century, the federal Juvenile Delinquents Act of 1908 allowed for the creation of juvenile courts in provinces across the country; subsequent provincial laws allowed Canadian municipalities to set up juvenile courts. The goal of these youth courts was to treat the problems at the root of delinquent behaviour rather than to simply punish the young offenders. In Montreal, for instance, the city's first juvenile court was established in 1912. The judge who presided over this court, François-Xavier Choquet, hoped to encourage a more "merciful" form of justice. In the eyes of observers across Canada, a more merciful form of juvenile justice would best be carried out by female authorities—policewomen, probation officers, and judges, such as Vancouver juvenile court judge Helen Gregory MacGill—who, together, would create and constitute a maternalist form of juvenile justice. Maternalist justice notwithstanding, coercion remained integral to court procedures: adolescent girls judged delinquent were sometimes subjected to gynecological exams, for instance, in order to determine whether they were sexually active or whether they had contracted a sexually transmitted infection. Questions of sexuality were frequently evoked in the case of girls considered delinquent. While girls' delinquency was sometimes blamed upon their sexual victimhood (girls who had been sexually harassed or assaulted, for instance), they were often judged delinquent because of what was considered to be their sexual precociousness or assertiveness.[41]

Nineteenth-century delinquent practices, such as loitering in the streets or stealing, continued to be reprimanded in the early twentieth century and were joined by new practices popular among adolescents such as smoking cigarettes, sneaking into cinemas, and frequenting dance-halls. Often, disobeying parents or refusing to contribute wages or work to the family economy was reason enough to be brought before the juvenile court. Juvenile court judges dealt with children and adolescents brought before them by members of the police force and, often, by members of their own families. Indeed, roughly half of the girls who appeared before Montreal's juvenile court in the early twentieth century were there on the initiative of their own parents. Take the example of a Montreal widow and mother of three, who occasionally earned money through paid domestic labour, but who was nonetheless dependent upon the wages earned by her children. In 1918, she complained to the juvenile court that she had lost control over her 14-year-old son, who stole goods from the household in order to sell them and used the profits in order to secure admission to the cinema.[42] What is interesting here is that new state institutions such as the juvenile court were integrated into the parenting strategies of families, especially the working-class families whose children were most likely to come to the attention of municipal authorities such as police officers and social reformers. Although juvenile justice authorities often blamed the delinquency of children or adolescents on their father's absence from the home or on their mother's paid work, clearly these parents were heavily involved in the disciplining—and the policing—of their own children. That said, the solutions envisaged by working-class parents could differ from those promoted by the new juvenile justice authorities. Working-class parents frequently asked authorities to imprison or institutionalize their children. Did parents want their children to be punished, protected, educated, or supervised? It is difficult to say. What is clear is that as the twentieth century progressed, social workers and judges, for their part, clearly preferred techniques of probation that allowed delinquent youth to remain in a family setting, albeit under surveillance.

Private Institutions for Children

Although the state increasingly intervened in the lives of children in the late nineteenth and early twentieth centuries, there were aspects of children's lives that remained largely untouched by government in these decades. The state had little to offer in the way of direct social assistance to poor or needy children, for example. Most nineteenth-century Canadians appeared to think that the poor or people caught in a bind should turn first to their own family for help, and then to private charities. Private charitable institutions, however, regularly received small grants from the state and were thus subject to a limited degree of state surveillance and regulation.[43] The Hamilton Ladies Benevolent Society and Orphan Asylum, for instance, operated with the help of municipal funding. Infants' homes in Ontario, such as the

Toronto Infants' Home and Ottawa's Bethlehem for the Friendless, functioned thanks to private donations and municipal funding, but also with the help of regular grants from the provincial government.[44] In the absence of direct state support for families, these private institutions and measures remained crucial. For children, these private institutions included the network of orphanages established across the country beginning in the nineteenth century. Many large cities housed several orphanages, run by different religious denominations or philanthropic organizations. In Halifax, orphaned or otherwise dependent or neglected children might find themselves in the Halifax Protestant Industrial School, in the Halifax Protestant Orphans' Home, in St. Joseph's Orphanage, in St. Patrick's Home for Boys, or in the Home of the Guardian Angel.[45] Depending on their family's religion, Montreal children could be sent to the Montreal Protestant Orphan Asylum, established in 1822, the Asile des orphelins catholiques, created in 1832, the Hospice Saint-Joseph, established in 1841, the St. Patrick's Orphan Asylum, set up in the midst of the Irish "famine migration" of 1846, or the Orphelinat Saint-Alexis, which opened its doors in 1853.[46] Most Catholic orphanages in Canada were run by nuns, while the vast majority of Protestant orphanages were managed by middle-class lay women, who were often required to answer to the bourgeois philanthropists who partially funded these institutions.

Private funds and energies were also crucial to the founding of the hospitals for children that were established in a few Canadian cities at the end of the nineteenth and the beginning of the twentieth centuries. Toronto's Hospital for Sick Children first opened its doors in 1875, thanks to initiatives undertaken by a group of educated, Protestant, middle-class women led by Elizabeth McMaster. The founding of the hospital, which later became known as "SickKids," owed much to the "intersection of charity, religion, and medicine that informed late Victorian Canadian society."[47] In 1908, Montreal's Hôpital Sainte-Justine emerged from a similar initiative on the part of Justine Lacoste-Beaubien and other bourgeois French-Catholic women active in social reform, in a context where Montreal's francophone and Catholic families were particularly badly hit by rates of infant mortality that, even at the turn of the twentieth century, were considered shocking.[48]

The State and the Regulation of Indigenous Families

The British North America Act and the Canadian Confederation of 1867 made all Indigenous peoples on what had become Canadian territory wards of the new federal government. The federal government, particularly the

Indian Department, later known as the Department of Indian Affairs (DIA), undertook these responsibilities in part by creating a system of reserved lands on territory to which Indigenous title had been extinguished; these "reserves" established on ceded and unceded lands were conceived in an effort to encourage the creation of sedentary, agricultural farm families. Between 1871 and 1899, the federal government negotiated a series of eight treaties with Indigenous nations, covering territory from today's northwestern Ontario, westward across the Prairies, to what is today the northeastern part of British Columbia. This involved securing authority over these territories and establishing clear boundaries between Indigenous reserves and land that the new Dominion government wished to make available to European settlers. Towards the end of the nineteenth century, the policy of the pass system was implemented in an effort to discourage the mobility of Indigenous peoples and limit them to their reserves. While the effectiveness of the pass system is debatable, there is no doubt that the intention was to keep Indigenous people largely separate from Euro-Canadian settlers.[49]

In 1869, the federal government adopted the Gradual Enfranchisement Act, a major piece of legislation that would have significant and long-lasting consequences for Indigenous family structures and for the rights of the individuals within these families. This legislation determined an Indigenous woman's "Indian" status in function of her husband's background. An Indigenous woman who married a non-Indigenous man lost "Indian" status and all that went with it—the right to live on the reserve, annual payments—for both herself and her children. This status was lost for good and was not regained when she was widowed, unless she remarried with an Indigenous man. Conversely, women of European background who married Indigenous men acquired "Indian" status and gained access to reserves and annuities for both themselves and their children. An Indigenous woman who married an Indigenous man of another band would be obliged to take his status, and their children would belong to the band of their father. Furthermore, the 1869 legislation ruled that Indigenous women could not vote in band elections; this right was reserved for Indigenous men over the age of 21.[50] This reasoning in terms of the paternal lineage ran directly counter to the matrilineal and matrilocal traditions of the majority of Indigenous peoples in Canada, and notably Iroquoian-speaking nations such as the Haudenosaunee and the Wendat. The Indian Act, adopted a few years later, in 1876, was a massive, comprehensive piece of legislation that incorporated and built upon the 1869 legislation. According to the 1876 Act, Indigenous peoples were legal minors, wards of the federal government; the legislation outlined a series of prohibitions and restrictions that affected the daily life of Indigenous families in areas ranging from property holding to religious practice. The overriding objective of the Act was the assimilation of Indigenous peoples, a goal to be achieved through Christian teaching and through encouraging Indigenous people to become sedentary farmers.[51] Moreover, as Indigenous scholars have pointed out, the successive pieces of colonial legislation consolidated in the Indian Act of 1876 bolstered the powers enjoyed by Indigenous men within band government and on the reserve, at the expense of Indigenous women.[52]

Métis Families and Webs of Kinship

The Canadian Confederation and European encroachment in the western part of the continent had an enormous and irreversible impact upon the Indigenous families who had occupied these lands for centuries. One of the best-known examples of Indigenous opposition to the Canadian colonization of the west was what has become known as the Red River Resistance of 1869–1870. Red River was the heart of the vast Métis territory that spread from the Great Lakes west through what are now the Prairie Provinces. The Métis have been referred to by historians and anthropologists as a "new nation," an example of ethnogenesis produced by relationships between First Nations women and European men, largely French Canadian, Scots, or Orcadian, involved in the western fur trade over the course of the eighteenth and nineteenth centuries.[53] These mixed-race fur-trade families were bound by "many tender ties" of love and affection, but also by relations that were economic and political, and sometimes exploitative.[54] In the eighteenth and very early nineteenth centuries, Indigenous women, notably Cree, Chipewyan, and Ojibwa, made the western fur trade possible by fabricating moccasins and snowshoes for traders, preparing, preserving, and providing food, and trapping smaller animals such as marten. Indigenous women who entered into intimate relationships with European men involved in the fur trade served as intermediaries, playing roles that were both economic and diplomatic. These domestic relationships, celebrated without the sanction of Church or state, were known as marriages *à la façon du pays* ("by the custom of the country"). By the early decades of the nineteenth century, Euro-Canadian men in fur-trade country often chose Métis women (the daughters of European-First Nations relationships) as their "country wives."[55] With the colonial policies of the federal government and the expansion of European settlement to western Canada, the situation of dual-heritage families—and of First Nation and Métis wives in particular—became more precarious. In the case of some mixed-race couples married *à la façon du pays*, First Nation or Métis wives were set aside, sometimes with a cash annuity ("turned off," to use the contemporary term), in favour of recently arrived British women or when the Euro-Canadian husband decided to return to eastern Canada. Marguerite Wadin, for example, a Métis woman, was abandoned by her husband Alexander McKay, a trader for the North West Company, when he left the fur-trade country in 1808.[56] Other mixed-race couples lived out their entire lives together. Justifying his decision to move back to eastern North America with his Métis companion Lisette and their children, trader Daniel Harmon, for instance, wrote in 1819:

> Having lived with this woman as my wife, though we were never formally contracted to each other, . . . and having children by her, I consider that I am under a moral obligation not to dissolve the connexion, if she is willing to continue it. The union which had been formed between us, in the providence of God, has not only been cemented by a long and mutual performance of kind offices, but, also, by a more sacred consideration. . . . I consider it to be my duty to take her to a christian [sic] land, where she may enjoy Divine ordinances, grow in grace, and ripen for glory. We have wept together over the early departure of several children, and especially, over the death of a beloved son. We have children still living, who are equally dear to us both. How could I spend my days in the civilized world, and leave my beloved children in the wilderness? The thought has in it the bitterness of death. How could I tear them from a mother's love, and leave her to mourn over their absence, to the day of her death? Possessing only the common feelings of humanity, how could I think of her, in such circumstances, without anguish?[57]

As late as the 1860s, the validity of marriages "by the custom of the country" was recognized by the Canadian courts in what became known as the Connolly case, a widely publicized suit that turned on the legitimacy of the decades-long relationship between fur trader William Connolly and his Cree companion (and mother of their six children), Susanne.[58] Métis women such as Amelia Connolly, the daughter of Susanne (and later the wife of James Douglas, governor of the Crown Colony of Vancouver Island), however, found their social status threatened by the arrival of increasing numbers of non-Indigenous women on the Canadian Prairies and in the west-coast colonies that formed the province of British Columbia in 1871.[59] In the Pacific Northwest, the Anglican Church, hoping to encourage marriages between settler men and European women, organized the arrival in Victoria of "brides' ships," carrying unmarried women from the United Kingdom, in 1862 and 1863.[60]

If the Métis people were born of the western fur trade, their identities and communities were shaped by shared economic practices, notably the Plains buffalo hunt, an event that annually mobilized over one thousand Métis men, women, and children well into the nineteenth century. Métis author Maria Campbell describes how "when the buffalo hunt was finished, the women would bring the meat in, while the girls worked to keep the fires going, creating smoke to keep the flies away as the meat was hung to dry.... [T]he meat was pounded into a pulp and mixed with sundried Saskatoon berries and grease to make pemmican, then sewn up in buffalo robes to help preserve it." Women also accompanied the hunt in their role as bonesetters and medicine women.[61] Métis men participated in the buffalo hunt, but also worked in trapping, trading, and transportation, provisioning the fur trade, or as guides and interpreters.[62] These various economic activities, especially the demands of the fur trade and the commercial buffalo hunt, meant that the Métis were a highly mobile people, attached to a vast territory stretching from the Red River settlement west through the northern Plains. The frontiers of this territory—the Métis homeland—were determined by the limits of Métis kinship networks, which were made up of webs of extended families, interwoven with fur trade networks and sometimes expanded through "fictive kinship practices" such as godparenting and adoption.[63] According to historians Brenda Macdougall, Carolyn Podruchny, and Nicole St-Onge, "family relationships sat at the center of [Métis] collective consciousness and way of being."[64] In some cases, these kinship networks

FIGURE 4.1 Trader [George] McPherson's family, North West Angle, Lake of the Woods, Ontario, 1872. Library and Archives Canada, Online MIKAN no. 3248463.

spanned the Atlantic. Some British-Métis children, part of a mid-nineteenth-century fur-trade elite, moved relatively easily within the British Empire, from their homes at Hudson's Bay Company fur trade posts to schools in Red River, the Canadas, or Great Britain. In these metropolitan schools, these boys and girls acquired the formal education and the savoir-faire necessary to consolidate their position in the colonial elite. The gravestones and burial sites of British-Métis children who died while away at school in Britain bear witness to the various illnesses that threatened nineteenth-century children, but also to the role of kin in caring for these children and thus the strength of "transnational fur-trade family relationships."[65]

By the mid-nineteenth century, Métis family networks and livelihoods were threatened by increasing European settlement. The new federal government purchased the vast territory of Rupert's Land from the Hudson's Bay Company in 1869 without bothering to consult the people who lived there; when it began sending surveyors to Red River, local residents mobilized. One of these residents was a well-educated Métis man named Louis Riel, who with his supporters established a provisional government in November 1869. The following year, the provisional government agreed to enter into the Canadian Confederation on the basis of the guarantees promised by the Manitoba Act, which included 1.4 million acres of land to be allocated to Métis families. Much of this land was never allocated, however, and in the years following the 1870 Manitoba Act many Métis families—indeed, groups of extended families—migrated west, to what is today Saskatchewan. This Métis out-migration, combined with the influx of settler families from Ontario and from Great Britain, meant that by 1885 only 7 per cent of Manitoba's population was officially Métis.[66]

The late 1870s and the 1880s would be years of deprivation, even starvation, for many of the Indigenous nations of the Canadian Prairies, such as the Plains Cree, the Assiniboine, and the Ojibwa. The disappearance of the buffalo in the late 1870s meant the eradication of a longstanding source of food, clothing, and footwear. Promises inscribed in the numbered treaties to provide Indigenous peoples with farming implements, livestock, and seeds were frequently broken, and the quality of the tools and the seed grain that did reach Indigenous farming families left much to be desired. When Indigenous farmers on reserves in the southern settlement belt of the Prairies managed to produce crops of hay and grain sufficiently abundant to sell, the federal government forced them to reduce the size of their landholdings and livestock herds and to use out-dated farm implements so as to diminish their agricultural returns and not compete with their European settler neighbours.[67]

Diseases, both epidemic and endemic, likewise had a devastating impact on Indigenous peoples on the Prairies. The federal government dictated racist policies of extreme parsimoniousness, resulting in the chronic malnutrition and deliberate starvation of many Indigenous peoples in the last decades of the nineteenth century.[68]

It is in the context of the flagrant violation of treaty promises, severe material deprivation, and the federal government's failure to recognize Métis rights to land along the South Saskatchewan River and elsewhere that the Northwest Resistance of 1885 must be understood. The suppression of the Métis resistance at Batoche by the North-West Mounted Police, aided by the newly completed Canadian Pacific Railway, resulted in, among other things, the hanging of Louis Riel for treason, an event that further exacerbated Indigenous and non-Indigenous relations.[69]

Residential Schools

In almost all parts of Canada, residential and industrial schools were established for Indigenous children beginning in 1879. Over the course of the next century, over 150,000 Indigenous children would attend some 134 residential schools, from British Columbia to the Maritimes.[70] Unlike the public schools for Canadian children of European descent, which were administered by the provinces, residential and industrial schools were funded and administered by the federal government and various religious communities, both Catholic and Protestant. Industrial schools, common in western Canada, were designed to teach Indigenous children useful trades seen to befit what the DIA assumed to be their lot in life: carpentry or shoemaking for boys, and domestic work for girls. At the All Hallows School for girls in Yale, British Columbia, a "semi-industrial" boarding school run by Anglican nuns, the Indigenous pupils were kept almost entirely separate from the Euro-Canadian girls, crossing paths only at the daily religious services. The Indigenous girls, unlike their Euro-Canadian counterparts, were expected to do the school's domestic work, and as the nineteenth century drew to a close, their classroom learning was increasingly interspersed with household chores and training in the art of European-style domestic labour.[71]

By the end of the nineteenth century, it had become clear that industrial schools were only minimally useful for Indigenous children and, perhaps more importantly to the DIA, were also costly to run.[72] Residential schools, however, lasted well into the twentieth century; the last closed its doors in 1997.[73] They were based on the premise that Indigenous children needed to be isolated from their own families if they were to eventually adapt to Euro-Canadian society. As journalist, lawyer, and Conservative politician Nicolas Flood Davin argued in 1879, "If anything is to be done with the Indian we must catch him very young. The children must be kept constantly in the circle of civilized conditions."[74] If the federal government and the various religious communities—Catholic, Anglican, Presbyterian, and United Church—with which it collaborated justified residential schooling in terms of the "care" of Indigenous children, their own archives reveal a century-long history of neglect and abuse.[75] Disease, particularly tuberculosis, ran rampant in residential schools, which were cheaply constructed, poorly lit and ventilated, overcrowded, and chronically underfunded.[76] One non-Indigenous Prairie man described a residential school in Prince Albert, Saskatchewan as "a disgrace to anybody. Ignorant teachers, pigsty boarding, poor clothing everything cheap and nasty...."[77] Mortality rates among pupils were shockingly high, a situation driven home by the fact that most residential schools had their own cemetery on the grounds. The spread of tuberculosis and other illnesses and chronic ailments owed much to overcrowding and unsanitary conditions in residential schools and to the lack of appropriate medical care, but also to the fact that the Indigenous pupils were malnourished and thus less resistant to infection. One boy at the Onion Lake Residential School in Saskatchewan wrote in 1923:

> We are going to tell you how we are treated. I am always hungry. We only get two slices of bread and one plate of porridge. Seven children ran away because there [sic] hungry.... I am going to hit the teacher if she is cruel to me again. We are treated like pigs, some of the boys always eat cats and wheat. I never ask anyone to give me anything to eat. Some of the boys cried because they are hungry. Once I cry to [sic] because I was very hungry.[78]

Not surprisingly, most Indigenous parents had no desire to send their children to these schools. Those who did so often withdrew their children from these institutions upon witnessing their unhappiness or mistreatment; children themselves often ran away from these institutions. The Indian Agent at Duck Lake, Saskatchewan, explained in 1910 that local Indigenous parents were resistant to the idea of sending their children to residential schools and demanded the creation of a day school. The Agent explained, "I know it is because so many of their children die at the Boarding school, or come home from the boarding school to die."[79]

The reports of the Truth and Reconciliation Commission of Canada, published in six volumes in 2015, bring to light both the extremely

FIGURE 4.2 These girls were students at the Blue Quills Residential School near St. Paul, Alberta. Provincial Archives of Alberta @ Flickr Commons.

difficult conditions for the children that lived in these residential schools and the physical and psychological scars left by the schools on many of their former pupils.[80] In addition to the devastating consequences of insufficient nourishment and widespread illness, former students recall the common use of corporal punishment (notably the administering of the strap, plus "pulling ears, slapping heads, and hitting knuckles") and the multiple occurrences of sexual abuse.[81] Other examples of the violation of children's bodies, such as cutting their hair short or shaving their heads, are recurrent in the memories of residential school survivors. Dan Kennedy, for example, remembers that "in keeping with the promise to civilize the little pagan, they went to work and cut off my braids, which, incidentally, according to Assiniboine traditional custom, was a token of mourning—the closer the relative, the closer the cut. After my haircut, I wondered in silence if my mother had died."[82] In an effort to bring about the assimilation of Indigenous people, children in residential schools were generally forbidden to use Indigenous languages and often punished when they did so. Peter Julian, a Mi'kmaw man who attended a residential school in Shubenacadie, Nova Scotia, recalls,

> Neither me nor Teresa could speak a word of English because at home we had spoken all Indian—our native tongue. So they started off with an interpreter who was one of the older kids who told me if I was caught talking Indian again I was to be beaten and that sort of put a fright into me . . . So inside of four or five years, I forgot all my Indian . . . . Well, just think, it was pounded out of me with a few strappings from the nuns.[83]

Small wonder, then, that the Truth and Reconciliation Commission Report characterizes the residential school system—and Canada's Indigenous policy more generally—as "cultural genocide."[84]

The Politics of Population: Immigration and the Federal Census

Between the mid-nineteenth century and the First World War, hundreds of thousands of immigrants arrived in the colonies that became Canada. From the 1850s through the 1890s, most of these migrants were from the United States, England, Scotland, Wales, and Ireland, some of them attracted by the possibility of homesteading or purchasing land on the Prairies. Mennonites from Russia and Icelanders also settled on the Prairies in the 1870s.[85] Towards the end of the nineteenth century, large numbers of migrants from the Ukraine, Italy, and the Austro-Hungarian Empire arrived in Canada. From 1896 to the beginning of the First World War, the numbers of immigrants to Canada increased most dramatically, around 2.5 million people arriving from the United States, Great Britain, and Europe. According to historian John Herd Thompson, "annual arrivals peaked at 400,000 in 1914."[86] Some of the arrivals from the United States were in fact returning Canadians, notably Franco-Americans returning to Quebec. Many of these two and a half million immigrants settled in the cities and towns of central and eastern Canada. These included the many thousands of Ashkenazi Jews who left Eastern Europe (Russia, Poland, Lithuania, Romania, Hungary, and Galicia), fleeing poverty, anti-Semitism, and the Russian pogroms. They often arrived as young families and settled principally in Montreal, Toronto, and Winnipeg. Between 1901 and 1911, for example, the Jewish population of Montreal rose from 7,000 to 28,000 people. Almost 9,000 Eastern European Jews settled in Winnipeg between 1882 and 1930.[87]

Around a million of the two and a half million migrants who arrived between 1896 and 1914 chose to settle in the Prairie Provinces and in British Columbia. Clifford Sifton, Liberal Prime Minister Wilfrid Laurier's Minister of the Interior, played a key role in organizing the arrival and settlement of these turn-of-the-twentieth-century migrants. Sifton, who like his contemporaries envisioned a Prairie economy propelled by commercial agriculture, had a marked preference for farmers from the American Midwest and agricultural families from northern England and Scotland, but he was willing to tolerate the arrival of European peasants in "sheepskin coats" with "stout wives" and several children. Family labour was key to the colonization of the

Canadian West. The 1872 Dominion Lands Act, for instance, adopted long before Sifton became Minister of the Interior, encouraged the formation of family farms headed by non-Indigenous adult men. These government land grants of 160 acres, known as homesteads, were far more affordable for most settlers than the land that was available to purchase. Yet they were not accessible to everyone. Married women were not allowed to apply for a homestead grant on the Canadian Prairies; after 1876, single women were also excluded from homesteading. Only adult men and female heads of households with minor children were permitted to homestead; in practice, these women were almost always widows. Under the provisions of the 1876 Indian Act, neither Indigenous men nor Indigenous women had access to homestead grants. Homesteading, then, a system founded on Indigenous dispossession, helped to "shape a society of male heads of household and dependent females."[88] Despite the fact that all contemporary observers were aware of the amount of work undertaken both in the house and on the farm by rural women, women's agricultural labour was not recognized as such in official tallies like those kept by the Dominion Bureau of Statistics. Farm households also included non-family members such as "hired men"; feeding and cleaning up after these hired men added to the domestic work of farm women and their daughters.[89]

Under Sifton and his predecessors such as Conservative T. Mayne Daly, the Canadian state thus played a central role in recruiting migrants and settling them on ceded or expropriated Indigenous lands. The colony known as "New Iceland," created on the southwest shore of Lake Winnipeg in the 1870s, exemplifies the settling of new colonists on lands from which their Indigenous inhabitants (in this case, Ojibwa and Cree) had only recently been removed—or to which they still laid claim.[90] The emerging Canadian state was also active in selecting what it perceived to be the right type of migrants. The numerous Canadian immigration agencies established in the United States, for instance, filtered out African-American migrants, ensuring that African-American immigration to Canada would remain minimal in this period.[91] Asian immigration to British Columbia after the 1858 gold rush was a source of controversy among Euro-Canadian settlers. While many Euro-Canadians wished to exclude Asian migrants from Canada altogether, some large employers—notably railway companies—insisted upon the need for Asian labour. In light of these debates, Canadian governments did their best to ensure that Asian immigration remained both limited and temporary.[92] In 1908, the Canadian and Japanese governments agreed to severely limit Japanese migration to Canada. Immigration from South Asia was minimal due to the "continuous journey" ruling, also adopted in 1908, which required

FIGURE 4.3 Wedding portrait of Yip Kew Him and Lee Lan Fan in Vancouver, British Columbia, 1914. City of Vancouver Archives/AM1108-S4-: CVA 689-60

migrants to have arrived in Canada via a single voyage. Over twenty years earlier, the federal government, responding to pressure from British Columbia, had imposed a prohibitive Head Tax on migrants from China. This Head Tax, which was increased in 1901 and again in 1904, prevented the many male sojourners from China living in British Columbia from sending for their wives and thus contributed to a dramatic sex imbalance within Chinese-Canadian communities. Politicians and many citizens reasoned that, without the possibility of bringing their female companions to Canada, male Asian migrants would eventually leave the country. There was, however, some turn-of-the-twentieth-century support for the immigration of Asian women. Those Euro-Canadians in favour of admitting Asian women to Canada hoped that the presence of Chinese, Japanese, or South Asian women would eliminate what they saw as the "risk" of Asian-European intermarriage and would instead lead to the creation of segregated "ethnic communities."[93]

The Canadian state, backed by many of its citizens, thus actively worked to build a settler society that would be white and, to a significant degree, of British descent. Historian Laura Ishiguro's analysis of letters sent "home" by British settlers in British Columbia shows that letter-writers sought to understand and assess their daily life in terms of metropolitan norms. Furthermore, Ishiguro points out the silences in this family correspondence, notably the remarkable absence of references to the Indigenous peoples who continued to inhabit the Pacific Northwest.[94] The family was central to colonization and the creation of this settler society.[95] Legislation around immigration, property, and citizenship, in addition to shaping the contours of a white settler society, spoke to particular, gendered visions of the family. Canada's 1881 Naturalization Act stipulated that a married woman was to automatically assume her husband's nationality; this stipulation was confirmed and reinforced in the Naturalization Act of 1914. In the early twentieth century, Canadian women lobbied the federal government to allow married women to keep their status as British subjects even if they married non-British subjects—a campaign that was ultimately successful, but not until 1946.[96]

One final way in which the state contributed to understandings of families in late nineteenth-century Canada was through the work of counting and classification that was the official census, conducted every ten years from 1851 on and, beginning in the twentieth century, every five years. The early census-takers, owing to a lack of experience and administrative infrastructure and thinking in terms of their own world-views, counted and classified unevenly and selectively. They systematically under-enumerated Indigenous peoples, for instance, and thus symbolically—and officially—reduced their importance within the population of Canada. Not surprisingly, as census-takers attempted to translate real life into census categories, they interpreted what they observed according to dominant visions of nineteenth-century families. In the 1851 and 1861 censuses, for instance, very few married women were attributed an occupation, and unmarried women were generally reported to be servants. Children were naturally assumed to be contributing to the family economy: John Beatty, census commissioner for Canada West's Northumberland County in 1861, observed that "'some Enumerators in entering 'Laborers' have included all the male children of a farmer for instance down to the age of one year'."[97] Early census-takers discovered, moreover, that many inhabitants of Canada did not think in terms of census categories and had yet to develop a sense of what historians and demographers call "age-consciousness," that is, an awareness of distinct stages of life, closely associated with different ages.[98] In parts of the country lacking "an effective system of civil registration, some people did not know the year of their birth or the ages of their children—a further example of census knowledge depending on administrative infrastructure."[99] This situation would change over the last decades of the nineteenth century as some of the English-Canadian provinces began establishing civil registration systems for the regular collection of vital statistics. Ontario, for instance, introduced a system of vital statistics registration through its municipalities in 1869. In Quebec, the state traditionally received copies of the meticulously kept parish records of Catholic marriages, baptisms, and burials. All this newfound state attention to the collection and diffusion of the "facts of life" took place within what historian George Emery has called a broader "nineteenth-century statistical movement." [100]

The British North America Act of 1867, the Criminal Code of 1892, and the legislation adopted by the different Canadian provinces in the last decades of the nineteenth century all played a role in determining the shape of Canadian families and the possibilities open to individual family members. The federal legislation pertaining more specifically to Indigenous peoples had an impact upon the lived experiences of First Nations and Métis families. These different legislative and judicial measures represented a sustained and ongoing attempt by the emerging Canadian state to impose a national framework on familial structures and practices that were both subnational—that is, smaller than the coast-to-coast country in the making—and supranational—that is, intimately linked to territories, countries, and empires of origin. Familial ties and webs of kinship could be more enduring and were often more expansive than the new ties of nationhood.

The late nineteenth-century state, in Canada as in most of the western world, was profoundly liberal. The state regulated, to some degree, the functioning of the market, but very few people assumed that it should provide direct assistance to the needy; most people appear to have thought that these were functions best left to private charity. However, the state did provide indirect aid to the ill and the needy through regular grants to private charitable institutions such as infants' homes and orphanages. Direct state assistance to families would increase, albeit in limited and selective ways, when Canada entered the First World War in August 1914.

5

Two World Wars, the Great Depression, and a Mixed Social Economy of Welfare, 1914–1945

THE PERIOD BETWEEN the beginning of the First World War and the end of the Second World War witnessed greater state intervention into the lives of families by provincial governments and then, from the 1940s onward, by the federal state. Within civil society, this was the era of the development of what some have called the "helping professions": new professions that attempted to play an increasingly important role in family life, such as paediatrics, social work, and psychology. Finally, the Great War, the Second World War and the devastating economic depression between these two military conflicts had an enormous impact on families across the country. This chapter explores all of these developments, against the larger backdrop of the timid entry of Canadian families into consumer society during these decades, a transformation that was particularly noticeable in urban areas during the years known by some as the "Roaring Twenties." These economic, social, and political changes were felt differently among families in cities and those in the countryside, among Indigenous families and those of European descent; region, race, and ethnicity continued to play a key role in the lives of Canadian families, as they had for centuries.

The Great War and Families in Canada

When the Great War broke out in August 1914, pitting England and France against Germany, the Austro-Hungarian Empire, and their allies, Canada was immediately swept up into wartime preparations. A former British colony consisting of some 7.5 million people in 1914, it was automatically at war once Great Britain declared war. It went without saying that Canada was expected to contribute to the British war effort by furnishing male soldiers, female nurses, weapons and munitions, and material contributions such as bacon, beef, and wheat to the well-being of soldiers and European civilians.[1] Recruiting posters melded imperial and familial themes and presented the Dominion of Canada as a lion cub coming readily to the aid of the "Old Lion" that was Great Britain.

FIGURE 5.1 Recruiting poster, Great War. McCord Museum, Montreal.

For many men only recently arrived in Canada from the United Kingdom, wartime recruitment exercised a visceral pull, attracting husbands, fathers, and sons into various Canadian regiments. In the early years of the war, approximately 70 per cent of the men who enrolled in the Canadian Expeditionary Force were British-born; by contrast, 37 per cent of Canada's population as a whole was reported by the 1911 census takers to have been born in Great Britain.[2] For French-Canadian families in Quebec and elsewhere in the country, roots in North America established centuries earlier meant that European military needs seemed much less urgent and the desire to enrol far less strong. Early twentieth-century military recruiters insisted upon the differential rates of recruitment among English Canadians and French Canadians respectively; the most jingoistic English Canadians, fuelled by wartime imperialist sentiment, accused French Canadians of being "the only white race of quitters."[3] Recent research suggests, however, that rates of volunteer enrolment were similar for French-Canadian men and for English-Canadian men born in Canada; it was the British-born who signed up the most quickly and in the greatest numbers.[4]

In addition to loyalty to Great Britain and to ideas of Empire, family motivations were important for many men, and notably the desire—and the need—to provide financially for one's family. The severe recession experienced by Canadians in 1913 and the resulting high rates of unemployment meant that many adult men had a difficult time fulfilling what Canadian society perceived to be these men's breadwinner obligations. Financial reasons thus motivated some husbands and fathers to enrol; nearly 20 per cent of soldiers and 35 per cent of officers in the Canadian Expeditionary Force were married.[5] Many unmarried men also joined up for financial reasons: some needed to help out their aging parents no longer able to work; others hoped to be able to save enough money to marry and start their own families.

Medical examinations were obligatory for men wishing to enrol in the armed services, and these examinations revealed the poor health of many Canadian men in the early twentieth century. Between 100,000 and 200,000 First World War volunteers were rejected for medical reasons ranging from flat feet, to poor eyesight, to hernias, to bad teeth. In 1916 alone, almost a quarter of the men who volunteered for military service were rejected as "unfit to serve."[6] Many men rejected for medical reasons experienced feelings of shame, even despondency, amid fears that others perceived them as unmanly "shirkers" or "slackers." The White Feather campaign—distributing white feathers, a sign of cowardice, to enlistment-aged men in the streets not in uniform—carried out by patriotic or imperialist civilians was designed to remind men that their duty lay overseas.[7] Martin Colby, a Canadian interviewed decades after the war, recalled:

> In them days it was rather annoying to go out at all because the men in uniform... they'd come up and tap you on the shoulder and say, "Why ain't you in the army?" And I used to have difficulty even when I told them I had bad ears because I had scarlet fever. "Go on, try again. Try again." I used to say, "What the hell's the use of trying after they turned me down?" I tried often enough. But, oh Jesus, they used to pressure the life out of you. It was hell.'[8]

Recruiting posters, too, played on masculine feelings of shame and familial obligation. Defenders of men who were unable to serve for medical reasons—including military regiments and the Honourably Rejected Volunteers of Canada Association—put into place badge campaigns so that strangers would understand that the men wearing them were not in fact "shirkers."[9] A wide range of early twentieth-century Canadians were involved in recruitment efforts—the militia, not surprisingly, alongside soldiers on leave and soldiers already returned from the war, but also civilians such as clergymen and other local notables. As historian Paul Maroney notes, "Recruiters addressed crowds wherever they could find them: at theatres, fairs, churches, sporting events, and at club meetings. Workplaces were also turned into makeshift recruiting halls, with some patriotic employers allowing recruiting parties into their establishments to address the men."[10]

A husband, son, father, or brother in the armed services was usually a source of worry for families, even if he had enrolled voluntarily. Patriotic mothers were expected to willingly sacrifice their sons to the imperial cause, but many, understandably, had no desire to send their boys off to battle.[11] One woman, Marion Presnail, wrote to Colonel Sam Hughes, Canada's Minister of Militia, pleading with him to send her son back home and describing herself as "a poor widow mother whose heart is almost broken over this impetuous act of a boy."[12] Parents' concern for their enlisted sons was exacerbated for underage boys. Over 20,000 boys under the age of 18 enlisted in the Canadian Expeditionary Force, although it is difficult to calculate the exact numbers, since these adolescents lied about their age in order to enrol. Some parents sent letters to military authorities, insisting that their underage son be sent home. After the death on the battlefield of one soldier son, Florence Brown wrote to the Young Soldiers' Battalion to reclaim her other son, 17-year-old Harold, arguing that he was "all I have in this world ... I think that I have done my part in giving all for King and country. I am a lonely mother and no means to support myself." The situation of underage soldiers underlines the ambiguous status of older adolescents. In this early twentieth-century society where most 16- and 17-year-old boys had already left school and were working for pay, it is not surprising that many of them considered themselves mature enough to join the armed services.[13] For younger children, the enlistment and subsequent absence from their home of their father could be a source of uncertainty and insecurity, and it often had an impact on their living arrangements and conditions. School-age children maintained contact with their absent fathers through correspondence. If letters written by fathers provided their children with glimpses, often sanitized, of unfamiliar European cities and life on the battlefront, children's letters revealed preoccupations with "[n]ew pets, report cards, school holidays, medical problems, and sibling rivalries."[14]

The threat and then the reality of military conscription also caused tensions within families. By 1917, as Canadian prime minister Robert Borden came to realize that the number of Canadian volunteers was insufficient to allow him to meet the military commitments he had made to Great Britain, discussion of obligatory military service became louder and more frequent. The question was decided in August 1917, when Borden's Military Service Act was passed, and in the federal election of December 1917, when Borden was decisively elected on a Unionist (pro-conscription) platform. Canadian historiography has long insisted, and with good reason, upon the fracture occasioned—or exacerbated—by the conscription debate and the Military Service Act of 1917 between English Canadians and French Canadians, particularly those French Canadians living in Quebec.[15] Residents of the English-Canadian provinces generally supported conscription; most residents of Quebec were opposed to military conscription. But the Quebec/English Canada divide overshadowed other, equally real, sources of division. French-speakers elsewhere in Canada were also markedly less enthusiastic about military conscription. Furthermore, the rural-urban divide was important in this debate. Farming families across the country—a country in which the majority of the population was rural in the 1910s—required a great deal of physical labour to keep the farms going, and had no desire to see husbands or adult sons drafted into the armed services.[16] In Ontario, the United Farmers of Ontario spoke for many rural families when it protested the Borden government's 1917 proposal to implement compulsory military duty and the government's 1918 decision to cancel farmers' military exemptions. The Military Service Act called attention to what was a longstanding problem in Ontario, that is, rural depopulation. Farm labourers, already in short supply, were being both lured into high-paying munitions jobs in the city and targeted by military recruiters. At its June 1918 convention in Toronto, the United Farmers of Ontario endorsed a resolution stating that

> Long before the war broke out, the rapid depletion of the population of the rural districts and corresponding increase in the towns and cities was creating a food shortage, which even at that time was becoming serious [. . .]. The war has withdrawn tens of thousands of our best farmers and farmers' sons who enlisted for military service. Thousands of other workers on the farm because of the high wages offered, have been drawn from the farms to engage in work in munitions factories. The effect of all this, has been to create a crisis in farm conditions through the shortage of labour that is alarmingly reducing the production of our farms and intensifying dangerous conditions previously existing.[17]

As the United Farmers of Ontario pointed out, Borden's wartime policies were contradictory: "on one hand urging greater [food] production and on the other conscripting the manpower necessary to increase production."[18]

Women were not accepted into the armed services as soldiers, but as military nurses, commonly referred to as nursing sisters. The vast majority of women who served as nursing sisters with the Canadian Army Medical Corps during the Great War were unmarried and the majority were Canadian-born. Some of these women enrolled in the CAMC in order to help support their aging parents or other family members. Nurse Ruth Hays, for example, used some of her salary to help out her widowed sister, Lois; nursing sister Blanche Lavallée allocated part of her salary to her father, who had cancer and was unable to work.[19] Great War nursing resulted in concrete citizenship rewards, such as the securing of the federal vote in 1917, before most other Canadian women. Contemporary observers were not duped by the unsubtle electoral ploys associated with the federal female suffrage. Borden's Military Voters Act and his Wartime Elections Act, both passed in 1917, gave the vote to nursing sisters and to the close female relatives of men enrolled in the armed services, on the assumption that these women would vote for the pro-conscription Union government. Most other adult women obtained the federal vote a year later, in 1918. Notable exceptions were women of Asian background and Indigenous women, who would not secure the federal suffrage until 1948 and 1960 respectively.

Men who volunteered to be part of the Canadian Expeditionary Force and were accepted earned a small salary that varied according to military rank. A portion of this salary could be "assigned" to someone else, for instance an elderly parent or a wife. The costs of soldiers' food, lodging, and clothing were also taken care of for the duration of the war. In addition, married soldiers were entitled to a modest $20 per month separation allowance for their wife— an amount that all contemporaries acknowledged was insufficient, especially for women attempting to raise children on this amount. Canada's military archives are full of letters from the wives of enlisted men who felt that their husbands' enrolment had left them "totally unprovided for."[20] The Canadian Patriotic Fund, a private association established by men belonging to Canada's socioeconomic elite, stepped into the breach, raising funds among civilians in order to help soldiers' wives cover the costs of rental or mortgage payments, grocery bills, clothing, and shoes.[21] Indeed, the material assistance provided by the Canadian Patriotic Fund was used as a recruitment argument; its very existence reassured men considering enlistment that their families would be taken care of in their absence.[22] The system set up by the Canadian Patriotic Fund in fact helped to inspire the more extensive system of military dependents' allowances established by the Department of Pensions and National Health during the Second World War, a generation later.

Family correspondence exchanged during the Great War shows the extent to which wartime separation strained relationships between husbands and wives and also created a physical and psychological distance between absent fathers and their children. Wives were faced with the difficulty of negotiating the application for, and budgeting of, soldiers' assigned pay and separation allowances and, when these were not enough, Canadian Patriotic Fund allowances. Some married women sought paid work to compensate for their husbands' absence and insufficient soldiers' pay. Rural women worked hard to keep the farm afloat despite the absence of a key source of male labour. Loneliness was felt and expressed even in cases where the soldier had not yet been shipped overseas. For example, the wife of one recruit based at the Valcartier military training camp, just north of Quebec City, wrote to him, "Dearest I saw in the papers that if any of you got drunk & kicked up now you got sent back Home [sic], why can't you do that Johnnie [?]."[23] Letter writing was in most cases the only way for family members separated by the war to maintain their relationships. Sidney and Isabelle Brook, a farming couple living in Craigmyle, Alberta, corresponded from June 1916 to April 1918 while Sidney was in training at Sarcee, a military camp near Calgary, and then overseas, in England and in France. Sidney, a British immigrant aged 44 at the time of his enlistment, claimed to have enrolled for reasons of patriotism, but financial motivations also appear to have played a role in his decision to enlist. The 200-odd letters exchanged by Sidney and Isabelle testify to the new challenges faced by Isabelle, obliged to manage the farm on her own while at the same time raising their five children with little assistance from extended family. Sidney was still overseas when one of these children, seven-year-old Arnott, died tragically of diphtheria; he learned of Arnott's death by telegram.[24]

For those men, unmarried women, and adolescent boys and girls untouched by military enlistment, the Great War could mean the opportunity to work in one of the many munitions factories that sprang up across the country, especially in Ontario and Quebec, or in one of the factories that contributed indirectly to the war effort by producing tents, blankets, military uniforms or cigarettes for soldiers. In Quebec, munitions production took place in the economic metropolis that was Montreal, but also in smaller towns and cities such as Hull, Rigaud, Beloeil, Trois-Rivières, Shawinigan, Drummondville, Sherbrooke, and Quebec City. In Ontario, production for war needs took place in such cities as Toronto, Brantford, and Hamilton. In other areas of the country, the Great War revitalized specific industries—such as shipbuilding in Saint John, New Brunswick.

Within a matter of months, the war put an end to the serious economic recession of 1913; war work resulted in financial stability for many families living in—or willing to move to—one of these urban centres. Arguably the changes to the economy occasioned by the Great War represented simply an economic "rebound" after the recession of 1913, rather than a great economic boom, but for many Canadian families, the difference between 1913 and 1915 or 1916 was nonetheless palpable.[25] So attractive was munitions work to many Canadians that it in fact counteracted military recruitment efforts: men had less incentive to enlist in the armed services if there was well-paying work to be had at home. In cases where men did enlist, or where there was no adult man in the family, war work could provide adolescent boys and girls with a wage to contribute to the household. Quebec's chief factory inspector, Louis Guyon, recounted stories of women pleading with him to let their underage children work in munitions factories. One widow, he claimed, had told him that the six dollars a week earned by her child allowed her to pay her rental and heating costs.[26] In such cases, working-class adolescents, occasionally as young as age 12 or 13, acted as breadwinners. In early-twentieth-century Canada, where in most places it was far more socially acceptable to send children out to work than for married women to seek paid work outside the home, relatively few married women took on work in munitions or other wartime factories; most of the female workers in these factories were single.[27] In a context where industrial employers eager to profit from the money to be made in wartime production hastily "did over" their out-dated factories and where many war workers, such as adolescents, were new to industrial production, received very little on-the-job training, and worked long and late hours, accidents such as burns, scalding, cuts, loss of digits or members, chemical intoxications, explosions, and electrocutions were frequent.[28]

Middle-class women, both single and married, were far less likely to work in munitions factories. In addition to carrying out their unpaid domestic labour under wartime conditions, many of them also took on voluntary war work, such as knitting socks, rolling bandages, and preparing care packages for local servicemen sent overseas. The Women's Patriotic Association (WPA) of Newfoundland (not yet part of Canada), for instance, was widely praised for the thousands of pairs of grey wool socks that it sent to soldiers on the western front and that helped to prevent trench foot. Haudenosaunee women of the Grand River Reserve in southern Ontario also knitted socks for soldiers overseas, and especially for the 300 Grand River Reserve men enrolled in the Canadian Expeditionary Force. Acting under the auspices of the

Six Nations Women's Patriotic League, formed in November 1914, these women undertook voluntary wartime labour that reinforced their historical allegiance to the British Crown. In addition to knitting socks, they embroidered a large regimental flag with the symbols of four Iroquois clans for the Brock Rangers and prepared packages of food (nuts, candy, chocolate, Christmas puddings) for Six Nations soldiers. Much of the unpaid wartime labour undertaken by women thus drew on skills long considered feminine, but earned them public recognition of their wartime role and encouraged some of them to undertake other kinds of political work in the public sphere.[29]

The Great War had a serious impact upon Canada's rural families.[30] Given the federal government's commitment to providing both its troops and the civilians of the Allied Powers with foodstuffs, Canadian agricultural products were in high demand, especially as a war initially expected to last a few months dragged on for years. The *Grain Growers' Guide* suggested in April 1918 that Canadians were well placed to "Fight the Huns with Food"; a month later, the *Canadian Food Bulletin* urged readers to "MAKE the KITCHEN (K)ONQUER the KAISER."[31] The problem was that in wartime many of the Canadian men who would normally have been farming had been recruited by the armed forces or attracted to the cities by the relatively high wages offered in munitions factories. The federal and provincial governments tried out various solutions to the agricultural labour crisis. Ontario's "Farmerettes," launched in 1917 and modelled on Great Britain's Women's Land Army, attempted to attract young women—many of them high school or university students—to work on farms for the duration of the war. The objective was to have these young urban women help out farmers' wives with their housekeeping duties, so that the latter could take on more of the agricultural work in their husbands' absence. Provincial governments and private associations such as the Boy Scouts encouraged young children to help out with agricultural tasks so as to do "their bit" for the war effort. In Quebec, for instance, the Department of Agriculture distributed seeds to schoolchildren so that they might plant vegetables in schoolyards. In the spring of 1916, the Saskatchewan government organized Gopher Day, whereby children spurred on by the incentive of monetary prizes hunted down gophers and thus helped to save the province's crops. Urban dwellers across the country were urged to plant vegetable gardens in vacant lots and back yards so as to become self-sufficient and thus relieve the pressure on the country's farmers, who could reserve their harvests for export to soldiers and overseas civilians. As the *Canadian Food Bulletin* noted in 1918,

There is only one reserve for our agricultural force – the man power of our cities and town [sic]. Those who are obliged to remain in the cities must help to feed themselves – by devoting a part of their time to growing their own vegetables.

We are holding the food line for ourselves, for our Allies, – for civilization.

IT'S UP TO THE RESERVES![32]

After several years of war, as food shortages in Europe grew more urgent, the federal government took concrete steps to intervene. The "Soldiers of the Soil," a federal initiative launched in 1918, aimed to send adolescent boys aged 15 to 19 to undertake agricultural labour on farms across the country.[33] The S.O.S. programme appears to have been particularly popular in Saskatchewan, Manitoba, and Nova Scotia.[34] These sporadic and relatively modest interventions on the part of the Canadian state foreshadowed the much more extensive state incursions into daily life that families would experience during the Second World War.

Many husbands, fathers, and sons never returned to Canada. Of the roughly 600,000 men and women who served with the Canadian Expeditionary Force, close to 66,000 died on the battlefields of Europe. 170,000 other Canadians returned wounded or injured.[35] War widows and orphans thus numbered in the tens of thousands.[36] One Montreal boy belonging to the city's Anglo-Protestant elite, for example, lost both of his uncles on Great War battlefields; his father, badly wounded during the war, died of his injuries some years after his return. This boy recalls growing up with a constant feeling of "profound sadness" at the same time that he idolized these three male relatives as war heroes.[37]

Those men who did return from the war found that government pensions for demobilized men were limited. This was the case even for those returned soldiers who had been wounded and were permanently incapacitated or disabled as a result of their wartime experience. Their campaign for decent pensions and health care in the wake of the Great War constituted a "second battle" waged by returned soldiers.[38] The federal government established modest measures for veterans, such as the Soldier Settlement Act, during and after the war, but these paled in comparison to the Veterans' Charter that would be enacted in 1944 for a subsequent generation of soldiers. The question of the employability of veterans, especially disabled veterans, was central to public debate in the wake of the Great War; defenders of returned soldiers brandished the spectre of men whose military service to their country had been loudly and publicly praised reduced to begging in the streets. Great War veterans faced with unemployment and underemployment during the Great Depression of the 1930s were quick to remind the government of their service to the country during the First World War. In return, they argued, the state had "a reciprocal duty" to ensure that they were able to earn a decent living. As one veteran wrote to the Ontario premier in 1934, "I myself am a returned man with four years of service for my country. It certainly does not make me feel very nice to think I helped to defend a country that will not help me in times when I and my family need it badly."[39]

In many ways, the influenza pandemic of 1918–1919 constituted the final chapter of the Great War story. The movement of military troops around the globe was in part responsible for the rapid spread of the virus known colloquially as "Spanish flu" and the often-fatal infections such as pneumonia that followed in its wake. Perhaps as many as 100 million people worldwide died of influenza in 1918–1919; in Canada, 50,000 deaths and many more cases of severe illness resulted from this epidemic.[40] In Newfoundland and in Quebec, the 1918–1919 epidemic was followed by another wave of influenza in the winter of 1920. The pandemic had a huge impact on families, as this particular strain of influenza appears to have wrought the most devastation among young adults aged 20 to 40, in Canada as elsewhere. In Winnipeg, Manitoba, fully 60 per cent of influenza deaths were of adults aged 20 to 39. Many of the dead were thus the parents of young children, and also the principal breadwinners in these families.[41]

Although influenza felled Canadians of all walks of life—rich and poor, men and women, Canadian-born and immigrant—it was by no means a "democratic" disease. On the Prairies, Indigenous communities "were disproportionately devastated by the disease: the estimated average for Canadian Aboriginals during the pandemic was 37.7 deaths per 1,000, compared to 6.1 deaths per 1,000 for Canada as a whole."[42] Indigenous children living in overcrowded residential and industrial schools were especially at risk of catching the virus.[43] Moreover, within the Euro-Canadian population, social class made a difference to survival and mortality rates. Mortality rates from influenza were higher in the working-class wards of the North End of Hamilton, Ontario than in the city's prosperous South End.[44]

In some ways, this could be considered the last nineteenth-century epidemic. Scientific medicine was largely helpless before the influenza virus; physicians were reduced to recommending fresh air and sunshine to sick and dying patients. Moreover, the war effort had siphoned off medical personnel such as doctors and nurses, leaving most victims to be cared for primarily by members of their own families. Private charity and assistance by social reformers, nuns, firemen, policemen, and civic-minded volunteers also played a crucial role in dealing with this medical and social crisis.[45] In the wake of the epidemic, private institutions such as orphanages and children's homes helped some families broken by influenza to put the pieces back together.[46] And yet, the pandemic probably acted as a spur to state intervention in the field of health and welfare in Canada; a federal Department of Health was established for the first time in 1919.[47] At the same time, some survivors of the epidemic relied upon—and tested—new provincial welfare measures such as mothers' allowances. By the end of 1920, the Mothers' Allowance Commission of Manitoba, established in 1916, was supporting some 131 working-class families in which the husband and father had died of influenza.[48]

Early State Interventions

State interventions into family life were timid in the 1920s and 1930s, but certainly more numerous and more extensive than before the Great War. During the interwar years, such measures were largely adopted by the different provincial governments; the British North America Act of 1867 made social welfare a provincial responsibility—inasmuch as it was perceived to be a state responsibility at all. Although the federal government was not entirely absent from the social welfare scene in the interwar years, its role remained relatively discreet.

One category of Canadians seen to be deserving of state assistance during the interwar years were needy mothers raising children on their own—that is, widowed or abandoned mothers, or mothers whose husbands were institutionalized (in hospitals, for example). Initiated in part out of a concern for war widows left with young children to support in the wake of the Great War, the first mothers' allowances were established in the years during and immediately following the war. So-called "first-wave" feminists were among their most fervent champions. Using maternalist arguments, activist women and men successfully persuaded provincial governments that "mother-work" deserved state support.[49] By 1920, five provinces—Manitoba, Saskatchewan, Alberta, British Columbia, and Ontario—had adopted mothers' allowances. Nova Scotia followed suit in 1930 and Quebec in 1937. In New Brunswick, mothers' allowances were implemented in 1943 and in Prince Edward Island, in 1949.[50]

Rates, residency requirements, and criteria for admissibility all varied among the different provinces. Unwed, separated, or divorced mothers were not always eligible for provincial mothers' allowances, nor were women whose husbands were in prison. Although administered by the state, then, these pensions were clearly moralizing, imbued with the nineteenth-century distinctions between the deserving and the undeserving poor. Moreover, the sums given to needy mothers were modest, preserving the time-honoured principle of "less eligibility" present in most state welfare initiatives since the nineteenth century; state welfare was not supposed to be so generous that it would discourage people from working to support themselves. The moralizing aspects of these allowances were evident not just in the selection of recipients deemed worthy, but also in the monitoring of the behaviour of those judged eligible for the allowances. The budgets, household and parenting skills, and social and sexual lives of women in receipt of mothers' allowances remained under constant scrutiny by neighbours, social workers, and government authorities.[51]

In 1927, in collaboration with the provinces, the federal government established the first Canadian old-age pension. Well aware that the British North America Act had made social assistance a provincial jurisdiction, Ottawa required the nine provinces to opt in to the programme and to share its costs. The old-age pensions adopted and administered by the provinces in the 1920s and 1930s were not viewed as fundamental rights of all citizens, but rather, like military pensions and mothers' allowances, were designed to alleviate the poverty of a needy and deserving category of citizen whose poverty did not appear to be their own fault. These pensions, consisting of very modest amounts of money, were thus restricted to persons over the age of 70 (and far fewer people reached the age of 70 in the interwar years than do today) who were British subjects residing in Canada for at least twenty years and who were demonstrably poor; means testing, often humiliating for the recipients, was an integral part of the administration of these early old-age pensions. Moreover, potential recipients were obliged to meet the residency requirements imposed by the various provinces.

By 1936, only two provinces—Quebec and New Brunswick—had not yet adopted the old-age pension. Elderly women and men wrote hundreds of letters to Quebec premier Louis-Alexandre Taschereau in the mid-1930s, after several years of economic depression. Elderly women, able to vote in federal elections since 1918, but not eligible to vote in provincial elections before 1940, were well aware of the interwar debates around old-age pensions and, more precisely, were acutely aware that Taschereau had not yet opted into the federal-provincial plan. They explained to the premier their need for the pension, a need that they justified on the basis of their age and on the basis of their poverty. While some of them wrote as supplicants, asking for a favour, others had clearly integrated the language of citizenship and entitlement circulating in Canada and abroad in the interwar years and demanded the old-age pension as their right or their due. Most of these women took care to underline the fact that they had already exhausted traditional sources of social assistance, namely, family, savings, and private charitable institutions. They were too old or too frail to work. Moreover, their adult children were unable to help them, being out of work themselves or having to take care of their own families. Finally, these letter-writers specified that their pension would be used for strict necessities, such as "spectacles and other things."[52] These letters surely played some role in making political authorities aware of the very real needs of Canadians and thus helping to pave the way for more generous, even universal, welfare-state measures in the post–Second World War period.

The state measures initiated in the 1920s were modest because they were seen by virtually everyone as supplementary measures, designed for those individuals unable to provide for themselves through "normal" market means and unable to turn to their own families for help. This was an attitude that made sense to many in the context of the "Roaring Twenties," when the capitalist economy appeared to be providing jobs and plenty for many Canadians. The economic deprivation occasioned by the Great Depression of the 1930s would lay bare the contradictions of capitalism and the limits of economic liberalism. To many, the hardships suffered during the Depression would provide solid arguments for the necessity of regular, sustained, and significant state intervention into family life.

Surviving the Great Depression

Perceptions of the 1920s have been shaped by Hollywood films and by magazine photos: the "Roaring Twenties" or "les années folles" are encapsulated for many by images of jazz, radio, automobiles, flappers wearing short skirts and bobbed hair, and a new youth culture reposing in part upon commercialized leisure such as cinemas and theatres. Heterosexual romance was another key component of this youth culture and rituals such as wedding showers were integrated into some women's workplaces in the 1920s.[53] In contrast, the "Dirty Thirties"—the years of the Great Depression—evoke a much more sombre portrait: the dust bowl, breadlines, soup kitchens, and men "riding the rods" in search of work. If young women appear to be at the heart of images of the Twenties,[54] it is adult men who figure most prominently in popular representations of the Thirties.[55]

The Great Depression was not limited to Canada, or even to North America. But Canada was particularly badly hit by the consequences of this economic crisis, in part because its economy was so reliant upon the export of natural resources, such as wheat and lumber, and the by-products of natural resources, such as pulp and paper. As international markets for these products dried up, Canadian producers such as farmers and Canadians employed in manufacturing all suffered. At the worst moment of the Depression, in 1933, somewhere between a quarter and a third of Canada's official labour force was out of work.[56] Naturally, those considered to be the dependents of the men considered to be part of the official labour force—women and their children—also suffered greatly from the lack of a breadwinner's income. Many children, for instance, failed to attend school because they did not have sufficiently decent clothing to wear. In 1936, one Ontario father explained to a family court that his two sons were kept home from school because "'they did not have shoes. I want them to go to school, but I certainly would not want to go to school myself with the clothes my children have.'"[57] A boy who grew up in a "respectable" working-class neighbourhood in Vancouver remembered that during the Depression he was obliged to wear "'a pair of hand-me-down boots worn in all seasons. Dad got them from the Infants' Hospital (from some dead infant, I now imagine) and for the first half-year or so they were too big, then for another half-year or so they were okay, and then for another interminable while they were too small.'"[58]

Unemployment during the Great Depression had a major impact on men's sense of themselves and on their masculine identity. In a context where society insisted so strongly upon the necessity of men's economic independence and upon their role as the family breadwinner, what did it mean for men to be unable to provide for their families—or even just for themselves? For young, unmarried men, the Depression represented a significant obstacle to their achievement of adult manhood, a stage of life identified with financial autonomy and the ability to marry and set up a household.[59] Married men and fathers caught up in the maelstrom of the Great Depression felt judged by their wives and children. Journalist Barry Broadfoot recounts the story told by a woman charged with distributing municipal relief during the Depression, who claimed that she had "seen tears in men's eyes, as though they were signing away their manhood, their right to be a husband and sit at the head of the table and carve the roast."[60] A similar story of masculine shame is that of the man who "recalled seeing his father performing relief work sweeping the streets of Toronto: 'I remember so vividly seeing my father one day with this push broom in the gutter. I ran up yelling to him. He wouldn't answer.

Wouldn't even look at me.'"[61] Ontario resident George Wilson wrote numerous times to Ontario Premier Mitchell Hepburn in the mid-1930s, detailing his attempts to hide his unemployment from his pregnant wife and explaining that his despair had led him to contemplate suicide.[62] This sense of shame among unemployed men was not merely self-imposed: institutions ranging from the state to churches to charitable associations to their own families constantly reminded them that they were failing to carry out their familial duties. In an effort to drive this point home, the town council of Timmins, Ontario, voted in 1932 to "publish the names and addresses of all direct relief recipients each month in the newspaper."[63]

Other men desperate to find work so as to be able to feed their families wrote to federal Prime Minister R.B. Bennett during the 1930s. Charles Grierson of Winnipeg, Manitoba, for example, penned over a half-dozen letters to Bennett during the Depression. Born in Winnipeg in 1901, Grierson secured work with the Manitoba Telephone System after leaving school at the age of thirteen in 1914. He worked for them until he lost his job in February 1930. Over the subsequent months of unemployment, he, his wife, and their three young children lost their home and all of their furniture. His letter to Bennett dated 8 June 1933 read as follows:

"Dear Sir:–
Sometime ago I wrote a letter to you appealing for help or employment.
It is now forty months since I had the pleasure of a pay check.
My family, are all undernourished, ill clothed and ill sheltered and are in need of Medical Assistance.
How long do you think we can carry on under these circumstances.
You stated that there would be no one starve in Canada I presume you meant not starve over night but slowly our family amongst thousands of others are doing the same slowly and slowly.
Possibly you have never felt the Pang of a Wolf. Well become a Father have children then have them come to you asking for a slice of bread between meals and have to tell them to wait. Wait until five of humanitys humans sleep all in one room no larger than nine square feet with one window in it....
I want work of a nature that will provide an honest living Now not ten years from now.
I am not radical, Red or unloyal but I would appreciate an honest chance in this world for my family.

I do not believe I am crazy but am reaching the breaking point.

My body, my muscles, my brain are like sodden wood crumbling under this strain. Though the lack of idleness.

I have knowledge of Electrical work – Chaffeur – Sailor – Telephone and Telegraph work.

For God's sake please make a personal endeavour to assist me toward a brighter outlook immediately.

Yours Very Sincerely."[64]

In Montreal, unemployed French-Canadian men expressed similar sentiments of frustration and shame. Despite the dramatic rates of unemployment among adult men in the 1930s, the gendered division of labour among married couples remained astonishingly resilient. Most unemployed men were extremely hostile to the idea of their wives seeking paid work outside the home; such a state of things would simply draw attention to their own incapacity to fulfill their breadwinner role, they thought. Nor were they willing to undertake domestic labour—even though they might well be spending the better part of their day at home. Participating in the unpaid work of the household—women's work—would be yet another affront to their masculinity, which had already taken a serious blow.[65] Some wives of unemployed men did seek casual work—as "cleaning ladies," for example. This was the case for the family of a Vancouver boy whose father lost his job during the Depression; his mother travelled across town to clean homes in a wealthy neighbourhood.[66]

One of the paradoxes of the Great Depression was the widespread sentiment of shame about being poor and out of work, even if over a quarter of Canada's labour force was unemployed during these years. A Montreal woman remembers turning the milkman sent by the Saint-Vincent-de-Paul Society away when he knocked at the door rather than admit to her own mother, who happened to be present in the room, that she and her husband were receiving unemployment relief.[67] A boy who grew up in British Columbia recalled that "'our school books were given to us because we were on relief. It was very embarrassing getting up in front of the class to get those books.'"[68] Small wonder that some children tried to help out during the Depression: young boys often obtained paper routes, for example, as a way of contributing small sums of money to the family economy.[69]

Men unable to find steady work resorted to short-term solutions such as odd jobs, municipal relief work, or scavenging. Some men, desperate or deeply frustrated by their situation, resorted to illegal solutions such as relief fraud, theft, bootlegging, or illegal gambling. George Tapp, for example, the father of seven children, was employed as a motorman by the Toronto Transit Commission, but also worked as a bookie on the side in order to supplement his income during the Depression.[70]

Some unemployed men, married and, especially, single, took to riding the trains west to British Columbia in search of work and more temperate climates.[71] Whole communities of adult men were on the move during the Depression and were perceived by some observers to be fleeing their family responsibilities. In these cases, adult women and their children were obliged to keep things together, materially and emotionally, back home. Moreover, leaving to "ride the rods" was often a form of marital desertion; some of the women left behind never saw their husbands again and were faced with the humiliating task of explaining to relief officials and the civil servants who administered the mothers' allowance why there was no adult man in their household.[72]

In the absence of fathers, or their income, adolescent girls and young women often became the family breadwinners during the Depression, at least in large cities such as Toronto that offered an abundance of jobs in the clerical

FIGURE 5.2 Men being served a meal in a church basement soup kitchen during the Great Depression (Montreal, c. 1930). © McCord Museum, Montreal. MP-1978.107.53.

and service sectors. Since it was less expensive to hire young women than adult men, the former were often preferred by employers hoping to cut costs. At the same time, the expansion of the tertiary sector during the 1920s meant that there existed jobs designated "feminine" to be filled (as secretaries, bookkeepers, receptionists, or waitresses, for instance). However, not all young women had access to the same opportunities: Jewish women and African-Canadian women found their choices circumscribed by anti-Semitism and racism in what was a predominantly white and Protestant city in the 1930s. Claire Clark, for example, a young Toronto woman of West Indian background who had done extremely well in school and who had acquired clerical training, was refused employment in offices or department stores. She instead used her sewing skills to earn a living, working out of her home as a dressmaker.[73] Those young women who were able to find employment during the Depression devoted some of their earnings to clothing; dressing decently was a way for these young women to "reaffirm their respectability in the face of the Great Depression."[74] Appearing respectable also made finding paid employment easier. The fact that young women continued to window-shop, consult department store catalogues, and make over old clothing so that it conformed to the latest fashions demonstrates that consumer culture was well established in Canada's interwar cities, even in the midst of an economic depression.[75]

What was absent during the Great Depression was any kind of sustained and sufficient state support. No unemployment insurance programme existed, at either the federal or the provincial level. Instead, faced with the devastating and durable nature of joblessness during the 1930s, the federal and provincial governments collaborated with the municipalities that were on the front lines in order to fund the sporadic and temporary form of assistance known as unemployment relief. This unemployment relief took various forms. Sometimes it was paid in kind, in the form of firewood, coal, or clothing. Sometimes it took the form of vouchers to be spent at the local grocer or butcher. Sometimes it was conditional upon participation in public works projects, such as road building. Almost always, relief was perceived as humiliating by those obliged to accept it. Discussions of a permanent system of unemployment insurance were tossed back and forth between the federal and provincial governments. Although social assistance was constitutionally a provincial jurisdiction, the provinces were in no financial shape to initiate such a programme during the 1930s. By the end of the Depression it had become clear that only the federal government had the financial and administrative capacity to do so. The federal branch of the state finally accepted responsibility for unemployment by adopting the Unemployment Insurance Act in 1940, once the economic crisis was over.[76]

It is little wonder that, given the collapse of the market and insufficient state support, ordinary Canadians began calling into question family forms judged "traditional." Rates of marriage declined during the 1930s, as young men did not have the savings or the wages required to establish a new household and young women often needed—or felt obligated—to continue supporting their aging parents before leaving to begin a family of their own.[77] Likewise, the costs of raising children were felt more acutely than ever during the Depression. One example that throws into sharp relief the questioning of familial practices during the 1930s was the trial of Ontario social worker Dorothea Palmer. Palmer was employed by the Parents' Information Bureau, an association founded by Ontario industrialist Alvin R. Kaufman to distribute birth control information to poor and working-class families. Kaufman, owner of Kitchener's Kaufman Rubber Company, employed some fifty nurses and social workers to visit mothers in poor neighbourhoods in cities across Canada. Like a number of middle-class, Protestant, English Canadians in the 1930s, he openly espoused eugenicist views. With his fellow members of the Eugenics Society of Canada, he argued that fewer children born to poor families would be a good thing for the nation (or "the race") and would impose less of a burden upon the state. Dorothea Palmer herself appears to have thought that information about contraception would allow women more autonomy over their lives. In September 1936, she was arrested in Eastview (now Vanier), Ontario, a largely French-speaking, Catholic suburb of Ottawa, for speaking to local families about contraception and showing them examples of contraceptive devices such as condoms and contraceptive jelly. In a context where the advertisement, distribution, and sale of contraceptives were illegal, Palmer was charged under Section 207 of the Criminal Code and brought to trial. A successful defence of Palmer's actions (and, by extension, of the work of the Parents' Information Bureau and similar clinics elsewhere in Canada) required demonstrating that Palmer had been working for the public good, the only condition under which the diffusion of birth control information was legally acceptable. Palmer was in fact acquitted for this reason in March 1937; the legal decision explicitly recognized the difficulty of bearing and raising numerous children in the material circumstances of the Great Depression. The twenty-one French-Canadian and Catholic housewives visited by Palmer who testified at her trial agreed that she had committed no harm. Clearly, the costs—material, physical, and emotional—of numerous, closely spaced pregnancies and births were becoming more widely recognized in the interwar years.[78]

Private Charity and the Emergence of the "Helping Professions"

That the Canadian state had little in the way of concrete measures to offer to the men who returned from the battlefields of Europe or to the men, women, and children who fell victim to the massive unemployment rates of the 1930s should not be surprising. This was a profoundly liberal state and mode of governance. Private charity remained important, even central, through the "boom and bust" years that were the 1920s and 1930s. To a certain degree, private charitable efforts were professionalized in the interwar years, as new family experts such as nurses, paediatricians, psychologists, and social workers glimpsed the potential to help, but also to shape, Canadian families. Often, members of these emerging "helping professions" worked with private associations that had existed since the nineteenth century and that had long been reliant upon the volunteer labour of middle-class women. Indeed, it was often difficult for professional social workers, usually women, to lay claim to a particular expertise, when work similar to theirs had for so long been undertaken by well-meaning women who were both untrained and unpaid.[79] Sometimes these new experts worked in tandem with the state; indeed, throughout the interwar years and during the Second World War, the state frequently relied upon social workers and private charitable associations to screen potential beneficiaries of new public welfare measures.[80]

New childcare experts argued that parents, but especially mothers, needed proper training in order to raise children fit for the twentieth century. No longer was a supposed "maternal instinct" sufficient: mothers needed to consult the advice manuals and parenting guides that proliferated in the wake of the Great War. After the slaughter of the war and the tens of thousands of deaths in Canada due to influenza, in a context where both infant and maternal mortality rates were exceedingly high, huge expectations were placed upon mothers to rear healthy children. Mothering needed to be "scientific," based upon ideas of routine, order, and regularity and upon laboratory standards of cleanliness. The latest ideas in scientific child-raising were tested in new nursery schools established in large cities such as Toronto and Montreal. Unlike the crèches that had taken care of working-class infants and children since the nineteenth century, these new nursery schools, run by experts such as paediatricians and psychologists, were aimed squarely at middle-class children not yet old enough to attend school.[81]

One of the best-known examples of the impact of childcare experts and the "helping professions" on Canadian families in the interwar years was the extraordinary story of the Dionne quintuplets. Identical sisters Yvonne, Marie, Émilie, Annette, and Cécile were born near the village of Corbeil, Ontario, in May 1934. The daughters of a farming couple that already had five children (a sixth child had died very young), the "Quints," as they were called in the press and on the radio, were the first known quintuplets to survive for more than a few days. Within months of their birth, the girls, judged physically fragile, were taken away from their parents and confined to the care of the Ontario government. It was not until 1938 that Oliva and Elzire Dionne, assisted by Franco-Ontarian associations such as the *Association canadienne-française de l'éducation de l'Ontario* and the *Fédération des femmes canadiennes-françaises*, would regain control of their daughters.[82] The girls' francophone, Catholic parents, farmers in northern Ontario, were perceived by interwar childcare experts to be conservative, poor, and out of touch with modern developments in childcare. One nurse, for instance, claimed that if the girls' mother "had realized and recognized the need of proper pre-natal care, not only for her own relief and comfort but to lessen the risks to her expected offspring, her five babies might not have been born so prematurely nor to such a degree afflicted with the worst curse of infancy—rickets."[83] Once in the care of the state, the quintuplets became a living laboratory for paediatricians and other medical doctors (Dr. Allan Roy Dafoe and Dr. Alan Brown) as well as child psychologists (Dr. William Blatz), who eagerly conducted experiments in modern childrearing upon the girls, while a North American public avid for details followed news of the girls' progress in the daily press. Mothers in search of childrearing advice even wrote to Dr. Dafoe, convinced that the man who had ensured the survival and good health of the Dionne sisters could provide good counsel as they raised their own children.[84] If the quintuplets fascinated these interwar childhood experts, they also nourished a burgeoning interwar consumer culture. Several Hollywood movies were made about the girls, and memorabilia such as dishes, paper dolls, china dolls, calendars and souvenir booklets were produced, all bearing the girls' image. Photographs of the five girls were also used to endorse products such as Colgate dental cream and Palmolive soap. "Quintland," the combined home and hospital in which the little girls were placed, became, for all intents and purposes, a twentieth-century amusement park, and the quintuplets a consumer spectacle. Visitors from all over North America made the road trip to the complex in Callander, Ontario to watch the girls play behind one-way glass—and left after having purchased souvenirs at one of the several Quintland gift shops.[85]

FIGURE 5.3 The Dionne Quintuplets. Wikimedia Commons.

The doctors who worked with the Dionne quintuplets, especially Brown and Blatz, were on the cutting edge of interwar expertise and had at their disposal almost unlimited resources. Most members of the interwar helping professions made do with far fewer resources, far from the media spotlight. And most children taken into care in this period lived in far more spartan circumstances than the Dionne girls. Across the country, private associations and institutions remained important during the interwar years, despite intense debate over the relative benefits of institutionalization for children. In cases where biological kin could not take care of their children, professional social workers increasingly promoted the merits of adoption or foster care rather than institutions. New Brunswick and Nova Scotia had had adoption laws in place since 1873 and 1896 respectively. In the 1920s, several other provinces passed adoption legislation: British Columbia in 1920, Ontario in 1921, and Quebec and Manitoba in 1924. These provincial laws severed the legal ties between biological parents and their child and created new, legally bound families.[86] Unlike large institutions for children, important in all Canadian provinces since the mid-nineteenth century, foster homes and adoptive homes were expected to mimic the structure and function of biological families, headed by a heterosexual married couple and with the authority residing with the father. As the twentieth century advanced, the infants and children considered most desirable—healthy white babies, especially girls—tended to be adopted quickly, while the children who ended up in foster homes tended to be older, often boys, sometimes with learning difficulties or physical disabilities. Indigenous children and non-white children were also overrepresented in foster homes through the second half of the twentieth century.[87]

The Canadian Council on Child Welfare (CCCW) was keen to modernize and standardize institutions for children across the country in the interwar years. CCCW director Charlotte Whitton—and her assistants and allies—attempted to eliminate what they perceived to be regional or provincial peculiarities.[88] The institutional model privileged in Quebec, where the majority of the population was Catholic, was exactly what Whitton was trying to eliminate.[89] However, institutions housing dozens or even hundreds of children could be found in every Canadian province in the interwar years. In the late 1920s, social workers dispatched by Whitton to assess the Boys Industrial Home in Saint John, New Brunswick were dismayed to discover an institution in terrible physical condition, where the boys were dirty, malnourished, and generally neglected, and where new social-work practices such as psychological assessments or the keeping of case files had made few or no inroads.[90]

Despite centralizing tendencies and the promotion of foster care and adoption by social workers, the 1920s actually saw the creation of some new private institutions for children. In the Maritimes, for example, the Nova Scotia Home for Colored Children opened its doors in Preston, six miles east of Dartmouth, in 1921. This was a project to which the African Nova Scotian community contributed both moral support and funds, in part because it was known that most other orphanages and children's homes in and around Halifax refused to admit Black children.[91] Several years later, in 1928, the married couple William and Lila Young opened the Ideal Maternity Home in Chester, Nova Scotia. This private (indeed, commercial) maternity home and adoption placement service was intended to assist unmarried mothers and their children. By the 1940s, both of these institutions were attracting considerable criticism for the lack of trained expertise and absence of professional practice within their walls. Far worse, the Nova Scotia Home for Colored Children would become notorious for the severe physical and emotional abuse inflicted upon some of the children who lived there.[92] The Ideal Maternity Home, for its part, by the 1940s the largest maternity home in eastern Canada, housed "severely malnourished and neglected children" and exploited both birth mothers and adoptive parents through black-market adoptions.[93] In 1944, George Davidson, the executive director of the Canadian Welfare Council, stated that

> Although the [Ideal Maternity] Home confines upwards of a hundred mothers or more a year, and cares for as many as seventy babies at a time, there is a total lack of qualified medical supervision, and a serious inadequacy of properly qualified, fully trained nursing care. The room in which the babies were kept was, on the occasion of the survey visit, distressingly overcrowded, with the obvious result that it was impossible to prevent the spread of colds (and this would apply to similar infectious diseases).... On at least one previous occasion, infant deaths at this institution have reached epidemic proportions, and it is the opinion of this survey that nothing except great good fortune has prevented similar tragedies from recurring on more frequent occasions.[94]

Members of the new helping professions, then, made significant inroads in Canada during the interwar years, as they refined their techniques and promoted new bureaucratic practices. Fostering and adoption were increasingly seen to be better choices for babies and children than large institutions. The impact of the efforts made by experts in child health and welfare was uneven, however, and institutions created in the mid-nineteenth century continued to house children in need of care a century later.

The Second World War and the Beginnings of the Canadian Welfare State

A scant twenty years after the Great War ended, the war that would quickly become known as the Second World War began, for Canada, on 10 September 1939. A "total war" like its predecessor, the Second World War had an impact on the daily lives of almost all Canadian families. Most directly touched were those where a family member—a husband, a father, a son, a daughter, a sibling—enrolled in one of the armed services, including the new services for women (the Canadian Women's Army Corps, the Women's Royal Canadian Naval Service, and the Royal Canadian Air Force—Women's Division). As with the generation that had lived through the Great War, military enlistment meant long absences, loneliness, and, sometimes, strained relationships between husbands and wives. For children, it meant long years without a father, and, eventually, the return of a father who they no longer knew or barely remembered. For married women, it meant making do on their husbands' assigned pay and separation allowances and sometimes seeking paid work themselves.[95] For families opposed to the idea of military conscription, the spectre of compulsory enrolment created an additional source of worry. Significant numbers of Canadian men (and a significantly smaller number of women) enrolled in the armed forces. An estimated 1,090,762 Canadian men and women were in uniform over the course of the war.[96] Enrolments ranged from a high of just over 50 per cent of men aged 18 to 45 in British Columbia to just over 25 per cent of men aged 18 to 45 in Quebec.[97] Clearly, many families across Canada experienced the direct impact of the war in this way, through the enrolment of a husband, a father, a son, a brother, or, occasionally, a daughter or a sister.

Some Canadian families also lived with the presence of troops on leave and in training in their towns and cities, even though the military front lay overseas. Towns near military bases from British Columbia to Nova Scotia experienced the influx of soldiers on leave; on Saturday nights, dance halls, restaurants, cinemas, and taverns were filled with men in uniform.[98] Air force personnel and students associated with the British Commonwealth Air Training Plan were present in the air schools set up in all nine provinces, from British Columbia to Prince Edward Island. Port cities such as Halifax, Sydney, Montreal, and Vancouver were transformed by the presence of warships and sailors. In still independent Newfoundland, Allied naval bases and a Royal Canadian Air Force station near St. John's housed American and Canadian servicemen for several years.[99] In all of these places, local citizens, including parents, worried that "khaki-mad" adolescent girls and young women might find in these soldiers on leave a source of romantic interest.[100]

Children and adolescents did in fact experience the impact of the war in particular ways. Older teenagers earning good wartime wages were able to participate in the various leisure options offered by towns and cities across Canada. They gathered to listen to big-band music in concert halls and high-school gymnasia and practised the jive and the jitterbug in commercial dance halls.[101] In St. John's, children and teenagers were fascinated by the Canadian and, especially, American servicemen who handed out chocolate bars, bottles of Coca Cola, and cigarettes throughout the war years, but who were also present in their homes, invited to dinner on Sundays or on holidays. Decades after the Second World War, one St. John's girl remembered finding chewing gum in her stocking one Christmas morning and assuming that it had been brought to her by Santa Claus, rather than by the "six burly sailors" who had spent Christmas Eve with her family.[102]

The Second World War and the continuing importance of imperial ties resulted in the arrival in Canada, in the summer of 1940, of some 3,200 British children, unaccompanied by their parents. These young evacuees were intended to stay in Canada for the duration of the war, so as to be safe from the bombing of Britain. These white, British girls and boys, frequently referred to in the newspapers as "war guests," were for the most part welcomed with open arms by Canadians. Roughly half of these children (1655 of them) arrived in Canada through private arrangements made among family members and friends, while the Children's Overseas Reception Board (CORB), an organization sponsored by the British government, arranged the travel and resettlement of the 1532 other children. The CORB conducted medical screenings of the children and also screened their Canadian foster parents for suitability. These British evacuees were placed in all nine Canadian provinces. They ranged in age from 5 to 15, but most of the children were aged 8 to 13. Some of them arrived with their siblings. Their stays in Canada were lengthy, often four to five years, and many of the British children, although not all, developed close and loving relationships with their foster parents and siblings. Most stayed until the summer of 1945, although those who turned seventeen before the end of the war were allowed to return to the United Kingdom earlier. The reunions of these children and adolescents with their biological parents at the end of the war, and their reinsertion in British life more generally, were not always easy.[103]

A booming wartime economy meant an abundance of jobs for adult men, for unmarried—and some married—women, and for adolescents of both sexes. It was very easy for teenagers to get jobs and many of them jumped at the chance to earn regular wages.[104] Adolescent boys and girls worked both part-time and full-time during the war, as messengers or couriers, for instance, but also in war industries. Some adult observers worried that the teenagers flocking to well-paid jobs in war industry were "mortgaging their futures by leaving school precipitously" for employment that ultimately proved temporary.[105]

As wartime production soaked up the unemployment of the 1930s and as military recruitment removed from the labour force an important number of adult men, the federal government and war industries began progressively to recruit women for the industrial cause. They began, naturally, with unmarried women, and then extended their search to married women without children. Finally, in a situation of full employment where the war effort (and industrial profits) depended upon keeping factories running around the clock, the National Selective Service Women's Division took the unusual step of recruiting married women with children. An even more unusual step was the establishment of government-funded day nurseries for the children of women working in essential war industries. Funded through cost-sharing agreements between the federal government and the participating provinces (Ontario, Quebec, and, initially, Alberta), these public day nurseries were unprecedented. Ultimately, Alberta never did establish any wartime day nurseries, but Ontario set up twenty-eight day nurseries and Quebec six—all in the Montreal region. Surveys conducted during the war found that the Quebec wartime day nurseries were used primarily by Protestant and Jewish mothers. Catholic mothers had to combat the opposition voiced by the clergy, who deemed these government day cares to be "socialist" measures. More generally, wariness of federal state intervention in the context of the war meant that most wage-earning Quebec mothers turned to the informal networks of care that they had used for years: neighbours, older daughters, or female members of their extended family.[106] The Dominion-Provincial Wartime Day Nurseries Agreement, established in cities where war production was important, was a measure "for the duration" only and was never intended to last into peacetime; mothers, it was assumed, would leave their paid jobs and return to their homes and children full-time once the war was over.[107] It was no surprise to anyone, then, when the Wartime Day Nurseries Agreement was abrogated in 1946. Yet many of the mothers who had benefited from these day nurseries were not willing to see the programme die without a protest. A number of Montreal mothers, for example, drafted petitions urging government officials to keep the day nurseries open beyond the final days of the war. This would, the mothers argued in 1945, "be a great help in enabling us to get our home life back to a stable basis."[108]

In many parts of the country, the Second World War did lead to a significant increase in the number of married women working for pay. As historian Lisa Pasolli finds, "By 1944, married women made up 34 percent of all female workers [across Canada], up from 22 percent in 1939."[109] Not all of these women were employed in war industries. In British Columbia, for instance, married women worked in factories, but also in laundries, restaurants and cafés, hotels, and private homes.[110] While some married women might have taken up paid employment for patriotic reasons, the vast majority worked because they and their families needed the income. Although encouraged, to a certain extent, by the federal government, this work was opposed by other members of society. Tilly Rolston, for example, a Conservative Member of the Legislative Assembly (MLA) in British Columbia, warned in 1944 that:

> Military victory will be a hollow mockery if we produce a generation of demoralized and delinquent Canadians while winning this war to preserve our way of life. Your daily newspaper and local police record

will show you how serious this threat has become. We have thousands of underfed, neglected children who are key carriers, while mother wields a blow torch.[111]

Across Canada, the paid work of mothers was in fact blamed by conservative commentators for familial woes ranging from adultery to divorce to juvenile delinquency.[112]

Industrial work—munitions work in particular—received the lion's share of public attention during the war. But such work was limited to a certain number of urban centres across the country. The war also had an impact on the nature of work in rural areas and in regions where resource extraction fuelled the economy. In Newfoundland, for instance, the Second World War meant the construction of numerous American and Canadian wartime bases on the island, employing some 20,000 Newfoundlanders.[113] This important new source of employment and wages was a boon to Newfoundlanders, many of whom had spent the 1920s and 1930s in dire economic straits. Most of these 20,000 workers were men, who, in keeping with a long tradition of occupational pluralism, often combined work on the bases with seasonal work in fishing or logging. Women also found work on these army, navy, and air bases as laundresses, waitresses, secretaries, or stenographers.[114]

Much more extensively than during the First World War, the federal government intervened in the daily life of civilians. In an effort to closely manage the wartime economy and prevent inflation, the state took it upon itself to control prices, rents, and wages. For the first time in Canada, official rationing limited the kinds and quantities of products—meat, sugar, alcohol, and gasoline—available to civilians. The federal government encouraged patriotic citizens to salvage, reuse, and recycle. It likewise mounted publicity campaigns encouraging citizens

FIGURE 5.4 Propaganda encouraging housewives to reduce, reuse, and recycle during the Second World War. Avenues.

to save their wartime earnings—through Victory Bonds, for example—so as to counter inflationary tendencies. In urban areas, especially, activist housewives, notebooks in hand, monitored prices in local shops and reported those business owners or landlords who failed to respect federal price and rent controls. This wartime price monitoring created a relationship between married women and the state at a time when the nature and potential of citizenship was a subject of public debate.[115] Alongside those citizens eager to conform to government regulations were those who took advantage of the opportunities for profits created by the war. An underground economy—what some call the "black market"—flourished in wartime Canada, suggesting the limits of—and opposition to—federal government controls.[116] Tensions between those citizens who felt that they had sacrificed a great deal for the war effort and those who had visibly profited from the war ran high by the mid-1940s. In the context of the severe housing shortage that was prevalent in centres of war production across the country (Halifax, Toronto, Montreal, Vancouver), one woman living in Verdun, Quebec, wrote to the local newspaper in February 1945:

> I was evicted three years ago and since have occupied an abandoned store for which I pay $25 per month. Each winter I use six tons of fuel. The thermometer is usually at 45 [degrees Fahrenheit] in the morning and may reach 66 during the daytime. My family (three school children) have no bath other than the swimming pool in summer. During the last three years a couch ... has been my bedroom, with a plentiful supply of mice for company. I have my three sons in the services since 1939. Three of my daughters are helping in the war effort by working in munitions plants. One of them has already had a nervous breakdown, owing to environment. I feel my duty to King and Country has far exceeded its limits. Where would King and Country be without sons such as mine, and what on earth are they fighting for? Of late I have begun to appreciate the word "sucker" when applied by a Zombie to a man in uniform .... Could I have foreseen what has happened to us since 1939, believe you me, my three boys would have donned overalls instead of khaki.[117]

In many ways, the federal government's management of daily life during the war paved the way for—and accompanied—its significantly increased intervention in the realm of social assistance and social welfare. A federally led welfare state took shape in Canada in the 1940s, beginning with federal

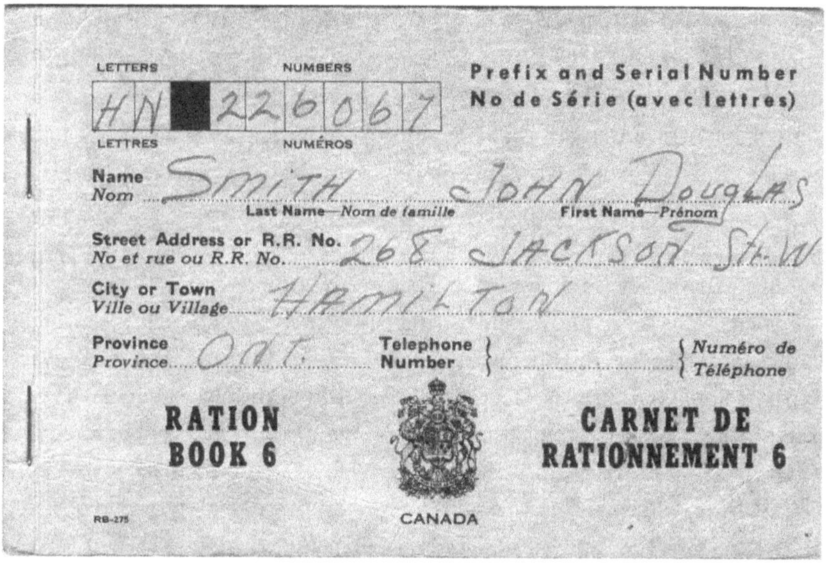

FIGURE 5.5 Rationing booklet, Second World War. Wartime Canada.

unemployment insurance, adopted in 1940, and continuing with measures for soldiers and veterans far more generous than what the state had provided to a previous generation of enlisted men and returned soldiers. These measures included rehabilitation credits to put towards the purchase of a home and furniture, guaranteed access to the job that the soldier had left behind, access to vocational training and university education, and the benefits included in the Veterans' Land Act.[118] It was the universal family allowance programme adopted in 1944 and implemented across the country in 1945, however, that was the highlight of federal intervention in social welfare in the immediate postwar period. Family allowances were both materially and symbolically important: they were provided to all Canadian families, regardless of their income, and thus did not stigmatize poor or working-class families in the way that the means-tested measures of the 1920s and 1930s had done. Family allowances were paid by cheque (and not in the form of humiliating vouchers, the way that unemployment relief had been distributed during the Depression) and were calculated according to the number of children in the family. Moreover, these cheques were sent to mothers, not fathers, and thus recognized the crucial role played by married women across the country in managing and stretching the family budget and in taking care of their children's needs. In most provinces, the receipt of family allowances was conditional upon children attending school. In Quebec, in particular, the 1940s thus witnessed the adoption of a particular constellation of legislation—compulsory schooling in 1943, family allowances in 1944, plus laws limiting paid child labour—that assured children of new social rights as young citizens.[119] Even in provinces that had adopted compulsory schooling decades earlier, family allowances made a significant difference to rates of children's school attendance. Not only could parents do without the modest wages formerly earned by their children, but they could also afford to buy the decent clothing and footwear necessary for children to attend school.[120]

There were limits, however, to this new universality. Until 1953, for instance, some Indigenous peoples (the majority of Inuit peoples and several First Nations communities) received their family allowance payments in kind and not in cash. They were required to use their family allowances to choose among a select range of authorized goods—powdered milk, baby cereal, processed food, children's clothes—using the Department of Indian Affairs' Indian agents as intermediaries. These were of course goods aimed at infants and children, but these were also goods that corresponded to the government objective of initiating Indigenous peoples into Euro-Canadian patterns of consumption. These requirements reflected a persistent paternalism by which

FIGURE 5.6 Treated as threats to public security during the Second World War, these Japanese-Canadian men were conscripted to work on the Hope-Princeton Highway Project (British Columbia, 1942). Their families were likely housed in the nearby Tashme Internment Camp. University of British Columbia Library. Rare Books and Special Collections. Japanese Canadian Research Collection. JCPC_03_007. @ Flickr Commons.

Indigenous families were treated as wards of the federal government. Even in the context of new social programmes touted as "universal," some Indigenous mothers were viewed as not sufficiently responsible to decide how to spend their family allowance.[121]

State intervention within families could be a progressive measure that effected positive change, as when it added regular sources of income to the family budget without subjecting the members of these families to humiliating means tests. However, as with military conscription, state intervention could also be coercive, especially in wartime. Nowhere was this coercion more evident than in the case of Canadian families of Japanese origin, 95 per cent of whom lived in British Columbia, where they worked in agriculture in the Fraser Valley and in the fishing industry along the coast, as well as in the small Japanese business community established along Powell Street in Vancouver. In the spring of 1942, these families were forcibly removed from their homes and relocated to camps in the interior of B.C. The displacement and confinement of some 22,000 Japanese nationals and Japanese Canadians, many of whom had been born in Canada, followed upon the bombing of the American naval base in Pearl Harbor, Hawaii, by Japan in December 1941. The ostensible reason for this federal policy was the fear of a Japanese attack upon the west coast of Canada. This fear, however, built upon longstanding racism and concerns about the threat posed by the so-called "yellow peril" to Canada's cultural make-up. The particular context of the war thus exacerbated longstanding racist sentiment. A similar policy of removal and confinement of Japanese-Americans was adopted in the United States.[122] Interviews with some of the Japanese Canadians who were interned as either adults or children reveal much about memories of family life in the internment camps in Greenwood, New Denver, Slocan, Kaslo, and other former ghost towns in the B.C. Interior. These internment settlements were often feminized places, inhabited by women, children, and the very elderly, as adult men were frequently interned in work camps or road camps elsewhere in B.C. or in Ontario. Some adult men—those who most actively resisted the internment—were sent to prisoner-of-war camps in Petawawa or Angler, in Ontario. Women interviewed decades after the war remember their mothers' efforts to pack the domestic goods—dishes, cutlery, tablecloths, stoves, and sewing machines—that would help them to set up a home wherever they were sent. Those who were children at the time of the internment recall having to leave their toys and books behind when they were rounded up. And they remember the constant worry felt by their mothers, obliged to parent alone in the absence of their husbands. Prohibited from returning to the west coast until

1949, many Japanese-Canadian families were forced to disperse and to relocate east of the Rockies after the war, taking long, uncomfortable train rides east before settling in Ontario or Quebec, often far from friends or relatives.[123]

In 1945, Canada was still a small country, a former colony of France, and then of Britain, relatively removed from the centres of international decision-making, its economy based to a significant degree upon the exploitation of natural resources. By the end of the Second World War, however, the country also had an extremely solid manufacturing base and the initial elements of a welfare state. The thirty years that followed the Second World War—the decades known in France as the "trente glorieuses"—would bring enormous changes to Canada and to Canadian families, including massive waves of immigration and unprecedented economic prosperity.

6
Thirty Glorious Years? Families and the Postwar Settlement, 1945–1975

THE THREE DECADES that followed the Second World War are known in France as the "trente glorieuses"—the thirty glorious years. What was viewed as glorious was the return to peace after the ravages of the war, in the context of a sustained period of prosperity that was, in Western Europe and in North America, unprecedented. This was a relatively widespread prosperity fuelled by both public and private spending. New welfare-state measures provided many families with a significant degree of social and economic security. Expenditures linked to the Cold War contributed to the health of what some have called "high capitalism" and to the development of a consumer society that included more and more members of that society. In the wake of the tragedies occasioned by the Holocaust and the Second World War, the family was viewed as an institution crucial to a healthy postwar society. The United Nations' Universal Declaration of Human Rights, issued in Paris in December 1948, deemed the family "the natural and fundamental group unit of society," a unit that was "entitled to protection by society and the State."[1] Across North America, the 1950s bore witness to a relatively conservative vision of the family that promoted ideological conformity, breadwinning husbands and dependent wives and children, and an intolerance of homosexuality. During the tumultuous years of the 1960s and early 1970s, however, longstanding models of family were called into question and often discarded altogether.[2]

A Period of Relative Prosperity

Historians of the workplace and industrial relations tend to refer to the decades that followed the Second World War as a "Fordist" moment. In return for union recognition and relatively high wages, workers agreed to cooperate with their employers and to work towards achieving industrial peace. Full employment and decent wages allowed these workers and their families to participate in consumer society; consumer spending in turn fuelled the capitalist economy and, more specifically, the production of goods. This is what historians have called the "postwar settlement" or "postwar compromise." "Businesses conceded unions a measure of legitimacy and citizen rights, while unions accepted managerial prerogatives and labour's place within a capitalist social order." However, a third actor, the state, had an important role to play in this regime premised upon industrial legality; during the postwar period, the state actively regulated the relationship between labour and capital through such key legislation as the Industrial Relations and Disputes Investigation Act (IRDIA) of 1948.[3] The Labour-Management Production Committees established in industries across Canada during the Second World War are an important example of this tendency toward cooperation among labour, capital, and the state.[4] Historian Craig Heron has enumerated the benefits of the postwar settlement important to male breadwinners like his father in the 1940s and 1950s: "regular wage increases, modest promotion opportunities . . ., a benefit plan, more leisure time in the form of 40-hour weeks and regular paid holidays and vacations, and, most important in his Depression-era consciousness, good job security."[5]

Historians of the state tend to refer to these decades as a "Keynesian" moment, that is, a moment when the Canadian state, like many Western European nations, opted for government spending as a way of fuelling the economy. The assumption was that state welfare measures would encourage consumer spending and that consumer spending would fuel the economy.[6] State spending was thus integral to the health of postwar capitalism; both state welfare measures and private-sector wages contributed to the flourishing of a postwar consumer society. The political and ideological context of the Cold War promoted participation in this consumer society. Cold War thinking "encouraged citizens to prize the private consumption and accumulation of products in the nuclear family household as proof of capitalism's success."[7]

A key factor fuelling the development of a consumer society in the postwar period was widespread advertising. Advertising was given a new medium of transmission with the arrival of television in Canada in 1952.[8] Television sets were of course themselves a consumer item, one that many Canadian households rushed to acquire. By 1958, 81 per cent of households in Ontario and 79 per cent of households in Quebec had acquired a television set. By the following year, fully 90 per cent of households in Canada's urban centres owned a television.[9] The regional and rural-urban differences in the acquisition of consumer goods revealed by these statistics are telling. Throughout the 1940s and 1950s, many families in rural areas were dependent upon the rhythm of rural electrification in order to buy new electrical appliances such as stoves, refrigerators, and washing machines. Nonetheless, the rate at which Canadian households across the country acquired a TV set in the 1950s and 1960s is impressive. The programmes developed by the public broadcasters, CBC and Radio-Canada, and by private broadcasters such as CTV, were accompanied—and rendered possible, in the case of private networks—by advertisements for products made by such companies as General Motors, Lowney's, and Molson's.[10] Of course, advertising had been present for three decades on Canadian radio stations and even longer in magazines and the daily press. In the postwar years, advertisers responded to pent-up consumer demand, which had been difficult to satisfy during the years of deprivation and then rationing.[11] Once the Second World War was finally over, the needs of industry were given priority over the wishes of domestic consumers. New household appliances such as electric stoves, refrigerators, and washing machines were thus coveted for months, even years, before they once again arrived on the market.

For many married women, postwar consumerism was best represented by the purchase of these household appliances, unaffordable during the Great Depression and unavailable during the war. Just about everyone assumed that women, and especially married women, would be the principal users of these appliances.[12] Whether these appliances made married women's domestic labour easier is a matter for debate: some have argued that their arrival was accompanied by higher standards of cleanliness necessarily involving "More Work for Mother."[13] New domestic appliances—and postwar consumer purchases more generally—were clearly gendered. Just as most household appliances judged essential were aimed at married women, consumer purchases involving leisure or hobbies—barbecues, lawnmowers, and high-fidelity stereos—were potential purchases aimed at married men.[14] Indeed, the popularity of high-fidelity stereo equipment among middle-class men in the post-Second World War years represented these men's desire to reclaim domestic space that they perceived to be overly feminized. "Before World War II, the phonograph and recorded music were not especially associated with men. By the 1960s, however, home audio sound reproduction equipment had hardened into masculinist technologies *par excellence*."[15]

Not all Canadian families enjoyed the material abundance evoked by the expression "postwar prosperity," however.[16] Writing in 1966, the authors of the Hawthorn Report (*A Survey of the Contemporary Indians of Canada: A Report on Economic, Political, Educational Needs and Policies*) claimed that Indigenous peoples, for instance, "want the material blessings other Canadians have in the way of incomes, houses, cars, furnishings, clothes, foods and so on, perhaps partly because they are advertised at and exhorted to want them equally with the rest of us. Their income levels and their average expenditures are rising but on the average are now far less than equal to national or regional averages and the gap is ever widening."[17] The Hawthorn Report suggested, in fact, that Indigenous peoples "occupied the lowest economic rung in Canada."[18] Judged by the usual, measurable indicators of wellbeing—wages, access to education, quality of housing, health—the conditions in which many Indigenous people lived were perceived by the authors of the report to be deeply inadequate. The two Hawthorn Reports (the first report, on Indigenous peoples in British Columbia, was published in 1958) constitute an example of the increasing interest of social scientists in Indigenous peoples—and of the impact of the social sciences on the Indian Affairs branch of the postwar federal Department of Citizenship and Immigration. These studies often revealed the real poverty in which many Indigenous peoples were living, while at the same time turning them into objects of scientific study.[19]

Among the most notorious of these studies were the various investigations of malnutrition conducted among Indigenous communities in northern Manitoba and northern Ontario and in residential schools across the country in the 1940s and the 1950s. These studies demonstrated, without a doubt, the real hunger and malnourishment present among the Cree First Nations and among children and adolescents attending residential schools in Nova Scotia, Ontario, Alberta, and British Columbia. Most shockingly, the individuals who were part of the scientific control groups were deliberately maintained in a state of malnutrition that the scientists and bureaucrats involved in the studies could have alleviated with vitamin supplements and nutrients.[20]

Even for those families fortunate to benefit from some measure of postwar prosperity, financial ease did not arrive as soon as victory in Europe and Japan was declared. The 1940s were a period of economic uncertainty for many, and many Canadian families purchased cautiously and selectively in the 1940s and early 1950s, often preferring to adapt and remake existing furniture, for example, rather than replace it with new purchases.[21] In Quebec, moreover, widespread automobile ownership and suburbanization were phenomena of the later 1950s and the 1960s rather than of the immediate postwar years.[22] Indeed, generalizations about "postwar material life" were often based on "the most prosperous parts of the United States in the most prosperous years of the 1950s and 1960s."[23]

In Canada, by contrast, the immediate postwar period was characterized, particularly in urban areas, by the continued negotiation of rationing and material scarcity and the battle by housewives—radical and less so—against inflation and the high prices of household necessities. In 1948, for example, Montreal housewives protested the high prices of meat and fresh produce, boycotted butchers and grocers, and demanded the legalization of margarine as a less costly alternative to butter.[24] Across Canada, "militant housewives" took issue with high grocery prices in the late 1940s. Some did so through the Canadian Association of Consumers, a Liberal Party-affiliated organization of largely middle-class, activist women. Other women, Communists or social democrats, participated in the Housewives Consumer Association (HCA). British Columbia social activist Effie Jones, for example, was a member of the social democratic Co-operative Commonwealth Federation (CCF) in the 1930s. By the 1950s, Jones had left the CCF and become active within the Communist Party of Canada; she was an active member of the HCA. Her fellow British Columbian Mona Bjarnason Morgan was also involved with the HCA in postwar Vancouver, where she participated in "the fight to lower food prices in order to attain a better standard of living for working families."[25] Communist and CCF women who mobilized in the postwar years braved the hostility and anticommunism of political authorities in the context of the international Cold War. Yet both women on the Left and women on the Right, such as supporters of the Social Credit Party in postwar Alberta, justified their political organizing using language that historians have termed "maternalist," related to married women's presumed responsibility for matters concerning the family and the household.[26]

For the thousands of Canadian families, including those recently arrived from Europe, living in large cities, the physical space and material comforts advertised by promoters of the new postwar suburban housing developments were largely unknown. Toronto families whose members had emigrated from Italy in the postwar years often doubled up, sharing houses in the older core of the city with boarders and sometimes with other immigrant families. Maria Rossi, for example, who arrived in Toronto with her daughter in 1956, moved into a flat rented by her husband, who had arrived in Canada a year earlier, in the basement of a west-end home owned by another Italian-Canadian family.[27] Historian Alvin Finkel recounts that in the 1940s and 1950s, his parents, both prewar immigrants from Eastern Europe, rented a flat in Finkel's grandmother's North Winnipeg home. Here "I slept in the living room, sharing this 'bedroom' with a brother, a sister, and the television set."[28] High rates of employment and wages considerably higher than those earned during the Depression years did mean, however, that even if prosperity remained elusive, many postwar Canadian families were able to enjoy a newfound sense of economic security.[29]

The Baby Boom and Visions of Family

The demographic phenomenon at the heart of postwar family life in North America was the explosion in births that has become known as the "baby boom." Marriage rates, which had declined during the Depression of the 1930s, rose again during the war. These increased marriage rates were followed shortly thereafter by a rise in birth rates. In some sense, then, the famous postwar baby boom actually had its roots in the Second World War.[30] "From a low of 227,000 live births in the mid-1930s, the number of Canadian babies born each year rose to 343,504 by 1946, and to a peak of 479,000 by the later 1950s." More families were formed in 1946 "than ever before in Canada."[31] It is important to understand, however, that the baby boom was not a return to the large families of the eighteenth or nineteenth centuries; most couples were not having families of seven or eight children. Rather, the phenomenon was the result of many young parents deciding to have their children in a relatively short space of time. Couples were marrying younger than before (most women married in their early twenties) and were waiting mere months before deciding to have a baby.[32] Couples who had married before the war, but who waited until the war was over before having children, also contributed to the postwar baby boom. At the peak of the baby boom, in the late 1950s, Canada's total fertility rate was 3.94 children per woman.[33] The fact that thousands of young couples made the decision to begin a family at the same time made it seem as though everyone was pregnant, giving birth, and raising children. Across North America, then, a society and a culture centred on babies and children appeared to reign. The baby boom was in fact a semi-international phenomenon, involving especially, it seemed, countries that had sent soldiers overseas during the war, such as Canada, the United States, Australia, and New Zealand.[34] Within Canada, the baby boom was not always experienced in the same ways. In Quebec, for instance, where family size had been dropping progressively since the late nineteenth century, the baby boom represented a temporary moment during which the decrease in family size stalled, before plunging in the 1960s and 1970s. At each stage of the life cycle, the baby-boom generation took Canadian society by storm, creating the need for new infrastructure first as babies, then as children attending elementary schools, then as teenagers and young adults frequenting high schools, then universities.[35] In both English Canada and Quebec, as in the United States, the babies born in the 1940s and 1950s would fuel the youth movements and social movements of the later 1960s and the 1970s.[36]

The family privileged during much of the postwar period, and certainly during the later 1940s and the 1950s, was one predicated on a breadwinning husband and a dependent wife and children. In the immediate postwar period, the very idea of full employment was contingent upon married women leaving the paid labour market at the end of the war. Many did so. By 1946, across Canada, the proportion of married women working for pay was very low.[37] Some married women conceivably left the labour market out of choice, in order to devote all of their time to domestic labour and their family, while some newly married women went straight from their parents' home to the homes that they established with their husbands. Prevailing discourses of femininity surely played some role in determining or constraining these women's choices. Female teachers in postwar secondary schools, for instance, were expected to promote "taken-for-granted" gendered expectations that included the nuclear family model and heteronormativity. They were also expected to adhere to these expectations themselves and adopt a conventional feminine appearance.[38] Other married women were forcibly encouraged to leave the labour market by federal government measures: public day nurseries that closed their doors; a civil service that fired married women so as to give their jobs to men; a tax structure modified so as to disadvantage men whose wives worked for pay.[39] As one scholar bluntly summarizes, "Postwar planning was designed explicitly to secure the withdrawal of women war workers from the formal economy."[40]

The postwar family wage structure thus rested upon an employed husband and father, a dependent wife, and dependent children, regularly attending school rather than earning wages. In many ways, this particular historical moment was the swan song of the family wage: one of the few—and last— moments in Canadian history when many adult men earned enough to support their families single-handedly. It was this period when both political and popular culture insisted upon the importance of the sole male breadwinner and the financial dependence of wives and children that has become known as the period of the "feminine mystique," after the title of American journalist Betty Friedan's famous work of investigative reporting.[41] Friedan's 1963 book described the malaise of thousands of white, middle-class, college-educated American women living in the suburbs who were clearly socially and economically privileged, but who were nonetheless dissatisfied with the daily routine of dropping children off at school, chatting with neighbours, and participating in Scouts and Home-and-School meetings. It was the gap between the education obtained by these middle-class women and their absence (or withdrawal) from the paid labour market that was seen by many women as problematic. The book had a devastating—and galvanizing—effect on many readers, well beyond the borders of the United States, and has often been cited as one of the formative moments in the creation of "second-wave" feminism.[42]

Even in the United States, however, this portrait of well-educated, but vaguely dissatisfied, married women, stranded in their recently built suburbs with babies and toddlers while their husbands were at work in the city and their older children at school, did not describe the reality of all postwar families.[43] In postwar Canadian cities and suburbs, many married women questioned—sometimes openly—the social norms that saw them confined to the home, the family, and the bedroom suburb. Furthermore, some married women developed forms of community activism within suburbs, lobbying for such essential services as "sewers, libraries, and garbage disposal."[44] Moreover, some married women mobilized on the international front during the 1950s, 1960s, and 1970s in order to help children orphaned, impoverished, or displaced by Cold War politics and military interventions. Many of these activist Canadian mothers, who joined associations such as the Voice of Women or the Women's International League for Peace and Freedom, justified their political activity in maternalist terms, arguing that it was precisely their experience as mothers in Canada that allowed them to understand the needs of children abroad.[45]

Young postwar families, particularly young mothers, were besieged by parenting advice, especially advice considered scientific and that had as its source doctors, nurses, social workers, and psychologists. Dr. Benjamin Spock's famous manual, *Dr. Spock's Baby and Child Care*, was first published in the United States in 1946 and was widely distributed in Canada over the course of the postwar decades. It constituted a departure, to some degree, from interwar manuals insisting upon strict routines, rigid diets, and carefully limited parental affection, and allowed for greater permissiveness on the part of parents. Yet childcare experts retained an important place in postwar society. By 1950, the medicalization of pregnancy and birth in Canada was fully realized.[46] One of the most obvious manifestations of this medicalization was the rising number of hospital births; by the early 1950s, 80 per cent of Canadian babies were born in the hospital.[47] In Quebec, the post-Second World War decades witnessed the increasing control of physicians and hospitals over the birthing process. Promising modern, "no-risk" deliveries, hospital births were accompanied by the generalized use of anaesthesia and by invasive techniques such as Caesarean sections.[48] As toddlers and children, many of these postwar babies would attend regular check-ups with paediatricians. These babies and children were healthier than previous generations of children—not simply because they were under the watchful eyes of family doctors and paediatricians, but also because of the higher wages earned by their fathers and, sometimes, mothers, and thus, improved living conditions, which meant that most children were better nourished than previous generations of young Canadians. As teenagers, these children were also subjected – to some degree—to the norms established by adolescent psychologists. Much of the work of postwar adolescent psychologists was devoted to ensuring that teenagers—a word newly popular in the postwar decades—would develop sexualities considered "normal" and "healthy," that is, heterosexual, and ultimately contained within the channels of legal marriage.[49]

Indeed, the ambient political conservatism and conformity encouraged an ethos of what American poet Adrienne Rich termed, in 1980, "compulsory heterosexuality."[50] Sex was supposed to take place only within the confines of marriage—and this was seen to be especially important for women. As various North American scholars have shown, Cold War politics were often accompanied by a virulent homophobia and fears of "deviant" or "abnormal" sexualities, seen to pose a threat to national security.[51] In Canada, homosexuality, like contraception and abortion, remained criminalized until 1969. State surveillance of homosexuality was extensive during the immediate postwar decades; in the 1960s alone, the RCMP investigated over 9,000 gay men across the country.[52]

Postwar Immigration and Canadian Cities

Wartime migration from the countryside to the city fuelled urbanization across Canada during the 1940s. Often, this was migration undertaken by men and unmarried women in search of paid work in war industries. In families where husbands and fathers had enrolled in the armed forces or been

FIGURE 6.1 British war brides and their children arrive in Halifax, Nova Scotia on 26 March 1946. Nova Scotia Archives accession no. 1992-304 no. 25/neg. no.: N-6965.

conscripted, married women and their children sometimes chose to live with extended family or in-laws as a way of securing emotional support and sharing childcare and other domestic responsibilities. Sometimes this decision was a response to the lack of housing options in centres of war production such as Halifax, Montreal, or Toronto; this "doubling-up" of families also contributed to the phenomenon of overcrowded housing common to these centres.

In the postwar period, urbanization was also fuelled by massive waves of immigration, principally from the United Kingdom and Europe. War brides—women who had married Canadian servicemen overseas—and their children were among the first postwar immigrants, arriving during and immediately after the war. These approximately 48,000 women came principally from the United Kingdom (England, Scotland, Wales), but also, to a lesser extent, from the Netherlands. Many of these women, used to the urban amenities of Great Britain, found life in rural or small-town Canada difficult. Conflicts with in-laws were frequent, particularly when the war brides did not share the same language or religion as their new husbands' family.

Evidence exists that some war brides, unable to adjust to their new life in Canada, made the decision to cut their losses and return to the United Kingdom.[53]

People rendered stateless by the Second World War, known as Displaced Persons or "DPs," also came to Canada in the wake of the war, some 165,000 of them by 1953.[54] Roughly ten per cent of these postwar refugees from Europe were Jews, both adolescents and adults, who had survived the Holocaust.[55] The War Orphans Project, initiated and carried out by the Canadian Jewish Congress (CJC) between 1947 and 1952, was originally intended to bring over to Canada orphaned Jewish children. Owing to a number of factors—the devastatingly low survival rates of children placed in the Nazi camps, competition from similar projects undertaken by the United States, Australia, and South Africa, and the attraction, for many young European Jews, of a new home in Palestine—the CJC had a more difficult time than expected recruiting orphans. Those 1,115 orphans who did respond to the CJC's invitation to apply for residence in Canada were older than anticipated (aged 15 to 18, rather than young children), were mostly boys (in a context where adoptive parents in Canada had long sought girls), and came from eastern and central Europe (Hungary, Romania, Poland) rather than, as expected, from Germany, France, or Belgium. Furthermore, Canadian families responded in very small numbers to the CJC's appeal for adoptive homes, to the extent that the plan to place these "children" with adoptive families was forced to give way to a Plan B, that of paying foster families to take in Jewish orphans temporarily. Many of the orphans who made their way to Canadian cities such as Montreal, Toronto, or Winnipeg in the late 1940s or early 1950s chose to move on again after a short stint in Canada, returning to Europe, or taking a chance on the United States or, after 1948, Israel.[56] Interviews with eighteen "child survivors," that is, Jewish refugees who arrived after the war as teenagers or young adults and who settled in Montreal, found that these young Jewish immigrants were resolutely focused upon the future. One male survivor noted that their youth was an asset: "the fact that we did not have the baggage of having had wives and children who were lost during the war. We started over again, we were young." The "first obligation" of these Jewish immigrants was "recreating family," and thus marrying and having children. "Most survivors married within two to three years of coming to Montreal and had children shortly thereafter, or when they could afford to do so." More often than not, these immigrants, considered by more established Jewish Montrealers and by non-Jews to be "'too broken' to be suitable candidates for marriage," married other Holocaust survivors.[57]

Most European immigration to Canada in the 1950s and 1960s was familial migration. Occasionally one member of the family, usually the husband and father, came first in order to establish himself in a job and find housing; his wife and children followed some months or, occasionally, years later.[58] Often, however, entire families arrived together. These postwar immigrants came from the United Kingdom (English, Scotland, Wales) in large numbers in the 1950s; they also came from Ireland, Italy, Portugal, Greece, Hungary, and Poland. Canadian immigration policy in the 1950s was "selectively more open" than before the Second World War.[59] The arrival of immigrants from southern and central Europe, in particular, had a significant impact on the ethnic, linguistic, and religious make-up of Canada's population, particularly within its larger cities and especially in central Canada. Roughly half of the immigrants who arrived in Canada between 1946 and 1962 settled in Ontario.[60] Canadian cities that had traditionally had heavy Protestant majorities, such as Vancouver or Toronto, became home to growing numbers of Catholic families. The Italian immigrants who settled in Vancouver, Toronto, and Montreal created "Little Italies" that were both residential neighbourhoods and sites of small businesses (groceries, butcher shops, bakeries, cafés, travel agencies, credit unions) catering to the daily needs of these immigrant communities. Many of these small businesses were family businesses, relying on the labour of all members of the household, including teenage children.[61]

FIGURE 6.2 Two Portuguese-Canadian sisters in Kensington Market, Toronto, 1957. York University Libraries, Clara Thomas Archives & Special Collections online exhibits.

In 1962, new Immigration Regulations abolished the explicitly racist dimensions of earlier Canadian Immigration Acts. Five years later, in 1967, the federal government adopted a new "points system" that established criteria other than nationality or race (such as skills, training, or education) for the selection of immigrants to Canada.[62] These new federal regulations, designed in large part to serve the needs of the labour market, help to explain why, in the 1960s and 1970s, the sources of immigration to Canada became more diverse, as families arrived from the West Indies, Latin America, and China. In 1962, 78 per cent of all immigrants to Canada came from Europe; by 1976, this number had fallen to 38 per cent.[63] Some immigrant households were multigenerational, a phenomenon that owed something to postwar family reunification policies. Within such households, power dynamics were influenced by gender, earning capacity, and age. A Chinese-Canadian fruit pedlar and storekeeper living with his children and grandchildren in Vancouver was described by his grandchild in 1965 as "the boss of our family [who] always gets his own way."[64]

Some postwar immigrants, both men and women, were educated and highly skilled and found work in professional or white-collar fields such as teaching, nursing, and medicine.[65] Among these middle-class workers were a significant number of highly trained Black nurses who arrived in Canada from the Caribbean in the 1950s, 1960s, and 1970s.[66] Other immigrants, however, particularly those who came from rural areas of southern Europe, became part of Canada's industrial workforce, in full swing during the postwar decades. The manufacturing sector in cities such as Hamilton, Toronto, and Montreal attracted both men and women, married and single, recently arrived in Canada.[67] Immigrant men were also employed in construction work, building the rapidly expanding cities and suburbs of the postwar era. In Toronto, "By 1961, more than 15,000 Italians, or fully one-third of Toronto's working Italian men, were employed in construction, and they represented one-third of the city's total construction workforce." These men were involved in two notable strikes in the early 1960s, in which they used "the image of the honourable family man" to justify their demands for better pay, safer working conditions, and the protection offered by unions.[68] Many married immigrant women worked in personal service jobs, as babysitters or cleaning ladies. Scholar Charmaine Crawford recalls the story of her own mother, who emigrated from Trinidad to Canada in the early 1970s:

> Like many other immigrants, my parents migrated to Canada to provide a better life for me. I don't remember my parents leaving me behind in Trinidad at the age of three but I do remember being reunited with them at the age of five. It was 1974. It was cold. I remember getting a coat and a pair of rubber boots to wear and keep me warm. Throughout the years I had to adapt to my new life and environment. I remember accompanying my mother to her little jobs where she cleaned homes that seemed like mansions compared to our cramped one-bedroom apartment. My mother didn't work as a domestic for too long. She hated the hours, the low pay, and not being able to speak her mind when she was unfairly treated.[69]

Suburbanization

Although cities did expand in the postwar years, between "1951 and 1961 the population in metropolitan areas around city cores grew far more than that in city centres."[70] Life in postwar Canada has often been associated with the suburbs and, more specifically, with the cookie-cutter bungalows and the crescents and cul-de-sacs favoured by postwar suburban planners. To some extent, this association reflects the prevalence of American media such as movies, television, publicity reels, and magazines that continually reproduced these images during and after the period in question. It is nevertheless true that Canada also continued to "suburbanize" during these years. There were already numerous Canadian suburbs before the Second World War, which were economically and architecturally diverse, frequently evolved beyond the reach of municipal regulation, and often included large numbers of worker-built homes.[71] By contrast, the new suburbs of the 1950s and 1960s were more likely to be the project of developers and were more likely to include corporate tract housing; many of these carefully planned postwar suburbs catered explicitly to middle-class buyers.[72] Nonetheless, neither postwar Canadian suburbs nor their residents were homogeneous.[73]

Some Canadian suburbs were leafy, wealthy enclaves such as Toronto's Forest Hill, immortalized as "Crestwood Heights" by sociologist John R. Seeley and his collaborators in 1956. This upper middle-class inner suburb, incorporated in the 1920s, was home to both Protestant and Jewish families. Seeley and his fellow researchers were particularly interested in questions of family structure, children, schooling, and mental health. Their detailed study of the daily lives of Forest Hill residents reveals the significant gap between the lived experiences of the husbands who went to work in "Big City" (downtown Toronto) most days of the week and their highly-educated wives who spent their days at home or in the shops and institutions of their suburban community. They found that "the institutions of Crestwood Heights tend ... to converge upon the family, existing as they do to regulate the life of a purely residential community devoted to child-rearing."[74]

Many of the new postwar suburbs, however, especially those on the furthest outskirts of big cities, were settled by young couples of more modest means, from working-class households or farm families, seeking affordable homes and green space where their young children could play.[75] In his memoirs, Pierre Vallières, a key intellectual leader of the *Front de liberation du Québec*, recalls his family's move from the flat that they rented in a working-class neighbourhood on the east side of Montreal to the south-shore suburb of Longueuil-Annexe (later Ville Jacques-Cartier) immediately after the war. He described the small house that his parents had purchased as follows:

> The shack was made of wood covered with *"papier brique,"* a kind of tarpaper designed to look like brick. In the center front was a little white porch. Inside, only three rooms: in the middle a kitchen, which also served as dining room, living room, bathroom, etc.; to the left, a large bedroom which my parents shared with Raymond (who was not yet walking); lastly, to the right, a tiny room with a double-decker bed and a chest of drawers: this was the room of the "two oldest," André and me. The rooms were separated by walls of *"donnacona,"* a kind of hard, thick cardboard which could be bought quite cheaply from any dealer in building materials. . . . Many of the shacks that went up in Ville Jacques-Cartier in the years following our arrival were built entirely out of two-by-fours and broad panels of this economical cardboard, which was then covered with tarpaper. It was not exactly warm in winter, but it didn't cost much, and with this miraculous material you could build a little house in two days![76]

This extract from Vallières' memoirs captures the importance both material and symbolic, for young parents dealing with the high rents, housing shortages, and aging housing stock of Canadian cities in wartime, of the purchase of a home and the accession to property ownership. Postwar developers catered to—and cultivated—Montreal families' desire to leave their overcrowded city flats for the suburbs through advertisements marketing the single-family home—notably the bungalow—in the many suburbs springing up around the Quebec metropolis in the 1950s and 1960s. Proximity to schools, churches, and shopping centres was seen as a selling point for these suburban homes. Moreover, many of the single-family homes marketed to Montreal families were relatively modest in size and price, particularly in the 1950s.[77] Small though they might have been, these new constructions offered space and modern conveniences unavailable in the flats and row housing of older city centres such as Halifax, Montreal, or Toronto.

Although advertisements and promotional literature often presented new suburban developments as springing up, fully formed, out of empty lots or farmers' fields, some suburban developments were achieved only by expelling the former residents of these territories. The Métis "fringe community" known as Rooster Town, for example, was a vibrant urban settlement on the outskirts of Winnipeg, in existence for the first sixty years of the twentieth century. Residents of Rooster Town worked mostly in labouring occupations in and around the settlement. In the late 1950s, Winnipeg newspapers published a series of sensationalist articles insisting upon the poverty of the community and depicting its residents as living in filth and squalor. By the end of the 1950s, the municipal government had intervened in order to move families out of Rooster Town, in the process making way for suburban development and projects that included a shopping centre and a high school. Many of these Métis residents, who had already been dispossessed of their lands in Manitoba and who were being forcibly encouraged to leave the urban community in which they had lived for two or three generations, moved a considerable distance, into the North End of Winnipeg.[78]

Postwar suburbanization meant homes in the suburbs ("bedroom suburbs," as they were called at the time), but it also meant daily lives and habits built around the automobile and increasing urban sprawl. Life in the suburbs was made possible by growing rates of automobile ownership and by abundant and inexpensive gasoline.[79] Increasingly important in the 1950s, 1960s, and 1970s were highways, shopping malls, parking lots, and drive-in services ranging from doughnut shops to dry cleaners. New drive-in restaurants such as McDonald's became popular among young parents seeking quick and affordable meals for their children, but also among teenagers with disposable income.[80] Automobiles also created opportunities for family leisure activities beyond the suburbs. In Ontario, rising rates of automobile ownership in the postwar decades allowed for the democratization of cottage ownership, as middle-class and even some working-class families were able to access and purchase inexpensive land in "cottage country," around Muskoka, Georgian Bay, and the Kawarthas.[81] Increased access to automobiles also allowed for family road trips within Canada or to the neighbouring United States during summer holidays.[82]

Over the course of the 1960s and especially the 1970s, Canadian suburbs became more ethnically diverse. The Tasher, a community of Hasidic Jews, decided, for example, to settle in Sainte-Thérèse-Ouest, some twenty-five kilometres north of Montreal, in the 1960s. A rural municipality whose inhabitants were largely francophone and Catholic, Sainte-Thérèse-Ouest (later Boisbriand) was in the midst of becoming an industrial suburb, in part thanks to the construction of the Laurentian Autoroute that linked the municipality to Montreal and the decision made by General Motors to open a plant employing a thousand workers next to the highway. The willingness of local authorities to bend municipal zoning regulations—and the lack of significant resistance to these changes on the part of local residents—allowed for the establishment of an orthodox Jewish community in the suburb; this community included single-family homes, a synagogue, and a *yeshiva*.[83]

Many of the immigrant families who had settled in Canada's large cities in the 1950s and 1960s worked several jobs and saved their wages so as to be able to move out of the older city neighbourhoods, so that their children might benefit from the back yards, community centres, and new public schools to be found in newer suburban areas. By the 1970s and 1980s, Canada's suburbs had become especially economically and ethnically diverse in large metropolitan areas such as those surrounding Toronto, Montreal, and Vancouver, where, by the very end of the period, families newly arrived in Canada were choosing to settle directly in suburbs rather than first trying out life in the older city core.[84]

Married Women in the Labour Market

By the time that Betty Friedan's *The Feminine Mystique* was published in 1963, rates of married women's paid employment in Canada had been rising again for almost a decade, since the mid-1950s. "Between 1951 and 1961," historian Craig Heron notes, "the proportion of married women in Ontario working for pay rose from one in ten to one in five. By the mid-1960s, half the province's female workforce was married."[85] In 1941, only 12.7 per cent of Canadian women in paid employment were married; by 1961, 49.8 per cent of all Canadian women in paid employment were married.[86] Many of the married women integrating or reintegrating the paid labour force in the 1950s were women over the age of thirty-five, returning to the formal labour force once their children were at school.[87] Almost all of the Peterborough, Ontario, women interviewed by historian Joan Sangster worked out of economic necessity, because their husband's wages were inadequate or inexistent. Gradually, married women's paid employment became more socially acceptable, but the "pregnancy bar" remained in place through the 1950s and early 1960s; many pregnant women were fired from their jobs or strongly encouraged to leave of their own accord. Furthermore, married women's work was acceptable as long as they were seen to be adequately tending to the needs of their families. Married women's part-time or seasonal work was often more easily tolerated by social commentators than full-time work; married women who worked full-time for wages nonetheless remained responsible for almost the entirety of domestic labour, including cooking and cleaning, leading to the phenomenon that has been called the "double day" or the "second shift."[88]

In many cases, these employed women had a significant level of formal instruction, a high school diploma and often more. With the expansion of the twentieth-century state and the corporate economy, there existed abundant new white-collar work opportunities—dubbed "pink-collar" jobs—for women in secretarial pools, banks, offices, and public service. This new female workforce, composed of both single and married women, provided members for many public-sector unions from the 1960s onward, as teachers, civil servants, and nurses across the country organized. Unionized public-sector jobs provided job security, reasonable wages and benefits and, increasingly, the right to strike. These advantages were often hard-won, however. When nurses at Montreal's Sainte-Justine Hospital for children struck illegally in 1963 in order to protest their extremely difficult working conditions, it served as a very public reminder of the heavily female nature of the nursing workforce. Convincing employers and the public of the economic value of work such as nursing, performed by women—and in Quebec and French Canada, performed for centuries by nuns working without pay—was extremely difficult. Nurses were expected to be self-sacrificing and to devote themselves to their charges—particularly when their charges were children, as in the Sainte-Justine Hospital strike—and striking for better pay and working conditions was often presented in the press as selfish. As New Brunswick Premier Louis Robichaud reminded nursing leaders in that province in 1964, nurses ought to "be 'dedicated' and work for less."[89]

Since Canada's industrial sector had emerged revitalized from the Second World War, a strong manufacturing sector provided "blue-collar"—often unionized—work for women, both immigrant and Canadian-born, through the 1970s. In the small industrial city of Peterborough, Ontario, women found work in factories owned by Quaker Oats and Westclox, and in the Bonnerworth woollens mill.[90] In larger cities such as Toronto and Montreal, some immigrant women with little formal education or still in the process of learning English or French worked in manufacturing jobs or else in low-paid jobs in the expanding postwar service sector, as cleaning ladies, nurses' aides, or in hotel laundries. Portuguese-Canadian women worked as "cleaning ladies" in private homes, but also in Toronto's offices and commercial buildings, in the 1970s and 1980s. While postwar immigrant women have often been portrayed as docile, the 1984 strike by 250 Portuguese cleaning women employed at a downtown Toronto office tower was evidence that immigrant women could be important actors in the postwar labour movement.[91] Yet the salaries earned by women workers, both immigrant and Canadian-born, remained lower than those of men throughout the postwar period, in part because the sectors in which women were hired paid less than those that hired men.

Indigenous, immigrant, or racialized married women worked outside the home to a greater extent than did white, Canadian-born women in the immediate postwar decades. Black, Canadian-born nurses, for instance, largely continued working for pay after the birth of their children, although through the 1960s very few Black women were admitted to Canadian nursing schools.[92] In the 1960s, the Medical Services Branch (MSB) of the Department of National Health and Welfare often preferred to hire married Indigenous women in their thirties and forties—rather than younger, single, Indigenous women—as Community Health Representatives (CHRs). For the MSB, hiring older married women was a way of ensuring that candidates were emotionally mature and that their children were old enough to be at school. The MSB even appears to have been willing to provide some help with childcare so that married women might take on this work. For example, "When she was asked to pursue CHR training in Norway House [Manitoba] in 1961–2, Dorothy Stranger recalls, 'They said, 'we'll find a babysitter' and my mother would babysit too sometimes, you know, like take charge? And I went'."[93] This receptivity to the hiring of married women as CHRs contrasted with the MSB's policy regarding the hiring of nurses, "who were nearly all young, unmarried, and without dependants, as suited the ideals of femininity and sexuality in the field of nursing."[94]

Despite the significantly increased numbers of married women working for wages in the immediate postwar decades, very little progress was made in systematically providing decent childcare in the form of public daycares. After the closing of the federal-provincial wartime day nurseries in Ontario and Quebec in 1945, working mothers in those provinces, like their counterparts in other provinces, made do by cobbling together the volunteer efforts of extended family such as grandparents and aunts or their own elder daughters, plus the paid work of female neighbours. The industrial town of Peterborough, Ontario, opened its first daycare in 1967, but many married women were reluctant to leave their children there, as, to them, public daycare smacked of poverty and welfare measures.[95] In British Columbia, the money provided by the shared-cost (federal-provincial) Canada Assistance Plan from 1966 on allowed for the creation of subsidized places in licensed daycares for low-income mothers. While this new measure helped some mothers and children, this remained a "welfarist" policy that did nothing to change the popular perception that public daycare was for the children of poor parents. Moreover, despite the infusion of federal money, the number of subsidized daycare spots in B.C. remained woefully inadequate. According to historian Lisa Pasolli,

> In January 1967, only nine day care centres were licensed and approved for subsidy payments: four in Vancouver, two in North Vancouver, and one each in Richmond, Surrey, and Terrace, for a total of only 331 subsidy-eligible child care spaces in the province. Considering that the Community Chest had identified 6,000 children in Vancouver alone who were in desperate need of day care, the province's initial efforts hardly made a dent, even with the promise to fast-track the approval of centres in Prince Rupert, Victoria, and Alert Bay.[96]

It would take the feminist activism of the 1970s for public daycare to be seen as both a right for employed mothers and as something that could benefit all children, regardless of the socioeconomic status of their parents.[97]

The Welfare State

Among the welfare state measures adopted in the postwar decades, the most important for families, in terms of impact both symbolic and real, were surely public hospital insurance and health insurance. These crucial measures meant that access to hospital care and to care by a physician was no longer dependent upon income or savings, putting decent health-care within the reach of most Canadians. Saskatchewan was the pioneering province, adopting universal, single-payer hospital insurance in 1947 under social democratic premier Tommy Douglas, formerly a Baptist minister. Other provinces followed suit—although not all on the universal, single-payer model—and in 1957 the federal government adopted Canada-wide, federal-provincial shared-cost hospital insurance based on the Saskatchewan model. A decade later, in 1966, the federal government adopted the Medical Care Act. This legislation provided for the creation of a system of national health insurance, popularly known as "Medicare" and covering a wide variety of medical services, inspired by the universal health-insurance model developed by Saskatchewan's CCF government in 1962.[98]

More generous old age pensions were also adopted in these decades. These new measures attempted to improve upon the shared-cost (federal-provincial) pensions adopted in the interwar years by providing more substantial payments, lowering the age of eligibility for means-tested pensions, and eliminating the means test altogether for persons over the age of seventy. This last reform meant that all people over the age of seventy would receive an old age pension, regardless of their financial situation. In 1951, the federal government adopted a universal measure known as Old Age Security, providing all Canadians over the age of 70, including Indigenous peoples, with a guaranteed monthly amount. In 1965, a contributory pension was superimposed upon Old Age Security. Known as the Canada Pension Plan (and in Quebec, the Quebec Pension Plan or *Régime des rentes du Québec*), this portable, public, contributory plan took into account the contributions made by Canadians over the course of their working lives.[99] Taken together, these measures meant that the elderly were no longer solely reliant upon the goodwill of their children or other family members or, failing family support, upon private charitable institutions, for their sustenance and survival. The monthly amount provided by the state was a measure of social citizenship that gave the retired and the elderly some degree of dignity and autonomy. For elderly women who had spent most of their adult life working at home, these were rare sources of income in their own name. Public pensions also served to demarcate more clearly the transition from "work" to "retirement" and helped to create a category of the elderly known as "pensioners."[100] By the 1960s, most Quebecers and Canadians had begun to associate "old age" (defined variously as 65 or 70) with the withdrawal from the labour market and the right to a pension.[101]

Most of the universal social welfare measures adopted between the 1940s and the 1960s were federal initiatives. The provinces, however, retained the responsibility for means-tested social assistance programmes, known colloquially as "welfare."[102] The 1966 Canada Assistance Plan, a national assistance programme adopted by the federal government, gave the provinces additional money with which to carry out provincial welfare initiatives and there is evidence that this infusion of money did make a difference to the living standards of many families. However, "even within Ontario, the nation's richest province, maximum welfare benefits for individuals and families of all sizes never came close to reaching existing federal government or social planning council definitions of a poverty line." In 1970, Ontario families eligible for welfare received payments equivalent only to 60 per cent "of their basic budgetary needs as measured by the most reliable existing guides to family spending."[103]

Despite—or perhaps because of—federal government initiatives, the 1960s witnessed a number of successful attempts by some provinces to remind the federal government that the British North America Act had made social welfare a provincial jurisdiction. The separate Quebec Pension Plan (*Régime des rentes du Québec*) adopted in 1965 and the universal provincial family allowances adopted by Quebec in 1967 were two examples of this desire for provincial autonomy. Although Quebec's Quiet Revolution is the classic example of greater state intervention combined with nationalism in these years, it was echoed, to a certain extent, in the other provinces.[104]

The social welfare measures adopted by the Canadian state in the three decades following the Second World War—in some ways the most generous public welfare measures in Canada's history—represent the benevolent dimensions of this twentieth-century welfare state. However, these new measures were not always applied evenly to all citizens. Moreover, even well-intentioned measures, conceived in the spirit of liberal humanitarianism, could have coercive and unfortunate consequences. Nowhere was this more evident than in the case of Indigenous families. During the same years in which the federal government announced universal health and hospital insurance, for example, it established what amounted to a parallel health system for Indigenous people. Across the country, Indigenous people suffered disproportionately from communicable diseases such as tuberculosis, a situation no doubt exacerbated by the malnutrition, overcrowded housing, and contaminated water characteristic of many of the communities in which they lived.[105] A network of "Indian Hospitals" designed by the Canadian Tuberculosis Association and funded by the federal government was established in the provinces west of the Ottawa River in the mid-twentieth century. Although tuberculosis was presented as the *raison d'être* for these hospitals, they admitted Indigenous patients suffering from various illnesses, for all intents and purposes creating a segregated hospital system whereby the new modern hospitals of the postwar era were reserved for white patients. Conditions in the Indian Hospitals were poor; most of these aging buildings had had previous lives as schools, military hospitals, or quarantine stations before being converted into Indian Hospitals. Many of the patients arrived directly from residential schools, underlining the similarly devastating conditions (overcrowding, inadequate heating, insufficient food) in these other federal institutions for Indigenous peoples. Patients, particularly those suffering from tuberculosis, could spend years in these hospitals. Historian Maureen Lux provides the example of Doreen Callihoo, eight years old in 1946, who

> would spend eleven of the next twelve years in the Charles Camsell Indian Hospital [in Edmonton]. She recalled that as a child she received streptomycin injections and twice-weekly painful pneumothorax treatments (air injected into the chest to collapse the lung). As an adolescent, she had two separate thoracoplasties (removal of several ribs at a time to collapse the lung), disfiguring procedures performed

under local anaesthetic. She left the hospital after a year of antimicrobial medications, but returned the following year to undergo a pneumonectomy (the surgical removal of her lung) because of bronchiectasis, a chronic lung infection.[106]

In the North (the Yukon, the Northwest Territories, and what are now Nunavut and Nunavik), tuberculosis was endemic in Inuit communities in the 1940s and 1950s. Federal government officials working for the Indian Health Service, which in 1945 was transferred from the Department of Indian Affairs to the brand-new Department of National Health and Welfare, chose to remove Inuit suffering from TB from their communities and transport them to sanatoria in southern Canadian cities such as Edmonton, Brandon, Hamilton, Toronto, or Montreal. By 1956, "approximately one out of every seven Inuit was in a sanatorium in the south."[107] Such forced removal for public health reasons occasioned huge disruptions of family life, separating family members for months and even years. Very often, family members were not kept informed of patients' medical progress—or even of their death. Numerous stories have been told by Inuit and by government officials and members of the Protestant and Catholic clergy of children sent to southern cities for tuberculosis treatment who were returned to the North once cured, but who had trouble locating their family and difficulty readjusting to life in an Inuit community after years of living in a southern hospital and speaking English or French rather than Inuktitut.[108]

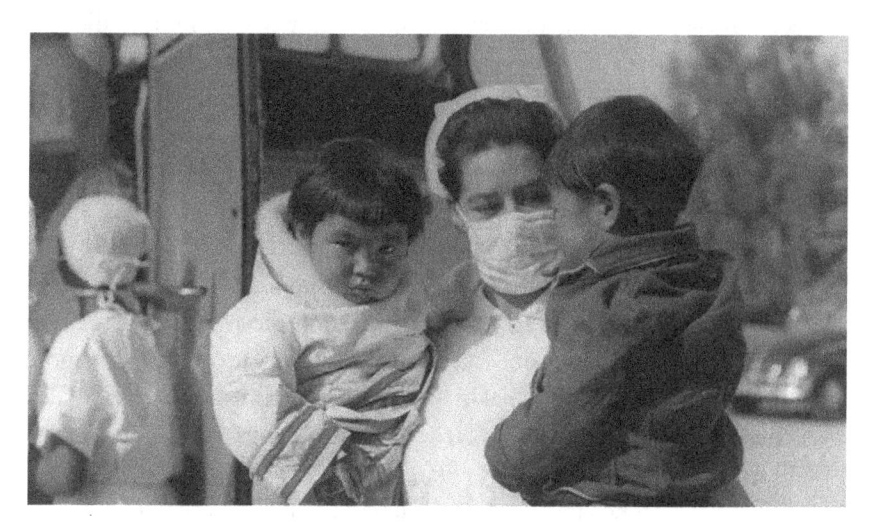

FIGURE 6.3 Inuit tuberculosis patients arriving at the Mountain Sanatorium in Hamilton, Ontario. CBC. Gerda Selway.

The fact that Canada was busy colonizing the North at the same time that it was implementing nation-wide social welfare measures had numerous consequences for the Inuit. The removal and relocation of Inuit families and communities was common, not just in the case of TB patients. In the 1950s, for instance, the federal government insisted upon the relocation of some Inuit family groups to Ellesmere Island, for reasons that were geopolitical and purely strategic, so as "to establish a Canadian presence in the High Arctic" in the context of the Cold War.[109] Throughout the postwar decades, Inuit families were encouraged to relocate in order to hunt and trap the Arctic fox, for schooling opportunities for their children, and for employment opportunities for adults on Canadian and American air bases.[110]

Furthermore, beginning in the 1940s, the federal government, in an attempt to keep track of the beneficiaries of new welfare-state measures, assigned identification discs bearing individual numbers to the Inuit. In 1945, the existence—and importance—of these identification discs was in fact written into Part 7 of the Family Allowance Regulations, which defined "Eskimos" and "Nomads."[111] As an additional way of identifying Inuit recipients of state welfare, the federal government and the Northwest Territories Government strongly encouraged the adoption of family names, or surnames, a practice that contravened the Inuit's own ideas of family. In 1970, the Northwest Territories Government in fact "launched Project Surname with the avowed intention of persuading all Eskimo adults to adopt a surname or family name."[112] The administration of family allowances and new old age pensions in the North was not always simple and payment in kind did not always meet the needs of beneficiaries. Jimmy Koodlooalook of Inukjuak, interviewed by a local schoolteacher and welfare administrator, Marjorie Hinds, about his wife's family allowance payment in August 1953, recounted the following:

QUESTION: What did you get from Family Allowances?
ANSWER: Very little, the least I have ever had from F.A. Some cottonade to make pants for the three children, 2 yards of duffle and 5 lbs. of milk to last all winter. I also got one sweater, but I put it back so as to get more milk. I didn't even get flannelette to make shirts for the children. I also had 2 bags of oats with 6 lbs. in each bag, that was for three children to last all winter.
QUESTION: How much money was to your credit on F.A. at this time?
ANSWER: I don't know. But I've never got so little when I've asked for Family Allowances.

QUESTION: Did you get cod liver oil and vitamin pills for the children from the nurse before you left last fall?

ANSWER: No, we got no cod liver oil at all and no vitamin pills. She wouldn't hear of it. We wanted medicine but the first time we went to ask she wouldn't give us any, so we went again and that time we got some cough medicine and aspirin. About one-third of a Winchester bottle of cough medicine, (i.e. approximately 24 ounces) and quite a lot of aspirin. We know how to use the medicine if there is a label on the bottle with it written in syllabic. We should like to take medicine back with us this time.[113]

One final example of state intervention in Indigenous family life in the decades following the end of the war is the administration of what has come to be known as the "Sixties Scoop"—that is, the adoption of Indigenous children by non-Indigenous parents in the 1960s and 1970s. Some of these adoptions had devastating consequences for Indigenous children, their birth parents, and even their adoptive parents. Métis educator Chelsea Vowel argues, "The Sixties Scoop picked up where residential schools left off, removing children from their homes, and producing cultural amputees."[114] The "kidnap" narrative evoked by the word "scoop" does not capture all of the complexity of these transracial adoptions, however, which need to be situated in the broader context of poverty, racism, and colonialism. In some cases, for instance, Indigenous mothers actively sought to have their children adopted so as to spare them a life of material deprivation or insecurity.[115] Moreover, an exclusive focus on the "scoop" of the 1960s and 1970s neglects the fact that Indigenous children continued to be significantly overrepresented among children taken into state care in the later twentieth and early twenty-first centuries.

Schooling and Youth Culture

Historians of North America agree that youth cultures became more cohesive and more easily identifiable in the wake of the Second World War. These youth cultures were predicated upon the sense that "youth"—children, adolescents, and young adults—had shared interests and motivations strong enough to form the basis of an identity separate and different from that of adults.[116] In Canada, this sense of a shared identity was fostered by the fact that children and adolescents were spending a longer period of their life in school. As more mothers sought paid work outside the home, teenage children, expected to be financially dependent upon their parents, stayed in school. Rates of high school attendance and completion varied according to region and social class, but statistics show that in Ontario, at least, "50 percent [of adolescents] were reaching Grade 12 on time."[117] In secondary schools across Canada—often co-educational institutions—teenagers learned to see themselves as belonging to a collectivity determined by age and, often, learned to see their interests as opposed to those of adults in positions of authority: parents, but also teachers, guidance counsellors, and high-school principals. University attendance remained the purview of a tiny minority in the 1950s and a slightly more important minority in the 1960s and 1970s. "Nearly 90 percent of youth moved directly into the paid labour market instead of post-secondary institutions after high school."[118] Access to university, even more than high-school completion rates, varied according to social class, parental income and savings, region, and mother tongue. The common youth culture created by prolonged high school attendance divided once high school ended.[119] While the children of middle-class parents continued on to university, working-class teenagers were expected to find jobs as soon as they left school.

In the postwar decades, mainstream youth cultures continued to be shaped by participation in clubs and associations aimed at kids and teenagers, such as the Boy Scouts, the Girl Guides, or, in Quebec, the Jeannettes. These clubs for children were as present in the new postwar suburbs as they had been in interwar cities.[120] Youth cultures were also influenced by the postwar consumer society. Young people became a market to be courted by record producers, magazine publishers, movie producers, and the owners of sites and vehicles of commercialized leisure such as radio stations, cinemas, and soda shops. Older children and teenagers used their allowances, pocket money, and wages from part-time work such as paper routes to participate in postwar consumer culture. Taste in music was a factor distinguishing youth from adults, and some youth from others; so was fashion. In English Canada, especially, the influence of popular culture and commercial culture emanating from the United States was key.[121] In the 1950s and early 1960s, popular icons of postwar youth—and of masculine rebellion in particular—included James Dean, Marlon Brando, and Elvis Presley. Within the broad category of people known as "youth," however, class, gender, and ethnic differences created various youth subcultures. As early as 1949, one observer, describing the working-class teenage boys who made up Vancouver's "North End Gang," wrote that these boys' "feeling of being 'different' was expressed concretely in their choice of clothing. At dances most of them wore long coats and expensive trousers called 'strides' specially tailored with extremely narrow cuffs. Some deliberately allowed their hair to grow long and unruly."[122]

Fewer models of rebellion were available to girls. Mainstream postwar youth cultures promoted heterosexuality and held out the promise of fulfilling sexual lives for both men and women within the confines of marriage.[123] "Going steady" was, for many teenage couples, practice for marriage. Large numbers of unmarried teenage couples in English Canada were having sex well before the sexual revolution of the 1960s and 1970s. The material and moral consequences of sexual behaviour viewed as illicit (such as premarital sex) were borne disproportionately by girls, however.[124] Non-Indigenous teenage girls who became pregnant were strongly encouraged to hide themselves away in maternity homes and to give up their babies for adoption. In Indigenous communities in British Columbia, in contrast, the babies of teenage girls were often kept on the reserve and sometimes cared for by grandmothers and aunties.[125]

By the end of the 1960s and throughout the 1970s, a current of youth culture known as the counterculture had emerged in opposition to youth cultures judged conservative, commercial, or mainstream. The media—newspapers, magazines, radio, movies, and television—made much of the development of what they called a "generation gap." This gap could be identified—and exacerbated—by matters related to personal style, clothing, and deportment, but, in addition, often spoke to differences in worldviews and political stances.[126] Linked to the counterculture, but more politicized than most manifestations of the counterculture, was youth participation in various social movements: the student movement, opposition to American involvement in Vietnam, the New Left, the sexual revolution, women's liberation, and gay liberation. Moreover, the protests of young people had an impact, during these years, within the labour movement and in the workplace.[127] In Quebec and Acadian New Brunswick, youth activism was often inflected with neo-nationalist convictions and sometimes intertwined with *indépendantiste* politics.[128] The soundtrack to the youth cultures of French-speaking Quebecers and Acadians was made up of the folk and rock music of the United States, but also the *chansonniers* of Quebec, the Maritimes, and French-speaking Europe.[129]

Youth countercultures were visible across the country, in part because Canadian teenagers and young adults were increasingly mobile in this period. At the end of the 1960s and through the 1970s, every summer saw tens of thousands of white, middle-class teenagers and university students take to hitchhiking as a cheap and sociable means of transportation and way of seeing the world. Wearing the long hair and backpacks associated with "hippie youth," some hitchhiked across the country on the Trans-Canada Highway (known by some as "Hippie Highway"), in pairs or in groups, with no particular timeline in mind. Others had concrete destinations, such as Banff, Alberta or Vancouver, British Columbia. The residents of these destinations, however, did not always welcome hitchhikers, who "generally contribute[d] nothing to the local economy."[130] In the late 1960s and very early 1970s, some young people hitched a ride to Banff and set up camp at the Echo Creek campground; others took summer jobs in the local tourist industry, including at the Banff Springs Hotel. Conservative local residents argued that the Echo Creek campground constituted a public health hazard and that the presence of large groups of "hippie kids" in the area, having sex, smoking drugs, and playing music, was a threat to the local tourist industry. Although older adults and local politicians tended to tar all counterculture youth with the same brush, this young and mobile generation was not homogeneous. In particular, the stakes of being on the road were different for young men and young women respectively. The dangers of hitchhiking (violence or theft, for instance) were present for everyone, but young women were at particular risk of sexual harassment and sexual assault. Likewise, some young women who spent their summer working in Banff and participated in its flourishing youth scene were confronted with an unintended and unwanted pregnancy. Parents were all too aware of these risks. While some teenage hitchhikers set off on their road trip with their parents' approval, others snuck away or openly defied their parents' authority.[131]

Postwar youth cultures had an impact upon mainstream politics. The strength and persuasiveness of Quebec's student and youth movements arguably convinced Quebec's Quiet Revolution Premier, Jean Lesage, to lower the voting age in provincial elections from 21 to 18 in 1963.[132] The federal government followed suit in 1970. The youth cultures of Quebec and Canada were domestic manifestations of what was an international phenomenon and were experienced differently in cities and in rural areas, among young men and among young women, and among the children of working-class families and of socioeconomic elites respectively.

On the Eve of Revolution?

Beginning at the end of the 1960s, the world as it had evolved in the immediate postwar years was turned upside down—or so it seemed at the time. "From the late 1950s to the mid-1980s old certainties were up for debate, and across the globe it seemed that power relations between men and women, church and state, colonizers and colonized subjects, parents and children, black and white people, West and East and North and South, were all shifting in extraordinary ways," writes scholar Liz Millward.[133] In North America, in Europe, and in former European colonies such as Vietnam and Cuba, social movements including the civil rights movement among African-Americans, opposition to American involvement in Vietnam, student movements such as *Mai 68* in France, the militancy of the New Left, the Red Power movement, and movements for women's liberation and gay liberation had an enormous impact upon public debate and personal relationships, and thus, upon the shape and significance of families.[134]

Canada, like all other western countries, participated in these debates and these shifting power relations. Many of the most profound transformations of these years were related to changes in the forms and meanings of family life, some of which were facilitated by the Canadian state. In response to pressure from organized women's groups, for instance, it agreed in 1967 (Canada's centenary) to create the Royal Commission on the Status of Women in Canada. The findings of this Commission—on numerous topics pertaining to women's experiences and their roles within the family, including marriage and divorce, paid and unpaid work, birth control, abortion, and daycare—were shared in a well-publicized report in the fall of 1970.[135]

Marriage breakdown and the accessibility of divorce were the topic of much public discussion in the late 1960s. The British North America Act had given the federal government exclusive jurisdiction over divorce, although several provinces already had divorce courts prior to entering into Confederation. In the immediate post-Second World War decades, divorce remained expensive and difficult to obtain, adultery being the principal admissible grounds for putting a legal end to a marriage. Liberal Prime Minister Lester B. Pearson and the Special Joint Committee of the Senate and the House of Commons on Divorce struck in 1966 to enquire into the reform of federal divorce laws received testimonials from many ordinary Canadians who felt stuck in unhappy marriages. Other letters came from husbands or wives who had been deserted decades earlier, but who in the absence of access to a divorce, were unable to remarry. "By the mid-1960s," writes historian Christina Burr, "it was estimated that in Canada 60,000 deserted people, a significant proportion of them women, were unable to obtain a divorce."[136] What is striking in the letters written to Prime Minister Pearson is the extent to which legal marriage remained the overriding goal for the vast majority of those who put pen to paper. More easily accessible, legal divorce was seen by these letter-writers as a way of putting an end to unhappy and irregular situations so that they might once again become part of a married couple and family. For example, Eleanor B., a Winnipeg woman, had left her husband in the mid-1950s after years of married life that included domestic violence, marital rape, and incest involving her husband and their five-year-old son. After a decade of raising her two boys alone, she had met another man. "'I now have a chance for a normal happy home life as I met a man who wants to marry me, adopt my boys, get me off welfare and out of this house,'" she wrote to Prime Minister Pearson. Yet in the absence of reformed divorce legislation, she was unable to legally extract herself from her first, miserable marriage.[137] In response to situations such as those endured by Eleanor B., the federal government adopted its first general divorce law. The Divorce Act of 1968 preserved older "fault-based" reasons for divorce such as adultery and enlarged this category of reasons to include mental or physical cruelty, separation, or desertion, but also introduced the permanent breakdown of the marriage as legitimate grounds for divorce, making these legal proceedings more accessible and, perhaps, less stigmatizing.

Other legislation adopted by the federal Liberal government in the 1960s that had a major impact upon the lives of Canadian families was the Omnibus Bill, famously introduced by Liberal Minister of Justice Pierre Elliott Trudeau's declaration that the state had no business in the bedrooms of the nation.[138] Once adopted, the Criminal Law Amendment Act of 1968–1969 partially decriminalized abortion, although access to this medical procedure remained uneven across the country. The same Act made contraception legal, and thus condoms, diaphragms, and new oral contraceptives (approved by the United States Food and Drug Administration for sale in 1960 and by the late 1960s known across North America simply as "the Pill") became easier to obtain by both married and unmarried couples.[139] The 1968–1969 legislation also decriminalized consensual sexual relationships between adult members of the same sex, as long as these were conducted in private.

In all of these instances, the state was reacting to changes that were already well underway in civil society and that had in fact been the object of organized campaigns by various social movements for years. The Sexual Revolution, the Women's Liberation Movement, the Gay Liberation Movement, and lesbian organizing (the latter inspired by both the women's liberation movement and the gay liberation movement) all helped to render conceivable and acceptable families radically different from the "traditional" model of a married heterosexual couple and their biological children. "Second-wave" feminists and university students, for instance, were among the most active proponents of better access to contraception and safe abortions.[140] Furthermore, state activities in this period were not always benevolent. Recent research has uncovered the extensive surveillance activities undertaken by the Royal Canadian Mounted Police from the late 1960s through the 1980s, whose officers spied and reported on the new groups associated with the Women's Liberation Movement and with gay liberation.[141] The concern and, often, incomprehension displayed by the RCMP is proof both of the far-reaching nature of the challenges posed in these years to family forms seen as traditional and of the criticism and backlash that these challenges provoked.

7

Metamorphosis and Persistence: Challenging the Nuclear Family, 1975–2005

LOOKING BACK FROM the vantage point of the twenty-first century, even historians, who stress incremental transformations over long periods of time, cannot help but be struck by the rapidity of changes in family life over the last quarter of the twentieth century. All of a sudden, it seemed, in the space of a generation or two, the hegemonic vision of the family—nuclear and heterosexual—that had held sway since at least the Industrial Revolution appeared to be poised on the brink of implosion or collapse. Some welcomed and celebrated these changes. For other, more conservative, commentators these transformations in family life appeared menacing and were frequently discussed in hyperbolic terms, as threatening the very foundations of western civilization.[1] Without denying the complexity and diversity of family forms over the nineteenth and twentieth centuries, the last decades of the twentieth century saw the nuclear and heterosexual family suddenly become a legitimate—and widespread—object of critique in Canada. Over time, these critiques were translated into new family forms.

Within the space of a quarter-century, family size decreased considerably, to the point where in both Quebec and English Canada, fertility rates hovered at 1.5—well below the replacement-level fertility rate of 2.1 children per woman. While birth rates had been declining progressively across the country since the end of the nineteenth century, the postwar baby boom had made relatively large families (on average, 3.7 children per woman) seem the norm.[2]

Moreover, from the 1970s on, church- or state-sanctioned marriage was no longer the only acceptable conjugal form, competing with common-law marriage and, by the end of the century, same-sex marriage and, in Quebec, civil unions. New forms of conjugal unions, plus a significant increase in divorce rates, also produced new forms of parenthood or renewed old forms of parenthood differently, such as reconstituted (or "blended") families, lone parenting, and same-sex parenting.

Significant numbers of children continued to be taken into state care and placed in foster homes in these years. Indigenous children were over-represented among children in provincial care in the last decades of the twentieth century; many lived with the consequences of the Sixties Scoop, which continued into the early 1980s. Some Canadians developed a greater awareness of the problematic nature of non-Indigenous adoptions of Indigenous children in these years. The increasing numbers of international adoptions in the 1980s and 1990s likewise raised questions about the politics of North-South adoptions, and, more precisely, about the ethics of relatively prosperous North American families adopting the babies of poorer families from the Global South. As international adoption became less accessible towards the end of the twentieth century, some women and couples who had known the frustration or heartache of infertility turned to new reproductive technologies in the hope of conceiving a baby. While these technologies showcased the extraordinary capacity of modern medicine, they also raised questions of a pragmatic and even of an ethical nature. Is parenthood a right? Is it a right that belongs to everyone? Should the state subsidize these efforts at conception?

In sum, the last decades of the twentieth century witnessed the multiplication of family forms. The dominant family model—a father and a mother, each married only once, living with their biological children—which had never been the sole family model in Canada, was slowly losing its status as the hegemonic model of family. These transformations were of course not specific to Canada: they were taking place, at roughly the same moment, in other North American and European societies. The rapid changes in family life that began in the 1970s accompanied, and were often the result of, other major kinds of social change. The formerly hegemonic model of family was chipped away at by certain "quiet" social revolutions and openly contested by other revolutions, noisier and more dramatic.

While these changes touched families everywhere in Canada, they did not always do so at the same speed and to the same degree. Some of these phenomena, such as divorce or same-sex parenting, appeared first or more prominently in large cities such as Vancouver, Toronto, or Montreal.[3] Relatively quickly, they also became part of life in suburbs and small towns across the country.[4] Furthermore, during these decades, differences between family life in Quebec and English Canada become ever more apparent, notably with regard to fertility rates and to the social legitimacy of marriage. Despite the welfare-state measures and nation-building policies adopted by Canadian governments over the course of the nineteenth and twentieth centuries, families in Canada were clearly not all the same at the dawn of the twenty-first century.

The Social Movements of the "Long Sixties" and Their Consequences

As early as the late 1950s, some social commentators were beginning to speak of a "generation gap," whereby adolescents and those in their early twenties appeared to have priorities and preoccupations radically different from those of their parents.[5] This "gap" intensified in the 1960s and 1970s, as many young adults criticized what they perceived to be the materialism, conservatism, and conformity of their parents' generation.[6] They demanded new kinds of romantic and sexual relations, freer of the constraints formerly imposed by churches, the state, and a moral code they saw as prudish and hypocritical.[7] They openly advocated premarital sex and demanded access to birth control for unmarried women. On campuses across the country, university students helped to spread the word about birth control techniques—including new technologies, such as oral contraceptives—and access to abortion, months and sometimes years before the Omnibus bill adopted by the federal Liberals in 1969 decriminalized the sale of contraceptives and allowed for therapeutic abortions in hospitals under certain circumstances. Literally hundreds of thousands of copies of the *Birth Control Handbook*, authored by the Birth Control Committee of the McGill Students' Council, were distributed across North American university campuses. The handbook's editorial staff included eight McGill students, led by undergraduates Donna Cherniak and Allan

FIGURE 7.1 The McGill *Birth Control Handbook*, 1968. apps.carleton.edu.

Feingold. First published in September 1968, the *Handbook* was reissued and reprinted several times, and the first French-language version of the manual was published in 1970 under the title *Pour un contrôle des naissances*.[8]

It was largely young adults such as these—many, but not all of them, university students—who participated in what some have called the Sexual Revolution. The link between access to reliable forms of contraception and greater (hetero)sexual freedom was clear, although some have argued that "the Pill" in fact placed all of the responsibility for birth control on women's shoulders, freeing men from thinking about the consequences of sex. Some of these young adults had cut their political teeth—and honed their sense of generational belonging—in the New Left, in the student movement, or in protests against American involvement in Vietnam, all movements central to the "Long Sixties," the period of social activism between the late 1950s and the mid-1970s.[9] Many others embraced the countercultural movements of this period, which were less overtly political, but still critical of the Establishment, and notably of one of the central pillars of that Establishment, the bourgeois family. Some aspects of the Sexual Revolution sprang from the countercultural conviction that the preceding generation had driven society down the road of hypocrisy and profits.[10]

Among the most important movements of the Long Sixties, in terms both of the numbers involved and of its impact, was what came to be known as "second-wave" feminism. Members of the Women's Liberation Movement (WLM) were explicitly concerned with deconstructing, critiquing, and transforming the heterosexual, nuclear family. Second-wave feminists criticized the imbalance of power and the unequal access to resources within families, inequities that in their eyes placed far too much power in the hands of the husband and father. They demanded recognition of the economic value of the unpaid labour undertaken by women, whether as wives, mothers, or daughters.[11] They sought to reduce the economic dependency of married women on their husbands, along with their inferiority in the eyes of the law. Second-wave feminists also sought to remind political leaders and the public that childcare was a social and political issue, not simply the problem of individual women. They demanded the creation of subsidized daycares, including on university campuses. In 1969, the University of Toronto Women's Group successfully occupied the university's Senate Chamber in order to obtain funding for a cooperative daycare near the campus.[12] When the Royal Commission on the Status of Women published its official *Report* in 1970, it included a detailed list of recommendations regarding the necessity of publicly funded daycares that would be accessible to women working both outside and inside the home.[13]

Finally, second-wave feminists mobilized around access to abortion. The partial decriminalization of abortion in the 1969 Omnibus bill, far from resolving the question, in fact spurred on feminist organizing. In 1970, younger feminists joined more experienced militants in the Abortion Caravan, a cross-country trek organized by the Vancouver Women's Caucus that ended in Ottawa with pro-choice demonstrations on Parliament Hill and at the Prime Minister's Residence on Sussex Drive.[14] The Omnibus bill decriminalized abortions that took place in accredited hospitals, on the recommendation of a TAC (Therapeutic Abortion Committee). Over the course of the 1970s and 1980s, it became apparent that access to safe abortions varied widely according to region. By the mid-1980s, anti-choice activism had virtually eliminated access to abortion in Prince Edward Island; women in New Brunswick likewise found their access to abortion increasingly restricted over the course of the 1980s. This lack of access might have been due to the strength of conservative Protestant denominations and of Catholic lobbies in New Brunswick and PEI; religious activism fuelled much of the anti-choice movement in the Maritimes.[15] Elsewhere in Canada, such as in British Columbia, feminists competed against anti-choice militants to be named to hospital boards.[16] One of the consequences of these regional inequalities was that many women seeking an abortion were forced to travel within Canada (from eastern Ontario or the Maritimes to the Morgentaler clinic in Montreal), or to the United States (from the Kootenays in B.C. to Spokane, Washington, or from the Maritimes to Maine or New York State), or even to the United Kingdom. For women without significant financial resources, the cost of travelling in order to secure a safe and legal abortion was often prohibitive.[17]

Gay liberation was another revolution of the 1970s that explicitly critiqued contemporary understandings of the family. Intimately linked to the Sexual Revolution in that it insisted upon the importance of uncoupling sexuality and procreation, the gay liberation movement also shared some of the critiques of the family emanating from youth rebellion and from second-wave feminism. Gay-rights activists demanded recognition of the existence, and then the rights, of same-sex couples and their families. They critiqued what American feminist poet and activist Adrienne Rich called, in 1980, "compulsory heterosexuality" and privileged definitions of family that emphasized the social rather than the biological. Of course, gay men and lesbians were themselves part of nuclear families, and their relationships with their heterosexual parents and siblings were not necessarily characterized by estrangement.[18] Nonetheless, many young gay men and lesbians had experienced homophobia and heterosexism, including within their own families. While gay men and

FIGURE 7.2 Pride Week in Toronto, 1973. © Jearld Moldenhauer. Image:\u00a9 JearldMoldenhauer.Jeraldmoldenhauer.com\r\n

lesbians often organized together to secure fundamental social, civil, and legal rights, their respective interests were not always identical and these alliances occasionally foundered. Likewise, while many lesbians were active participants in the feminist movement of the 1970s and early 1980s, organized feminism was not always a comfortable home for lesbians; homophobia could also be found within the women's liberation movement.[19]

In Quebec, the various movements for liberation had been preceded by the Quiet Revolution of the 1960s: a thoroughgoing movement of political reform that sought to modernize Quebec's political and economic institutions and also reclaim the control of these institutions for Quebec's French-speaking majority.[20] In the wake of this period of *rattrapage* ("catching-up") and a desire to break with the old order, liberation movements such as second-wave feminism and gay liberation flourished. They accompanied, and sometimes drew inspiration from, the *indépendantiste* (independence) movement of the 1960s and 1970s. Occasionally, however, feminists and gay liberationists clashed with the sovereignty movement, some of whose participants were less than open to feminist or gay-rights demands.[21] Concretely, the women's movement in Quebec was aided by some of the reforms of the Quiet Revolution, which had made schooling—particularly public secondary schools—and university education far more accessible to francophone girls and women. The expansion of the public sector also opened up new kinds of white-collar employment for lay women, including married women; by the end of the 1960s, one employed woman in two in Quebec was married. Increased educational and employment opportunities facilitated some women's participation in second-wave feminism, while the limits of these reforms spurred others to action. A long sought-after reform of the Civil Code in 1964 finally gave married women relative legal equality with their spouses. After decades of lobbying by Quebec feminists, married women's legal incapacity was abolished, alongside a husband's authority within marriage. While paternal authority remained in place in 1964, it would be replaced in 1977 by parental authority.

Even before the gains attributable to the Quiet Revolution, many women in Quebec had seen daily life transformed by what some have called the "contraceptive revolution," the decrease in family size that had begun at the end of the nineteenth century, but that accelerated dramatically in the late 1950s. This rapid decrease in family size from the 1950s onward owed something to new contraceptive methods such as the sympto-thermic method (which relied on tracking ovulation through a combination of the calendar and the thermometer) promoted by *Seréna*, a method popular among married Catholic couples who preferred not to defy the teachings of the Catholic Church by resorting to mechanical methods of contraception. It owed even more to the spread of knowledge about contraceptive methods (by Planned Parenthood/*L'Association pour la planification des naissances*, among others, founded in 1964) and to better access to such methods.[22] In the 1960s, as the birth control pill became available and more widely prescribed, the decrease in family size became even more marked, to the point where, between 1960 and 1970, the number of children born to every fertile woman in Quebec, on average, dropped from four to two. Fewer and fewer Quebec women, or couples, chose to respect the taboos on contraception imposed by the Catholic Church.

Families Transformed?

During what historians have called the Long Sixties, then, various social actors, including radicalized youth, feminists, and gay men and lesbians, articulated trenchant critiques of existing social relations, including family life as they knew it. From the 1970s on, these critiques would be translated into actual changes in lived experiences of family, as well as in the family forms considered broadly acceptable.

One of the most obvious of these major changes was a rapid and dramatic drop in the size of families, across the country, but perhaps most dramatically in Quebec. From a high of 3.9 in 1961, the fertility rate (defined as the average number of children a woman has in her lifetime) in Canada dropped to 2.1 in 1971, and then to 1.6 in 1981.[23] In the case of Quebec more specifically, the province went from being "one exception to the other." From the end of the nineteenth century through the 1960s, it was the Canadian province with the largest families; by the 1970s, Quebec had the lowest fertility rate in

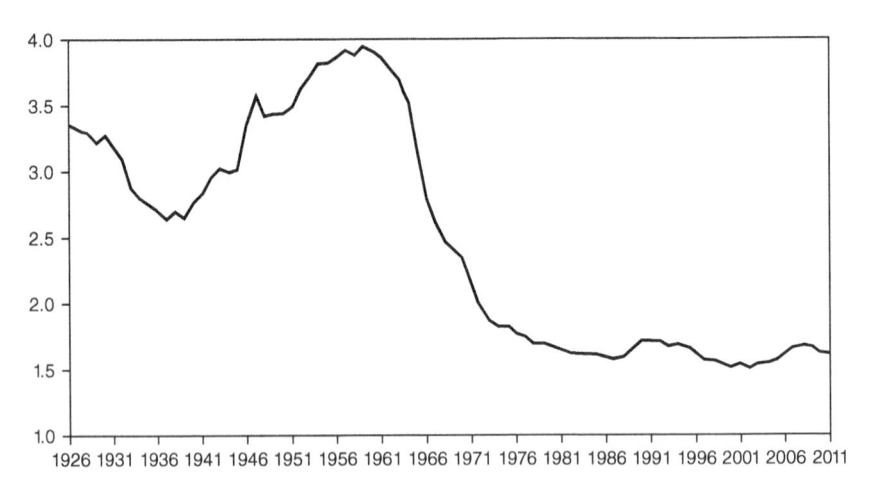

FIGURE 7.3 Total fertility rate, Canada, 1926 to 2011. Statistics Canada, Demography Division, Population Estimates Program, Canadian Vital Statistics, Births Database, 1926 to 199, Survey 3231.

Canada.[24] Even if some Quebec couples were controlling their fertility as early as the 1870s, the drop in the fertility rate beginning in the late 1950s was dramatic, to the point where Quebec had landed in the category of what demographers call "below-replacement fertility" by the 1970s.

By the early twenty-first century, Quebec's fertility rate (1.69) was actually slightly higher than that of Canada as a whole (1.61), that of Ontario (1.52), and that of British Columbia (1.42). There are of course differences within the province, and even within particular cities. In Montreal, for example, the fertility rate is 1.45 for francophone and anglophone women, but higher for Indigenous women and women belonging to some "allophone" communities (communities whose mother tongue is neither French nor English).[25] There are also important internal differences within Canada more broadly. In general, the Atlantic Provinces have fertility rates lower than the national average: this is the case for New Brunswick (1.54), Nova Scotia (1.47), and Newfoundland and Labrador (1.45). Only Prince Edward Island has a fertility rate slightly higher than the national average (1.62). In 2011, with the exception of Quebec, all of the fertility rates higher than the national average were to be found in the northern and Prairie provinces: Nunavut (2.97 children per woman), Saskatchewan (1.99), the Northwest Territories (1.97), Manitoba (1.86), Alberta (1.81), and the Yukon (1.73).[26] In part, these higher rates in the northern and western regions of the country reflect the significant proportion of these populations that is Indigenous (First Nations,

Métis, and Inuit). The fertility rates of "Registered Indian" women have gradually declined over the past decades: while the rate was 4.0 in 1976, it had dropped to 2.9 by the year 2000.[27] But these rates, well above the replacement-fertility rate, are still considerably higher than those of non-Indigenous women in Canada.

Across the country, then, as the twentieth century drew to a close, there were fewer children per family. In a consumer society where children were expensive to raise and more and more parents determined that their children be properly educated (that is, that they finish high school and obtain some post-secondary training or education), most couples appeared to want fewer children than their own parents had had. The smaller number of children per family was also related to the increasing age of parents, especially mothers, at the birth of the first child. This increased age at first birth was in turn related to the increasing age at first marriage, an age that increased steadily, from the 1970s onward, for both women and men. Across Canada, in 1971, men first married, on average, at age 25 and women at age 22.6; by 2008, men first married, on average, at age 31.1 and women at 29.1. Average ages in Quebec were slightly older: in 1971, the average age at first marriage was 25.6 for men and 23.5 for women; forty years later, in 2011, it had increased to 32.7 for men and to 31 for women.[28] This later age at first marriage was due in part to better educational and economic perspectives for women by the end of the twentieth century, which meant that many women postponed marriage until their studies were completed and they had settled into steady employment.[29] It was also due to the increasing popularity of common-law relationships, which, across the country, often served as a precursor to legal marriage. In many parts of Canada, by the end of the twentieth century, heterosexual couples lived together for years before marrying and having children.

The second major change in family life over the last quarter of the twentieth century was the increased frequency of divorce. For those couples that chose legal marriage, the substance of that relationship was clearly under review. Fewer and fewer marriages were for life. Rates of separation and, especially, of legal divorce rose steadily from the late 1960s onward.

Until the mid-twentieth century, most unhappy couples across the country stayed together, although desertions, informal separations, and even legal separations were not unknown. Divorce courts were established in three Canadian provinces (Nova Scotia, New Brunswick, and British Columbia) prior to the First World War and in three others (Alberta, Saskatchewan, and Ontario) during the interwar years. In Quebec, the Civil Code consecrated a double standard whereby a husband could request a legal separation in the event of his wife's adultery, but a husband's adultery was not sufficient reason for a wife to request a legal separation unless her husband had also moved his mistress into the family home.[30] Quebec's Civil Code made no provision for divorce until 1968. Quebec couples who wished to divorce despite the opposition of the Catholic Church and the opprobrium of their family were required, like residents of Newfoundland and Labrador, which also had no provincial divorce courts, to seek a private act of Parliament from the federal government—a procedure that was both costly and very public. Not surprisingly, in the early 1960s, Quebec had the lowest divorce rate of all Canadian provinces. That said, in most Canadian provinces, and perhaps especially in rural areas and small towns, divorce remained an infrequent phenomenon until the 1970s. Divorced individuals often lived in a context of social marginality, on the fringes of respectable society, which helps to explain why most unhappy couples stayed together. Good material reasons for staying together existed as well: for many, perhaps most, women, a separation or a divorce meant living with her children in poverty.

The first federal Divorce Act, adopted in 1968, made a difference. Compared to the various provincial divorce laws that had preceded it, the federal legislation broadened the spectrum of admissible reasons for divorce, to include not only adultery, mental or physical cruelty, and desertion, but also, quite simply, permanent marital breakdown and a separation that had lasted at least three years. After a revision of federal divorce law went into effect with the Divorce Act of 1985, this mandatory separation period was reduced to one year.[31] That the Catholic Church was aware of its loss of influence on the social and familial practices of parishioners is evident from the fact that it did not even bother to oppose the new divorce law presented in the federal Chamber of Commons in 1967 and adopted in 1968.

Across Canada, the divorce rate was just under 55 per 100,000 people in 1968; by the next year, after the adoption of the new legislation, it had jumped to 124 per 100,000, and by 1981, the divorce rate had reached 278 per 100,000 Canadians.[32] In the 1970s, then, what had been minimal rates of divorce in Canada began to rapidly increase. Issues that had been factors of marital tension in the 1960s became motivations for divorce in the 1970s.[33] Legal reform accompanied, and perhaps contributed to, increasing social acceptance, or at least tolerance, of divorce. By 2008, it was estimated that 40.7 per cent of marriages in Canada would end in divorce before the thirtieth wedding anniversary. Provincial estimates, by way of comparison, were 47.4 per cent in Quebec, 42.1 per cent in Ontario, and 37.1 per cent in British Columbia. Older language about "failed" marriages no longer seemed relevant in a context where marriage was clearly no longer necessarily viewed as an institution, or relationship, "for life."

The greater accessibility of divorce no doubt brought a great deal of emotional relief to unhappy couples and their children, especially in cases where the conflict had been overt and frequent. Yet divorce generally had a negative impact on the standard of living of many individuals, especially women, who usually earned less than men and who had often withdrawn from the paid labour force in order to raise young children. The case of Albertan woman Irene Murdoch captured public attention and had a significant impact upon subsequent jurisprudence. Murdoch was a farm-woman who had been integral to the maintenance and expansion of the family cattle ranch, and who had in fact managed it single-handedly five months a year during her husband's frequent and regular absences. Upon her separation from her husband in 1968, after twenty-five years of marriage, Irene Murdoch, who had been subjected to domestic violence, discovered that she was not entitled to half of the ranch's worth. In 1973, Murdoch received a one-time, lump sum "maintenance payment." The Supreme Court case *Murdoch v Murdoch* upheld the earlier decisions of Alberta courts, arguing that Murdoch had simply done what was expected of any farm wife. This decision laid bare women's legal inequality within (and after) marriage and provoked a number of feminist organizations to mobilize for the reform of family property law. Over the course of the late 1970s and 1980s, all Canadian provinces and territories adopted matrimonial property legislation that tended toward the equal division of property upon marriage breakdown.[34]

In the 1970s and early 1980s, divorced women and their children often found themselves living in poverty and, in the early part of the period, stigmatized by relatives and those in their communities. Divorced parents negotiated, and sometimes fought over, alimony and child-support payments. Custody battles became the stuff of popular and media discussion; the Hollywood film *Kramer versus Kramer*, which appeared on North American movie screens in 1979 and which depicted a divorced husband and wife fighting before the courts for custody of their son, no doubt resonated for at least some divorced parents and their children.[35]

By the later 1980s and the 1990s, divorce had become much more widely accepted in most Canadian communities and the benefits for both spouses and children of living in situations free from intense daily conflict were widely recognized. For most school-age children, divorce was a mainstream phenomenon, common among their peers. But most divorced women continued to experience a drop in their standard of living once they were no longer living with a male spouse, and children often experienced dramatically different living conditions with their mothers and their fathers. Divorce was in fact one of many factors contributing to the increased labour-force participation of women during these decades. The widespread participation in the paid labour force of mothers (both divorced and married) led some social workers, teachers, and journalists to decry the plight of so-called "latch-key" children, that is, children who let themselves in to empty homes at the end of the school day. One American study published in 1982 argued that the "absence of appropriate child supervision, especially during the portion of the day when the child is home from school but the parent is not yet home from work, [is] the most pressing national problem in the social policy and health care of children." Latch-key children, at home alone or in the care of only slighter older siblings, were perceived to be at greater risk of household accidents and domestic fires and were deemed "easy targets for child molesters."[36]

Divorce, of course, led to new kinds of reconstituted or "blended" families. Families reconstituted after the death of a husband or wife were a frequent phenomenon in the eighteenth and nineteenth centuries, but families reconstituted after a divorce had their specificities. Children and former spouses had to renegotiate family relationships in a context where the other spouse or parent was still in the picture and often living not very far away. Children often found themselves, not long after the separation or divorce, with two families, one per parent, plus, sometimes, the children of their parents' new partners. By 2001, 19 per cent of Canadian children aged 0 to 14 did not live with their two biological parents. In Quebec, the proportion of children aged 0 to 14 not living with their two biological parents was the highest in the country, at a full thirty per cent.

A third major change in Canadian family life over the last decades of the twentieth century was what demographers have referred to as the newly "optional" nature of marriage.[37] Increasingly, legal marriage coexisted with other conjugal forms, most notably common-law relationships. Common-law marriage was a rare phenomenon in Canada before the 1970s, generally the purview of those who were unable to marry because one of the partners was already married, but separated or deserted. By the end of the 1960s, the existence of common-law relationships was beginning to be recognized indirectly in federal and provincial welfare measures regulating pensions, social assistance, and adoption such as, in Quebec, the *Loi instituant le régime des rentes du Quebec* (1965); *la Loi de l'aide sociale* (1969), and the new *Loi sur l'adoption* (1969).

Common-law relationships became progressively more frequent in the 1970s. In these years, this was often the option favoured by young couples in their twenties and was frequently a temporary form of relationship that would lead, down the road, to legal marriage. In some cases, especially in Quebec, common-law relationships increasingly became a substitute for legal marriage. Interestingly, by the end of the twentieth century, older couples embarking upon a new relationship after the termination of a first marriage were tending to opt for common-law relationships as well.

In 1971, 10 per cent of all conjugal unions in Quebec were common-law relationships. The particular propensity of Quebecers to opt for common-law relationships would only become more obvious over subsequent decades. In 1981, common-law relationships represented over 20 per cent of all conjugal unions in Quebec, compared to just 6 per cent across Canada. At the beginning of the new century, in 2001, 14 per cent of Canadian couples were living common-law, compared to over 30 per cent in Quebec. This difference continues to increase: according to the 2011 census, the number of Canadian couples in common-law relationships had dropped slightly, to 12.5 per cent, while 37.8 per cent of Quebec couples lived outside of legal marriage. Equally interesting, 31.5 per cent of Quebec families were headed by a common-law couple, which was the case for only 16.7 per cent of families across Canada.

Unlike the English-Canadian common-law provinces, Quebec's Civil Code makes almost no provision for common-law spouses in the event of a separation. This Quebec specificity was highlighted by the notorious legal battle between "Lola" and "Eric," the extremely well publicized case of a Quebec billionaire and his ex-common-law partner, who claimed that she was entitled to a substantial alimony payment after their separation. The Supreme Court of Canada put an end to this legal saga in January 2013, when it ruled that the Quebec common-law regime was in fact constitutional and that the exclusion of common-law unions from certain rights given to married couples, as laid out in the Civil Code, did not contravene the Canadian Charter of Rights and Freedoms. Essentially, then, the Supreme Court upheld the status quo as it pertains to common-law unions in Quebec, a judgment that is not without consequences for the almost 40 per cent of Quebec couples who currently opt for this type of union. Interestingly, many in Quebec appear to agree with the Court's ruling, arguing that the decision not to marry means freedom from the long arm of the state.[38]

Another instance of Quebec divergences in the realm of the family was the creation of a new form of conjugal relationship in 2002, *l'union civile* (civil union). Not to be confused with either civil marriage or common-law marriage, civil union is a form of conjugal union unique to Quebec (in the Canadian context) that essentially makes an official, marriage-like relationship available to both different-sex and same-sex couples. The rights and obligations of civil union are virtually identical to those belonging to legal marriage, but in 2002, in a context where same-sex marriage had not yet been legalized, the legislation known as Law 84 made a form of marriage available to gay couples and also established rules of parental filiation between same-sex couples and their adopted children or children born with the help of new reproductive technologies. Almost twenty years after its creation, however, civil union remains a somewhat marginal institution. On average, only between 200 and 300 civil unions are celebrated each year in Quebec.[39] This is largely, of course, because civil union was rapidly superseded by an even newer form of conjugal union, namely same-sex marriage.

The legalization of same-sex marriage in Canada was a complicated process, in part because marriage is a shared constitutional jurisdiction. According to the British North America Act of 1867, the capacity to contract marriage belongs to the federal government, while that of celebrating marriage belongs to the provinces. Until recently, even if no federal law explicitly forbade gay marriage, it was not permitted in Canada because of the common-law definition of marriage, which explicitly stipulated that it be a union between two people of the opposite sex. This definition was contested by the Court of Appeals of Ontario and the Court of Appeals of British Columbia, as well as by Quebec's Superior Court. The first three Canadian provinces to allow same-sex marriage were Ontario, in June 2003, British Columbia, in July 2003, and Quebec, in March 2004. In June 2003, then-Prime Minister Jean Chrétien announced that he would opt for the progressive legalization of same-sex marriage across the country. His Bill (C-38), which extended the definition of civil marriage to same-sex unions, was approved by the Supreme Court of Canada and presented to the House of Commons in June 2005, where it was the object of debate and a free vote and was finally adopted by 158 votes to 133. On 20 July 2005, the Senate approved the text of the bill, and same-sex marriage became law in Canada. Worldwide, Canada was the fourth country to legalize gay marriage, after the Netherlands, Belgium, and Spain.

Many same-sex couples quickly took advantage of the new legislation. Within a half dozen years, the 2011 census showed that across Canada, 32.5 per cent of declared same-sex couples were legally married. Debates within gay and lesbian communities over the desirability or necessity of marriage were longstanding.[40] Why, many wondered, would same-sex couples want to participate in or reproduce a historically conservative, patriarchal, and heterosexist institution? Yet clearly many same-sex couples in Canada decided to embrace the possibility of marriage. In the United States, historian George Chauncey has argued, campaigns for the legalization of same-sex marriage acquired force in the 1990s and were spurred on by the catastrophic consequences of the AIDS epidemic, which included the partners of those who fell ill not having hospital visitation rights, the legal right to make medical decisions for their partner, or, after the death of their partner, not having legal access to the home that they had shared. What Chauncey has identified as a "lesbian baby boom" in the United States in the 1980s also increased support for same-sex marriage within lesbian communities, in order to ensure both partners' access to, and rights over, their children, especially in the case of the illness or death of one of the partners, or in the event of a conjugal separation.[41] Some instances of same-sex marriages existed before the institution was legalized at the beginning of the twenty-first century. Entertainer Michel Girouard and pianist Réjean Tremblay organized a much-publicized wedding in Montreal in 1972, and Winnipeg couple Chris Vogel and Richard North applied for a marriage license in 1974. These two couples, like other gay couples who held public wedding ceremonies in the 1960s and 1970s, were not motivated by what some have called the "homonormative" politics of the current marriage-equality movement. Instead, Girouard and Tremblay, like Vogel and North, sought to marry in order "to generate a public conversation about homosexual oppression": these were political actions rooted in the gay liberation movement and designed to explicitly critique the conventional nuclear family.[42]

The fourth major way in which families were transformed across the course of this quarter-century was by the creation of new forms—and the adaptation of old forms—of parenthood. Lone parenthood was far from a novel phenomenon: all kinds of families had been headed by widows and widowers, or by deserted or separated parents, usually, but not always, mothers, in the Canadian past. What was new was the numerical importance of lone parenthood. Across Canada in 2001, for instance, 15.7 per cent of all families were lone-parent families; in Quebec, the same year, single parents were at the head of 26.5 per cent of all families.[43] The other change in these years, of course, was the fact that fewer and fewer of these families were headed by widows or widowers, and more and more of them by parents who were divorced, separated, or never married. The most typical single parent was a woman with young children: most of the time, through the end of the twentieth century, the children remained the responsibility of the mother. In 2001, around 80 per cent of single parent families in Canada were headed by a woman.[44]

Single mothers in these decades were, generally speaking, financially disadvantaged compared both to women living with a partner and to single fathers. In 2003, 38 per cent of lone-parent families headed by women were living in poverty (below what Statistics Canada called "the after-tax low income cut-offs"). Only 13 per cent of lone-parent families headed by men were in this situation; only 7 per cent of two-parent families with children were below the low-income cut-off. Canada-wide statistics appear to show some improvement in the financial situation of female-headed lone-parent families over the course of the 1980s and the 1990s, although the difference between their financial situation and that of two-parent families remains striking.[45] One study conducted using earlier data has found that "the 1999 poverty rate of 51.8% for single mothers was almost threefold higher than that for single fathers (18%); and fivefold higher than the rate (10.4%) for couples with children."[46] These female-headed lone-parent families remain the majority (roughly four in five) of all lone-parent families and so represent large numbers of Canadian children living in poverty.

Gay parenthood was another form of parenthood far more common at the end of the twentieth century than in the 1970s. Same-sex parenting took many forms in the last decades of the twentieth century: a man or a woman who adopted the children of his or her partner; the sharing of parental authority within same-sex couples; same-sex couples who adopted a child, or children, together; and the recourse by lesbian couples—and, more recently, gay male couples—to medically assisted procreation. The "lesbian baby boom" in the United States appears to have had a Canadian equivalent in the 1990s.[47] In Quebec, same-sex parenthood was first institutionalized by Law 84, establishing civil union in 2002. Estimates are that between 7 per cent and 33 per cent of same-sex couples in Quebec today have children. In 2006, across Canada, roughly 9 per cent of those who declared themselves to be living in same-sex couples had children.[48] Same-sex parents have had to contend with significant prejudice and heterosexism; in the case of lesbian-parented households, much of this prejudice is based upon the assumption that "the adequate psychosocial development of children requires the availability and presence of a biological father."[49]

Many adults became parents in these years through domestic or international adoption. Informal adoption had a long history in Canada, but by the first decades of the twentieth century most provinces had established formal adoption legislation. In the nineteenth century, adopted children tended to be "illegitimate"—that is, babies or children whose parents had not been legally married—or else orphans, whose biological parents had died. In a society where a baby born out of wedlock was a stain on the family name and where unmarried women had great difficulty providing for the material needs of their child, these babies were often given up for adoption. By the 1970s, however, the private orphanages and Catholic crèches that had long housed such babies across the country were seeing more and more empty cribs. On the one hand, changing morals and standards of respectability made premarital sex less taboo and allowed some unmarried women to consider keeping their baby. Improved state welfare measures made it financially possible for them to do so.[50] And greater access to reliable forms of birth control reduced the risk of unwanted pregnancies. In such a context, individuals or couples who sought to adopt a child were faced with child "shortages," particularly if they wished to adopt a white infant in good health. Older children, children with physical or intellectual disabilities, and children of colour suffered from the prejudices of most adoptive parents and waited longer to be chosen.

Transracial adoptions were far from unknown in Canada in this period, however. Montreal's Open Door Society facilitated the adoption of African-Canadian children by white, middle-class parents in the 1960s.[51] Likewise, the hugely controversial "Sixties Scoop" continued through the 1970s and into the early 1980s.[52] In a context where legal adoption severed the ties between a child and its birth family, adoption by even the most well intentioned non-Indigenous family effectively cut children off from their Indigenous heritage and community, despite the fact that a 1976 Supreme Court of Canada decision confirmed that children adopted by non-Indigenous parents would retain their Indian status.[53] The social workers employed by provincial child protection services justified the apprehension of Indigenous children by the poverty and lack of material resources on reserves, conditions that were the result of centuries of colonialism. The children apprehended by these social workers were separated from their parents, but also from their siblings and their wider kin network. They often suffered from racism at the hands of adoptive family members, as well as in their new neighbourhoods and schools. Testimonials by many adoptees reveal physical abuse, hunger, confusion, anxiety, and shame. Moreover, while some children were permanently adopted, more Indigenous children moved through a series of foster homes; even adoptees were sometimes returned to the child welfare system by their adoptive parents. This lack of stability and permanence occasioned feelings of rejection and real material and emotional insecurity for children. When former adoptees attempted to reintegrate Indigenous communities as adults, they often faced numerous obstacles.[54]

From the 1970s on, Indigenous communities frequently and vociferously protested the apprehension of their children by provincial child protection agencies. Towards the end of the twentieth century, as a response to the intergenerational trauma bequeathed by residential schools, transracial adoption, and foster care, individual First Nations established healing initiatives and healing centres in communities on and off reserves.[55] Both the Aboriginal Healing Foundation and the First Nations Child and Family Caring Society were founded in 1998, in the wake of the publication of the Report of the Royal Commission on Aboriginal Peoples in 1996. The Caring Society, created at the Squamish First Nation, is a Canada-wide association devoted to networking, research, and public education; one of its key principles is the conviction that Indigenous children should be able "to grow up safely at home."[56]

Increasingly, by the 1990s, non-Indigenous parents hoping to adopt a child were turning to private adoption agencies working abroad. Between 1999 and 2009, between 1,500 and 2,200 internationally adopted children arrived in Canada each year. Many of these children came from China; others arrived from the United States, Ethiopia, Vietnam, and Haiti.[57] Patterns were similar in Quebec: since 1990, several hundred adopted children have arrived in Quebec each year, most of them from China, Vietnam, Haiti, Russia, South Korea, Colombia, and Taiwan. A peak was reached in 1996, when 977 internationally adopted children arrived in Quebec. After the turn of the twenty-first century, the number of international adoptions each year dropped, principally because sending countries modified the legislation around international adoption, responding to internal political pressure to have their babies adopted domestically.[58]

A final development in the realm of parenthood in the late twentieth century was the recourse to new reproductive technologies that assisted conception in the case of women, or couples, experiencing infertility, such as in vitro fertilization (IVF), the freezing of embryos, or genetic testing. For many women and couples, these treatments, when they worked, were a boon, allowing them to have a child, or children, when they had given up hope. But they came at the cost of the invasive medicalization of women's bodies, reproduction, and parenthood, and also had huge financial implications. Debates over whether governments should assume these costs were vigorous, and debates over where the limits to such government support should lie even more so. Should governments subsidize the recourse to new reproductive technologies on the part of older women? Postmenopausal women? Unmarried or single women? Lesbian women? A 2014 case in Quebec of a gay male couple resorting to state-subsidized reproductive technologies caused a furore in the media. Journalist Lysiane Gagnon, for example, argued that no one has "the right to a child," but that children do have the right to know their biological origins, something that would be impossible in the case of this particular male couple whose twin girls were conceived using an egg purchased in the United States and brought to term in the uterus of a surrogate.[59] New reproductive technologies also raise serious ethical issues about the relationship among nature, biology, technology, and society. What are the ethics, for instance, of deliberately risking more dangerous multiple births by implanting two or more ova? Alternatively, what are the ethics of "selective termination" in the event of multiple pregnancies? Do advanced prenatal testing techniques that allow medical professionals to detect congenital defects in foetuses, for instance, foster the development of a society where children living with disabilities are unwelcome? Many Canadians for whom women's right to choose if and when to have children is an absolute credo are appalled by decisions made by some couples, enabled by prenatal testing, to abort female foetuses.[60]

While all of these transformations in family life had deep roots, many of them seemed—both to contemporaries and to historians—to take place very quickly. One tendency is clear: Canadians are having fewer and fewer children. The fertility rate in most parts of Canada is below the replacement rate. Only Indigenous communities and some immigrant communities are attaining the replacement rate of 2.1 children per woman. This is a phenomenon common to the western world (Canadian fertility rates are similar to those in Italy, Portugal, and Poland, for instance), and is thus neither unique nor, necessarily, worrisome. It does, however, underline the importance of immigration if Canada is to maintain its active workforce and sustain state welfare programmes such as public pensions. It also suggests the importance of family-friendly state policies (including, but not limited to, affordable, accessible childcare) that will help to close the wage gap between men and women and that will enable parents to share more equitably the work of child-raising and to find a more satisfying balance between family life and paid work.

It is clear, too, that in certain regards, family practices in Quebec are very different from those in most parts of English Canada. These differences appear to be growing over time. In Quebec, for instance, there appears to be a firm and widespread desire to form couples and families without seeking the approval of either churches or the state. Fewer and fewer legal marriages are celebrated in Quebec. And, in contrast to the English-Canadian provinces, Quebec's Civil Code provides few legal protections for common-law spouses, particularly in the event of a separation. Common-law relationships in Quebec are very often long-term relationships that produce children, but increasingly such unions are legitimated by the presence and approval of family, kin, and community, rather than by religion or the law. This might be a rejection of the Catholic teachings that held so much weight for so long in Quebec, or a refusal of what is perceived to be a North American political culture of conformism and conservatism. Finally, it could be the result of the impact of second-wave feminism, so strong in Quebec for so long.

Media pundits occasionally paint gloomy portraits of solitary Canadians aging alone, without the support of spouses, children, or social safety nets. Before buying into such apocalyptic predictions, however, it is important to understand that couples, and more globally, families, persist and remain important to many. Even legal marriage, clearly on the decline, remains numerically important; even in Quebec, 52 per cent of families in 2011 were headed by married couples. The 2011 census also shows that the majority of people aged 65 and over (56 per cent) are part of couples, a greater percentage than in 2001. And the percentage of women over the age of 65 living alone has also fallen.[61] More importantly, perhaps, new family configurations and new forms of solidarity are being created, in rural areas and in cities; they are perhaps all the stronger for being forged out of motivations other than obligation or tradition.

Conclusion
Twenty-First-Century Families

TWO DECADES INTO the twenty-first century, it is difficult to say how future historians will view the evolution of families in Canada at the turn of the new century. It is largely the work of demographers, sociologists, and social-work researchers that discerns larger patterns and trends amid the everyday activity of the world in which we live. Among a multitude of new practices and family forms is the decision made by many Canadian provinces (such as Ontario, British Columbia, and Alberta) from the 1990s on to regulate the practice of midwifery. This has changed the experience—and often, the location—of childbirth for many women and their partners. Another example is the recognition, in some provinces, of multiple parents on a birth certificate, a precedent set by legislation in British Columbia in 2013, but also allowed by a court decision in Newfoundland and Labrador in 2018. A third example is the increasing opposition, in Canada as elsewhere, to surgeries performed on children born with intersex traits.[1] A half-century ago, none of these developments was on the horizon, or even, for most Canadians, within the realm of possibility.

Among the many recent changes in family life in Canada, four transformations stand out. The first is that the population of Canada is aging and now resembles what demographers call the inverted (or "upside-down") pyramid. This has major implications for healthcare, social services, the labour market and, not least, family arrangements. The second is what some have called the Tanguy or "boomerang" phenomenon, that is, adult children who remain in their parents' home through university, their first real job, and beyond—or who return to their parents' home, often in the wake of a crisis such as the end of a serious relationship or the loss of a job, after living for some time on their own. The third phenomenon that bears exploring are new sources of immigration. Immigration is crucial to a country with an aging population: Canadian families are more diverse than ever in terms of racial, ethnic, and religious background. Migrants bring with them the family forms and practices that they knew in the societies in which they previously lived; sometimes (but not always), this makes for difficult adjustments and for conflicts between parents and children, and between husbands and wives. A final, striking, phenomenon is the considerable growth of the Indigenous (First Nations, Métis, and Inuit) population in Canada. Indigenous populations are growing in number, and are on average younger than non-Indigenous populations. In some of the western provinces, such as Saskatchewan and Manitoba, Indigenous people make up a significant, and increasing, proportion of the total population. Yet Indigenous families continue to face considerable challenges in Canada. Testimony before the Truth and Reconciliation Commission of Canada between 2008 and 2014, for example, brought to the attention of the non-Indigenous public the major and often tragic impact that the legacy of the residential school experience continues to have on Indigenous families in Canada, alongside the remedies to intergenerational trauma proposed by Indigenous communities.

An Aging Population

What demographers call the upside-down pyramid is the result of the aging of the large cohorts of children born in the wartime and postwar decades, combined with increased life expectancy and the low birth rates of the 1970s, 1980s, and 1990s. Canada's population as a whole is aging: the 2016 census showed that for the first time in the country's history, there are more Canadians aged 65 and over than there are aged 15 and under. To be sure, there are variations among the provinces. In Alberta, Saskatchewan, Manitoba, and the three territories—regions with significant Indigenous populations, and regions that have been attracting young people for work opportunities (notably in Alberta's oil and gas sector) over the past few decades—people under the age of 15 continue to outnumber people of retirement age.[2] However, the Atlantic Provinces, Quebec, and British Columbia reflect the nationwide trend of an aging population. In British Columbia, the temperate climate has long attracted retired people.[3] In the Atlantic Provinces and Quebec, the aging of the population can be explained by a combination of regional outmigration, lower immigration rates, and low birth rates. In Quebec, persons aged 65 and over constituted only about 5 per cent of the population in the early twentieth century; in 2026, they will likely make up a quarter of the Quebec population. This is also the case because Quebec's birth rate has been particularly low since the beginning of the 1970s, especially for Quebec-born francophones, whose birth rates have been described as "croissance zéro" (zero growth).[4]

In provinces such as Quebec, then, the proportion of the labour force considered "active" will be smaller in the years to come and will be required to support the economic burden of an aging population, notably the costs of old-age pensions and of healthcare. The public costs of housing elderly people will also be significant, in a context where older adults and persons approaching the age of retirement have fewer children than previous generations of elderly people—and thus, at least in theory, less family support than previous generations. More far-flung families also mean fewer children in the same city or region as their aging parents. Finally, older adults without spouses or children can be particularly isolated. Elderly single men in twentieth-century British Columbia, retired from resource-extraction industries such as logging, mining, or fishing, often found themselves alone once their working life

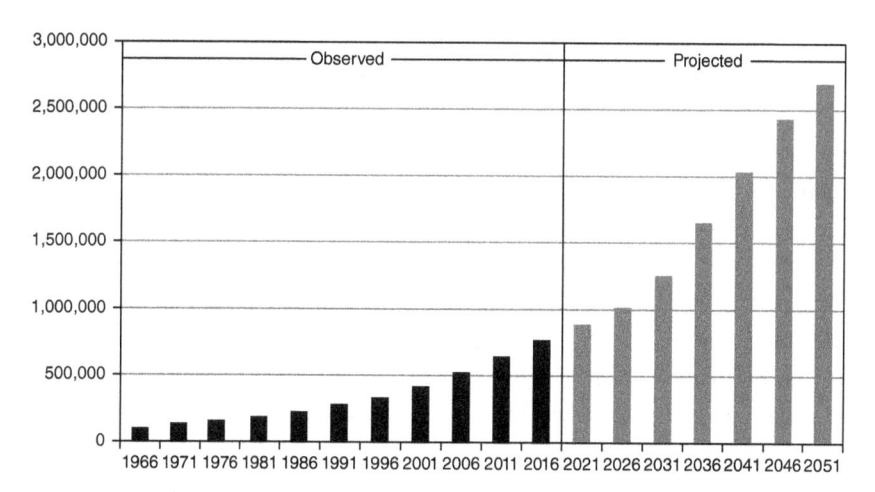

FIGURE C.1 Population aged 85 and over, Canada, 1966 to 2051. Statistics Canada, Census of Population, 1966 to 2016. Data for 2021 to 2061 are population projections. From the M1 medium-growth scenario of national projects. The projection data have as a base population the population estimates based on the 2011 Census, adjusted for net undercoverage. For more information, see the report Population Projects for Canada (2013 to 2063), Provinces and Territories (2013 to 2038). Statistics Canada Catalogue no. 91-520-X.

was over.[5] In most places in Canada today, however, older adult women outnumber older adult men; there are slightly fewer than two women for every man among those aged 85 and over, and five women for every man among centenarians.[6]

The fact that the Canadian population is aging becomes even more worrisome when the ambient political context is taken into account, that is, neoliberalism and the gradual dismantling of the welfare state. What role will the state take in caring for the elderly over decades to come? Stories in the media about the ill treatment and the neglect of older adults in both public facilities such as Quebec's *Centres d'hébergement de soins de longue durée* (CHSLD) and private old-age homes are frequent. In Woodstock, Ontario, for example, a nurse was convicted in 2017 of killing eight people between the ages of 75 and 96 in long-term care with overdoses of insulin: this has been cited by lobby groups such as CARP (formerly the Canadian Association for Retired Persons) as an extreme example of the chronic abuse of elderly people in long-term residential care.[7] "Elder abuse," a category of behaviour that includes verbal aggression, physical mistreatment, neglect, and the victimization of older adults through theft or fraud, has emerged in recent decades as a troubling issue.[8] As early as the interwar years, though, civil servants and social reformers worried about the neglect and the abuse of the elderly. By the 1960s, there appeared to have emerged a consensus that the state had a responsibility towards older adults—a responsibility that manifested itself in more generous old-age pensions, but also in decent public residential care for the aged.[9] A half-century later, at a moment when most states are reducing their commitments to citizens in the realm of social welfare, there is a very real possibility that elderly people will be faced with the choice between expensive private residential care and more affordable, but Spartan, public institutions. Older people without considerable financial resources could find themselves in the shabbiest and the most understaffed of nursing homes. Moreover, historically, in English Canada, elderly people have resisted being placed in institutions; the workhouses of the Poor Law era cast a long shadow that continued to shape people's perceptions of institutions for older adults well into the twentieth century.[10] Understandably, most older people appear to prefer to remain in the community, thus preserving some degree of autonomy. In a context, however, where their ability to do so depends upon the state of their health and their finances and on the extent to which they have support from their families, there is every chance that questions of hospital care and long-term residential care for the elderly will be major issues for provincial and federal governments in the years to come. Moreover, in an era when the vast majority of adult women work outside the home, the state can no longer assume that older adults will be entirely looked after by their daughters or their daughters-in-law.[11] The absolute devastation wrought by the COVID-19 pandemic in long-term care homes for the elderly in British Columbia, Ontario, and especially Quebec in the spring of 2020 laid bare both the risks inherent to the institutionalization of a vulnerable population and the fact that many existing care homes, both public and private, are chronically understaffed. The higher number of COVID-19 deaths in Quebec, in particular, owes a great deal to the prevalence of the institutional model in that province (a greater proportion of the elderly are in long-term care homes in Quebec than in other Canadian provinces) and to the fact that a large percentage of these institutions are private and thus less subject to regular state inspections.[12]

In recent years, the close association established during the postwar decades between the age of 65 and withdrawal from the labour force has become more tenuous. The most recent census data appears to indicate a trend towards people over the age of 65 working for pay in relatively large numbers. In 2015, one person in five over the age of 65—some 1.1 million Canadians—earned a salary. Not since the 1981 census had such a large proportion of retirement-aged Canadians reported working for pay. Among people over the age of 65, men are particularly likely to work for pay, as are people living in rural areas. Highly educated senior citizens are also especially likely to continue working after the age of 65.[13] Some of these Canadians work out of financial necessity: ironically, increased longevity—normally seen as a good thing—means that old-age pensions and personal savings are no longer enough to maintain a decent standard of living for what can be some twenty years or more of life after retirement. Others work because they continue to take pleasure in their jobs and in the contact with others that this implies, and because their health and energy levels allow them to do so. Many Canadians, however, appear to adhere to the idea that the period of life after age 65 should be devoted to non-wage-earning activities. Conservative Prime Minister Stephen Harper's 2012 decision to raise the age of eligibility for Old Age Security (OAS) from 65 to 67 met with popular protest, and this decision was subsequently reversed by Liberal Prime Minister Justin Trudeau's government in 2016.[14]

While some observers decry the fact that large numbers of retirement-age adults are obliged to continue working for pay or to reintegrate into the workforce, this trend does constitute a reminder that older citizens should not be regarded simply as an economic burden. Moreover, the unpaid labour that they perform—as grandparents, or as volunteer workers—represents a significant contribution to the Canadian economy, in addition to making the country a more caring and humane place. Researchers who have studied the question of intergenerational solidarities have discovered that relationships between the generations remain important in Canada today. Grandparents, for example, continue to play an important role in the lives of their grandchildren. The relationships between grandparents and grandchildren tend to be based on play rather than discipline, however; the latter is generally left to parents. Likewise, although many grandparents help out by occasionally babysitting their grandchildren, many are reluctant to take on child minding as a regular task. In better health and often more at ease financially than previous generations of elderly people, twenty-first-century grandparents tend to wish to maintain control over their own schedule and preserve their involvement in various social activities.[15]

Generation Boomerang?

What has come to be known as the boomerang or "Tanguy" phenomenon (named after the title character of a 2001 French film about a middle-aged couple who resort to desperate measures in order to convince their 28-year-old son to leave home) refers to adults in their twenties or even thirties who remain in their parents' home.[16] Some of these adult children (the "Tanguys") have never left the family home; others (the "boomerangs") return to their parents' home after months or years of living on their own or with roommates. These adult children return seeking their parents' financial help, but also their emotional and logistical support, particularly in moments of personal crisis, such as the loss of a job or the end of a romantic relationship. This phenomenon is so widespread that it is now considered a generational characteristic: sociologists and demographers speak of the "stay-at-home generation."[17] Other scholars argue for the existence of a new demographic category, what they call "emerging adulthood," namely, the period between the ages of 18 and 25.[18] These emerging adults are often perceived to be the beneficiaries of the phenomenon known as "helicopter parenting," that is, "intense parental involvement during young adulthood" leading to a "prolonged period of dependence."[19] In popular culture, the Tanguy or boomerang generation is often the object of humour (as in the eponymous 2001 film), but also of derision, as in the story, widely covered by the media in 2018, of 30-year-old Michael Rotondo of New York State, who was (successfully) sued by his parents so that he would finally move out of their home.[20] It is worth noting that the stay-at-home generation is always contrasted with the generation of its parents, the baby boomers, for whom "achieving financial, residential, and emotional independence [was] seen as a normative mode of development from youth into adulthood."[21] Of course, the first cohorts of baby boomers came of age at a time of exceptional prosperity, when well-paying jobs were plentiful and were often obtainable without a university education.[22]

The Tanguy phenomenon began attracting the attention of the media and of scholars in the early 2000s. In Canada, it appears to be a phenomenon traceable to the early 1980s and the early 1990s—two moments of economic recession, when young people had difficulty finding paid work. In 1991, across the country, 32 per cent of young adults aged 20 to 29 lived with their parents. Twenty years later, in 2011, 42 per cent of Canadian adults in their twenties lived with their parents. The Tanguy phenomenon is also shaped by factors other than the economy, however. A detailed Canadian study of this phenomenon has found that region matters: young adults in Quebec, for example, have a tendency to remain in their parents' home longer than young adults elsewhere in Canada, but they are less likely to return to their parents' home once they do leave. The same study found that children raised in small towns or cities tend to leave the parental home earlier than those who grew up in big cities. Family configurations also make a difference. Children raised in blended or recomposed families tend to leave home earlier than those raised in a home with their two parents. The presence of a stepparent in the home tends to encourage young adults to leave the home earlier; this is particularly the case for young women. The children of large families—that is, with numerous brothers or sisters—are more likely to leave the parental home earlier than those who grew up in smaller families.[23] In a 1998 sample of Canadians in their late twenties, "in all geographic and post-secondary status groups, men were more likely than women to live with their parents."[24]

Despite the bad press given to the Tanguy or boomerang generation—derogatory comments about men still living in their parents' basements are particularly common, suggesting that the social acceptability of boomerangs varies according to gender—one could argue that a longer cohabitation between generations has positive consequences, and not just for the adult children. For aging parents, the presence of their adult children in the home can be a source of tangible assistance, of emotional support, and of company. Some researchers have argued that generational cohabitation "provides increased opportunities for mentoring each other." And many adult children clearly appreciate their parents. One 18-year-old Canadian woman told researchers, "I think I'll stay home forever [laugh]. It's a good place... I love 'em.

I have a good family."[25] Scholars have also suggested that the cohabitation of parents and adult children is built on the unspoken assumption that parents' financial support will be repaid by support from their adult children as the parents themselves age.[26] The success of the cohabitation of parents and adult children can vary, however, according to the degree of dependence (financial and otherwise) at work in these relationships.

Integral to the "Tanguy" or "boomerang" phenomenon is of course the ability of young people to become independent or autonomous, alongside the very definition of what constitutes autonomy. For young people today, independence consists of a place of residence, a romantic partner, a regular salary, and stable employment. But there is no longer necessarily any one linear path to achieving these goals. For example, life as part of a stable couple can begin before one's studies are finished.[27] Young Quebecers tend to achieve some kind of independence between the ages of 20 and 30, but they are particularly vulnerable to the impact of larger socio-economic factors, such as a shortage of reasonably priced accommodation, an economic recession, or an oversaturated labour market.[28] Young adults who choose to pursue higher education often take longer to achieve other goals associated with autonomy. For instance, on average, young adults with university education take ten years longer than their peers who did not attend university to buy a home. This reflects the opportunity costs of a delay of several years before entering the full-time labour force, plus the costs of repaying student loans. University attendance also delays marriage and parenthood, particularly for women.[29] In a context where more young Canadians are attending university than before and where tuition fees continue to rise, these factors contribute to the more general tendency, among members of this generation, to delay pregnancy and parenthood until their thirties.

New Sources of Immigration

Since the changes in federal immigration policy adopted in the 1970s, the racial, ethnic, and religious origins of Canadian families have become much more diverse. In 2016, the top five countries of birth of recent immigrants to Canada were the Philippines, India, China, Iran, and Pakistan.[30] Immigrant families have primarily settled in the cities and suburbs of the large metropolitan regions—Toronto, Vancouver, Montreal, and Calgary. The home countries of recent immigrants to Quebec differ from those of immigrants to the English-speaking provinces because of Quebec's immigration policy, which favours immigrants with prior knowledge of the French language.[31]

Between 2006 and 2015, the top sending countries of immigrants to Quebec were, in order, Algeria, France, China, Morocco, and Haiti.[32]

Haiti has in fact been an important source of immigration to Quebec since the 1960s.[33] Interviews conducted with Montreal families of Haitian origin reveal that immigration to Quebec almost always occurred in several stages. Usually one parent left Haiti first, sometimes accompanied by one or more of the children. The other spouse and the remaining children followed some months or years later. Often the children left behind in Haiti were resentful of the parent who left, and the family reunifications that followed were occasionally difficult, involving bitterness or disappointment, especially when the families that were reunited were "reconstituted" families that included a stepparent. Once in Montreal, families often experienced a precarious economic situation, owing in part to the reluctance of Canadian governments and employers to recognize diplomas and skills acquired in Haiti. Parents attempted to reconcile their own past practices of child-rearing with the norms of local schools and other parents and with their children's own expectations. Parents of adolescents, in particular, often faced conflicts over how strict they ought to be with their children.[34]

Many of the families interviewed by scholar Gina Lafortune lived a transnational existence, in the sense that their family members were dispersed in several countries. These families were conscious of being part of a diaspora that included Haiti, the United States, and Quebec.[35] In an era of less expensive air travel and of electronic communications, migration no longer necessarily means a definitive rupture with the family left behind. This facilitates, in ways that are perhaps more tangible than before, the persistence of transnational families, even though letter-writing served to bind the ties of extended families in the nineteenth and early twentieth centuries.[36] Migrants continue to send money, goods, and gifts of all kinds to family back "home."[37] Remembering her own childhood in Toronto, scholar Charmaine Crawford recounts,

> My mother and I made occasional shopping trips to Honest Ed's and Bi-way to purchase non-perishable items that would then be packed in a barrel along with clothes and shoes to be shipped to my aunts and cousins in Trinidad. My major task during the holiday season as a teenager entailed carefully writing out Christmas cards for relatives under the watchful eye of my mother who, while instructing me on what to write, calculated how much money (or change) to include in each envelope from her meager [sic] salary. Our transnational family functioned in a triangular pattern between Canada, the United States and Trinidad.[38]

The internationalization of the domestic labour market means that over the past few decades many women with children have left the Caribbean or the Philippines, for example, in order to work as caregivers (nannies, home helpers, nurses' assistants) in North America. Between 1992 and 2014, the federal Live-in Caregiver Program allowed foreign live-in caregivers to apply for permanent residency in Canada after two years of work.[39] Some of these migrants planned to send for their children after months or years of working abroad; others hoped to return to their children, whom they had left in the care of extended family members. Crawford recalls:

> My mother tells me that one of her sisters, my aunt, is visiting my grandmother in the United States. It's the mid-1980s. My aunt says things are hard in Trinidad. You can't even rub two pennies together. My aunt got a visa for six months so she decides to get a job, first as a domestic, then taking care of an elderly person. Her employer likes her because she is a good worker and she doesn't have to pay her much. My aunt sends money back home to support her three children. They need food, clothes, and school supplies. She stays on without papers, hoping that her employer will sponsor her. She misses her children who she hasn't seen in three years. Time passes and she finds a way to send for them – but how do they cope when they finally meet?[40]

In some ways, departures are less definitive today than they were even thirty or forty years ago. Interviews conducted with Vietnamese-Chinese refugees who settled in Montreal in the late 1970s revealed that these refugees, particularly those over the age of forty, thought constantly of the possibility of family reunification, to the extent that family reunions occupied their dreams at night. Yet in a context where these refugees had left a war-torn country and made extremely difficult voyages overseas, reunion with family members left behind was at that time often complicated, even unfathomable.[41]

Many researchers have found that resettlement and adaptation to life in Canada is easier for younger immigrants and refugees such as children and teenagers. In part, this is because of the work done by public schools in welcoming immigrant children and helping them to integrate to the host society. Immigrant parents interviewed in the early 2000s frequently noted that their children were well received by teachers and other members of the personnel at their school and that they in fact integrated into Quebec and Canadian society much more quickly than did their parents. School attendance allows children to make friends in the host society, something that is often much more difficult for their immigrant parents.[42] The public school teaches language skills and elements of academic disciplines, of course, but is also designed to inculcate Canadian or Quebec values in school children—and to reach adult immigrants through their children. The fact that most recent immigrants to Quebec and Canada—particularly those whom the state calls "economic immigrants"—are highly educated appears to facilitate their children's adaptation to the local school system, as these parents are familiar with educational institutions and are not intimidated by the school personnel or afraid to ask questions of their children's teachers.[43] Of course, immigration can also produce conflicts between parents attached to the ways of doing things "back home" and their children, immersed in the practices of their North American peers. These conflicts tend to centre upon important questions related to parental authority and individual autonomy and are often manifested around concrete issues such as the choice of fields of study or teenagers' freedom to go out with friends. One second-generation Vietnamese-Canadian student wrote in 1998, "Growing up an Asian-Canadian is not an easy task. Sure, I was born a Canadian but my parents are Vietnamese. I clearly look Vietnamese, but am I a true Vietnamese girl? Behind this Asian face I wear, two different cultures are at war. At home, the Vietnamese mentality reigns; at school, I must act differently to integrate myself."[44] Children and teenagers who adapt more easily to life in Canada than do their parents, who learn English or French more quickly, who make Canadian friends, and who come to better understand "the system" acquire a relative degree of power in relation to their parents that they might not have had in the country of their birth.[45]

If generational conflicts occasionally erupt within immigrant families, conflicts between immigrant husbands and wives are often related to frustrations owing to the inability to obtain satisfactory work. Sociologist Gertrude Mianda, who interviewed francophone African women living in Toronto and Montreal, discovered that most of these women had come to Canada to join their husbands, who were studying.[46] Although many of these couples hoped to return to their country of origin, political events in their home country forced them to remain in Canada. Both these women and their husbands were obliged to take jobs well below the level of their formal qualifications—even the men, who had Canadian diplomas—and racism clearly limited their job opportunities in both of these cities. Furthermore, life in Ontario or Quebec forced these couples to renegotiate their vision of conjugal relations. In Canada, these couples and their children lived within the confines of a nuclear family, without the significant material and in-kind assistance provided by extended family members. In this situation, African women found the burden of domestic work while at the same time working for pay overwhelming: not only could they not count upon the help of extended family members for household chores, but they could often not count upon the help of their own husbands. The expectation, quite common in Ontario and Quebec, that husbands would or should contribute to housework was new to many of these women; some of the women felt as though they were the objects of condescension on the part of white Canadian and Québécois women, who assumed that African women were subordinate to and exploited by their own husbands. One interviewee explained that most of her friends in Canada were African women, who better understood the situation in which she and her husband found themselves. "You see," she said, "with all the racism that one encounters here, already my husband can't find work easily. He feels humiliated, and if, on top of that, I force him to do housework, you see what that ends up like. That's why my friends are African; I don't count on finding friends among the women here."[47]

The difficulties faced by adult immigrants in finding work in their fields are imposing and remain very common. One recent Eastern European migrant, for instance, found relatively satisfying work soon after her arrival in Canada, but her husband, a professional engineer, faced the double obstacle of having his foreign education and training recognized and then acquiring Canadian work experience in his field. Frequently, husbands and fathers used to being the family breadwinner experience years of working in jobs other than those for which their education and training had prepared them, which can lead to sentiments of frustration and sometimes depression.[48] Reliant upon the income of their spouses or their older children, some immigrant husbands and fathers feel keenly their loss of stature as the breadwinner and the shift in power dynamics that this produces between spouses or between parents and children.

Immigration specialists have thus studied in depth the difficult situations experienced by husbands and fathers, accustomed to bringing home a significant part of the family income. However, married heterosexual women also experience particular problems. When there is a choice to make about who will return to university in order to obtain a Canadian postsecondary degree, for example, it is often the husband whose needs are prioritized. The same goes for language classes, particularly since, in the absence of affordable or accessible childcare, the presence of young children often retains women at home. The family reunification policies of the Canadian and Quebec governments allow for a solution to some of these problems. Immigrant couples might attempt, for instance, to bring their elderly parents to Canada. The presence of grandparents constitutes a source of childcare that allows women to absent themselves from the home in order to take language classes or to undertake further study. It can also provide help with domestic labour such as cleaning and laundry. Finally, multigenerational families help to alleviate the loneliness and sense of loss often experienced by recent immigrants.[49]

In a country where the population is aging and birth rates are low, the need for immigrants is undeniable. Despite official policies of multiculturalism in Canada and interculturalism in Quebec, debates over the numbers and kinds of immigrants that Canada should admit are nonetheless numerous and, occasionally, vociferous. Among some Canadians, there exists the fear that immigrants—particularly non-white immigrants and non-Christian immigrants—will refuse to "integrate." Visible markers of belonging to non-Christian religions, such as the turban for Sikh men or the veil or headscarf for Muslim women, continue to be a source of controversy. The adoption of Quebec's *Loi sur la laïcité de l'État* (known as Bill 21) in 2019 provoked intense debate and contestation within the province: this law banned the wearing of religious symbols such as a hijab, a kippah, or a turban at work by public servants in positions of authority (judges, police officers, and teachers, for example). The controversy over whether Baltej Singh Dhillon, a Sikh man who grew up in Surrey, British Columbia, should be allowed to keep his beard and wear a turban after being recruited by the Royal Canadian Mounted Police in 1988, is another example of these debates. However, these media controversies often have little to do with the priorities of immigrant families themselves, who are concerned above all with making a place for themselves within the host society and ensuring a safe and prosperous future for their children.[50] They are more relevant, perhaps, in the case of refugee families, some of whom are in fact seeking refuge in Canada from religious persecution in their country of origin.

Indigenous Families in the Twenty-First Century

In 2016, Indigenous peoples constituted 4.9 per cent of Canada's total population, that is, 1,673,785 people. In some provinces (notably Saskatchewan and Alberta) and territories, they make up a much larger proportion of the population.[51] The Truth and Reconciliation Commission of Canada, assembled in 2008 to examine the workings and consequences of Canada's residential school system, demonstrated the durable and often traumatic impact of residential schools on various areas of the lives of Indigenous peoples today, including the forced loss of Indigenous languages and the relationship of Indigenous peoples to the criminal justice system. One of the most striking findings of the Commission was the major overrepresentation of Indigenous children in today's child-protection system. Across the country, in 2011, Indigenous children represented 48.1 per cent of all children aged 14 and under in foster care. Again, the statistics vary by province. In Manitoba, 23 per cent of the province's children are Indigenous, but Indigenous children make up fully 85 per cent of the children in care. In Ontario, where only 3 per cent of the total child population is Indigenous, 21 per cent of children in care are Indigenous.[52] As the authors of the Final Report of the Truth and Reconciliation Commission of Canada note, more Indigenous children are now "placed in foster care each year than attended residential school in any one year."[53] The kinds of child welfare to which Indigenous children are exposed vary: traditional foster care, for the most part, but also, more recently, Indigenous-run child and family service agencies and Indigenous kinship care.

The individuals who testified before the Truth and Reconciliation Commission of Canada and the commissioners who contributed to the writing of the Final Report agreed that there was a direct link between the residential school experience and the overwhelming numbers of Indigenous children in care today. They speak of "an intergenerational cycle of neglect and abuse" that began with the residential school system.[54] Many survivors of residential schools testified to the effect that they had had no models or experience of good parenting. The federal government and residential school administrators had plucked them from their own families and separated them from their parents for years at a time; their daily life within the schools was often characterized by physical abuse and sexual violence. Tim McNeil, for instance, testified before the Commission when it visited Newfoundland and Labrador:

> I was a good parent until my kids turned thirteen, and when my kids turned thirteen then I started parenting them the way that I was when I was in school. So suddenly my love was gone, my affection was gone, my time was gone. I started treating them the way I was treated in the dorm. And that was with strict rules, strict discipline, you had to follow a certain order, there was no love, there was no affection.[55]

Moreover, the residential school system left former pupils with inadequate education and training, poorly preparing them for the labour market either off or on the reserves. Many Indigenous peoples thus find themselves living in poverty today and dealing with problems of addiction and substance misuse—factors that make it difficult for them to parent and that increase the likelihood that provincial authorities will take their children into care. As the authors of the Final Report point out, a long history of racism within Canada's child-protection structures means that non-Indigenous child welfare authorities and social workers are very quick to suspect or assume neglect within Indigenous families, often equating poverty with a lack of care. This makes them even more likely to remove Indigenous children from their homes and to separate them from their families.[56] At the same time, historically, child removal and foster care placement has provided absolutely no guarantee that Indigenous children would be better cared for. The case of Richard Cardinal, a Métis teenager who hanged himself in 1984 at the age of seventeen, brought to public attention the appalling experience of some Indigenous children removed from their parents and placed in foster care. "From the age of four until his death," the authors of the Final Report note, "this Métis boy lived in twenty-eight different child welfare placements across Alberta, including sixteen foster homes and twelve group homes, shelters, and locked facilities."[57] Likewise, a woman who met with the Commission in Alberta spoke of the time that she spent in a foster home:

> In that foster home there was a pedophile, and I don't [know] what was happening to anybody else, but I became his target. The mother used to always send me to do errands with him. And so every time, he would make me do things to him and then he would give me candy. Also, in that home there was no hugging of us foster kids or anything like that. And I carried a great guilt for many, many years, because sometimes I didn't want to resist it, I just . . . .. But I knew it was very bad.[58]

The "intergenerational cycle of neglect and abuse" identified by the authors of the Final Report has also had an impact upon the health of Indigenous families. The Final Report details the legacy of years of malnutrition, substandard living conditions, and communicable disease experienced in residential schools. Its authors show that infant mortality rates are much higher in Indigenous communities than among non-Indigenous Canadians, and that life expectancy is shorter for both Indigenous women and men than for their non-Indigenous counterparts. Addiction and substance misuse linked to centuries of colonialism and racism have contributed to phenomena such as foetal alcohol spectrum disorder, mental illness, and high rates of HIV infection. Suicide rates are very high in Indigenous communities, particularly among Inuit youth. The average annual rate of tuberculosis is 290 times higher among Inuit than among Canadian-born non-Indigenous people, a situation that scientists who have studied the case of Nunavut attribute to overcrowded housing, food insecurity, and, especially, inadequate access to healthcare professionals.[59] One particular challenge has been obtaining health services for high-needs children on reserves, who were disadvantaged by the gap between the federal government, responsible for Indigenous peoples under the terms of the Indian Act, and provincial governments, responsible for health and social services. This service gap has led to some Indigenous children living with disabilities being placed in foster homes off reserve so as to have access to better medical services. The death in a Winnipeg hospital of Jordan Rivers Anderson, a Cree boy from Norway House, Manitoba, who spent all of his short life in the hospital while the federal and provincial governments disputed who should be responsible for paying for the medical care and equipment that would be needed were he to return to his family's home on the reserve, led to the adoption in 2007 of Jordan's Principle. The Principle states that, henceforth, the government initially in contact with the child must pay for the necessary medical care up front so that the patient can be treated, before settling accounts with the other level of government. However, this federal legislation has not yet been ratified by all of Canada's provincial and territorial governments.[60]

Many observers, both Indigenous and non-Indigenous, have called into the question the sincerity or the usefulness of recent federal government initiatives undertaken in the name of reconciliation. Although the federal government apologized in 2008 for the role that it played in residential schooling over the course of a century, Professor Cindy Blackstock, the executive director of the First Nations Child and Family Caring Society, points out that Ottawa has also spent considerable sums of money contesting attempts by Indigenous associations to secure better funding for health and welfare measures for Indigenous children. A case in point is the complaint filed by the Assembly of First Nations and the Caring Society before the Canadian Human Rights Commission in 2007, criticizing the federal government's under-funding of health and welfare measures for children living on reserves. In 2016, the Canadian Human Rights Tribunal ruled that Ottawa had in fact discriminated against children living on reserves. In 2019, after a dozen years of legal battles and significant federal government opposition, this legal victory resulted in a financial settlement to Indigenous children and, in some cases, their parents and grandparents.⁶¹ Little wonder, then, that many Indigenous activists favour Indigenous-led strategies over reliance on the goodwill of the Canadian state. Anishinaabe activist and scholar Leanne Betasamosake Simpson, for instance, argues that what she calls "trauma-based mobilizations" directed by the state, such as the Truth and Reconciliation Commission or the National Inquiry into Missing and Murdered Indigenous Women and Girls (MMIWG), are not the best way forward. In order to achieve Indigenous freedom, she insists, what is needed are actions "initiated by Indigenous peoples on Indigenous terms."⁶²

Writing of Indigenous peoples in Canada, Simpson states, "Our presence is our weapon."⁶³ The extent to which the Indigenous population is in fact increasing, both on and off the reserve, is striking: Canada's Indigenous population has grown by 42.5 per cent since 2006. Furthermore, this population is younger than the country's non-Indigenous population: in 2016, the average age of an Indigenous person in Canada was 32.1 years, while the average age of a non-Indigenous person was 40.9 years. Almost one third of the Indigenous population is under the age of 15. These two demographic trends (population growth and the relative youth of this population) can be explained by relatively high fertility rates, by life expectancy that is longer than it was before (although still less than that of non-Indigenous Canadians), and by the increased tendency to self-identify in the census as Indigenous.⁶⁴

※ ※ ※

This book has covered a great deal of ground, from the Indigenous families who encountered, to varying degrees and at different rhythms, French explorers, missionaries, fur traders, and settlers in the sixteenth and seventeenth centuries, to the twenty-first-century Indigenous families who testified before the Truth and Reconciliation Commission of Canada. Despite the variety of periods, regions, and peoples explored in this historical synthesis, however, it is possible to draw some overarching conclusions.

The first is the extent to which the lives of all families are inextricably bound up with larger political processes, involving conquest, colonization, dispossession, settlement, and migration. This is true whether it is the impact of European colonization on Indigenous families, the impact of the British Conquest on *Canadien* families, or the impact of the two world wars and other international political and military events on families in Canada and families who, as a result of these conflicts, would decide to settle in Canada. In a sense, then, the family is one fascinating lens through which to view the historical evolution of the political entity that has come to be known as Canada and the various nations that coexist within this federal state.

The second conclusion, which holds true as much for the twenty-first century as for seventeenth-century New France, is the fact that historians must always attempt to peer into families and to examine the inner workings of these formations, which were very rarely entirely unified or homogeneous. It is essential to recognize, and to study, the differing interests and objectives of parents and children respectively, of girls and boys respectively, and of the respective spouses. Gender and age are crucial categories of analysis. Families in the past were sites of conflict at least as often as they were sites of harmony and goodwill. Families could, and did, provide love and protection. But they were also sites of abuses of power and, sometimes, of physical violence. Members of families, in the past as in the present, might have had the best of intentions, but they were not always free or able to carry them out.

The third conclusion has to do with the diversity of families in Canada, beginning long before European settlement in North America. A study of families in Canada must take into account differences of nation, political organization, ethnic and racial background, religion, language, region, wealth, and, from the mid-nineteenth century onward, social class. Studies of families must also examine the difference made by legal status, a more and more determinate factor by the twenty-first century, as the experiences of citizens, immigrants, and refugee families can vary widely. Families can take a variety of shapes. If so-called nuclear families, made up of a man, a woman, and their biological children living together, have been, for most of Canada's history, the predominant family form, nuclear or conjugal families have coexisted with extended or multigenerational families, with households that included non-family members, such as servants or boarders, with same-sex parents, with childless couples, and with couples or single persons with adopted children. Indeed, there is no single or simple answer to the question "What makes a family, today, in Canada?" Is family the networks of kinfolk and close friends that some scholars call "chosen families"—the people that one cares *for* and *about*?[65] Or is it the individuals, in Canada or in far-away countries or continents, with whom one shares ties of biology or history? Or is it simply those who "have to take you in," to quote American poet Robert Frost's definition of "home"?[66] The distinction made by cultural theorist Stuart Hall between "roots" and "routes" is important here. Hall argued in the 1990s, "Instead of asking what are people's roots, we ought to think about what are their routes, the different points by which they have come to be now;

they are, in a sense, the sum of those differences."[67] Both roots and routes are part of family history.

The final conclusion is that of families' historical agency. Families were in constant interaction with other institutions, and sometimes with institutions more powerful than them: churches, notably Catholic and Protestant, the various levels and components of the state, schools, the labour market, the hospital, or the asylum. These institutions helped to shape families. Sometimes they were a source of assistance to families; sometimes they exerted control over families and their members. Families could also use these institutions, and not always in ways that the institutions themselves intended. Sometimes families relied upon them. And sometimes they lobbied, petitioned, or demonstrated in public in order to transform these institutions. Those families who have worked for change—or those individuals who have worked for change in the name of the family—have benefited from the fact that "the family," as a concept, has almost always had good press. For centuries now, "family" has been a powerful rallying-cry and a useful tool in campaigns for new or better rights. Indeed, it is difficult to argue against the needs and interests of families—even if neither the definition nor the lived experiences of families have been fixed or constant.

Notes

INTRODUCTION

1. Bettina Bradbury, *Working Families: Age, Gender, and Daily Survival in Industrializing Montreal* (Toronto: McClelland & Stewart, 1993).
2. Kristin Burnett with Geoff Read, "Introduction: Indigenous Histories," in *Aboriginal History: A Reader*, 2nd edition, ed. Kristin Burnett and Geoff Read (Don Mills: Oxford University Press Canada, 2016), p. xix.
3. Statistics Canada, Dictionary, Census of Population, 2016, "Census family." Consulted on-line at https://www12.statcan.gc.ca/census-recensement/2016/ref/dict/fam004-eng.cfm
4. Peter Laslett, *The World We Have Lost* (New York: Scribner, 1965). Michael Katz, for instance, used census and other data in order to study social structure and family structure in Canada West, now Ontario. Michael Katz, *The People of Hamilton, Canada West: Family and Class in a Mid-Nineteenth-Century City* (Cambridge: Harvard University Press, 1975). See also Bettina Bradbury, *Working Families: Age, Gender, and Daily Survival in Industrializing Montreal* (Toronto: McClelland & Stewart, 1993); Danielle Gauvreau, "À propos de la mise en nourrice à Québec pendant le régime français," *Revue d'histoire de l'Amérique française*, XLI, 1 (été 1987): 53–62; Lisa Dillon, *The Shady Side of Fifty: Age and Old Age in Late Victorian Canada and the United States* (Montreal: McGill-Queen's University Press, 2008).
5. Hubert Charbonneau, *Vie et mort de nos ancêtres—Étude démographique* (Montréal: Les Presses de l'Université de Montréal, 1975). Such population reconstitutions have more recent equivalents in the work of Gérard Bouchard and his team, who studied population characteristics in Quebec's Saguenay region over long periods of time. Gérard Bouchard, *Quelques arpents d'Amérique: population, économie, famille au Saguenay, 1838–1971* (Montréal: Boréal, 1996).

6. On this last question, see Élisabeth Badinter, *L'amour en plus: histoire de l'amour maternel (XVIIe–XXe siècle)* (Paris: Flammarion, 1980). British historian Lawrence Stone's pioneering work on the family, which drew on quantitative analysis but also involved extensive inquiry into family sentiments, has been the object of some criticism, but it has nonetheless inspired studies of Canadian families such as Peter Ward's *Courtship, Love, and Marriage*. Lawrence Stone, *The Family, Sex, and Marriage in England, 1500–1800* (New York: Harper and Row, 1977); Stone, *Road to Divorce: England 1530–1987* (Oxford: Oxford University Press, 1990); Stone, *Uncertain Unions: Marriage in England, 1660–1753* (Oxford: Oxford University Press, 1992); Stone, *Broken Lives: Separation and Divorce in England, 1660–1857* (Oxford: Oxford University Press, 1993); Peter Ward, *Courtship, Love and Marriage in Nineteenth-Century English Canada* (Montreal and Kingston: McGill-Queen's University Press, 1990).
7. Ivy Pinchbeck, *Women Workers and the Industrial Revolution 1750–1850* (London: Routledge, 1930); Ellen Ross, *Love and Toil: Motherhood in Outcast London, 1870–1918* (New York: Oxford University Press, 1993).
8. Canadian studies include Bettina Bradbury's *Working Families* and Peter Gossage's *Families in Transition: Industry and Population in Nineteenth-Century Saint-Hyacinthe* (Montreal and Kingston: McGill-Queen's University Press, 1999).
9. Bruno Ramirez, *On the Move: French-Canadian and Italian Migrants in the North Atlantic Economy, 1860–1914* (Toronto: McClelland & Stewart, 1991); Franca Iacovetta, *Such Hardworking People: Italian Immigrants in Postwar Toronto* (Montreal and Kingston: McGill-Queen's University Press, 1992); Franca Iacovetta, *Gatekeepers: Reshaping Immigrant Lives in Cold War Canada* (Toronto: Between the Lines, 2006); Elizabeth Jane Errington, *Emigrant Worlds and Transatlantic Communities: Migration to Upper Canada in the First Half of the Nineteenth Century* (Montreal and Kingston: McGill-Queen's University Press, 2007); Sonia Cancian, *Families, Lovers, and Their Letters: Italian Postwar Migration to Canada* (Winnipeg: University of Manitoba Press, 2010).
10. Oscar Handlin, *The Uprooted: The Epic Story of the Great Migrations that Made the American People* (Boston: Little, Brown, 1951); John Bodnar, *The Transplanted: A History of Immigrants in Urban America* (Bloomington: Indiana University Press, 1985).
11. Magda Fahrni and Yves Frenette, "'Don't I long for Montréal': l'identité hybride d'une jeune migrante franco-americaine pendant la Première Guerre mondiale," *Histoire sociale/Social History*, XLI, 81 (mai 2008): 75–98.
12. France Gagnon, "Parenté et migration: le cas des Canadiens français à Montréal entre 1845 et 1875," *Historical Papers/Communications historiques*, Volume 23, numéro 1, 1988, pp. 63–85; Anthony B. Chan, *Gold Mountain: the Chinese in the New World* (Vancouver: New Star Books, 1983); Iacovetta, *Such Hardworking People*.

13. Gagnon, "Parenté et migration."
14. See Bruno Ramirez's discussion of market gardens among the first Italians to settle in Montreal. Bruno Ramirez, *Les premiers Italiens de Montréal: l'origine de la Petite Italie du Québec* (Montréal: Boréal Express, 1984).
15. Royden Loewen, *Village among Nations: "Canadian" Mennonites in a Transnational World* (Toronto: University of Toronto Press, 2013); Charmaine Crawford, "Sending Love in a Barrel: The Making of Transnational Families in Canada," *Canadian Woman Studies*, 22, 3-4 (2003): 104-9.
16. Katherine Arnup, *Education for Motherhood: Advice for Mothers in Twentieth-Century Canada* (Toronto: University of Toronto Press, 1994); Cynthia R. Comacchio, *Nations Are Built of Babies: Saving Ontario's Mothers and Children 1900-1940* (Montreal and Kingston: McGill-Queen's University Press, 1993); Denyse Baillargeon, *Un Québec en mal d'enfants. La médicalisation de la maternité 1910-1970* (Montréal: Éditions du remue-ménage, 2004); Veronica Strong-Boag, *The New Day Recalled: Lives of Girls and Women in English Canada, 1919-1939* (Toronto: Copp Clark Pitman, 1988).
17. Lara Campbell, *Respectable Citizens: Gender, Family, and Unemployment in Ontario's Great Depression* (Toronto: University of Toronto Press, 2009); Christopher Dummitt, "Finding a Place for Father: Selling the Barbecue in Postwar Canada," *Journal of the Canadian Historical Association*, Volume 9, Number 1 (1998), pp. 209-23; Robert Rutherdale, "New 'Faces' for Fathers: Memory, Life-Writing, and Fathers as Providers in the Postwar Consumer Era," in Magda Fahrni and Robert Rutherdale, eds., *Creating Postwar Canada: Community, Diversity, and Dissent* (Vancouver: University of British Columbia Press, 2008); Vincent Duhaime, "'Les pères ont ici leur devoir': le discours du mouvement familial québécois et la construction de la paternité dans l'après-guerre, 1945-1960," *Revue d'histoire de l'Amérique française*, 57, 4 (printemps 2004): 535-66; Magda Fahrni, *Household Politics: Montreal Families and Postwar Reconstruction* (Toronto: University of Toronto Press, 2005), esp. Chapter 6, "In the Streets: Fatherhood and Public Protest"; Peter Gossage, "On Dads and Damages: Looking for the 'Priceless Child' and the 'Manly Modern' in Quebec's Civil Courts, 1921-1960," *Histoire sociale/Social History*, 49, 100 (November 2016): 603-23.
18. Joy Parr, *Labouring Children: British Immigrant Apprentices to Canada* (Toronto: University of Toronto Press, 1980); Patricia Rooke and R.L. Schnell, *Discarding the Asylum: From Child Rescue to the Welfare State in English Canada* (Lanham, MD: University Press of America, 1983); Sylvie Ménard, *Des enfants sous surveillance. La rééducation des jeunes délinquants au Québec (1840-1950)* (Montréal, VLB Éditeur, 2003); Tamara Myers, *Caught: Montreal's Modern Girls and the Law, 1869-1945* (Toronto: University of Toronto Press, 2006); Mona Gleason, *Small Matters: Canadian Children in Sickness and Health, 1900-1940* (Montreal and Kingston: McGill-Queen's University Press, 2013), especially Chapter 5; Carmen J. Neilson, *Private Women and the Public Good:*

Charity and State Formation in Hamilton, Ontario, 1846–93 (Vancouver: UBC Press, 2014), Chapter 6; Veronica Strong-Boag, *Finding Families, Finding Ourselves: English Canada Encounters Adoption from the Nineteenth Century to the 1990s* (Don Mills: Oxford University Press, 2006); Veronica Strong-Boag, *Fostering Nation? Canada Confronts Its History of Childhood Disadvantage* (Waterloo: Wilfrid Laurier University Press, 2011), especially Chapter 2.

19. Neil Sutherland, *Growing Up: Childhood in English Canada from the Great War to the Age of Television* (Toronto: University of Toronto Press, 1997); Louise Bienvenue, *Quand la jeunesse entre en scène* (Montréal: Boréal, 2003); Sharon Wall, *The Nurture of Nature: Childhood, Antimodernism, and Ontario Summer Camps, 1920–55* (Vancouver: University of British Columbia Press, 2009); Kristine Alexander, *Guiding Modern Girls: Girlhood, Empire, and Internationalism in the 1920s and 1930s* (Vancouver: UBC Press, 2017).

20. Strong-Boag, *The New Day Recalled*; Mary Louise Adams, *The Trouble with Normal: Postwar Youth and the Making of Heterosexuality* (Toronto: University of Toronto Press, 1997); Mark Moss, *Manliness and Militarism: Educating Young Boys in Ontario for War* (Don Mills: Oxford University Press, 2001).

21. Katrina Srigley, "Clothing Stories: Consumption, Identity, and Desire in Depression-era Toronto," *Journal of Women's History* 19, 1: 82–104; Jenny Ellison, "Let Me Hear Your Body Talk: Aerobics for Fat Women Only, 1981–1985," pp. 205–26, in Cheryl Krasnick Warsh, ed., *Gender, Health and Popular Culture: Historical Perspectives* (Waterloo: Wilfred Laurier University Press, 2011).

22. Tamara Myers, *Caught: Montreal's Modern Girls and the Law, 1869–1945* (Toronto: University of Toronto Press, 2006); Christine Hudon, "L'éducation sentimentale et sexuelle dans les collèges pour garçons, du milieu du XIXe siècle à la Révolution tranquille," in Jean-Philippe Warren, ed., *Une histoire de la sexualité au Québec au XXe siècle* (Montréal: VLB Éditeur, 2012), pp. 32–53; Louise Bienvenue et Christine Hudon, "Les prêtres, les parents et la sexualité des collégiens dans les années 1940," in V. Blanchard, R. Revenin and J.-J. Yvorel, eds., *Les jeunes et la sexualité* (Paris: Éditions Autrement, 2010), pp. 99–107.

23. Sandra Rollings-Magnusson, *Heavy Burdens on Small Shoulders: The Labour of Pioneer Children on the Canadian Prairies* (Edmonton: University of Alberta Press, 2009); Dominique Marshall, *Aux origines sociales de l'État-providence. Familles québécoises, obligation scolaire et allocations familiales, 1940–1955* (Montréal: Presses de l'Université de Montréal, 1998).

24. Viviana A. Zelizer, *Pricing the Priceless Child: The Changing Social Value of Children* (Princeton: Princeton University Press, 1994); Magda Fahrni, "Glimpsing Working-Class Childhood through the Laurier Palace Fire of 1927: The Ordinary, the Tragic, and the Historian's Gaze," *Journal of the History of Childhood and Youth*, 8, 3 (Fall 2015): 426–50.

25. Cynthia Comacchio, *The Dominion of Youth: Adolescence and the Making of a Modern Canada, 1920–1950* (Waterloo: Wilfrid Laurier University Press,

2006); Jacinthe Archambault, "'Pour la personne la plus précieuse de votre vie': représentation des enfants dans la publicité et construction d'une norme sociale concernant la famille et l'enfance à Montréal (1944-1954)," *Revue d'histoire de l'Amérique française* 65, 1 (2011): 5-27; Jason Reid, *Get Out of My Room! A History of Teen Bedrooms in America* (Chicago: University of Chicago Press, 2016).

26. Kathryn Harvey, "Amazons and Victims: Resisting Wife-Abuse in Working-Class Montréal, 1869-1879," *Journal of the Canadian Historical Association*, Volume 2, Number 1 (1991): 131-48; Marie-Aimée Cliche, "Du péché au traumatisme: l'inceste, vu de la Cour des jeunes délinquants et de la Cour du bien-être social de Montréal, 1912-1965," *Canadian Historical Review*, 87, 2 (June 2006): 199-222; Marie-Aimée Cliche, *Maltraiter ou punir? La violence envers les enfants dans les familles québécoises 1850-1969* (Montréal: Boréal, 2007).

27. Hélène Guay, "Abus et maltraitance envers les aînés: quel est l'apport du droit?", *Revue du Barreau*, 73 (2014): 263-317.

28. James G. Snell, *The Citizen's Wage: The State and the Elderly in Canada, 1900-1951* (Toronto: University of Toronto Press, 1996); Aline Charles, *Quand devient-on vieille? Femmes, âge et travail au Québec, 1940-1980* (Québec: Presses de l'Université Laval, 2007); Lisa Dillon, *The Shady Side of Fifty: Age and Old Age in Late Victorian Canada and the United States* (Montreal and Kingston: McGill-Queen's University Press, 2008); Bettina Bradbury, *Wife to Widow: Lives, Laws, and Politics in Nineteenth-Century Montreal* (Vancouver: University of British Columbia Press, 2011).

29. Heidi MacDonald, "Singleness and Choice: The Impact of Age, Time, and Class on Three Female Youth Diarists in 1930s Canada," in Catherine Carstairs and Nancy Janovicek, eds., *Feminist History in Canada: New Essays on Women, Gender, Work, and Nation* (Vancouver: University of British Columbia Press, 2013).

30. James Struthers, "'A Nice Homelike Atmosphere': State Alternatives to Family Care for the Aged in Post–World War II Ontario," pp. 335-54, in Lori Chambers and Edgar-André Montigny, eds., *Family Matters: Papers in Post-Confederation Canadian Family History* (Toronto: Canadian Scholars Press, 1998); Megan J. Davies, *Into the House of Old: A History of Residential Care in British Columbia* (Montreal and Kingston: McGill-Queen's University Press, 2003).

31. Aline Charles, "Femmes âgées, pauvres et sans droit de vote, mais . . . citoyennes? Lettres au premier ministre du Québec, 1935-1936," *Recherches féministes*, 26, 2 (2013): 51-70.

32. Dominique Marshall, *Aux origines sociales de l'État-providence. Familles québécoises, obligation scolaire et allocations familiales, 1940-1955* (Montréal: Presses de l'Université de Montréal, 1998); Nancy Christie, *Engendering the State: Family, Work, and Welfare in Canada* (Toronto: University of Toronto Press, 2000); Fahrni, *Household Politics*.

33. Thérèse Hamel, "Obligation scolaire et travail des enfants au Québec: 1900–1950," *Revue d'histoire de l'Amérique française*, 38, 1 (1984): 39–58; Marshall, *Aux origines sociales de l'État-providence*; Jacques Paul Couturier and Wendy Johnston, "L'État, les familles et l'obligation scolaire au Nouveau-Brunswick dans les années 1940," *Histoire sociale/Social History*, 35, 69 (2002): 1–34.
34. Cynthia S. Fish, "La puissance paternelle et les cas de garde d'enfants au Québec, 1866–1928," *Revue d'histoire de l'Amérique française*, 57, 4 (printemps 2004): 509–33.
35. Cynthia Comacchio, *Nations Are Built of Babies*; Baillargeon, *Un Québec en mal d'enfants*; Mona Gleason, *Normalizing the Ideal: Psychology, Schooling, and the Family in Postwar Canada* (Toronto: University of Toronto Press, 1999); Tamara Myers, *Caught: Montreal's Modern Girls and the Law, 1869–1945* (Toronto: University of Toronto Press, 2006).
36. For a useful discussion of these terms and categories, see Chelsea Vowel, *Indigenous Writes: A Guide to First Nations, Métis and Inuit Issues in Canada* (Winnipeg: HighWater Press, 2016), Chapter 1.
37. For instance, Carolyn Podruchny and Kathryn Magee Labelle, "Jean de Brébeuf and the Wendat Voices of Seventeenth-Century New France," *Renaissance and Reformation/Renaissance et Réforme*, 34, 1–2 (Winter-Spring 2011): 97–126; Roland Viau, *Femmes de personne. Sexes, genres et pouvoirs en Iroquoisie ancienne* (Montreal: Boréal, 2005). Older work on Innu women's reactions to the Jesuit presence in New France includes Eleanor Burke Leacock, "Montagnais Women and the Jesuit Program for Colonization," in Leacock, *Myths of Male Dominance: Collected Articles on Women Cross-Culturally* (Chicago: Haymarket Books, 2008 [1981]), pp. 43–62.
38. Jean Barman, "Separate and Unequal: Indian and White Girls at All Hallows School, 1884–1920," pp. 215–33, in Veronica Strong-Boag and Anita Clair Fellman, eds., *Rethinking Canada: The Promise of Women's History*, 2nd edition (Toronto: Copp Clark Pitman, 1991); John S. Milloy, *A National Crime: The Canadian Government and the Residential School System, 1879 to 1986*, 2nd edition (Winnipeg: University of Manitoba Press, 2017).
39. Sarah Carter, *Lost Harvests: Prairie Indian Reserve Farmers and Government Policy* (Montreal and Kingston: McGill-Queen's University Press, 1990); Sarah Carter, *The Importance of Being Monogamous: Marriage and Nation Building in Western Canada to 1915* (Edmonton: University of Alberta Press, 2008); Sarah Carter, *Imperial Plots: Women, Land, and the Spadework of British Colonialism on the Canadian Prairies* (Winnipeg: University of Manitoba Press, 2016); Elizabeth Elbourne, "Broken Alliance: Debating Six Nations' Land Claims in 1822," *Cultural and Social History*, 9, 4 (2012): 497–525.
40. Early work includes Sylvia Van Kirk, *Many Tender Ties: Women in Fur-Trade Society in Western Canada, 1670–1870* (Winnipeg: Watson & Dwyer, 1980); Jennifer S.H. Brown, *Strangers in Blood: Fur Trade Company Families in Indian*

Country (Vancouver: University of British Columbia Press, 1980); Jacqueline Peterson and Jennifer S.H. Brown, eds., *The New Peoples: Being and Becoming Métis in North America* (Winnipeg: University of Manitoba Press, 1985).

41. Heather Devine, *The People Who Own Themselves: Aboriginal Ethnogenesis in a Canadian Family, 1660–1900* (Calgary: University of Calgary Press, 2004); Brenda Macdougall, *One of the Family: Metis Culture in Nineteenth-Century Northwestern Saskatchewan* (Vancouver: University of British Columbia Press, 2010); Chris Andersen, *"Métis": Race, Recognition, and the Struggle for Indigenous Peoplehood* (Vancouver: UBC Press, 2014); Adam Gaudry, "Respecting Métis Nationhood and Self-Determination in Matters of Métis Identity," pp. 152–63, in *Aboriginal History: A Reader*, 2nd edition, ed. Kristin Burnett and Geoff Read (Don Mills: Oxford University Press Canada, 2016); Brenda Macdougall, "The Myth of Metis Cultural Ambivalence," p. 435, in Nicole St-Onge, Carolyn Podruchny, and Brenda Macdougall, eds., *Contours of a People: Metis Family, Mobility and History* (Norman: University of Oklahoma Press, 2012).

42. Harriet Gorham, "Families of Mixed Descent in the Western Great Lakes Region," pp. 37–55, in *Native People, Native Lands: Canadian Indians, Inuit and Metis*, ed. Bruce Alden Cox (Montreal and Kingston: McGill-Queen's University Press, 2002); Gilles Havard, *Empire et métissages. Indiens et Français dans le Pays d'en Haut, 1660–1715* (Paris: Presses de l'Université Paris-Sorbonne; Sillery: Septentrion, 2003), Chapter 10, "Sexualité et intermariage: le pays du métissage," pp. 625–80; Jacqueline Peterson, "Red River Redux: Métis Ethnogenesis and the Great Lakes Region," pp. 22–58, in Nicole St-Onge, Carolyn Podruchny, and Brenda Macdougall, eds., *Contours of a People: Metis Family, Mobility and History* (Norman: University of Oklahoma Press, 2012).

43. Karen Dubinsky, *Babies Without Borders: Adoption and Migration across the Americas* (Toronto: University of Toronto Press, 2010), pp. 79–92; Veronica Strong-Boag, *Finding Families, Finding Ourselves: English Canada Encounters Adoption from the Nineteenth Century to the 1990s* (Don Mills: Oxford University Press, 2006); Christine Smith (McFarlane), "A Legacy of Canadian Child Care: Surviving the Sixties Scoop," pp. 209–12, in *Aboriginal History: A Reader*, 2nd edition, ed. Kristin Burnett and Geoff Read (Don Mills: Oxford University Press, 2016); Chelsea Vowel, *Indigenous Writes: A Guide to First Nations, Métis and Inuit Issues in Canada* (Winnipeg: HighWater Press, 2016), Chapter 21. Vowel prefers the terms "stolen generations" or "lost generations" to "Sixties Scoop," as the adoption of First Nations and Métis children by non-Indigenous families continued well beyond the 1960s.

44. Truth and Reconciliation Commission of Canada, *The Final Report of the Truth and Reconciliation Commission of Canada*, Volume 5, *Canada's Residential Schools: The Legacy* (Montreal and Kingston: McGill-Queen's University Press, 2015); Phil Fontaine, Aimée Craft, and the Truth and Reconciliation Commission of Canada, *A Knock on the Door: The Essential History of Residential Schools*

from the Truth and Reconciliation Commission of Canada (Winnipeg: University of Manitoba Press, 2015).

45. Veronica Strong-Boag, *Fostering Nation? Canada Confronts Its History of Childhood Disadvantage* (Waterloo: Wilfrid Laurier University Press, 2011); Chelsea Vowel, *Indigenous Writes: A Guide to First Nations, Métis and Inuit Issues in Canada* (Winnipeg: HighWater Press, 2016), pp. 184–7.

46. Karen Dubinsky, *The Second Greatest Disappointment: Honeymooning and Tourism at Niagara Falls* (New Brunswick, New Jersey: Rutgers University Press, 1999); Elise Chenier, *Strangers in our Midst: Sexual Deviancy in Postwar Ontario* (Toronto: University of Toronto Press, 2008).

47. Mary Louise Adams, *The Trouble with Normal: Postwar Youth and the Making of Heterosexuality* (Toronto: University of Toronto Press, 1997).

48. Line Chamberland, *Mémoires lesbiennes. Le lesbianisme à Montréal entre 1950 et 1972* (Montréal: Éditions du remue-ménage, 1996); Steven Maynard, "'Horrible temptations': Sex, Men, and Working-Class Male Youth in Urban Ontario, 1890–1935," *Canadian Historical Review*, 78 (June 1997): 191–235; Elise Chenier, "Rethinking Class in Lesbian Bar Culture: Living 'The Gay Life' in Toronto, 1955–1965," *Left History*, 9, 2 (2004): 85–118; Cameron Duder, *Awfully Devoted Women: Lesbian Lives in Canada, 1900–65* (Vancouver: University of British Columbia Press, 2010); Valerie J. Korinek, *Prairie Fairies: A History of Queer Communities and People in Western Canada, 1930–1985* (Toronto: University of Toronto Press, 2018); Dominic Dagenais, *Grossières indécences. Pratiques et identités homosexuelles à Montréal, 1880–1929* (Montreal and Kingston: McGill-Queen's University Press, 2020); Wesley Thomas and Sue-Ellen Jacobs, "'…And We Are Still Here': From *Berdache* to Two-Spirit People," *American Indian Culture and Research Journal*, 23, 2 (1999): 91–107.

49. Kath Weston, *Families We Choose: Lesbians, Gays, Kinship* (New York: Columbia University Press, 1991); Heather Murray, *Not in this Family: Gays and the Meaning of Kinship in Postwar North America* (Philadelphia: University of Pennsylvania Press, 2010).

50. Elise Chenier, "Love-Politics: Lesbian Wedding Practices in Canada and the United States from the 1920s to the 1970s," *Journal of the History of Sexuality* 27, 2 (2018), p. 302; George Chauncey, *Why Marriage? The History Shaping Today's Debate over Gay Equality* (New York: Basic Books, 2004).

51. Lisa Dillon, *The Shady Side of Fifty: Age and Old Age in Late Victorian Canada and the United States* (Montreal and Kingston: McGill-Queen's University Press, 2008).

52. I think here of critical histories of empire such as the transnational family of James Douglas and Amelia Connolly, studied by Adele Perry, and the British families who settled in British Columbia at the turn of the twentieth century, examined by Laura Ishiguro, who wrote frequently to extended family in the United Kingdom and whose descriptions of daily domestic life created what

Laura Ishiguro calls a "trans-imperial family form of colonial knowledge." Adele Perry, "James Douglas, Amelia Connolly, and the Writing of Gender and Women's History," in Catherine Carstairs and Nancy Janovicek (eds.), *Feminist History in Canada: New Essays on Women, Gender, Work, and Nation* (Vancouver: University of British Columbia Press, 2013), pp. 23–40; Laura Ishiguro, "'A Dreadful Little Glutton Always Telling You About Food': The Epistolary Everyday and the Making of Settler Colonial British Columbia," *Canadian Historical Review*, 99, 2 (June 2018): 258–83.

53. Veronica Strong-Boag uses the term "first families" to describe birth families. Strong-Boag, *Finding Families, Finding Ourselves: English Canada Encounters Adoption from the Nineteenth Century to the 1990s* (Don Mills: Oxford University Press, 2006); Strong-Boag, *Fostering Nation? Canada Confronts Its History of Childhood Disadvantage* (Waterloo: Wilfrid Laurier University Press, 2011).

54. Karen Dubinsky, *Babies without Borders: Adoption and Migration Across the Americas* (Toronto: University of Toronto Press, 2010); Karen Balcom, *The Traffic in Babies: Cross-Border Adoption and Baby-Selling between the United States and Canada, 1930–1972* (Toronto: University of Toronto Press, 2011).

55. Cynthia Comacchio, *The Infinite Bonds of Family: Domesticity in Canada, 1850–1940* (Toronto: University of Toronto Press, 1999), p. 4.

56. Sherry Olson's and Patricia Thornton's recent *Peopling the North American City: Montreal, 1840–1900*, for example, doesn't mention families in the title, but within its over 500 pages it deals with topics central to family history, such as the formation of couples and the founding of households, the nature of marriages, and rates of infant mortality. Sherry Olson and Patricia Thornton, *Peopling the North American City: Montreal, 1840–1900* (Montreal and Kingston: McGill-Queen's University Press, 2011).

57. A sympathetic yet critical analysis of the practice of genealogy is to be found in Caroline-Isabelle Caron, *Se créer des ancêtres. Un parcours généalogique nord-américain XIXe-XXe siècles* (Sillery: Septentrion, 2006). On the usefulness of genealogy for academic historians, see Tanya Evans, "Secrets and Lies: The Radical Potential of Family History," *History Workshop Journal*, 71, 1 (2011): 49–73.

58. In addition to the work of Sherry Olson and Patricia Thornton, mentioned earlier, we might think of Bettina Bradbury who, in her book *Wife to Widow*, undertakes "collective genealogies." Bradbury, *Wife to Widow*, p. 5. Other examples include the painstaking work carried out by Heather Devine and Brenda Macdougall, both of whom have used the tools of genealogists in order to reconstruct Métis histories on the northern Plains. Devine, *The People Who Own Themselves*; Macdougall, *One of the Family*.

59. We thus know about the diaries of William Lyon Mackenzie King, Elizabeth Smith, Lucy Maud Montgomery, Henriette Dessaulles, Joséphine Marchand, Lucy Peel, and Alice Chown, to take only a few well-known examples. See, e.g., Veronica Strong-Boag, ed., *"A woman with a purpose": The Diaries of Elizabeth*

Smith 1872–1884 (Toronto: University of Toronto Press, 1980); J.I. Little, ed., *Love Strong as Death: Lucy Peel's Canadian Journal, 1833–1836* (Waterloo: Wilfrid Laurier University Press, 2001).

60. For example, Vera K. Fast, ed., *Companions of the Peace: Diaries and Letters of Monica Storrs, 1931–1939* (Toronto: University of Toronto Press, 1999); Susan Jackel, *A Flannel Shirt and Liberty: British Emigrant Gentlewomen in the Canadian West, 1880–1914* (Vancouver: University of British Columbia Press, 1982).

61. See Gail G. Campbell, "Using Diaries to Explore the Shared Worlds of Family and Community in Nineteenth-Century New Brunswick," in *Feminist History in Canada: New Essays on Women, Gender, Work, and Nation*, ed. Catherine Carstairs and Nancy Janovicek (Vancouver: University of British Columbia Press, 2013); Gail G. Campbell, *"I wish to keep a record": Nineteenth-Century New Brunswick Women Diarists and Their World* (Toronto: University of Toronto Press, 2017).

62. Françoise Noel, *Family Life and Sociability in Upper and Lower Canada, 1780–1870: A View from Diaries and Family Correspondence* (Montreal and Kingston: McGill-Queen's University Press, 2003); Jean Barman, *Sojourning Sisters: the Lives and Letters of Jessie and Annie McQueen* (Toronto: University of Toronto Press, 2003); Cancian, *Families, Lovers, and Their Letters*; Elizabeth Jane Errington, *Emigrant Worlds and Transatlantic Communities: Migration to Upper Canada in the First Half of the Nineteenth Century* (Montreal and Kingston: McGill-Queen's University Press, 2007); Magda Fahrni and Yves Frenette, "'Don't I long for Montréal': l'identité hybride d'une jeune migrante franco-américaine pendant la Première Guerre mondiale," *Histoire sociale/Social History*, XLI, 81 (May 2008): 75–98.

63. For example, Thérèse Casgrain, *Une femme chez les hommes* (Montréal: Éditions du Jour, 1971).

64. Sylvie Dépatie, "La transmission du patrimoine au Canada (XVIIe-XVIIIe siècle): qui sont les défavorisés?", *Revue d'histoire de l'Amérique française*, 54, 4 (Spring 2001): 558–70; Thierry Nootens, *Fous, prodigues et ivrognes: familles et déviance à Montréal au XIXe siècle* (Montreal and Kingston: McGill-Queen's University Press, 2007); Bradbury, *Wife to Widow*; Thierry Nootens, *Genre, patrimoine et droit civil. Les femmes mariées de la bourgeoisie québécoise en procès, 1900–1930* (Montreal and Kingston: McGill-Queen's University Press, 2019).

65. Marshall, *Aux origines sociales de l'État-providence*.

66. Adèle Clapperton-Richard, "Reconnue, altérisée, occultée: l'agentivité des figures historiques dans les manuels québécois d'histoire nationale, 1954–1980" (Mémoire de maîtrise, Université du Québec à Montréal, 2020).

67. Annmarie Adams and Peter Gossage, "Chez Fadette: Girlhood, Family, and Private Space in Late-Nineteenth-Century Saint-Hyacinthe," *Urban History Review/Revue d'histoire urbaine*, 26, 2 (March 1998): 56–68; Sherry Farrell

Racette, "Looking for Stories and Unbroken Threads: Museum Artifacts as Women's History and Cultural Legacy," pp. 283–312, in *Restoring the Balance: First Nations Women, Community, and Culture*, ed. Gail Guthrie Valaskakis, Madeleine Dion Stout, and Eric Guimond, eds. (Winnipeg: University of Manitoba Press, 2009).

68. Sutherland, *Growing Up*; Gleason, *Small Matters*; Stacey Zembrzycki, "'There Were Always Men in Our House': Gender and the Childhood Memories of Working-Class Ukrainians in Depression-Era Canada," *Labour/Le Travail* 60 (Fall 2007): 77–105; Barbara Lorenzkowski, "The Children's War," in Steven High, ed., *Occupied St John's: A Social History of a City at War, 1939–1945* (Montreal and Kingston: McGill-Queen's University Press, 2010).

69. Denyse Baillargeon, *Ménagères au temps de la Crise* (Montréal: Les Éditions du Remue-ménage, 1993); Katrina Srigley, *Breadwinning Daughters: Young Working Women in a Depression-Era City, 1929–1939* (Toronto: University of Toronto Press, 2010).

70. Spyros Spyrou, "The Limits of Children's Voices: From Authenticity to Critical, Reflexive Representation," *Childhood*, 18, 2 (2011): 151–65. The methodological literature on oral history is abundant: see, e.g., Joan Sangster, "Telling our Stories: Feminist Debates and the Use of Oral History," *Women's History Review*, 3, 1 (1994): 5–28; Katrina Srigley, Stacey Zembrzycki, and Franca Iacovetta, eds., *Beyond Women's Words: Feminisms and the Practices of Oral History in the Twenty-First Century* (New York: Routledge, 2018).

71. See David Lowenthal, *The Past is a Foreign Country* (New York: Cambridge University Press, 1985); Jill Lepore, "Historians Who Love Too Much: Reflections on Microhistory and Biography," *The Journal of American History*, 88, 1 (June 2001): 129–44.

72. On sibling relations in Britain, see Leonore Davidoff, *Thicker Than Water: Siblings and their relations, 1780–1920* (Oxford: Oxford University Press, 2012). On grandparents in Canada and the United States, see Dillon, *The Shady Side of Fifty*, Chapter 6; on grandparents—and especially grandmothers—in Canada, see Veronica Strong-Boag, *Fostering Nation? Canada Confronts Its History of Childhood Disadvantage* (Waterloo: Wilfrid Laurier University Press, 2011), pp. 18, 21–5.

73. One of the few Canadian syntheses to have been published, Cynthia Comacchio's *The Infinite Bonds of Family*, is very useful for the period stretching from the Industrial Revolution until the beginning of the Second World War. Two good collections of articles in Canadian family history are Bettina Bradbury, ed., *Canadian Family History: Selected Readings* (Toronto: Copp Clark Pitman, 1992); and E.-A. Montigny and Lori Chambers, eds., *Family Matters: Papers in Post-Confederation Canadian Family History* (Toronto: Scholars Press, 1998).

CHAPTER 1

1. Jean-François Lozier, *Flesh Reborn: The Saint Lawrence Valley Mission Settlements through the Seventeenth Century* (Montreal; Kingston: McGill-Queen's University Press, 2018), p. 23.
2. Jean Barman, *The West Beyond the West: A History of British Columbia* (Toronto: University of Toronto Press, 1991), p. 13.
3. Michael Witgen, *An Infinity of Nations: How the Native New World Shaped Early North America* (Philadelphia: University of Pennsylvania Press, 2012), p. 17.
4. Susan M. Hill, *The Clay We Are Made Of: Haudenosaunee Land Tenure on the Grand River* (Winnipeg: University of Manitoba Press, 2017), pp. 84, 86–7.
5. Audra Simpson, *Mohawk Interruptus: Political Life Across the Borders of Settler States* (Durham: Duke University Press, 2014), p. 112.
6. Susan M. Hill, *The Clay We Are Made Of: Haudenosaunee Land Tenure on the Grand River* (Winnipeg: University of Manitoba Press, 2017), pp. 20, 37; Heidi Bohaker, "'Nindoodemag': The Significance of Algonquian Kinship Networks in the Eastern Great Lakes Region, 1600–1701," *The William and Mary Quarterly*, Third Series, 63, 1 (January 2006): 23–52.
7. Susan M. Hill, *The Clay We Are Made Of: Haudenosaunee Land Tenure on the Grand River* (Winnipeg: University of Manitoba Press, 2017), pp. 93, 110; Kathryn Magee Labelle, *Dispersed but Not Destroyed: A History of the Seventeenth-Century Wendat People* (Vancouver: UBC Press, 2013), p. 2.
8. Georges Sioui, "Why Canada Should Look for, Find, Recognize and Embrace its True, Aboriginal Roots. The Time of the Toad," p. 154, in *Histoires de Kanatha vues et contées. Essais et discours, 1991–2008/Histories of Kanatha Seen and Told. Essays and Discourses, 1991–2008* (Ottawa: University of Ottawa Press, 2008).
9. Michael Witgen, *An Infinity of Nations: How the Native New World Shaped Early North America* (Philadelphia: University of Pennsylvania Press, 2012), p. 89.
10. Georges Sioui insists upon the importance of captives acquired during warfare for the Wendat and Haudenosaunee peoples. Sioui, "1992: The Discovery of Americity," p. 24, and Sioui, "Canada's Past, Present and Future from a Native Canadian Perspective," p. 100, in *Histoires de Kanatha vues et contées. Essais et discours, 1991–2008/Histories of Kanatha Seen and Told. Essays and Discourses, 1991–2008* (Ottawa: University of Ottawa Press, 2008).
11. Susan M. Hill, *The Clay We Are Made Of: Haudenosaunee Land Tenure on the Grand River* (Winnipeg: University of Manitoba Press, 2017), pp. 3, 63, 66, 76, 91.
12. Peter E. Pope, *Fish into Wine: The Newfoundland Plantation in the Seventeenth Century* (Chapel Hill: University of North Carolina Press, 2004); Philip Girard, Jim Phillips, and R. Blake Brown, *A History of Law in Canada*, Vol. 1, *Beginnings to 1866* (Toronto: University of Toronto Press, 2018), p. 88.

13. Audra Simpson, *Mohawk Interruptus: Political Life Across the Borders of Settler States* (Durham: Duke University Press, 2014), pp. 39, 46–7; Jean-François Lozier, *Flesh Reborn: The Saint Lawrence Valley Mission Settlements through the Seventeenth Century* (Montreal; Kingston: McGill-Queen's University Press, 2018).
14. Susan M. Hill, *The Clay We Are Made Of: Haudenosaunee Land Tenure on the Grand River* (Winnipeg: University of Manitoba Press, 2017); Heidi Bohaker, "'Nindoodemag': The Significance of Algonquian Kinship Networks in the Eastern Great Lakes Region, 1600–1701," *The William and Mary Quarterly*, Third Series, 63, 1 (January 2006): 23–52.
15. H.P. Biggar, *The Voyages of Jacques Cartier, Published from the Originals with Translations, Notes and Appendices* (Ottawa, F.A. Acland, 1924), p. 56.
16. Michael Witgen, *An Infinity of Nations: How the Native New World Shaped Early North America* (Philadelphia: University of Pennsylvania Press, 2012), p. 45–6.
17. Biggar, *The Voyages of Jacques Cartier*, pp. 62–3.
18. Dominique Deslandres, *Croire et faire croire. Les missions françaises au XVIIe siècle* (Paris: Fayard, 2003).
19. Carolyn Podruchny and Kathryn Magee Labelle, "Jean de Brébeuf and the Wendat Voices of Seventeenth-Century New France," *Renaissance and Reformation*, 34, 1–2 (Winter–Spring 2011): 97–126.
20. Eleanor Burke Leacock, "Montagnais Women and the Jesuit Program for Colonization," in Leacock, *Myths of Male Dominance: Collected Articles on Women Cross-Culturally* (Chicago: Haymarket Books, 2008 [1981]), pp. 43–62.
21. Gabriel Sagard, *The Long Journey to the Country of the Hurons*, ed. George M. Wrong, trans. H.H. Langton (Toronto: The Champlain Society, 1939 [1632], reprinted by Greenwood Press, Publishers, New York, 1968), pp. 124–5.
22. Sagard, *The Long Journey to the Country of the Hurons*, p. 124.
23. Quoted in Leacock, "Montagnais Women and the Jesuit Program for Colonization," p. 49. French explorer Samuel de Champlain claimed that divorce existed among the seventeenth-century Algonquin (Anishinaabeg). Edward Gaylord Bourne, ed., *The Voyages and Explorations of Samuel de Champlain (1604–1616) Narrated by Himself*, trans. Annie Nettleton Bourne, *Volume 1* (Toronto: The Courier Press, 1911), p. 179.
24. Dominique Deslandres, *Croire et faire croire. Les missions françaises au XVIIe siècle* (Paris: Fayard, 2003), p. 366.
25. Allan Greer, *Mohawk Saint: Catherine Tekakwitha and the Jesuits* (New York: Oxford University Press, 2005).
26. Sagard, *The Long Journey to the Country of the Hurons*, pp. 127–31.
27. Quoted in Leacock, "Montagnais Women and the Jesuit Program for Colonization," p. 46.

28. Cornelius J. Jaenen, "Amerindian Views of French Culture in the Seventeenth Century," *Canadian Historical Review*, 55, 3 (1974), p. 286.
29. Georges Sioui, "Personal Reactions of Indigenous People to European Ideas and Behaviour," p. 65, in *Histoires de Kanatha vues et contées. Essais et discours, 1991–2008/Histories of Kanatha Seen and Told. Essays and Discourses, 1991–2008* (Ottawa: University of Ottawa Press, 2008).
30. Leacock, "Montagnais Women and the Jesuit Program for Colonization," pp. 46–7; Dominique Deslandres, *Croire et faire croire. Les missions françaises au XVIIe siècle* (Paris: Fayard, 2003), pp. 357, 364.
31. On the importance of food for these Indigenous pupils, see Dominique Deslandres, *Croire et faire croire. Les missions françaises au XVIIe siècle* (Paris: Fayard, 2003), p. 368. Ursuline Marie de l'Incarnation wrote in 1668 of turning away Anishinaabe (Algonquin) boarders because they did not have enough food for them. Joyce Marshall, ed. and trans., *Word from New France. The Selected Letters of Marie de l'Incarnation* (Toronto: Oxford University Press, 1967), p. 335. The red dresses are mentioned by Joyce Marshall in *Word from New France*, p. 23.
32. Marshall, *Word from New France*, p. 336.
33. Thwaites, *Jesuit Relations*, Volume XXII (1642), Chapter 8, "Of the Seminary of the Ursulines"; see also Dominique Deslandres, *Croire et faire croire. Les missions françaises au XVIIe siècle* (Paris: Fayard, 2003), pp. 364–5, 376; and Kathryn Magee Labelle, *Dispersed but Not Destroyed: A History of the Seventeenth-Century Wendat People* (Vancouver: UBC Press, 2013), pp. 165–8.
34. Marshall, *Word from New France*, p. 341.
35. Victoria Jackson, "Silent Diplomacy: Wendat Boys' 'Adoptions' at the Jesuit Seminary, 1636–1642," *Journal of the Canadian Historical Association*, 27, 1 (2016), p. 141.
36. For example, Bruce G. Trigger, *The Children of Aataentsic: A History of the Huron People to 1660* (Montreal: McGill-Queen's University Press, 1987).
37. Audra Simpson, *Mohawk Interruptus: Political Life Across the Borders of Settler States* (Durham: Duke University Press, 2014), p. 70.
38. Chelsea Vowel points out that linguistic groupings are vast categories that include peoples with quite different cultural practices. Vowel, *Indigenous Writes: A Guide to First Nations, Métis and Inuit Issues in Canada* (Winnipeg: Highwater Press, 2016), p. 12.
39. Jonathan Lainey and Thomas Peace, "Louis Vincent Sawatanen: A Life Forged by Warfare and Migration," p. 109, in *Aboriginal History: A Reader*, 2nd edition, eds Kristin Burnett and Geoff Read (Don Mills: Oxford University Press Canada, 2016).
40. Dominique Deslandres, *Croire et faire croire. Les missions françaises au XVIIe siècle* (Paris: Fayard, 2003), p. 366; Olive Patricia Dickason, *Canada's First Nations: A History of Founding Peoples from Earliest Times* (Toronto: McClelland & Stewart, 1992), pp. 69–71.

41. Susan M. Hill, *The Clay We Are Made Of: Haudenosaunee Land Tenure on the Grand River* (Winnipeg: University of Manitoba Press, 2017), pp. 35, 53–67.
42. Norman Clermont, "La place de la femme dans les sociétés iroquoiennes de la période du contact," *Recherches amérindiennes au Québec*, 13, 4 (1983), Table; Alain Beaulieu, Stéphanie Béreau and Jean Tanguay, *Les Wendats du Québec. Territoire, économie et identité, 1650–1930* (Quebec City: Les Éditions GID, 2013), pp. 35–52.
43. Dickason, *Canada's First Nations*, p. 73; Heidi Bohaker, "'Nindoodemag': The Significance of Algonquian Kinship Networks in the Eastern Great Lakes Region, 1600–1701," *The William and Mary Quarterly*, Third Series, 63, 1 (January 2006), pp. 34, 37, 39.
44. Cornelius J. Jaenen, "Amerindian Views of French Culture in the Seventeenth Century," *Canadian Historical Review*, 55, 3 (1974), pp. 271–2.
45. Georges Sioui, "Relecture autochtone de l'événement des 500 ans," pp. 6–7, and Sioui, "L'autohistoire amérindienne: l'histoire mise en presence de la nature," pp. 237–8, in *Histoires de Kanatha vues et contées. Essais et discours, 1991–2008/Histories of Kanatha Seen and Told. Essays and Discourses, 1991–2008* (Ottawa: University of Ottawa Press, 2008); Susan M. Hill, *The Clay We Are Made Of: Haudenosaunee Land Tenure on the Grand River* (Winnipeg: University of Manitoba Press, 2017), pp. 66–7.
46. Dickason, *Canada's First Nations*, pp. 132–5; Carolyn Podruchny and Kathryn Magee Labelle, "Jean de Brébeuf and the Wendat Voices of Seventeenth-Century New France," *Renaissance and Reformation*, 34, 1–2 (Winter–Spring 2011), p. 117; Susan M. Hill, *The Clay We Are Made Of: Haudenosaunee Land Tenure on the Grand River* (Winnipeg: University of Manitoba Press, 2017), p. 90.
47. Georges Sioui, "Canada's Past, Present and Future from a Native Canadian Perspective," p. 102, in *Histoires de Kanatha vues et contées. Essais et discours, 1991–2008/Histories of Kanatha Seen and Told. Essays and Discourses, 1991–2008* (Ottawa: University of Ottawa Press, 2008).
48. Kathryn Magee Labelle, *Dispersed but Not Destroyed: A History of the Seventeenth-Century Wendat People* (Vancouver: UBC Press, 2013), p. 13.
49. Heidi Bohaker makes this same argument with respect to the Anishinaabeg. Bohaker, "'Nindoodemag': The Significance of Algonquian Kinship Networks in the Eastern Great Lakes Region, 1600–1701," *The William and Mary Quarterly*, Third Series, 63, 1 (January 2006), pp. 43–5.
50. Kathryn Magee Labelle, *Dispersed but Not Destroyed: A History of the Seventeenth-Century Wendat People* (Vancouver: UBC Press, 2013). The quotation regarding Jacques Otratenkoui is to be found on page 188. Other examples of marriages within the Wendat diaspora can be found on pages 178–9. Marie Félix Arontio's marriage to Laurent du Bocq is discussed on pages 110–11.
51. Sioui, "Why Canada Should Look for, Find, Recognize and Embrace its True, Aboriginal Roots. The Time of the Toad," p. 153, in *Histoires de Kanatha vues et*

contées. Essais et discours, 1991–2008/Histories of Kanatha Seen and Told. Essays and Discourses, 1991–2008 (Ottawa: University of Ottawa Press, 2008).

52. Georges Sioui, "Our Responsibility as Indigenous Peoples: Suggestions to Anthropology," p. 82, in *Histoires de Kanatha vues et contées. Essais et discours, 1991–2008/Histories of Kanatha Seen and Told. Essays and Discourses, 1991–2008* (Ottawa: University of Ottawa Press, 2008). Sioui argues that "the coming of the Europeans, with the devastating sicknesses that they brought, spelled a rapid and drastic depopulation of all our peoples, *principally the sedentary and agricultural populations*" (my emphasis).

53. Michael Witgen, *An Infinity of Nations: How the Native New World Shaped Early North America* (Philadelphia: University of Pennsylvania Press, 2012), pp. 28, 107.

54. Richard White, *The Middle Ground. Indians, Empires and Republics in the Great Lakes Region, 1650–1815* (Cambridge: Cambridge University Press, 1991); Gilles Havard, *Empire et métissages. Indiens et Français dans le Pays d'en Haut, 1660–1715* (Paris: Presses de l'Université Paris-Sorbonne; Sillery: Septentrion, 2003).

55. Gilles Havard, *Empire et métissages. Indiens et Français dans le Pays d'en Haut, 1660–1715* (Paris: Presses de l'Université Paris-Sorbonne; Sillery: Septentrion, 2003), Chapter 10, "Sexualité et intermarriage: le pays du métissage," pp. 625–80. André Lachance and Sylvie Savoie have found 53 Indigenous–European marriages in the *Pays d'en haut* recorded in parish registers between 1644 and 1760, but Havard argues (on page 652) that these numbers significantly underrepresent the importance of mixed marriages in the region.

56. Gilles Havard, *Empire et métissages. Indiens et Français dans le Pays d'en Haut, 1660–1715* (Paris: Presses de l'Université Paris-Sorbonne; Sillery: Septentrion, 2003), p. 776. My translation.

57. Allan Greer, *Property and Dispossession: Natives, Empires and Land in Early Modern North America* (Cambridge: Cambridge University Press, 2018), pp. 73–81.

58. Leslie Choquette, *Frenchmen into Peasants: Modernity and Tradition in the Peopling of French Canada* (Cambridge, Mass.: Harvard University Press, 1997).

59. Leslie Choquette, *Frenchmen into Peasants: Modernity and Tradition in the Peopling of French Canada* (Cambridge, Mass.: Harvard University Press, 1997), p. 4.

60. Didier Poton, "Le Canada: un espace économique marginal dans l'empire colonial français," dans *1763. Le Traité de Paris bouleverse l'Amérique* (Sillery, Septentrion, 2013), pp. 116–17.

61. Choquette, *Frenchmen into Peasants*, pp. 19, 21.

62. Allan Greer, *The People of New France* (Toronto: University of Toronto Press, 1997), p. 12.

63. Choquette, *Frenchmen into Peasants*, p. 38.

64. Greer, *The People of New France*, p. 17.

65. Gilles Havard, *Empire et métissages. Indiens et Français dans le Pays d'en Haut, 1660–1715* (Paris: Presses de l'Université Paris-Sorbonne; Sillery: Septentrion, 2003), pp. 646–51.
66. Gilles Havard, *Empire et métissages. Indiens et Français dans le Pays d'en Haut, 1660–1715* (Paris: Presses de l'Université Paris-Sorbonne; Sillery: Septentrion, 2003), p. 652.
67. See, e.g., Gustave Lanctôt, *Filles de joie ou Filles du Roi. Étude sur l'émigration féminine en Nouvelle-France* (Montréal: 1952).
68. Yves Landry, *Les Filles du roi au XVIIe siècle. Orphelines en France, pionnières au Canada* (Montréal: Éditions Leméac, 1992).
69. Marshall, *Word from New France*, p. 353.
70. Jan Noel, *Along a River: The First French-Canadian Women* (Toronto: University of Toronto Press, 2013), p. 77.
71. Noel, *Along a River*, p. 80.
72. Marshall, *Word from New France*, pp. 353, 314.
73. Marshall, *Word from New France*, pp. 330–1, 353–4, 361.
74. Marshall, *Word from New France*, p. 331.
75. Marshall, *Word from New France*, p. 345.
76. Greer, *The People of New France*, pp. 15–16. A small minority of these *engagés* were women, almost all of whom worked as domestic servants. On female *engagées*, see Robert Larin, *Brève histoire du peuplement européen en Nouvelle-France* (Sillery: Septentrion, 2000), p. 84n10.
77. Noel, *Along a River*, pp. 80, 82.
78. Cole Harris, *The Reluctant Land: Society, Space, and Environment in Canada before Confederation* (Vancouver: UBC Press, 2008), pp. 67, 73.
79. Lisa Dillon, "Parental and Sibling Influences on the Timing of Marriage, XVIIth and XVIIIth Century Québec," *Annales de démographie historique*, 2010/1, 119, pp. 155, 158, 173–4.
80. Dillon, "Parental and Sibling Influences on the Timing of Marriage," pp. 174–5.
81. Marshall, *Word from New France*, p. 354.
82. Noel, *Along a River*, p. 81.
83. Harris, *The Reluctant Land*, p. 73.
84. Danielle Gauvreau, "À propos de la mise en nourrice à Québec pendant le régime français," *Revue d'histoire de l'Amérique française*, 41, 1 (été 1987): 53–61. Émilie Robert, who has studied wet-nursing on the Island of Montreal during the French regime, argues that over the course of the eighteenth century, artisans and members of the bourgeoisie, and not just colonial elites, began to make use of wet-nurses. Émilie Robert, "La mise en nourrice en Nouvelle-France: l'île de Montréal, 1680–1768" (M.A. thesis, Université de Montréal, 2011).
85. Noel, *Along a River*, p. 81; Greer, *The People of New France*, p. 24.
86. Réal Bates, "Les conceptions prénuptiales dans la Vallée du Saint-Laurent avant 1725," *Revue d'histoire de l'Amérique française*, 40, 2 (automne 1986): 253–72;

Josette Brun, *Vie et mort du couple en Nouvelle-France. Québec et Louisbourg au XVIIIe siècle* (Montreal: McGill-Queen's University Press, 2006), pp. 42–4.
87. Marshall, *Word from New France*, p. 330.
88. Marshall, *Word from New France*, p. 315.
89. Benoît Grenier, *Brève histoire du régime seigneurial* (Montréal: Boréal, 2012), p. 63.
90. Harris, *The Reluctant Land*, p. 76; Greer, *The People of New France*, pp. 33, 55–6.
91. Marshall, *Word from New France*, p. 345.
92. Greer, *The People of New France*, pp. 23–6; Gilles Archambault, "La question des vivres au Canada au cours de l'hiver 1757–1758," *Revue d'histoire de l'Amérique française*, 21, 1 (1967), 16–50.
93. Rénald Lessard, *Au temps de la petite vérole. La médecine au Canada au XVIIe et XVIIIe siècles* (Quebec: Septentrion, 2012), p. 28.
94. https://www.ined.fr/fr/tout-savoir-population/graphiques-cartes/graphiques-interpretes/esperance-vie-france; Noel, *Along a River*, pp. 81–3.
95. Marshall, *Word from New France*, p. 337.
96. Deslandres, *Croire et faire croire*.
97. Serge Gagnon, *Mariage et famille au temps de Papineau* (Sainte-Foy: Presses de l'Université Laval, 1993); Harris, *The Reluctant Land*, p. 77.
98. Harris, *The Reluctant Land*, pp. 77, 84.
99. Sylvie Dépatie, "Maîtres et domestiques dans les campagnes montréalaises au XVIIIe siècle: bilan préliminaire," *Histoire, économie et société*, 2008/4 27e année: 51–65.
100. Harris, *The Reluctant Land*, pp. 73–9.
101. Allan Greer, *Peasant, Lord, and Merchant: Rural Society in Three Quebec Parishes, 1740–1840* (Toronto: University of Toronto Press, 1985); Grenier, *Brève histoire du régime seigneurial*, p. 23 and elsewhere; Harris, *The Reluctant Land*, pp. 79–80.
102. Grenier, *Brève histoire du régime seigneurial*, p. 22.
103. Grenier, *Brève histoire du régime seigneurial*, p. 52.
104. This debate is discussed in Gregory M.W. Kennedy, *Something of a Peasant Paradise? Comparing Rural Societies in Acadie and the Loudunais, 1604–1755* (Montreal; Kingston: McGill-Queen's University Press, 2014), Chapter 4, "The Seigneury."
105. Gregory Kennedy, "Marshland Colonization in Acadia and Poitou during the 17th Century," *Acadiensis*, XLII, 1 (2013): 37–66. The quotation is on page 52. See also Harris, *The Reluctant Land*, pp. 55–65. On the specific origins of Acadian families, see Gregory M.W. Kennedy, *Something of a Peasant Paradise? Comparing Rural Societies in Acadie and the Loudunais, 1604–1755* (Montreal; Kingston: McGill-Queen's University Press, 2014), pp. 9–12.
106. On these various bonuses, see Noel, *Along a River*, p. 80; Philip Girard, Jim Phillips, and R. Blake Brown, *A History of Law in Canada*, Vol. 1, *Beginnings to 1866* (Toronto: University of Toronto Press, 2018), p. 154.

107. Philip Girard, Jim Phillips, and R. Blake Brown, *A History of Law in Canada*, Vol. 1, *Beginnings to 1866* (Toronto: University of Toronto Press, 2018), pp. 154–5, 158–60.
108. Harris, *The Reluctant Land*, pp. 76, 79; Dillon, "Parental and Sibling Influences on the Timing of Marriage," pp. 144–6.
109. Sylvie Dépatie, "La transmission du patrimoine au Canada (XVIIe–XVIIIe siècle): qui sont les défavorisés?", *Revue d'histoire de l'Amérique française*, 54, 4 (2001): 558–70.
110. See, e.g., Jan Noel, "New France: Les Femmes Favorisées," in Veronica Strong-Boag and Anita Clair Fellman, eds, *Rethinking Canada: The Promise of Women's History*, 2nd edition (Toronto: Copp Clark Pitman, 1991); Micheline Dumont, "Les femmes de la Nouvelle-France étaient-elles favorisées?", *Atlantis*, 8, 1 (1982), pp. 118–24.
111. These women figure in all syntheses of the history of women in Quebec or Canada, e.g. Denyse Baillargeon, *Brève histoire des femmes au Québec* (Montréal: Boréal, 2012); Collectif Clio, *L'histoire des femmes au Québec depuis quatre siècles*, 2e édition (Montréal: Le Jour, 1992); Gail Cuthbert Brandt, Naomi Black, Paula Bourne, and Magda Fahrni, *Canadian Women: A History*, 3rd edition (Toronto: Nelson, 2011).
112. Deslandres, *Croire et faire croire*, pp. 361–4.
113. Josette Brun, *Vie et mort du couple en Nouvelle-France. Québec et Louisbourg au XVIIIe siècle* (Montreal: McGill-Queen's University Press, 2006).
114. As author Frank Mackey points out, however, slavery's "historical significance far outstrips its demographic weight." Mackey, *Done with Slavery: The Black Fact in Montreal, 1760–1840* (Montreal: McGill-Queen's University Press, 2010), p. 109. Brett Rushforth estimates that Indigenous slaves "never constituted more than 5 percent of the colony's total population." Rushforth, "'A Little Flesh We Offer You': The Origins of Indian Slavery in New France," *William and Mary Quarterly*, 3rd series, 60, 4 (October 2003), p. 777.
115. These numbers, calculated by historian Marcel Trudel, are cited in Denyse Beaugrand-Champagne, *Le procès de Marie-Josèphe-Angélique* (Outremont: Libre Expression, 2004), p. 61, second [un-numbered] footnote. Frank Mackey claims that Trudel's numbers are unreliable, however. Mackey, *Done with Slavery*, p. 13.
116. Brett Rushforth, "'A Little Flesh We Offer You': The Origins of Indian Slavery in New France," *William and Mary Quarterly*, 3rd series, 60, 4 (October 2003): 777–808. The quotations are on pages 793 and 802.
117. Kenneth Donovan, "Slaves and Their Owners in Ile Royale, 1713–1760," *Acadiensis*, 25, 1 (Autumn 1995): 3–32.
118. Beaugrand-Champagne, *Le procès de Marie-Josèphe-Angélique*; Afua Cooper, *The Hanging of Angélique: The Untold Story of Canadian Slavery and the Burning of Old Montréal* (Toronto: HarperCollins, 2006); André Vachon, "MARIE-JOSEPH-ANGÉLIQUE," in *Dictionary of Canadian Biography*, vol. 2,

University of Toronto/Université Laval, 2003–, accessed February 5, 2020, http://www.biographi.ca/en/bio/marie_joseph_angelique_2E.html.
119. According to Gregory Kennedy, "even conservative estimates suggest that the Mi'kmaw population diminished by three-quarters between 1500 and 1700." Kennedy, "Marshland Colonization in Acadia and Poitou during the 17th Century," *Acadiensis*, XLII, 1 (2013), p. 59.

CHAPTER 2

1. Jacques Mathieu et Sophie Imbeault, *La Guerre des Canadiens 1756–1763* (Quebec: Septentrion, 2013), pp. 179–80.
2. Marcel Fournier, "L'apport démographique des soldats de Montcalm au cours de la guerre de Sept Ans et ses répercussions sur la population canadienne," pp. 184–6, in *1763. Le traité de Paris bouleverse l'Amérique*, dir. Sophie Imbeault, Denis Vaugeois, et Laurent Veyssière (Quebec: Septentrion, 2013).
3. Jacques Mathieu et Sophie Imbeault, *La Guerre des Canadiens 1756–1763* (Quebec: Septentrion, 2013), chapitre 5, pp. 151–208.
4. Robert Larin, "Les Canadiens passés en France à la Conquête. Les nécessiteux secourus à La Rochelle en 1761–1762," *Revue d'histoire de l'Amérique française*, 68, 1–2 (été-automne 2014): 101–24; Mathieu et Imbeault, *La Guerre des Canadiens 1756–1763* (Quebec: Septentrion, 2013), chapitre 6, pp. 209–34.
5. Sophie Imbeault, *Les Tarieu de Lanaudière. Une famille noble après la Conquête 1760–1791* (Quebec: Septentrion, 2004). See also the case of the Taschereau family as analysed in Brian Young, *Patrician Families and the Making of Quebec: The Taschereaus and McCords* (Montreal; Kingston: McGill-Queen's University Press, 2014), p. 21.
6. For the numbers of French soldiers from the *Troupes de Terre* and the *Troupes de la Marine* who married and stayed in Canada after the Seven Years War, see Marcel Fournier, "L'apport démographique des soldats de Montcalm au cours de la guerre de Sept Ans et ses répercussions sur la population canadienne," p. 188. The numbers of Acadian refugees are listed on page 190.
7. Donald Fyson, "The Canadiens and the Conquest of Quebec: Interpretations, Realities, Ambiguities," in *Quebec Questions: Quebec Studies for the Twenty-First Century*, eds Stéphan Gervais, Christopher Kirkey, and Jarrett Rudy (Don Mills: Oxford University Press Canada, 2011), pp. 20–1. For the difference between these two terms, see Michel De Waele, "Conquête et cession. La Nouvelle-France et le traité de Paris, 1755–1763," p. 86, in *1763. Le traité de Paris bouleverse l'Amérique*, dir. Sophie Imbeault, Denis Vaugeois, et Laurent Veyssière (Québec, Septentrion, 2013).
8. The authors of one of the major syntheses in Quebec women's history, for instance, argue that the period extending from 1701 to 1832 was one of stability and continuity for most people in the colony, despite the Conquest and its aftermath.

Collectif Clio, *L'histoire des femmes au Québec depuis quatre siècles*, 2e édition (Montréal: Éditions Le Jour, 1992), pp. 75, 78.

9. This might also have reflected a longstanding British practice of indirect rule in its colonies and in the British "hinterland." Fyson, "The Canadiens and the Conquest of Quebec," pp. 25–6, 28, 31.

10. The extent to which habitants actually did subdivide their land is the subject of an extensive historiographical debate. See, e.g., Allan Greer, *Peasant, Lord, and Merchant: Rural Society in Three Quebec Parishes, 1740–1840* (Toronto: University of Toronto Press, 1985).

11. Sylvie Dépatie, "La transmission du patrimoine au Canada (XVIIe–XVIIIe siècle): qui sont les défavorisés?", *Revue d'histoire de l'Amérique française*, 54, 4 (2001): 558–70.

12. Christine Hudon, *Prêtres et fidèles dans le diocèse de Saint-Hyacinthe, 1820–1875* (Sillery: Septentrion, 1996); Serge Gagnon, *Quand le Québec manquait de prêtres: la charge pastorale au Bas-Canada* (Sainte-Foy: Les Presses de l'Université Laval, 2006).

13. Marcel Fournier, "L'apport démographique des soldats de Montcalm au cours de la guerre de Sept Ans et ses répercussions sur la population canadienne," p. 185.

14. An 1831 law gave non-British immigrants civil and political rights and allowed for their naturalization. See Marcel Fournier on indirect French immigration to the British colony between 1765 and 1831. Fournier, *Les Français au Québec, 1765–1865. Un mouvement migratoire méconnu* (Sillery: Septentrion, 1995).

15. Jonathan Lainey and Thomas Peace, "Louis Vincent Sawatanen: A Life Forged by Warfare and Migration," in *Aboriginal History: A Reader*, 2nd edition, eds Kristin Burnett and Geoff Read (Don Mills: Oxford University Press Canada, 2016), p. 111.

16. Susan M. Hill, *The Clay We Are Made Of: Haudenosaunee Land Tenure on the Grand River* (Winnipeg: University of Manitoba Press, 2017), p. 120.

17. Jonathan Lainey and Thomas Peace, "Louis Vincent Sawatanen: A Life Forged by Warfare and Migration," in *Aboriginal History: A Reader*, 2nd edition, eds Kristin Burnett and Geoff Read (Don Mills: Oxford University Press Canada, 2016), p. 110.

18. Jonathan Lainey and Thomas Peace, "Louis Vincent Sawatanen: A Life Forged by Warfare and Migration," in *Aboriginal History: A Reader*, 2nd edition, eds Kristin Burnett and Geoff Read (Don Mills: Oxford University Press Canada, 2016), p. 111.

19. Michael Witgen, *An Infinity of Nations: How the Native New World Shaped Early North America* (Philadelphia: University of Pennsylvania Press, 2012), p. 218; Susan M. Hill, *The Clay We Are Made Of: Haudenosaunee Land Tenure on the Grand River* (Winnipeg: University of Manitoba Press, 2017), p. 121.

20. Alain Beaulieu, "Sous la protection de Sa Majesté. La signification de la Conquête pour les Autochtones," pp. 278–301, in *1763. Le Traité de Paris bouleverse*

l'Amérique, eds Sophie Imbeault, Denis Vaugeois, and Laurent Veyssière (Quebec: Septentrion, 2013); Jonathan Lainey and Thomas Peace, "Louis Vincent Sawatanen, premier bachelier autochtone canadien (Canada, 1745–Canada, 1825)," in *Vivre la Conquête à travers plus de 25 parcours individuels*, Tome I, eds Gaston Deschênes et Denis Vaugeois (Quebec: Septentrion, 2013), pp. 207–9.

21. Naomi Griffiths, "The Golden Age: Acadian Life, 1713–1748," *Histoire sociale/Social History*, 17, 33 (May 1984): 21–34; Naomi E.S. Griffiths, *From Migrant to Acadian: A North American Border People, 1604–1755* (Montreal; Kingston: McGill-Queen's University Press, 2004), p. 285; Gregory M.W. Kennedy, *Something of a Peasant Paradise? Comparing Rural Societies in Acadie and the Loudunais, 1604–1755* (Montreal; Kingston: McGill-Queen's University Press, 2014), Chapter 2, "The Political and Military Environment," p. 72.

22. Gregory M.W. Kennedy, *Something of a Peasant Paradise? Comparing Rural Societies in Acadie and the Loudunais, 1604–1755* (Montreal; Kingston: McGill-Queen's University Press, 2014), Chapter 2, "The Political and Military Environment," pp. 66–8.

23. Nicolas Landry and Nicole Lang, *Histoire de l'Acadie*, 2e édition (Québec: Sillery, 2014), pp. 42–4, 76, 99–118, 154–5.

24. Nicolas Landry and Nicole Lang, *Histoire de l'Acadie*, 2e édition (Québec: Sillery, 2014), p. 155.

25. Margaret Conrad, Toni Laidlaw, and Donna Smyth, eds., *No Place Like Home* (Halifax: Formac Publishing Company, 1988), pp. 6–7.

26. Quoted in Janice Potter McKinnon, *While the Women Only Wept: Loyalist Refugee Women* (Montreal; Kingston: McGill-Queen's University Press, 1993), p. 74.

27. E.J. Errington, *Wives and Mothers, School Mistresses and Scullery Maids: Working Women in Upper Canada, 1790–1840* (Montreal: McGill-Queen's University Press, 1995), p. 5.

28. Margaret Conrad, Toni Laidlaw, and Donna Smyth, eds., *No Place Like Home* (Halifax: Formac Publishing Company, 1988), p. 8; Channon Oyeniran, "Black Loyalists in British North America," *The Canadian Encyclopedia*, Historica Canada, Article published 25 March 2019; Last Edited 25 March 2019. https://www.thecanadianencyclopedia.ca/en/article/black-loyalists-in-british-north-america

29. Gretchen Green, "Molly Brant, Catharine Brant, and Their Daughters: A Study in Colonial Acculturation," *Ontario History*, 81, 3 (September 1989): 235–50. On the forging of the Covenant Chain of Friendship, see Susan M. Hill, *The Clay We Are Made Of: Haudenosaunee Land Tenure on the Grand River* (Winnipeg: University of Manitoba Press, 2017), pp. 94–100.

30. Susan M. Hill, *The Clay We Are Made Of: Haudenosaunee Land Tenure on the Grand River* (Winnipeg: University of Manitoba Press, 2017), pp. 127–39, 147.

31. Gretchen Green, "Molly Brant, Catharine Brant, and Their Daughters: A Study in Colonial Acculturation," *Ontario History*, 81, 3 (September 1989): 235–50.

32. Christopher Moore notes that there existed among the Royal Highland Emigrants, a loyalist military unit, "the prior existence of a familiar hierarchy built on the social and economic ascendancy of the officer class." Moore, "The Disposition to Settle: The Royal Highland Emigrants and Loyalist Settlement in Upper Canada, 1784," p. 71, in *Historical Essays on Upper Canada: New Perspectives*, eds J.K. Johnson and Bruce G. Wilson (Ottawa: Carleton University Press, 1989). On the ethnic and religious makeup of the Loyalists, see Janice Potter McKinnon, *While the Women Only Wept: Loyalist Refugee Women* (Montreal; Kingston: McGill-Queen's University Press, 1993), pp. 12–20.
33. David Mills, *The Idea of Loyalty in Upper Canada, 1784–1850* (Montreal; Kingston: McGill-Queen's University Press, 1988).
34. Rebecca Byles, 8 November 1777, reproduced in Margaret Conrad, Toni Laidlaw, and Donna Smyth, eds., *No Place Like Home* (Halifax: Formac Publishing Company, 1988), p. 48.
35. See E.J. Errington, *Wives and Mothers, School Mistresses and Scullery Maids: Working Women in Upper Canada, 1790–1840* (Montreal: McGill-Queen's University Press, 1995), p. 5, on men's decisions to move and women's stoicism regarding these decisions; also Janice Potter McKinnon, *While the Women Only Wept: Loyalist Refugee Women* (Montreal; Kingston: McGill-Queen's University Press, 1993), p. xv.
36. See, e.g., David Gagan, *Hopeful Travellers: Families, Land, and Social Change in Mid-Victorian Peel County, Canada West* (Toronto: University of Toronto Press, 1981); Darrell A. Norris, "Migration, Pioneer Settlement, and the Life Course: The First Families of an Ontario Township," p. 179, in *Historical Essays on Upper Canada: New Perspectives*, eds J.K. Johnson and Bruce G. Wilson (Ottawa: Carleton University Press, 1989).
37. Marianne McLean, "Peopling Glengarry County: The Scottish Origins of a Canadian Community," pp. 151–73, in *Historical Essays on Upper Canada: New Perspectives*, eds J.K. Johnson and Bruce G. Wilson (Ottawa: Carleton University Press, 1989).
38. Peter A. Russell, "Forest into Farmland: Upper Canadian Clearing Rates, 1822–1839," pp. 137, 144, in *Historical Essays on Upper Canada: New Perspectives*, eds J.K. Johnson and Bruce G. Wilson (Ottawa: Carleton University Press, 1989).
39. Wendy Cameron, Sheila Haines and Mary McDougall Maude, *English Immigrant Voices: Labourers' Letters from Upper Canada in the 1830s* (Montreal; Kingston: McGill-Queen's University Press, 2000), p. 29.
40. Catharine Parr Traill, *The Backwoods of Canada* (Toronto: McClelland & Stewart, 1966).
41. Susanna Moodie, *Roughing it in the Bush* (Toronto: McClelland and Stewart, 1962), pp. 236–7. The italics are in the original.
42. Glenn J. Lockwood, "Irish Immigrants and the 'Critical Years' in Eastern Ontario: The Case of Montague Township, 1821–1881," in *Historical Essays on*

Upper Canada: New Perspectives, eds J.K. Johnson and Bruce G. Wilson (Ottawa: Carleton University Press, 1989).

43. Donald H. Akenson, "Ontario: Whatever Happened to the Irish?", in *Canadian Papers in Rural History*, eds D.H. Akenson (Gananoque: Langdale Press, 1982), pp. 204–56.

44. Margaret Conrad, Toni Laidlaw, and Donna Smyth, eds., *No Place Like Home* (Halifax: Formac Publishing Company, 1988), pp. 7, 9.

45. Frank Mackey, *Done with Slavery: The Black Fact in Montreal, 1760–1840* (Montreal; Kingston: McGill-Queen's University Press, 2010), pp. 36–40, 320; Natasha Henry, "If Black lives truly matter in Canada, an apology for slavery is only a first step," *Spacing Toronto*, 9 June 2020, http://spacing.ca/toronto/2020/06/09/if-black-lives-truly-matter-in-canada-an-apology-for-slavery-is-only-a-first-step/

46. Peter Ward, *Courtship, Love, and Marriage in Nineteenth-Century English Canada* (Montreal; Kingston: McGill-Queen's University Press, 1990), Chapter 1, "The Christian Setting of Courtship and Marriage."

47. Serge Gagnon, *Plaisir d'amour et crainte de Dieu. Sexualité et confession au Bas-Canada* (Québec: Les Presses de l'Université Laval, 1990); Serge Gagnon, *Mariage et famille au temps de Papineau* (Sainte-Foy: Presses de l'Université Laval, 1993).

48. Françoise Noël, *Family Life and Sociability in Upper and Lower Canada, 1780–1870* (Montreal; Kingston: McGill-Queen's University Press, 2003), p. 19.

49. Serge Gagnon, *Mariage et famille au temps de Papineau* (Sainte-Foy: Presses de l'Université Laval, 1993).

50. Brian Young, "Getting around Legal Incapacity: The Legal Status of Married Women in Trade in Mid-Nineteenth Century Lower Canada," in *Canadian Papers in Business History*, Volume 1, ed. Peter Baskerville (Victoria: University of Victoria Press, 1989), pp. 1–16.

51. Peter Ward, *Courtship, Love, and Marriage in Nineteenth-Century English Canada* (Montreal; Kingston: McGill-Queen's University Press, 1990), pp. 120–4.

52. Serge Gagnon, *Mariage et famille au temps de Papineau* (Sainte-Foy: Presses de l'Université Laval, 1993).

53. Quoted in Françoise Noël, *Family Life and Sociability in Upper and Lower Canada, 1780–1870* (Montreal; Kingston: McGill-Queen's University Press, 2003), p. 136.

54. Margaret Conrad, *Recording Angels: The Private Chronicles of Women from the Maritime Provinces of Canada, 1750–1850* (Ottawa: CRIAW, 1982), p. 10.

55. J.I. Little, ed., *Love Strong as Death: Lucy Peel's Canadian Journal, 1833–1836* (Waterloo: Wilfrid Laurier University Press, 2001), pp. 130–6; Françoise Noël, *Family Life and Sociability in Upper and Lower Canada, 1780–1870* (Montreal; Kingston: McGill-Queen's University Press, 2003), Chapter 7, "Childhood Accidents, Illness, and Death," pp. 165–72.

56. Françoise Noël, *Family Life and Sociability in Upper and Lower Canada, 1780–1870* (Montreal; Kingston: McGill-Queen's University Press, 2003), pp. 144–7.
57. Sylvie Dépatie, "Maîtres et domestiques dans les campagnes montréalaises au XVIIIe siècle: bilan préliminaire," *Histoire, économie et société*, 2008/4 (27e année), pp. 51–65.
58. J.I. Little, ed., *Love Strong as Death: Lucy Peel's Canadian Journal, 1833–1836* (Waterloo: Wilfrid Laurier University Press, 2001), p. 5.
59. Darrell A. Norris, "Migration, Pioneer Settlement, and the Life Course: The First Families of an Ontario Township," p. 180, in *Historical Essays on Upper Canada: New Perspectives*, eds J.K. Johnson and Bruce G. Wilson (Ottawa: Carleton University Press, 1989).
60. Susan M. Hill, *The Clay We Are Made Of: Haudenosaunee Land Tenure on the Grand River* (Winnipeg: University of Manitoba Press, 2017), especially pp. 167–85; Elizabeth Elbourne, "Broken Alliance: Debating Six Nations' Land Claims in 1822," *Cultural and Social History*, 9, 4 (2012): 497–525.
61. E.J. Errington, *Wives and Mothers, School Mistresses and Scullery Maids: Working Women in Upper Canada, 1790–1840* (Montreal: McGill-Queen's University Press, 1995), p. 9.
62. Darrell A. Norris, "Migration, Pioneer Settlement, and the Life Course: The First Families of an Ontario Township," pp. 191–2, in *Historical Essays on Upper Canada: New Perspectives*, eds J.K. Johnson and Bruce G. Wilson (Ottawa: Carleton University Press, 1989); Glenn J. Lockwood, "Irish Immigrants and the 'Critical Years' in Eastern Ontario: The Case of Montague Township, 1821–1881," in *Historical Essays on Upper Canada: New Perspectives*, eds. J.K. Johnson and Bruce G. Wilson (Ottawa: Carleton University Press, 1989), p. 231. J.I. Little points to the example of Thomas Peel, who "struggled as a bachelor settler" clearing land in Lower Canada's Eastern Townships before giving up and returning to England in 1836. J.I. Little, ed., *Love Strong as Death: Lucy Peel's Canadian Journal, 1833–1836* (Waterloo: Wilfrid Laurier University Press, 2001), p. 3; see also Lucy Peel's comment that "a labouring man with a family of Sons might soon clear a number of acres," p. 7.
63. This was the case of Edmund and Lucy Peel in Lower Canada's Eastern Townships, for instance. J.I. Little, ed., *Love Strong as Death: Lucy Peel's Canadian Journal, 1833–1836* (Waterloo: Wilfrid Laurier University Press, 2001), p. 3.
64. Susanna Moodie, *Roughing it in the Bush* (Toronto: McClelland and Stewart, 1962), p. 156.
65. Peter A. Russell, "Forest into Farmland: Upper Canadian Clearing Rates, 1822–1839," pp. 131–49, in *Historical Essays on Upper Canada: New Perspectives*, eds J.K. Johnson and Bruce G. Wilson (Ottawa: Carleton University Press, 1989). Darrell A. Norris, who examined the case of Euphrasia Township in Grey County, writes that "The average Euphrasia farm household managed to clear four or five acres annually up to 1851." Norris, "Migration, Pioneer Settlement,

and the Life Course: The First Families of an Ontario Township," p. 193, in *Historical Essays on Upper Canada: New Perspectives*, eds J.K. Johnson and Bruce G. Wilson.

66. E.J. Errington, *Wives and Mothers, School Mistresses and Scullery Maids: Working Women in Upper Canada, 1790–1840* (Montreal: McGill-Queen's University Press, 1995), p. 7.
67. Susanna Moodie, *Roughing it in the Bush* (Toronto: McClelland and Stewart, 1962), p. 166.
68. Douglas McCalla, "The Internal Economy of Upper Canada: New Evidence on Agricultural Marketing before 1850," *Agricultural History*, 59, 3(1985): 397–416.
69. Glenn J. Lockwood, "Irish Immigrants and the 'Critical Years' in Eastern Ontario: The Case of Montague Township, 1821–1881," pp. 210, 231, in *Historical Essays on Upper Canada: New Perspectives*, eds J.K. Johnson and Bruce G. Wilson (Ottawa: Carleton University Press, 1989).
70. E.J. Errington, *Wives and Mothers, School Mistresses and Scullery Maids: Working Women in Upper Canada, 1790–1840* (Montreal: McGill-Queen's University Press, 1995), p. 12.
71. Julia Roberts, "'A Mixed Assemblage of Persons': Race and Tavern Space in Upper Canada," *Canadian Historical Review* 83, 1 (March 2002): 1–28.
72. Douglas McCalla, "The Internal Economy of Upper Canada: New Evidence on Agricultural Marketing before 1850," *Agricultural History*, 59, 3(1985): 397–416.
73. E.J. Errington, *Wives and Mothers, School Mistresses and Scullery Maids: Working Women in Upper Canada, 1790–1840* (Montreal: McGill-Queen's University Press, 1995), pp. 14–15.
74. J.I. Little, ed., *Love Strong as Death: Lucy Peel's Canadian Journal, 1833–1836* (Waterloo: Wilfrid Laurier University Press, 2001), pp. 7–8. The quotation from Lucy Peel's diary is cited by Little on page 7 of his Introduction.
75. E.J. Errington, *Wives and Mothers, School Mistresses and Scullery Maids: Working Women in Upper Canada, 1790–1840* (Montreal: McGill-Queen's University Press, 1995), pp. 14–15; Margaret Conrad, Toni Laidlaw, and Donna Smyth, eds., *No Place Like Home* (Halifax: Formac Publishing Company, 1988), p. 11.
76. Catharine Parr Traill, *The Backwoods of Canada* (Toronto: McClelland & Stewart, 1966), pp. 53–4. The italics are in the original.
77. Béatrice Craig, Judith Rygiel, and Elizabeth Turcotte, "The Homespun Paradox: Market-Oriented Production of Cloth in Eastern Canada in the Nineteenth Century," *Agricultural History*, 76, 1 (2002): 28–57.
78. Louisa Collins Diary, 15 August 1815, reproduced in Margaret Conrad, Toni Laidlaw, and Donna Smyth, eds., *No Place Like Home* (Halifax: Formac Publishing Company, 1988), p. 65.
79. Margaret Conrad, Toni Laidlaw, and Donna Smyth, eds., *No Place Like Home* (Halifax: Formac Publishing Company, 1988), pp. 66, 68.

80. Gail G. Campbell, *"I wish to keep a record": Nineteenth-Century New Brunswick Women Diarists and Their World* (Toronto: University of Toronto Press, 2017), pp. 211–12.
81. E.J. Errington, *Wives and Mothers, School Mistresses and Scullery Maids: Working Women in Upper Canada, 1790–1840* (Montreal: McGill-Queen's University Press, 1995), p. 8.
82. Catharine Parr Traill, *The Backwoods of Canada* (Toronto: McClelland & Stewart, 1966), p. 53.
83. Julia Roberts, "'A Mixed Assemblage of Persons': Race and Tavern Space in Upper Canada," *Canadian Historical Review* 83, 1 (March 2002), p. 5.
84. On prostitution and the early nineteenth-century household economy, see Mary Anne Poutanen, *Beyond Brutal Passions: Prostitution in Early Nineteenth-Century Montreal* (Montreal; Kingston: McGill-Queen's University Press, 2015), Chapter 2.
85. E.J. Errington, *Wives and Mothers, School Mistresses and Scullery Maids: Working Women in Upper Canada, 1790–1840* (Montreal: McGill-Queen's University Press, 1995), p. 15–16.
86. J.I. Little, ed., *Love Strong as Death: Lucy Peel's Canadian Journal, 1833–1836* (Waterloo: Wilfrid Laurier University Press, 2001), pp. 4, 7, 9–11.
87. David Mills, *The Idea of Loyalty in Upper Canada, 1784–1850* (Montreal; Kingston: McGill-Queen's University Press, 1988); Katherine M.J. McKenna, "Options for Elite Women in Early Upper Canadian Society: The Case of the Powell Family," pp. 401–2, in *Historical Essays on Upper Canada: New Perspectives*, eds J.K. Johnson and Bruce G. Wilson (Ottawa: Carleton University Press, 1989).
88. E.J. Errington, *Wives and Mothers, School Mistresses and Scullery Maids: Working Women in Upper Canada, 1790–1840* (Montreal: McGill-Queen's University Press, 1995).
89. Rainer Baehre, "Paupers and Poor Relief in Upper Canada," in *Historical Essays on Upper Canada: New Perspectives*, eds J.K. Johnson and Bruce G. Wilson (Ottawa: Carleton University Press, 1989).
90. Katherine M.J. McKenna, *A Life of Propriety: Anne Murray Powell and Her Family, 1755–1849* (Montreal; Kingston: McGill-Queen's University Press, 1994), p. 192.
91. Cecilia Morgan, *Public Men and Virtuous Women: The Gendered Languages of Religion and Politics in Upper Canada, 1791–1850* (Toronto: University of Toronto Press, 1996), pp. 24, 219.
92. Colin M. Coates and Cecilia Morgan, *Heroines and History: Representations of Madeleine de Verchères and Laura Secord* (Toronto: University of Toronto Press, 2002), Part 2. For an interesting reflection on Laura Secord, sexual violence, and the gendered dimensions of the War of 1812, see Elsbeth Heaman, "Constructing Innocence: Representations of Sexual Violence in Upper Canada's War of 1812," *Journal of the Canadian Historical Association*, 24, 2 (2013): 114–55.

93. E.J. Errington, *Wives and Mothers, School Mistresses and Scullery Maids: Working Women in Upper Canada, 1790–1840* (Montreal: McGill-Queen's University Press, 1995), p. 9.

94. Jarvis Brownlie, "'Our fathers fought for the British': Racial Discourses and Indigenous Allies in Upper Canada," *Histoire sociale/Social History*, 50, 102 (November 2017): 259–84.

95. Elizabeth Elbourne, "Broken Alliance: Debating Six Nations' Land Claims in 1822," *Cultural and Social History*, 9, 4 (2012), especially pp. 497, 501; Michael Witgen, *An Infinity of Nations: How the Native New World Shaped Early North America* (Philadelphia: University of Pennsylvania Press, 2012), p. 321.

96. Susan M. Hill, *The Clay We Are Made Of: Haudenosaunee Land Tenure on the Grand River* (Winnipeg: University of Manitoba Press, 2017), pp. 153, 184.

97. Cecilia Morgan, *Public Men and Virtuous Women: The Gendered Languages of Religion and Politics in Upper Canada, 1791–1850* (Toronto: University of Toronto Press, 1996), pp. 6, 18; Alain Beaulieu, "Sous la protection de Sa Majesté. La signification de la Conquête pour les Autochtones," p. 280, in *1763. Le Traité de Paris bouleverse l'Amérique*, eds Sophie Imbeault, Denis Vaugeois, and Laurent Veyssière (Quebec: Septentrion, 2013).

98. Françoise Noël, *Family Life and Sociability in Upper and Lower Canada, 1780–1870* (Montreal; Kingston: McGill-Queen's University Press, 2003), pp. 119–23.

99. Julie Bruneau Papineau, *Une femme patriote. Correspondance 1823–1862* (Sillery: Septentrion, 1997); Louis Joseph Papineau, *Lettres à Julie*, texte établi et annoté par Georges Aubin et Renée Blanchet (Québec: Septentrion, 2000).

100. Allan Greer, *The Patriots and the People: The Rebellion of 1837 in Rural Lower Canada* (Toronto: University of Toronto Press, 1993), Chapter 7, "The queen is a whore!"

101. Margaret Conrad, Toni Laidlaw, and Donna Smyth, eds., *No Place Like Home* (Halifax: Formac Publishing Company, 1988), p. 10.

102. Denyse Baillargeon, *Brève histoire des femmes au Québec* (Montréal: Boréal, 2012), pp. 61–4; Bettina Bradbury, *Wife to Widow: Lives, Laws, and Politics in Nineteenth-Century Montreal* (Vancouver: University of British Columbia Press, 2011), Chapter 4.

103. E.J. Errington, *Wives and Mothers, School Mistresses and Scullery Maids: Working Women in Upper Canada, 1790–1840* (Montreal: McGill-Queen's University Press, 1995), p. 6.

104. Statistics Canada, Publications, *Censuses of Canada 1665 to 1871*, available online at http://www.statcan.gc.ca/pub/98-187-x/4064809-eng.htm

105. Elizabeth Vibert, "Real Men Hunt Buffalo: Masculinity, Race and Class in British Fur Traders' Narratives," *Gender & History*, 8, 1 (1996), p. 14.

106. Sylvia Van Kirk, *"Many Tender Ties": Women in Fur-Trade Society in Western Canada, 1670–1870* (Winnipeg: Watson & Dwyer Publishing, 1980); Jennifer S.H. Brown, *Strangers in Blood: Fur Trade Company Families in Indian*

Country (Vancouver: University of British Columbia Press, 1980); Jean Barman, *The West beyond the West: A History of British Columbia* (Toronto: University of Toronto Press, 1991), Chapter 3, "The Trade in Furs 1789–1849," pp. 32–51.

107. Jean Barman, *French Canadians, Furs, and Indigenous Women in the Making of the Pacific Northwest* (Vancouver: UBC Press, 2014). Short biographies of Toussaint Charbonneau and Pierre Charles can be found on page 341.

CHAPTER 3

1. Statistics Canada, "Population, Urban and Rural, by Province and Territory," http://www.statcan.gc.ca/tables-tableaux/sum-som/l01/cst01/demo62e-eng.htm, consulted 15 December 2015.
2. Betsy Beattie, "'Going Up to Lynn': Single, Maritime-Born Women in Lynn, Massachusetts, 1879–1930," *Acadiensis*, 22, 1 (Autumn 1992), p. 69.
3. Cited in Robert C.H. Sweeny, *Why Did We Choose to Industrialize? Montreal, 1819–1849* (Montreal; Kingston: McGill-Queen's University Press, 2015), p. 77.
4. Sherry Olson and Patricia Thornton, *Peopling the North American City: Montreal 1840–1900* (Montreal; Kingston: McGill-Queen's University Press, 2011), pp. 185–6.
5. Robert C.H. Sweeny, *Why Did We Choose to Industrialize? Montreal, 1819–1849* (Montreal; Kingston: McGill-Queen's University Press, 2015), pp. 46–7.
6. Betsy Beattie, "'Going Up to Lynn': Single, Maritime-Born Women in Lynn, Massachusetts, 1879–1930," *Acadiensis*, 22, 1 (Autumn 1992), p. 81.
7. Ian McKay, "Capital and Labour in the Halifax Baking and Confectionery Industry during the Last Half of the Nineteenth Century," *Labour/Le Travail*, 3 (1978), p. 65; Ben Forster and Kris Inwood, "The Diversity of Industrial Experience: Cabinet and Furniture Manufacture in Late Nineteenth-Century Ontario," *Enterprise & Society*, 4 (June 2003): 326–71.
8. Robert C.H. Sweeny, *Why Did We Choose to Industrialize? Montreal, 1819–1849* (Montreal; Kingston: McGill-Queen's University Press, 2015), p. 29.
9. Yvon Desloges et Alain Gelly, *Le canal de Lachine: du tumulte des flots à l'essor industriel et urbain, 1860–1950* (Sillery: Septentrion, 2002).
10. Gregory S. Kealey and Bryan D. Palmer, "The Bonds of Unity: The Knights of Labor in Ontario, 1880–1900," *Histoire sociale/Social History*, 28 (November 1981): 369–412.
11. Gerald Friesen, *The Canadian Prairies: A History* (Toronto: University of Toronto Press, 1987), p. 186.
12. Jean Barman, *The West beyond the West: A History of British Columbia* (Toronto: University of Toronto Press, 1991), p. 125.
13. Jean Barman, "Beyond Chinatown: Chinese Men and Indigenous Women in Early British Columbia," *BC Studies*, 177 (Spring 2013), pp. 51–3.

14. Jean Barman, *The West beyond the West: A History of British Columbia* (Toronto: University of Toronto Press, 1991), p. 124.
15. John Lutz, "After the Fur Trade: The Aboriginal Labouring Class of British Columbia, 1849–1890," *Journal of the Canadian Historical Association*, New Series, 3 (1992): 69–94.
16. Andrew Parnaby, "'The best men that ever worked the lumber': Aboriginal Longshoremen on Burrard Inlet, B.C., 1863–1939," *Canadian Historical Review*, 87 (March 2006): 53–78.
17. John Lutz, "Gender and Work in Lekwammen Families, 1843–1970," in Kathryn McPherson, Cecilia Morgan, and Nancy M. Forestell, eds, *Gendered Pasts: Historical Essays in Femininity and Masculinity in Canada* (Don Mills: Oxford University Press, 1999), especially pp. 91–3.
18. Paige Raibmon, "The Practice of Everyday Colonialism: Indigenous Women at Work in the Hop Fields and Tourist Industry of Puget Sound," *Labor: Studies in Working-Class Histories of the Americas*, 3, 3 (2006): 23–56.
19. John Lutz, "Gender and Work in Lekwammen Families, 1843–1970," in Kathryn McPherson, Cecilia Morgan, and Nancy M. Forestell, eds, *Gendered Pasts: Historical Essays in Femininity and Masculinity in Canada* (Don Mills: Oxford University Press, 1999), especially pp. 91–3.
20. Louise A. Tilly and Joan W. Scott, *Women, Work, and Family* (New York: Holt, Rinehart and Winston, 1978), Part 2, pp. 61–145. See also Sherry Olson and Patricia Thornton, *Peopling the North American City: Montreal 1840–1900* (Montreal; Kingston: McGill-Queen's University Press, 2011), pp. 183–4.
21. Michael S. Cross, "The Shiners' War: Social Violence in the Ottawa Valley in the 1830s," *Canadian Historical Review*, 54, 1 (1973): 1–26.
22. Ruth Bleasdale, "Class Conflict on the Canals of Upper Canada in the 1840s," *Labour/Le Travailleur*, 7 (Spring 1981), pp. 9–10; Dan Horner, "Solemn Processions and Terrifying Violence: Spectacle, Authority, and Citizenship during the Lachine Canal Strike of 1843," *Urban History Review/Revue d'histoire urbaine*, 38, 2 (2010): 36–47.
23. Francois Guérard, *Histoire de la santé au Québec* (Montréal: Boréal, 1996), p. 22; Maude Charest, "Prosélytisme et conflits religieux lors de l'épidémie de typhus à Montréal en 1847," *Cap-aux-Diamants: la revue d'histoire du Québec*, 112 (Hiver 2013), pp. 8–12.
24. Betsy Beattie, "'Going Up to Lynn': Single, Maritime-Born Women in Lynn, Massachusetts, 1879–1930," *Acadiensis*, 22, 1 (Autumn 1992): 65–86.
25. Betsy Beattie, "'Going Up to Lynn': Single, Maritime-Born Women in Lynn, Massachusetts, 1879–1930," *Acadiensis*, 22, 1 (Autumn 1992), p. 74.
26. France Gagnon, "Parenté et migration: le cas des Canadiens français à Montréal entre 1845 et 1875," *Historical Papers/Communications historiques*, 23, 1 (1988): 63–85. Sherry Olson and Patricia Thornton have also shown that in nineteenth-century Montreal, despite frequent moves, "kinfolk remained neighbours."

Sherry Olson and Patricia Thornton, *Peopling the North American City: Montreal 1840–1900* (Montreal; Kingston: McGill-Queen's University Press, 2011), p. 79.

27. Sherry Olson and Patricia Thornton, *Peopling the North American City: Montreal 1840–1900* (Montreal; Kingston: McGill-Queen's University Press, 2011), p. 183.

28. Bruno Ramirez, *On The Move: French-Canadian and Italian Migrants in the North Atlantic Economy, 1861–1914* (Toronto: Oxford University Press, 1991); Bruno Ramirez (with the assistance of Yves Otis), *Crossing the 49th Parallel: Emigration from Canada to the USA, 1900–1930* (Ithaca: Cornell University Press, 2001); Yves Frenette, Étienne Rivard, and Marc St-Hilaire, eds, *La francophonie nord-américaine* (Québec: Presses de l'Université Laval, 2012), Chapter 3, "Les grandes migrations, 1860–1920," pp. 107–205.

29. Yves Frenette, Étienne Rivard, and Marc St-Hilaire, eds, *La francophonie nord-américaine* (Québec: Presses de l'Université Laval, 2012), pp. 123, 125–6.

30. Tamara Hareven, "The Dynamics of Kin in an Industrial Community," *American Journal of Sociology*, 84, Supplement: Turning Points: Historical and Sociological Essays on the Family (1978), pp. S158–S160. See also Tamara K. Hareven, *Family Time and Industrial Time* (New York: Cambridge University Press, 1983).

31. Yves Frenette, Étienne Rivard, and Marc St-Hilaire, eds, *La francophonie nord-américaine* (Québec: Presses de l'Université Laval, 2012), pp. 129–30.

32. Tamara Hareven, "The Dynamics of Kin in an Industrial Community," *American Journal of Sociology*, 84, Supplement: Turning Points: Historical and Sociological Essays on the Family (1978), p. S156.

33. Joy Parr, *The Gender of Breadwinners: Women, Men, and Change in Two Industrial Towns, 1880–1950* (Toronto: University of Toronto Press, 1990); Betsy Beattie, "'Going Up to Lynn': Single, Maritime-Born Women in Lynn, Massachusetts, 1879–1930," *Acadiensis*, 22, 1 (Autumn 1992): 65–86.

34. Yves Frenette, Étienne Rivard, and Marc St-Hilaire, eds, *La francophonie nord-américaine* (Québec: Presses de l'Université Laval, 2012), p. 129.

35. Greg Kealey, ed., *Canada Investigates Industrialism: The Royal Commission on the Relations of Labor and Capital 1889* (Toronto: University of Toronto Press, 1973), pp. 113–14.

36. The expression comes from Jamie L. Bronstein, *Caught in the Machinery: Workplace Accidents and Injured Workers in Nineteenth-Century Britain* (Stanford: Stanford University Press, 2008).

37. Greg Kealey, ed., *Canada Investigates Industrialism: The Royal Commission on the Relations of Labor and Capital 1889* (Toronto: University of Toronto Press, 1973), pp. 395–6.

38. Greg Kealey, ed., *Canada Investigates Industrialism: The Royal Commission on the Relations of Labor and Capital 1889* (Toronto: University of Toronto Press, 1973), pp. 385–6.

39. Bettina Bradbury, *Working Families: Age, Gender, and Daily Survival in Industrializing Montreal* (Toronto: McClelland & Stewart, 1993), pp. 133, 143.

40. Greg Kealey, ed., *Canada Investigates Industrialism: The Royal Commission on the Relations of Labor and Capital 1889* (Toronto: University of Toronto Press, 1973), pp. 321–2.
41. Greg Kealey, ed., *Canada Investigates Industrialism: The Royal Commission on the Relations of Labor and Capital 1889* (Toronto: University of Toronto Press, 1973), pp. 225–7.
42. Bettina Bradbury, *Working Families: Age, Gender, and Daily Survival in Industrializing Montreal* (Toronto: McClelland & Stewart, 1993), p. 165.
43. John Bullen, "Hidden Workers: Child Labour and the Family Economy in Late Nineteenth-Century Urban Ontario," *Labour/Le Travail*, vol. 18 (Fall 1986): 163–87. On newsboys in the United States, see Vincent DiGirolamo, *Crying the News: A History of America's Newsboys* (New York: Oxford University Press, 2019).
44. Magda Fahrni, "'Ruffled' Mistresses and 'Discontented' Maids: Respectability and the Case of Domestic Service, 1880–1914," *Labour/Le Travail*, 39 (Spring 1997): 69–97.
45. Carolyn Strange, "Wounded Womanhood and Dead Men: Chivalry and the Trials of Clara Ford and Carrie Davies," in Franca Iacovetta and Mariana Valverde, eds, *Gender Conflicts: New Essays in Women's History* (Toronto: University of Toronto Press, 1992).
46. Quoted in Magda Fahrni, "'Ruffled' Mistresses and 'Discontented' Maids: Respectability and the Case of Domestic Service, 1880–1914," *Labour/Le Travail*, 39 (Spring 1997), p. 83.
47. Magda Fahrni, "'Ruffled' Mistresses and 'Discontented' Maids: Respectability and the Case of Domestic Service, 1880–1914," *Labour/Le Travail*, 39 (Spring 1997): 69–97; Genevieve Leslie, "Domestic Service in Canada, 1880–1920," in Janice Acton, et al., eds, *Women at Work: Ontario, 1850–1930* (Toronto 1974), 71–125; Helen Lenskyj, "A 'Servant Problem' or a 'Servant–Mistress Problem'? Domestic Service in Canada, 1890– 1930," *Atlantis*, 7 (Fall 1981), 3–11; Claudette Lacelle, *Urban Domestic Servants in Nineteenth Century Canada* (Ottawa: 1987).
48. Magda Fahrni, "'Ruffled' Mistresses and 'Discontented' Maids: Respectability and the Case of Domestic Service, 1880–1914," *Labour/Le Travail*, 39 (Spring 1997), p. 71n7.
49. Nicolas Kenny, "From body and home to nation and world: the varying scales of transnational urbanism in Montreal and Brussels at the turn of the twentieth century," *Urban History*, 36, 2 (2009), p. 232; see also Nicolas Kenny, *The Feel of the City: Experiences of Urban Transformation* (Toronto: University of Toronto Press, 2014).
50. Robert Gagnon, *Questions d'égouts. Santé publique, infrastructures et urbanisation à Montréal au XIXe siècle* (Montréal: Boréal, 2006), pp. 15–18, 62–4, 108, 128, 216.
51. Greg Kealey, ed., *Canada Investigates Industrialism: The Royal Commission on the Relations of Labor and Capital 1889* (Toronto: University of Toronto Press, 1973), p. 252.

52. Michael S. Cross, ed., *The Workingman in the Nineteenth Century* (Toronto: University of Toronto Press, 1974), pp. 148–50.
53. Bettina Bradbury, *Working Families: Age, Gender, and Daily Survival in Industrializing Montreal* (Montreal: McClelland & Stewart, 1993), p. 37.
54. Mary Anne Poutanen, *Beyond Brutal Passions: Prostitution in Early Nineteenth-Century Montreal* (Montreal: McGill-Queen's University Press, 2015); Kathryn Harvey, "To Love, Honour, and Obey: Wife-battering in Working-Class Montreal, 1869–79," *Urban History Review/Revue d'histoire urbaine*, 19, 2 (1990): 128–40.
55. See, e.g., Roderick MacLeod, "The Road to Terrace Bank: Land Capitalization, Public Space, and the Redpath Family Home, 1837–1861," *Journal of the Canadian Historical Association*, 14, 1 (2003): 165–92.
56. Sherry Olson et Patricia Thornton, "Familles montréalaises du XIXe siècle: trois cultures, trois trajectoires," *Cahiers québécois de démographie*, 21, 2 (1991): 51–75; Denyse Baillargeon, *Un Québec en mal d'enfants. La médicalisation de la maternité, 1910–1970* (Montréal: Éditions du Remue-ménage, 2004); Terry Copp, *The Anatomy of Poverty: The Condition of the Working Class in Montreal, 1897–1929* (Toronto: McClelland & Stewart, 1974).
57. Most Canadian provinces did not systematically collect statistics on maternal mortality before the 1920s. In 1925, Dr. Helen MacMurchy found that maternal mortality rates in Canada, at 5.5 deaths per thousand births, were higher than in many European countries. Nanci Langford, "Childbirth on the Canadian Prairies, 1880–1930," *Journal of Historical Sociology*, 8, 3 (September 1995), p. 299n7; H. MacMurchy, "On Maternal Mortality in Canada," *Canadian Medical Association Journal*, 15, 3 (1925): 293–7.
58. Christina Simmons, "'Helping the Poorer Sisters': The Women of the Jost Mission, Halifax, 1905–1945," *Acadiensis*, 14, 1 (Autumn 1984): 3–27.
59. Judith Fingard, "The Winter's Tale: The Seasonal Contours of Pre-industrial Poverty in British North America, 1815-1860," *Historical Papers/Communications historiques*, 9, 1 (1974): 65–94.
60. On the "renouveau religieux," see René Hardy, *Contrôle social et mutation de la culture religieuse au Québec, 1830–1930* (Montreal: Boréal, 1999); Louis Rousseau, "À propos du 'réveil religieux' dans le Québec du XIXe siècle: où se loge le vrai débat?", *Revue d'histoire de l'Amérique française*, 49, 2, automne 1995, pp. 223–45. On Ignace Bourget, see Roberto Perin, *Ignace de Montréal. Artisan d'une identité nationale* (Montréal: Boréal, 2008).
61. Huguette Lapointe-Roy, *Charité bien ordonnée: le premier réseau de lutte contre la pauvreté à Montréal au 19e siècle* (Montreal: Boréal, 1987).
62. Sherry Olson and Patricia Thornton, *Peopling the North American City: Montreal 1840–1900* (Montreal; Kingston: McGill-Queen's University Press, 2011), p. 182.

CHAPTER 4

1. Constance Backhouse, *Petticoats and Prejudice: Women and Law in Nineteenth-Century Canada* (Toronto: The Osgoode Society and Women's Press, 1991), p. 45.
2. Margaret Conrad, Toni Laidlaw, and Donna Smyth, eds, *No Place Like Home* (Halifax: Formac Publishing Company, 1988), p. 10.
3. Constance Backhouse, *Petticoats and Prejudice: Women and Law in Nineteenth-Century Canada* (Toronto: The Osgoode Society and Women's Press, 1991), p. 39; Bettina Bradbury, *Wife to Widow: Lives, Laws, and Politics in Nineteenth-Century Montreal* (Vancouver: UBC Press, 2011), pp. 62–8.
4. Constance Backhouse, "'Pure Patriarchy': Nineteenth-Century Canadian Marriage," *McGill Law Journal*, 31 (1986), pp. 271–2.
5. Constance Backhouse, "'Pure Patriarchy': Nineteenth-Century Canadian Marriage," *McGill Law Journal*, 31 (1986).
6. Lori Chambers, "Women's Labour, Relationship Breakdown, and Ownership of the Family Farm," *Canadian Journal of Law and Society*, 25 (2010), p. 78. On married women's "civil death" under Quebec's Civil Code, see Marie Lacoste Gérin-Lajoie, *Traité de droit usuel* (Montréal: 1902).
7. Constance Backhouse, *Petticoats and Prejudice: Women and Law in Nineteenth-Century Canada* (Toronto: The Osgoode Society and Women's Press, 1991), p. 177.
8. Constance Backhouse, "'Pure Patriarchy': Nineteenth-Century Canadian Marriage," *McGill Law Journal*, 31 (1986), p. 272; James Snell, "Marital Cruelty: Women and the Nova Scotia Divorce Court, 1900–1939," *Acadiensis*, 18 (Autumn 1988), p. 5.
9. Constance Backhouse, *Petticoats and Prejudice: Women and Law in Nineteenth-Century Canada* (Toronto: The Osgoode Society and Women's Press, 1991), p. 170; Backhouse, "'Pure Patriarchy'," p. 270.
10. Constance Backhouse, *Petticoats and Prejudice: Women and Law in Nineteenth-Century Canada* (Toronto: The Osgoode Society and Women's Press, 1991), p. 187. Margaret Conrad, Toni Laidlaw, and Donna Smyth mention the divorce law passed by Nova Scotia in 1857 on p. 12 of Conrad, Laidlaw, and Smyth, eds, *No Place Like Home* (Halifax: Formac Publishing Company, 1988).
11. James Snell, "Marital Cruelty: Women and the Nova Scotia Divorce Court, 1900–1939," *Acadiensis*, 18 (Autumn 1988), pp. 10, 16.
12. Quoted in Constance Backhouse, *Petticoats and Prejudice: Women and Law in Nineteenth-Century Canada* (Toronto: The Osgoode Society and Women's Press, 1991), p. 167.
13. Constance Backhouse, *Petticoats and Prejudice: Women and Law in Nineteenth-Century Canada* (Toronto: The Osgoode Society and Women's Press, 1991), p. 189.

14. Constance Backhouse, *Petticoats and Prejudice: Women and Law in Nineteenth-Century Canada* (Toronto: The Osgoode Society and Women's Press, 1991), Chapter 6, "Divorce and Separation," esp. pp. 174–6; Backhouse, "'Pure Patriarchy': Nineteenth-Century Canadian Marriage," *McGill Law Journal*, 31 (1986), pp. 303–12.
15. Constance Backhouse, *Petticoats and Prejudice: Women and Law in Nineteenth-Century Canada* (Toronto: The Osgoode Society and Women's Press, 1991), p. 190.
16. Constance Backhouse, *Petticoats and Prejudice: Women and Law in Nineteenth-Century Canada* (Toronto: The Osgoode Society and Women's Press, 1991), p. 170 and Chapter 7.
17. Cynthia S. Fish, "La puissance paternelle et les cas de garde d'enfants au Québec, 1866–1928," *Revue d'histoire de l'Amérique française*, 57, 4 (printemps 2004): 509–33.
18. Constance Backhouse, *Petticoats and Prejudice: Women and Law in Nineteenth-Century Canada* (Toronto: The Osgoode Society and Women's Press, 1991), p. 179–80; Margaret Conrad, Toni Laidlaw, and Donna Smyth, eds, *No Place Like Home* (Halifax: Formac Publishing Company, 1988), p. 12.
19. Peter Baskerville, *A Silent Revolution? Gender and Wealth in English Canada, 1860–1930* (Montreal; Kingston: McGill-Queen's University Press, 2008); Lori Chambers, "Women's Labour, Relationship Breakdown, and Ownership of the Family Farm," *Canadian Journal of Law and Society*, 25 (2010), p. 78.
20. Peter Baskerville, "Women and Investment in Late-Nineteenth-Century Urban Canada: Victoria and Hamilton, 1880–1901," *Canadian Historical Review*, 80, 2 (1999): 191–218; Baskerville, *A Silent Revolution?*
21. Christopher A. Clarkson, "Property Law and Family Regulation in Pacific British North America, 1862–1873," *Histoire sociale/Social History*, 30, 60 (1997): 386–416. The quotations are from pages 392 and 414. See also Chris Clarkson, *Domestic Reforms: Political Visions and Family Regulation in British Columbia, 1862–1940* (Vancouver: University of British Columbia Press, 2007).
22. Constance Backhouse, *Petticoats and Prejudice: Women and Law in Nineteenth-Century Canada* (Toronto: The Osgoode Society and Women's Press, 1991), pp. 40–80.
23. Cited in Angus McLaren and Arlene Tigar McLaren, *The Bedroom and the State: The Changing Practices and Politics of Contraception and Abortion in Canada, 1880–1980* (Toronto: McClelland & Stewart, 1986), p. 19.
24. Angus McLaren and Arlene Tigar McLaren, *The Bedroom and the State: The Changing Practices and Politics of Contraception and Abortion in Canada, 1880–1980* (Toronto: McClelland & Stewart, 1986), p. 18.
25. Constance Backhouse, *Petticoats and Prejudice: Women and Law in Nineteenth-Century Canada* (Toronto: The Osgoode Society and Women's Press, 1991), p. 166.

26. Angus McLaren and Arlene Tigar McLaren, *The Bedroom and the State: The Changing Practices and Politics of Contraception and Abortion in Canada, 1880–1980* (Toronto: McClelland & Stewart, 1986), pp. 32–53.
27. Marie-Aimée Cliche, "L'infanticide dans la région de Québec (1660–1969)," *Revue d'histoire de l'Amérique française*, 44, 1 (été 1990): 31–59; Constance Backhouse, *Petticoats and Prejudice: Women and Law in Nineteenth-Century Canada* (Toronto: The Osgoode Society and Women's Press, 1991), pp. 112–39; Andrée Lévesque, *La norme et les déviantes. Des femmes au Québec pendant l'entre-deux-guerres* (Montréal: Éditions du remue-ménage, 1989), Chapter 5.
28. Magda Fahrni, "'Ruffled' Mistresses and 'Discontented' Maids: Respectability and the Case of Domestic Service, 1880–1914," *Labour/Le Travail*, 39 (Spring 1997), p. 92.
29. On domestic violence in the United States, see Linda Gordon, *Heroes of Their Own Lives: The Politics and History of Family Violence—Boston, 1880–1960* (Urbana-Champaign: University of Illinois Press, 2002). On Great Britain, see Anna Clark, *Women's Silence, Men's Violence: Sexual Assault in England, 1770–1845* (London: Pandora, 1987).
30. Kathryn Harvey, "Amazons and Victims: Resisting Wife-Abuse in Working-Class Montréal, 1869–1879," *Journal of the Canadian Historical Association*, 2, 1 (1991): 131–48.
31. Catherine Cleverdon, *The Woman Suffrage Movement in Canada*, 2nd edition (Toronto: University of Toronto Press, 1974); Joan Sangster, *One Hundred Years of Struggle: The History of Women and the Vote in Canada* (Vancouver: UBC Press, 2018). See also the other books in the UBC Press series entitled "Women's Suffrage and the Struggle for Democracy."
32. Chad Gaffield, "Schooling, the Economy, and Rural Society in Nineteenth-Century Ontario," p. 71, in Joy Parr, ed., *Childhood and Family in Canadian History* (Toronto: McClelland & Stewart, 1982).
33. Alison Prentice, *The School Promoters: Education and Social Class in Mid-Nineteenth Century Upper Canada* (Toronto: McClelland and Stewart, 1977); Susan E. Houston and Alison Prentice, *Schooling and Scholars in Nineteenth-Century Ontario* (Toronto: University of Toronto Press, 1988).
34. Cited in Alison Prentice, *The School Promoters*, p. 170.
35. Chad Gaffield, "Schooling, the Economy, and Rural Society in Nineteenth-Century Ontario," p. 79, in Joy Parr, ed., *Childhood and Family in Canadian History* (Toronto: McClelland & Stewart, 1982).
36. Chad Gaffield, "Schooling, the Economy, and Rural Society in Nineteenth-Century Ontario," p. 71, in Joy Parr, ed., *Childhood and Family in Canadian History* (Toronto: McClelland & Stewart, 1982).
37. Bettina Bradbury, "Canadian Children Who Lived with One Parent in 1901," p. 37, in *Bringing Children and Youth into Canadian History: The Difference Kids Make*, eds Mona Gleason and Tamara Myers (Don Mills: Oxford University Press Canada, 2017).

38. Susan E. Houston, "The 'Waifs and Strays' of a Late Victorian City: Juvenile Delinquents in Toronto," p. 134, in Joy Parr, ed., *Childhood and Family in Canadian History* (Toronto: McClelland & Stewart, 1982).
39. Jean-Marie Fecteau et al., "Une politique de l'enfance délinquante et en danger: la mise en place des écoles de réforme et d'industrie au Québec (1840–1873)," *Crime, Histoire & Sociétés/Crime, History & Societies* 2, 1 (1998), pp. 75–110; Dale Gilbert, "Assister les familles de Québec. L'école de réforme et l'école d'industrie de l'Hospice Saint-Charles, 1870–1950," *Revue d'histoire de l'Amérique française*, 61, 3–4 (hiver 2008): 469–500; Tamara Myers, "Embodying Delinquency: Boys' Bodies, Sexuality, and Juvenile Justice History in Early Twentieth-Century Quebec," *Journal of the History of Sexuality*, 14, 4 (2005).
40. Tamara Myers and Joan Sangster, "Retorts, Runaways, and Riots: Patterns of Resistance in Canadian Reform Schools for Girls," *Journal of Social History*, 34, 3 (Spring 2001): 669–97.
41. Tamara Myers, "'Qui t'a débauchée?' Female Adolescent Sexuality and the Juvenile Delinquents' Court in Early Twentieth-Century Montreal," pp. 377–94, in *Family Matters: Papers in Post-Confederation Canadian Family History*, eds Lori Chambers and Edgar-André Montigny (Toronto: Canadian Scholars Press, 1998); Tamara Myers, *Caught: Montreal's Modern Girls and the Law, 1869–1945* (Toronto: University of Toronto Press, 2006).
42. Tamara Myers, "The Voluntary Delinquent: Parents, Daughters, and the Montreal Juvenile Delinquents' Court in 1918," *Canadian Historical Review*, 80, 2 (June 1999), p. 255, note 50.
43. Mariana Valverde, "The Mixed Social Economy as a Canadian Tradition," *Studies in Political Economy*, 14 (1995): 33–60.
44. Carmen J. Nielson, *Private Women and the Public Good: Charity and State Formation in Hamilton, Ontario, 1846–1893* (Vancouver: UBC Press, 2014); Charlotte Neff, "Ontario Government Funding and Supervision of Infants' Homes 1875–1893," *Journal of Family History*, 38, 1 (2012): 17–54.
45. Renée N. Lafferty, *The Guardianship of Best Interests: Institutional Care for the Children of the Poor in Halifax, 1850–1960* (Montreal; Kingston: McGill-Queen's University Press, 2013).
46. Jean-Marie Fecteau et al., "Une politique de l'enfance délinquante et en danger: la mise en place des écoles de réforme et d'industrie au Québec (1840–1873)," *Crime, Histoire & Sociétés/Crime, History & Societies* 2, 1 (1998), pp. 75–110.
47. David Wright, *SickKids: The History of The Hospital for Sick Children* (Toronto: University of Toronto Press, 2016), p. 27.
48. Denyse Baillargeon, *Naître, vivre, grandir. Sainte-Justine, 1907–2007* (Montréal: Boréal, 2007); Denyse Baillargeon, *Un Québec en mal d'enfants. La médicalisation de la maternité, 1910–1970* (Montréal: Éditions du Remue-ménage, 2004).
49. Sarah Carter, *Aboriginal People and Colonizers of Western Canada to 1900* (Toronto: University of Toronto Press, 1999), pp. 162–4.

50. The text of the 1869 legislation (32–33 Victoria, chapter 42) can be found here: https://www.aadnc-aandc.gc.ca/DAM/DAM-INTER-HQ/STAGING/texte-text/a69c6_1100100010205_eng.pdf
51. John Herd Thompson, *Forging the Prairie West* (Toronto: Oxford University Press, 1998), p. 60.
52. Joanne Barker, "Gender, Sovereignty, Rights: Native Women's Activism against Social Inequality and Violence in Canada," *American Quarterly*, 60, 2 (June 2008): 259–66.
53. Gerhard J. Ens and Joe Sawchuk, *From New Peoples to New Nations: Aspects of Métis History and Identity from the Eighteenth to the Twenty-first Centuries* (Toronto: University of Toronto Press, 2015).
54. Sylvia Van Kirk, *"Many Tender Ties": Women in Fur-Trade Society in Western Canada, 1670–1870* (Winnipeg: Watson & Dwyer Publishing, 1980); Jennifer S.H. Brown, *Strangers in Blood: Fur Trade Company Families in Indian Country* (Vancouver: University of British Columbia Press, 1980); Robin Jarvis Brownlie and Valerie J. Korinek, eds, *Finding a Way to the Heart: Feminist Writings on Aboriginal and Women's History in Canada* (Winnipeg: University of Manitoba Press, 2012).
55. Sylvia Van Kirk, "The Role of Native Women in the Fur Trade Society of Western Canada, 1670–1830," *Frontiers: A Journal of Women Studies*, 7, 3 (1984): 9–13.
56. Sylvia Van Kirk, *"Many Tender Ties": Women in Fur-Trade Society in Western Canada, 1670–1870* (Winnipeg: Watson & Dwyer Publishing, 1980), p. 121.
57. Quoted in Sylvia Van Kirk, *"Many Tender Ties": Women in Fur-Trade Society in Western Canada, 1670–1870* (Winnipeg: Watson & Dwyer Publishing, 1980), p. 139. On Daniel Harmon and Lisette, see also Jennifer S.H. Brown, *Strangers in Blood: Fur Trade Company Families in Indian Country* (Vancouver: University of British Columbia Press, 1980), pp. 103–7.
58. Constance Backhouse, *Petticoats and Prejudice: Women and Law in Nineteenth-Century Canada* (Toronto: The Osgoode Society and Women's Press, 1991), pp. 9–22.
59. Sylvia Van Kirk, "The Role of Native Women in the Fur Trade Society of Western Canada, 1670–1830," *Frontiers: A Journal of Women Studies*, 7, 3 (1984), p. 12; Adele Perry, "'Is your Garden in England, Sir': James Douglas's Archive and the Politics of Home," *History Workshop Journal*, 70 (2010), esp. pp. 75–6; Sarah Carter, *Aboriginal People and Colonizers of Western Canada to 1900* (Toronto: University of Toronto Press, 1999), pp. 79–80.
60. Jean Barman, *The West Beyond the West: A History of British Columbia* (Toronto: University of Toronto Press, 1991), p. 90.
61. Maria Campbell, "Foreword: Charting the Way," pp. xxii–xxiii, in Nicole St-Onge, Carolyn Podruchny, and Brenda Macdougall, eds, *Contours of a People: Metis Family, Mobility, and History* (Norman: University of Oklahoma Press, 2012). Campbell's description of the buffalo hunt draws on the recollections of Victoria Belcourt Callihoo.

62. Brenda Macdougall, Carolyn Podruchny, and Nicole St-Onge, "Introduction: Cultural Mobility and the Contours of Difference," pp. 8–9, in Nicole St-Onge, Carolyn Podruchny, and Brenda Macdougall, eds, *Contours of a People: Metis Family, Mobility, and History* (Norman: University of Oklahoma Press, 2012); Nicole St-Onge and Carolyn Podruchny, "Scuttling along a Spider's Web: Mobility and Kinship in Metis Ethnogenesis," pp. 61–2, in Nicole St-Onge, Carolyn Podruchny, and Brenda Macdougall, eds, *Contours of a People: Metis Family, Mobility, and History* (Norman: University of Oklahoma Press, 2012).

63. Nicole St-Onge and Carolyn Podruchny, "Scuttling along a Spider's Web: Mobility and Kinship in Metis Ethnogenesis," p. 81, in Nicole St-Onge, Carolyn Podruchny, and Brenda Macdougall, eds, *Contours of a People: Metis Family, Mobility, and History* (Norman: University of Oklahoma Press, 2012).

64. Brenda Macdougall, Carolyn Podruchny, and Nicole St-Onge, "Introduction: Cultural Mobility and the Contours of Difference," p. 6, in Nicole St-Onge, Carolyn Podruchny, and Brenda Macdougall, eds, *Contours of a People: Metis Family, Mobility, and History* (Norman: University of Oklahoma Press, 2012).

65. Erin Millions, "Portraits and Gravestones: Documenting the Transnational Lives of Nineteenth-Century British-Métis Students," *Journal of the Canadian Historical Association*, 29, 1 (2018), pp. 13, 22.

66. Sarah Carter, *Aboriginal People and Colonizers of Western Canada to 1900* (Toronto: University of Toronto Press, 1999), pp. 105–11; Jacqueline Peterson, "Red River Redux: Métis Ethnogenesis and the Great Lakes Region," p. 24, in Nicole St-Onge, Carolyn Podruchny, and Brenda Macdougall, eds, *Contours of a People: Metis Family, Mobility, and History* (Norman: University of Oklahoma Press, 2012).

67. Sarah Carter, *Aboriginal People and Colonizers of Western Canada to 1900* (Toronto: University of Toronto Press, 1999), pp. 132–40, 168–70.

68. James Daschuk, *Clearing the Plains: Disease, Politics of Starvation, and the Loss of Aboriginal Life* (Regina: University of Regina Press, 2013).

69. Sarah Carter, *Aboriginal People and Colonizers of Western Canada to 1900* (Toronto: University of Toronto Press, 1999), p. 150.

70. Chelsea Vowel, *Indigenous Writes: A Guide to First Nations, Métis and Inuit Issues in Canada* (Winnipeg: Highwater Press, 2016), p. 171; Celia Haig-Brown, "Always Remembering: Indian Residential Schools in Canada," p. 247, in *Aboriginal History: A Reader*, 2nd edition, eds Kristin Burnett and Geoff Read (Don Mills: Oxford University Press Canada, 2016).

71. Jean Barman, "Separate and Unequal: Indian and White Girls at All Hallows School, 1884–1920," pp. 215–33, in Veronica Strong-Boag and Anita Clair Fellman, eds, *Rethinking Canada: The Promise of Women's History*, 2nd edition (Toronto: Copp Clark Pitman, 1991).

72. Sarah Carter, *Aboriginal People and Colonizers of Western Canada to 1900* (Toronto: University of Toronto Press, 1999), p. 165.

73. Celia Haig-Brown, "Always Remembering: Indian Residential Schools in Canada," p. 245, in *Aboriginal History: A Reader*, 2nd edition, eds Kristin Burnett and Geoff Read (Don Mills: Oxford University Press Canada, 2016).

74. Quoted in Sarah De Leeuw, "'If Anything Is to Be Done with the Indian, We Must Catch Him Very Young': Colonial Constructions of Aboriginal Children and the Geographies of Indian Residential Schooling in British Columbia, Canada," p. 335, in *Bringing Children and Youth into Canadian History: The Difference Kids Make*, eds Mona Gleason and Tamara Myers (Don Mills: Oxford University Press Canada, 2017).

75. John S. Milloy, *A National Crime: The Canadian Government and the Residential School System, 1879 to 1976* (Winnipeg: University of Manitoba Press, 1999).

76. See Milloy, *A National Crime: The Canadian Government and the Residential School System, 1879 to 1976* (Winnipeg: University of Manitoba Press, 1999), Chapter 5, "'The Charge of Manslaughter': Disease and Death, 1879–1946."

77. Quoted in Milloy, *A National Crime: The Canadian Government and the Residential School System, 1879 to 1976* (Winnipeg: University of Manitoba Press, 1999), p. 80.

78. Quoted in Milloy, *A National Crime: The Canadian Government and the Residential School System, 1879 to 1976* (Winnipeg: University of Manitoba Press, 1999), p. 109.

79. Quoted in Milloy, *A National Crime: The Canadian Government and the Residential School System, 1879 to 1976* (Winnipeg: University of Manitoba Press, 1999), p. 88.

80. *Canada's Residential Schools*, 6 volumes (Montreal; Kingston: McGill-Queen's University Press, 2015). In the summary of the final report of the Truth and Reconciliation Commission, an entire section is devoted to "Les séquelles" ("after-effects" or "aftermath"): *Honorer la vérité, réconcilier pour l'avenir. Sommaire du rapport final de la Commission de vérité et réconciliation du Canada* (Montreal; Kingston: McGill-Queen's University Press, 2015), pp. 137–92.

81. The quotation is to be found in Celia Haig-Brown, "Always Remembering: Indian Residential Schools in Canada," p. 252, in *Aboriginal History: A Reader*, 2nd edition, eds Kristin Burnett and Geoff Read (Don Mills: Oxford University Press Canada, 2016). On corporal punishment in residential schools, see Milloy, *A National Crime: The Canadian Government and the Residential School System, 1879 to 1976* (Winnipeg: University of Manitoba Press, 1999), p. 139; *Honorer la vérité, réconcilier pour l'avenir. Sommaire du rapport final de la Commission de vérité et réconciliation du Canada* (Montreal; Kingston: McGill-Queen's University Press, 2015), pp. 105–14.

82. Quoted in Celia Haig-Brown, "Always Remembering: Indian Residential Schools in Canada," p. 249, in *Aboriginal History: A Reader*, 2nd edition, eds Kristin Burnett and Geoff Read (Don Mills: Oxford University Press Canada, 2016).

83. Quoted in Celia Haig-Brown, "Always Remembering: Indian Residential Schools in Canada," p. 251, in *Aboriginal History: A Reader*, 2nd edition, eds Kristin Burnett and Geoff Read (Don Mills: Oxford University Press Canada, 2016). On efforts to suppress the use of Aboriginal languages in the residential schools, see *Honorer la vérité, réconcilier pour l'avenir*, pp. 83–7.
84. Quoted in Chelsea Vowel, *Indigenous Writes: A Guide to First Nations, Métis and Inuit Issues in Canada* (Winnipeg: Highwater Press, 2016), p. 173.
85. Sarah Carter, *Imperial Plots: Women, Land, and the Spadework of British Colonialism on the Canadian Prairies* (Winnipeg: University of Manitoba Press, 2016); John Herd Thompson, *Forging the Prairie West* (Toronto: Oxford University Press, 1998), pp. 67–8; Ryan Eyford, *White Settler Reserve: New Iceland and the Colonization of the Canadian West* (Vancouver: UBC Press, 2016).
86. John Herd Thompson, *Forging the Prairie West* (Toronto: Oxford University Press, 1998), p. 77.
87. Pierre Anctil, *Histoire des Juifs du Québec* (Montreal: Boréal, 2017), p. 81; Arthur Ross, *Communal Solidarity: Immigration, Settlement, and Social Welfare in Winnipeg's Jewish Community, 1882–1930* (Winnipeg: University of Manitoba Press, 2019).
88. Sarah Carter, *Imperial Plots: Women, Land, and the Spadework of British Colonialism on the Canadian Prairies* (Winnipeg: University of Manitoba Press, 2016), p. 4. See also John Herd Thompson, *Forging the Prairie West* (Toronto: Oxford University Press, 1998), p. 52.
89. John Herd Thompson, *Forging the Prairie West* (Toronto: Oxford University Press, 1998), p. 83; Lori Chambers, "Women's Labour, Relationship Breakdown, and Ownership of the Family Farm," *Canadian Journal of Law and Society*, 25 (2010), pp. 75–7.
90. Ryan C. Eyford, "Quarantined Within a New Colonial Order: The 1876–1877 Lake Winnipeg Smallpox Epidemic," *Journal of the Canadian Historical Association*, 17, 1 (2006): 55–78.
91. Freda Hawkins, *Critical Years in Immigration: Canada and Australia Compared*, 2nd edition (Montreal; Kingston: McGill-Queen's University Press, 1991), Chapter 1.
92. Lisa Lowe, *Immigrant Acts: On Asian American Cultural Politics* (Durham: Duke University Press, 1996); Enakshi Dua, "Exclusion through Inclusion: Female Asian Migration in the Making of Canada as a White Settler Nation," *Gender, Place and Culture*, 14, 4 (2007), pp. 449, 463; Anthony B. Chan, *Gold Mountain: The Chinese in the New World* (Vancouver: New Star Books, 1983).
93. John Herd Thompson, *Forging the Prairie West* (Toronto: Oxford University Press, 1998), p. 73; Enakshi Dua, "Exclusion through Inclusion: Female Asian Migration in the Making of Canada as a White Settler Nation," *Gender, Place and Culture*, 14, 4 (2007), p. 462.

94. Laura Ishiguro, "'A Dreadful Little Glutton Always Telling You about Food': The Epistolary Everyday and the Making of Settler Colonial British Columbia," *Canadian Historical Review*, 99, 2 (June 2018): 258–83.
95. Laura Ishiguro, "'Growing Up and Grown Up... in our Future City': Discourses of Childhood and Settler Futurity in Colonial British Columbia," *BC Studies*, 190 (Summer 2016): 15–38.
96. Philip Girard, "'If two ride a horse, one must ride in front': Married Women's Nationality and the Law in Canada, 1880–1950," *Canadian Historical Review*, 94, 1 (March 2013): 28–54.
97. Quoted in Bruce Curtis, *The Politics of Population: State Formation, Statistics, and the Census of Canada, 1840–1875* (Toronto: University of Toronto Press, 2001), pp. 206, 220.
98. Howard P. Chudacoff, *How Old Are You? Age Consciousness in American Culture* (Princeton, NJ: Princeton University Press, 1989); Howard P. Chudacoff, "The Life Course of Women: Age and Age Consciousness, 1865–1915," *Journal of Family History* 5, 3 (1980): 274–92.
99. Bruce Curtis, *The Politics of Population: State Formation, Statistics, and the Census of Canada, 1840–1875* (Toronto: University of Toronto Press, 2001), p. 216.
100. George Emery, *Facts of Life: The Social Construction of Vital Statistics, Ontario, 1869–1952* (Montreal; Kingston: McGill-Queen's University Press, 1993), p. 5.

CHAPTER 5

1. For Canada's population in 1914, see Cynthia Toman, *Sister Soldiers of the Great War: The Nurses of the Canadian Army Medical Corps* (Vancouver: University of British Columbia Press, 2016), p. 11.
2. Desmond Morton, *When Your Number's Up: The Canadian Soldier in the First World War* (Toronto: Vintage Canada, 1994), p. 9.
3. Jonathan Vance, *Death So Noble: Memory, Meaning, and the First World War* (Vancouver: UBC Press, 1997), p. 260.
4. Yves Tremblay, "Le service militaire des Canadiens français en 1914–1918," in *Le Québec dans la Grande Guerre. Engagements, refus, heritages*, ed. Charles-Philippe Courtois and Laurent Veyssière (Québec: Septentrion, 2015), p. 65.
5. Mélanie Morin-Pelletier, "'The Anxious Waiting Ones at Home': Deux familles canadiennes plongées dans le tourment de la Grande Guerre," *Histoire sociale/Social History*, 47, 94 (2014), p. 362.
6. Nic Clarke, *Unwanted Warriors: Rejected Volunteers of the Canadian Expeditionary Force* (Vancouver: UBC Press, 2015), p. 3.
7. Jonathan Vance, *Death So Noble: Memory, Meaning, and the First World War* (Vancouver: UBC Press, 1997), p. 112.

8. Quoted in Paul Maroney, "'The Great Adventure': The Context and Ideology of Recruiting in Ontario, 1914–17," *Canadian Historical Review*, 77, 1 (March 1996), p. 62.
9. Nic Clarke, *Unwanted Warriors: Rejected Volunteers of the Canadian Expeditionary Force* (Vancouver: UBC Press, 2015), pp. 155–6.
10. Paul Maroney, "'The Great Adventure': The Context and Ideology of Recruiting in Ontario, 1914–17," *Canadian Historical Review*, 77, 1 (March 1996), p. 76.
11. Jonathan Vance, *Death So Noble: Memory, Meaning, and the First World War* (Vancouver: UBC Press, 1997), pp. 125–6.
12. Desmond Morton, *Fight or Pay: Soldiers' Families in the Great War* (Vancouver: UBC Press, 2004), p. 30.
13. Tim Cook, "'He was determined to go': Underage Soldiers in the Canadian Expeditionary Force," *Histoire sociale/Social History*, 41, 81 (May 2008): 41–74. The quotation from Florence Brown is on page 69.
14. Kristine Alexander, "An Honour and a Burden: Canadian Girls and the Great War," p. 183, in *A Sisterhood of Suffering and Service: Women and Girls of Canada and Newfoundland During the First World War*, ed. Sarah Glassford and Amy Shaw (Vancouver: UBC Press, 2012).
15. Béatrice Richard, "Le Québec face à la conscription (1917–1918). Essai d'analyse sociale d'un refus," pp. 113–30, in *Le Québec dans la Grande Guerre. Engagements, refus, héritages*, ed. Charles-Philippe Courtois and Laurent Veyssière (Québec: Sillery, 2015).
16. John Thompson, *The Harvests of War: The Prairie West, 1914–1918* (Toronto: McClelland and Stewart, 1978); Mourad Djebabla-Brun, *Combattre avec les vivres. L'effort de guerre alimentaire canadien en 1914–1918* (Québec: Septentrion, 1915).
17. W.R. Young, "Conscription, Rural Depopulation, and the Farmers of Ontario, 1917–19," *Canadian Historical Review*, 53, 3 (1972), p. 314.
18. W.R. Young, "Conscription, Rural Depopulation, and the Farmers of Ontario, 1917–19," *Canadian Historical Review*, 53, 3 (1972), p. 308.
19. Cynthia Toman, *Sister Soldiers of the Great War: The Nurses of the Canadian Army Medical Corps* (Vancouver: University of British Columbia Press, 2016), pp. 8, 49, 51, 58–9, 66.
20. The words are those of Mary Elizabeth Agnew, quoted in Desmond Morton, *Fight or Pay: Soldiers' Families in the Great War* (Vancouver: UBC Press, 2004), p. 30.
21. Desmond Morton, *Fight or Pay: Soldiers' Families in the Great War* (Vancouver: UBC Press, 2004).
22. Paul Maroney, "'The Great Adventure': The Context and Ideology of Recruiting in Ontario, 1914–17," *Canadian Historical Review*, 77, 1 (March 1996), p. 67.
23. Quoted in Nic Clarke, *Unwanted Warriors: Rejected Volunteers of the Canadian Expeditionary Force* (Vancouver: UBC Press, 2015), p. 18.

24. Mélanie Morin-Pelletier, "'The Anxious Waiting Ones at Home': Deux familles canadiennes plongées dans le tourment de la Grande Guerre," *Histoire sociale/Social History*, 47, 94 (2014).
25. Douglas McCalla, "The Economic Impact of the Great War," in *Canada and the First World War: Essays in Honour of Robert Craig Brown*, edited by David Mackenzie (Toronto: University of Toronto Press, 2005), pp. 138–53.
26. Magda Fahrni, "La Première Guerre mondiale et l'intervention étatique au Québec. Le cas des accidents du travail," in *Le Québec dans la Grande Guerre. Engagements, refus, héritages*, edited by Charles-Philippe Courtois and Laurent Veyssière (Québec: Sillery, 2015), p. 137.
27. On women's work during the First World War, see Joan Sangster, "Mobilizing Women for War," in *Canada and the First World War: Essays in Honour of Robert Craig Brown*, edited by David Mackenzie (Toronto: University of Toronto Press, 2005).
28. Magda Fahrni, "La Première Guerre mondiale et l'intervention étatique au Québec. Le cas des accidents du travail," in *Le Québec dans la Grande Guerre. Engagements, refus, héritages*, edited by Charles-Philippe Courtois and Laurent Veyssière (Québec: Sillery, 2015), pp. 131–41; and Magda Fahrni, "'Victimes de la tâche journalière': La gestion des accidents du travail au Québec pendant la Grande Guerre," in *Mains-d'œuvre en guerre, 1914–1918*, edited by Laure Machu, Isabelle Lespinet-Moret, and Vincent Viet (Paris: La Documentation française, 2018).
29. Margot I. Duley, "The Unquiet Knitters of Newfoundland: From Mothers of the Regiment to Mothers of the Nation," pp. 51–74, and Alison Norman, "'In Defense of the Empire': The Six Nations of the Grand River and the Great War," pp. 29–50, in *A Sisterhood of Suffering and Service: Women and Girls of Canada and Newfoundland During the First World War*, ed. Sarah Glassford and Amy Shaw (Vancouver: UBC Press, 2012).
30. *Canadian Food Bulletin*, 15 (4 May 1918), p. 3.
31. Quoted in Mourad Djebabla-Brun, *Combattre avec les vivres. L'effort de guerre alimentaire canadien en 1914–1918* (Québec: Septentrion, 2015), p. 9; *Canadian Food Bulletin*, 15 (4 May 1918), p. 4.
32. *Canadian Food Bulletin*, 15 (4 May 1918), p. 3.
33. Mourad Djebabla-Brun, *Combattre avec les vivres. L'effort de guerre alimentaire canadien en 1914–1918* (Québec: Septentrion, 2015).
34. *Canadian Food Bulletin*, 15 (4 May 1918), p. 7.
35. Mélanie Morin-Pelletier, "'The Anxious Waiting Ones at Home': Deux familles canadiennes plongées dans le tourment de la Grande Guerre," *Histoire sociale/Social History*, 47, 94 (2014); Jonathan Vance, *Death So Noble: Memory, Meaning, and the First World War* (Vancouver: UBC Press, 1997), p. 11.
36. Desmond Morton and Glenn Wright, *Winning the Second Battle: Canadian Veterans and the Return to Civilian Life, 1915–1930* (Toronto: University of Toronto Press, 1987), p. ix.

37. Margaret W. Westley, *Grandeur et déclin. L'élite anglo-protestante de Montréal, 1900–1950* (Montréal: Libre Expression, 1990), p. 136. See also Jonathan Vance, *Death So Noble: Memory, Meaning, and the First World War* (Vancouver: UBC Press, 1997), pp. 265–6.

38. Desmond Morton and Glenn Wright, *Winning the Second Battle: Canadian Veterans and the Return to Civilian Life, 1915–1930* (Toronto: University of Toronto Press, 1987).

39. Lara Campbell, "'We Who Have Wallowed in the Mud of Flanders': First World War Veterans, Unemployment and the Development of Social Welfare in Canada, 1929–1939," *Journal of the Canadian Historical Association*, New Series, 11 (2000), pp. 129, 131–2.

40. Mark Osborne Humphries, *The Last Plague: Spanish Influenza and the Politics of Public Health in Canada* (Toronto: University of Toronto Press, 2013), pp. 3–4.

41. Esyllt W. Jones, *Influenza 1918: Disease, Death, and Struggle in Winnipeg* (Toronto: University of Toronto Press, 2007), p. 141.

42. Karen Slonim, "Beyond Biology: Understanding the Social Impact of Infectious Disease in Two Aboriginal Communities," p. 119, in *Epidemic Encounters: Influenza, Society, and Culture in Canada, 1918–20*, ed. Magda Fahrni and Esyllt W. Jones (Vancouver: University of British Columbia Press, 2012). See also Mary-Ellen Kelm, "British Columbia First Nations and the Influenza Pandemic of 1918–1919," *BC Studies*, 122 (Summer 1999): 23–48; Maureen Lux, "'The Bitter Flats': The 1918 Influenza Epidemic in Saskatchewan," *Saskatchewan History*, 49, 1 (Spring 1997): 3–13.

43. Mark Osborne Humphries, *The Last Plague: Spanish Influenza and the Politics of Public Health in Canada* (Toronto: University of Toronto Press, 2013), pp. 128–9.

44. D. Ann Herring and Ellen Korol, "The North–South Divide: Social Inequality and Mortality from the 1918 Influenza Pandemic in Hamilton, Ontario," pp. 97–112, in *Epidemic Encounters: Influenza, Society, and Culture in Canada, 1918–20*, ed. Magda Fahrni and Esyllt W. Jones (Vancouver: University of British Columbia Press, 2012).

45. Magda Fahrni, "'Elles sont partout': les femmes et la ville en temps d'épidémie, Montréal, 1918-1920," *Revue d'histoire de l'Amérique française*, 58, 1 (2004): 67–85.

46. Esyllt W. Jones, *Influenza 1918: Disease, Death, and Struggle in Winnipeg* (Toronto: University of Toronto Press, 2007), pp. 154–64.

47. Janice Dickin McGinnis, "The Impact of Epidemic Influenza: Canada, 1918-1919," pp. 447–77, in *Medicine in Canadian Society*, ed. S.E.D. Shortt (Montreal; Kingston: McGill-Queen's University Press, 1981); Esyllt W. Jones, *Influenza 1918: Disease, Death, and Struggle in Winnipeg* (Toronto: University of Toronto Press, 2007); Magda Fahrni and Esyllt W. Jones, eds, *Epidemic Encounters:*

Influenza, Society, and Culture in Canada, 1918–20 (Vancouver: University of British Columbia Press, 2012); Mark Osborne Humphries, *The Last Plague: Spanish Influenza and the Politics of Public Health in Canada* (Toronto: University of Toronto Press, 2013).

48. Esyllt W. Jones, *Influenza 1918: Disease, Death, and Struggle in Winnipeg* (Toronto: University of Toronto Press, 2007), p. 146.
49. Molly Ladd-Taylor, *Mother-Work: Women, Child Welfare and the State* (Urbana and Chicago: University of Illinois Press, 1994); Veronica Strong-Boag, "'Wages for Housework': Mothers' Allowances and the Beginnings of Social Security in Canada," *Journal of Canadian Studies*, 14, 1 (Spring 1979): 24–34; Nancy Christie, *Engendering the State: Family, Work, and Welfare in Canada* (Toronto: University of Toronto Press, 2000).
50. Dennis Guest, *The Emergence of Social Security in Canada* (Vancouver: University of British Columbia Press, 1980), pp. 62–3.
51. Margaret Jane Hillyard Little, *"No Car, No Radio, No Liquor Permit": The Moral Regulation of Single Mothers in Ontario, 1920–1997* (Toronto: Oxford University Press, 1998). See also Esyllt W. Jones, *Influenza 1918: Disease, Death, and Struggle in Winnipeg* (Toronto: University of Toronto Press, 2007), pp. 147–54, on the surveillance of influenza widows receiving Mothers' Allowances.
52. Aline Charles, "Femmes âgées, pauvres et sans droit de vote, mais ... citoyennes? Lettres au premier ministre du Québec, 1935–1936," *Recherches féministes*, 26, 2 (2013): 51–70. The quotation is from page 65.
53. Suzanne Morton, *Ideal Surroundings: Domestic Life in a Working-Class Suburb in the 1920s* (Toronto: University of Toronto Press, 1995), pp. 147–9.
54. Suzanne Morton, *Ideal Surroundings: Domestic Life in a Working-Class Suburb in the 1920s* (Toronto: University of Toronto Press, 1995), p. 131.
55. Lara Campbell, *Respectable Citizens: Gender, Family, and Unemployment in Ontario's Great Depression* (Toronto: University of Toronto Press, 2009), p. 57.
56. John Herd Thompson with Allen Seager, *Canada, 1922–1939: Decades of Discord* (Toronto: McClelland & Stewart, 1985), p. 350.
57. Lara Campbell, *Respectable Citizens: Gender, Family, and Unemployment in Ontario's Great Depression* (Toronto: University of Toronto Press, 2009), p. 75.
58. Quoted in Neil Sutherland, *Growing Up: Childhood in English Canada from the Great War to the Age of Television* (Toronto: University of Toronto Press, 1997), p. 25.
59. Heidi Macdonald, "'Being in Your Twenties, in the Thirties': Liminality and Masculinity during the Great Depression," pp. 156–67, in *Bringing Children and Youth into Canadian History: The Difference Kids Make*, ed. Mona Gleason and Tamara Myers (Don Mills: Oxford University Press Canada, 2017).
60. Barry Broadfoot, *Ten Lost Years*, quoted in Lara Campbell, *Respectable Citizens: Gender, Family, and Unemployment in Ontario's Great Depression* (Toronto: University of Toronto Press, 2009), p. 60.

61. Robert Collins, *You Had to Be There: An Intimate Portrait of the Generation That Survived the Depression, Won the War, and Re-invented Canada* (Toronto: McClelland & Stewart, 1997), p. 22, quoted in Lara Campbell, *Respectable Citizens: Gender, Family, and Unemployment in Ontario's Great Depression* (Toronto: University of Toronto Press, 2009), p. 60.
62. Lara Campbell, *Respectable Citizens: Gender, Family, and Unemployment in Ontario's Great Depression* (Toronto: University of Toronto Press, 2009), pp. 64–5.
63. Lara Campbell, *Respectable Citizens: Gender, Family, and Unemployment in Ontario's Great Depression* (Toronto: University of Toronto Press, 2009), p. 62.
64. Reproduced in L.M. Grayson and Michael Bliss, eds, *The Wretched of Canada: Letters to R.B. Bennett, 1930–1935* (Toronto: University of Toronto Press, 1973), pp. 46–7. This transcription is faithful to the spelling in the original letter.
65. Denyse Baillargeon, *Ménagères au temps de la Crise* (Montréal: Les Éditions du Remue-ménage, 1993), Chapters 5 and 6.
66. Neil Sutherland, *Growing Up: Childhood in English Canada from the Great War to the Age of Television* (Toronto: University of Toronto Press, 1997), p. 42.
67. Denyse Baillargeon, *Ménagères au temps de la Crise* (Montréal: Les Éditions du Remue-ménage, 1993), p. 220.
68. Quoted in Neil Sutherland, *Growing Up: Childhood in English Canada from the Great War to the Age of Television* (Toronto: University of Toronto Press, 1997), p. 207.
69. Neil Sutherland, *Growing Up: Childhood in English Canada from the Great War to the Age of Television* (Toronto: University of Toronto Press, 1997), p. 138.
70. Lara Campbell, *Respectable Citizens: Gender, Family, and Unemployment in Ontario's Great Depression* (Toronto: University of Toronto Press, 2009), pp. 58, 66–8; Katrina Srigley, *Breadwinning Daughters: Young Working Women in a Depression-Era City, 1929–1939* (Toronto: University of Toronto Press, 2010), pp. 39–42.
71. See Todd McCallum, *Hobohemia* (Athabasca University Press, 2014).
72. Lara Campbell, *Respectable Citizens: Gender, Family, and Unemployment in Ontario's Great Depression* (Toronto: University of Toronto Press, 2009), pp. 79–82.
73. Katrina Srigley, *Breadwinning Daughters: Young Working Women in a Depression-Era City, 1929–1939* (Toronto: University of Toronto Press, 2010), pp. 29, 31, 42–3.
74. Katrina Srigley, *Breadwinning Daughters: Young Working Women in a Depression-Era City, 1929–1939* (Toronto: University of Toronto Press, 2010), p. 30.
75. On young women and consumer culture in the interwar years, see Suzanne Morton's work on 1920s Halifax. Suzanne Morton, *Ideal Surroundings: Domestic Life in a Working-Class Suburb in the 1920s* (Toronto: University of Toronto Press, 1995), Chapter 7, especially pages 146–50.

76. James Struthers, *No Fault of their Own: Unemployment and the Canadian Welfare State 1914–1941* (Toronto: University of Toronto Press, 1983).
77. On the decline in Montreal marriage rates between 1929 and 1933, see Denyse Baillargeon, *Ménagères au temps de la Crise* (Montréal: Les Éditions du Remue-ménage, 1993), p. 245, n1.
78. Diane Dodd, "The Canadian Birth Control Movement on Trial, 1936–1937," *Histoire sociale/Social History*, 16, 32 (November 1983): 411–28.
79. Suzanne Morton, *Wisdom, Justice, and Charity: Canadian Social Welfare Through the Life of Jane B. Wisdom, 1884–1975* (Toronto: University of Toronto Press, 2014), p. 133.
80. Veronica Strong-Boag, "'Wages for Housework': Mothers' Allowances and the Beginnings of Social Security in Canada," *Journal of Canadian Studies*, 14, 1 (Spring 1979): 24–34; Magda Fahrni, *Household Politics: Montreal Families and Postwar Reconstruction* (Toronto: University of Toronto Press, 2005), Chapters 2 and 3; Suzanne Morton, *Wisdom, Justice, and Charity: Canadian Social Welfare Through the Life of Jane B. Wisdom, 1884–1975* (Toronto: University of Toronto Press, 2014). This collaboration between the state and private agencies is what sociologist Mariana Valverde refers to as a "mixed social economy" of welfare. Mariana Valverde, "The Mixed Social Economy as a Canadian Tradition," *Studies in Political Economy*, 47 (Summer 1995): 33–60.
81. Veronica Strong-Boag, "Intruders in the Nursery: Childcare Professionals Reshape the Years One to Five, 1920–1940," in *Childhood and Family in Canadian History*, ed. Joy Parr (Toronto: McClelland & Stewart, 1982), pp. 160–78; Katherine Arnup, *Education for Motherhood: Advice for Mothers in Twentieth-Century Canada* (Toronto: McClelland & Stewart, 1994).
82. For a useful article that situates the girls within the larger context of French-speaking Ontario, see David Welch, "The Dionne Quintuplets: More Than an Ontario Showpiece—Five Franco-Ontarian Children," in *Journal of Canadian Studies*, 29, 4 (Winter 1994–1995): 36–64.
83. Quoted in Veronica Strong-Boag, "Intruders in the Nursery: Childcare Professionals Reshape the Years One to Five, 1920–1940," in *Childhood and Family in Canadian History*, ed. Joy Parr (Toronto: McClelland & Stewart, 1982), p. 175.
84. Katherine Arnup, "Raising the Dionne Quintuplets: Lessons for Modern Mothers," *Journal of Canadian Studies*, 29, 4 (Winter 1994–1995): 65–85.
85. Cynthia Wright, "They Were Five: The Dionne Quintuplets Revisited," pp. 5–14, and Mariana Valverde, "Families, Private Property, and the State: The Dionnes and the Toronto Stork Derby," pp. 15–35, both in *Journal of Canadian Studies*, 29, 4 (Winter 1994–1995).
86. Karen A. Balcom, *The Traffic in Babies: Cross-Border Adoption and Baby-Selling between the United States and Canada, 1930–1972* (Toronto: University of Toronto Press, 2011), p. 28; Veronica Strong-Boag, "Interrupted Relations: The Adoption of Children in Twentieth-Century British Columbia," *BC Studies*, 144

(Winter 2004/2005): 5–30; Dominique Goubau and Claire O'Neill, "L'adoption, l'Église et l'État. Les origines tumultueuses d'une institution légale," pp. 97–130, in Renée Joyal, ed., *L'évolution de la protection de l'enfance au Québec: des origines à nos jours* (Quebec City: Presses de l'Université du Québec, 2000).
87. Veronica Strong-Boag, *Fostering Nation? Canada Confronts Its History of Childhood Disadvantage* (Waterloo: Wilfrid Laurier University Press, 2011), especially Chapters 2 and 3.
88. Sharon Myers, "'Suffering from a sense of injustice': Children's Activism in Liberal State Formation at the Saint John Boys Industrial Home, 1927–1932," *Histoire sociale/Social History*, 52, 105 (May 2019), pp. 2–5.
89. Karen A. Balcom, *The Traffic in Babies: Cross-Border Adoption and Baby-Selling between the United States and Canada, 1930–1972* (Toronto: University of Toronto Press, 2011), p. 27.
90. Sharon Myers, "'Suffering from a sense of injustice': Children's Activism in Liberal State Formation at the Saint John Boys Industrial Home, 1927–1932," *Histoire sociale/Social History*, 52, 105 (May 2019): 1–30. On case files and the helping professions, see the chapter by Lykke de la Cour and Geoffrey Reaume, as well as the chapter by Franca Iacovetta, in Wendy Mitchinson and Franca Iacovetta, eds, *On the Case: Explorations in Social History* (Toronto: University of Toronto Press, 1998).
91. Renée N. Lafferty, *The Guardianship of Best Interests: Institutional Care for the Children of the Poor in Halifax, 1850–1960* (Montreal; Kingston: McGill-Queen's University Press, 2013), Chapter 2, "Race Uplift, Racism, and the Childhood Ideal: Founding and Funding the Nova Scotia Home for Colored Children."
92. Renée N. Lafferty, *The Guardianship of Best Interests: Institutional Care for the Children of the Poor in Halifax, 1850–1960* (Montreal; Kingston: McGill-Queen's University Press, 2013), Chapter 2, "Race Uplift, Racism, and the Childhood Ideal: Founding and Funding the Nova Scotia Home for Colored Children"; Wanda Lauren Taylor, *The Nova Scotia Home for Colored Children* (Halifax: Nimbus Publishing, 2015).
93. Karen A. Balcom, *The Traffic in Babies: Cross-Border Adoption and Baby-Selling between the United States and Canada, 1930–1972* (Toronto: University of Toronto Press, 2011), Chapter 2, "Border-Crossing Responses to the Ideal Maternity Home, 1945–1947."
94. Quoted in Karen A. Balcom, *The Traffic in Babies: Cross-Border Adoption and Baby-Selling between the United States and Canada, 1930–1972* (Toronto: University of Toronto Press, 2011), p. 59.
95. Magda Fahrni, *Household Politics: Montreal Families and Postwar Reconstruction* (Toronto: University of Toronto Press, 2005), Chapter 3.
96. Desmond Morton, *1945: When Canada Won the War*, Historical Booklet no. 54 (Ottawa: Canadian Historical Association, 1995), p. 1. Canada's total population in 1941 was 11,506,655.

97. Magda Fahrni, *Household Politics: Montreal Families and Postwar Reconstruction* (Toronto: University of Toronto Press, 2005), p. 199, n118.

98. Rémi Marquette, "Portrait d'un 'zombie': le récit de guerre et la construction identitaire d'un soldat inactif de la Seconde Guerre mondiale à travers sa correspondance (1942–1945)" (M.A. thesis, Université du Québec à Montréal, 2016).

99. Steven High, ed., *Occupied St John's: A Social History of a City at War, 1939–1945* (Montreal; Kingston: McGill-Queen's University Press, 2016).

100. Tamara Myers, *Caught: Montreal's Modern Girls and the Law, 1869–1945* (Toronto: University of Toronto Press, 2006), p. 189.

101. Cynthia Comacchio, *The Dominion of Youth: Adolescence and the Making of Modern Canada* (Waterloo: Wilfrid Laurier University Press, 2006), pp. 176–7.

102. Barbara Lorenzkowski, "The Children's War," p. 134, in Steven High, ed., *Occupied St John's: A Social History of a City at War, 1939–1945* (Montreal; Kingston: McGill-Queen's University Press, 2016).

103. Claire L. Halstead, "From Lion to Leaf: The Evacuation of British Children to Canada During the Second World War" (PhD dissertation, University of Western Ontario, 2015).

104. Neil Sutherland, *Growing Up: Childhood in English Canada from the Great War to the Age of Television* (Toronto: University of Toronto Press, 1997), p. 135.

105. Cynthia Comacchio, *The Dominion of Youth: Adolescence and the Making of Modern Canada* (Waterloo: Wilfrid Laurier University Press, 2006), pp. 130, 156.

106. Magda Fahrni, *Household Politics: Montreal Families and Postwar Reconstruction* (Toronto: University of Toronto Press, 2005), pp. 59–60.

107. Ruth Roach Pierson, *"They're Still Women After All": The Second World War and Canadian Womanhood* (Toronto: McClelland & Stewart, 1986), pp. 55–6; Lisa Pasolli, *Working Mothers and the Child Care Dilemma: A History of British Columbia's Social Policy* (Vancouver: UBC Press, 2015), Chapter 3, "'It takes real mothers and real homes to make real children': Child Care Debates during and after the Second World War."

108. Magda Fahrni, *Household Politics: Montreal Families and Postwar Reconstruction* (Toronto: University of Toronto Press, 2005), p. 58. See also Ruth Roach Pierson, *"They're Still Women After All": The Second World War and Canadian Womanhood* (Toronto: McClelland & Stewart, 1986), p. 56.

109. Lisa Pasolli, *Working Mothers and the Child Care Dilemma: A History of British Columbia's Social Policy* (Vancouver: UBC Press, 2015), p. 78.

110. Lisa Pasolli, *Working Mothers and the Child Care Dilemma: A History of British Columbia's Social Policy* (Vancouver: UBC Press, 2015), p. 81.

111. Lisa Pasolli, *Working Mothers and the Child Care Dilemma: A History of British Columbia's Social Policy* (Vancouver: UBC Press, 2015), p. 87.

112. Jeffrey A. Keshen, *Saints, Sinners, and Soldiers: Canada's Second World War* (Vancouver: UBC Press, 2004), pp. 158–67, 204–13; Magda Fahrni, *Household*

Politics: Montreal Families and Postwar Reconstruction (Toronto: University of Toronto Press, 2005), p. 57.

113. Steven High, "Working for Uncle Sam: The 'Comings' and 'Goings' of Newfoundland Base Construction Labour, 1940–1945," *Acadiensis*, 32, 2 (Spring 2003), p. 84.

114. Steven High, "Working for Uncle Sam: The 'Comings' and 'Goings' of Newfoundland Base Construction Labour, 1940–1945," *Acadiensis*, 32, 2 (Spring 2003), pp. 84–107.

115. Magda Fahrni, *Household Politics: Montreal Families and Postwar Reconstruction* (Toronto: University of Toronto Press, 2005), Chapter 5, "A Politics of Prices: Married Women and Economic Citizenship," pp. 108–23. See also Geneviève Auger and Raymonde Lamothe, *De la poêle à frire à la ligne de feu. La vie quotidienne des Québécoises pendant la guerre,"* 39–45 (Montréal: Boréal Express, 1981).

116. Jeffrey A. Keshen, *Saints, Sinners, and Soldiers: Canada's Second World War* (Vancouver: UBC Press, 2004), Chapter 4, "Black Market Profiteering: 'More than a fair share,'" pp. 94–120. See also Jeff Keshen, "One for All or All for One: Government Controls, Black Marketing and the Limits of Patriotism, 1939–47," *Journal of Canadian Studies*, 29, 4 (Winter 1994–1995), pp. 111–43.

117. Quoted in Serge Marc Durflinger, *Fighting from Home: The Second World War in Verdun, Quebec* (Vancouver: University of British Columbia Press, 2006), pp. 143–4.

118. Desmond Morton and Glenn Wright, *Winning the Second Battle: Canadian Veterans and the Return to Civilian Life, 1915–1930* (Toronto: University of Toronto Press, 1987), pp. 221–2; Peter Neary and J.L. Granatstein, eds, *The Veterans' Charter* and Post–World War II Canada (Montreal; Kingston : McGill-Queen's University Press, 1998).

119. Dominique Marshall, *Aux origines sociales de l'État-Providence* (Montréal: Les Presses de l'Université de Montréal, 1998).

120. On the uses to which parents put their new family allowances, see Magda Fahrni, *Household Politics: Montreal Families and Postwar Reconstruction* (Toronto: University of Toronto Press, 2005), p. 56.

121. Dominique Marshall, *Aux origines sociales de l'État-Providence* (Montréal: Les Presses de l'Université de Montréal, 1998), pp. 137–8. Emily Arrowsmith's PhD thesis uncovers similar tendencies in the administration of Dependents' Allowances to the families of Indigenous soldiers during the Second World War. Emily Arrowsmith, "Fair Enough? How Notions of Race, Gender, and Soldiers' Rights Affected Dependents' Allowance Policies Towards Canadian Aboriginal Families During World War II" (PhD thesis, Carleton University, 2006).

122. Greg Robinson, *By Order of the President: FDR and the Internment of Japanese Americans* (Cambridge, Mass.: Harvard University Press, 2001); Greg Robinson, *A Tragedy of Democracy: Japanese Confinement in North America* (New York: Columbia University Press, 2009).

123. Pamela H. Sugiman, "Memories of Internment: Narrating Japanese Canadian Women's Life Stories," *Canadian Journal of Sociology*, 29, 3 (Summer 2004): 359–88; Pamela Sugiman, "Passing Time, Moving Memories: Interpreting Wartime Narratives of Japanese Canadian Women," *Histoire sociale/Social History*, 36, 73, pp. 51–79. See also Ken Adachi, *The Enemy That Never Was: A History of the Japanese Canadians* (Toronto: McClelland & Stewart, 1991); Ann Gomer Sunahara, *The Politics of Racism: The Uprooting of Japanese Canadians During the Second World War* (Toronto: James Lorimer, 1980).

CHAPTER 6

1. http://www.un.org/en/universal-declaration-human-rights/, consulted 20 November 2017.
2. See, for example, Magda Fahrni and Robert Rutherdale, eds, *Creating Postwar Canada: Community, Diversity, and Dissent, 1945–1975* (Vancouver: University of British Columbia Press, 2008), especially the Introduction.
3. Peter S. McInnis, *Harnessing Labour Confrontation: Shaping the Postwar Settlement in Canada, 1943–1950* (Toronto: University of Toronto Press, 2002), pp. 2, 3.
4. Peter S. McInnis, *Harnessing Labour Confrontation: Shaping the Postwar Settlement in Canada, 1943–1950* (Toronto: University of Toronto Press, 2002), Chapter 4, "Teamwork for Harmony: Labour–Management Production Committees and the Postwar Settlement in Canada," pp. 113–44.
5. Craig Heron, "Harold, Marg, and the Boys: The Relevance of Class in Canadian History," *Journal of the Canadian Historical Association*, 20, 1 (2009), pp. 14–15.
6. Doug Owram, *The Government Generation: Canadian Intellectuals and the State, 1900–1945* (Toronto: University of Toronto Press, 1986).
7. Veronica Strong-Boag, "Home Dreams: Women and the Suburban Experiment in Canada, 1945–60," *Canadian Historical Review*, 72, 4 (December 1991), p. 474.
8. Paul Rutherford, *When Television Was Young: Primetime Canada, 1952–1957* (Toronto: University of Toronto Press, 1990).
9. Paul Rutherford, *When Television Was Young: Primetime Canada, 1952–1957* (Toronto: University of Toronto Press, 1990), p. 50.
10. Paul Rutherford, *When Television Was Young: Primetime Canada, 1952–1957* (Toronto: University of Toronto Press, 1990), Chapter 9, "'And Now a Word from Our Sponsor'," pp. 309–47.
11. Michael Dawson, *Selling British Columbia: Tourism and Consumer Culture, 1890–1970* (Vancouver: University of British Columbia Press, 2005).
12. Joy Parr, *Domestic Goods: The Material, the Moral, and the Economic in the Postwar Years* (Toronto: University of Toronto Press, 1999), especially Chapter 9, "Shopping for a Good Stove," pp. 199–217.

13. Ruth Schwartz Cohen, *More Work for Mother: The Ironies of Household Technology from The Open Hearth to The Microwave* (New York: Basic Books, 1983).
14. Chris Dummitt, "Finding a Place for Father: Selling the Barbecue in Postwar Canada," *Journal of the Canadian Historical Association*, 9 (1998): 209–23.
15. Keir Keightley, "'Turn it down!' She Shrieked: Gender, Domestic Space, and High Fidelity, 1948–59," *Popular Music*, 15, 2 (May 1996), p. 150.
16. See James Struthers, *The Limits of Affluence: Welfare in Ontario, 1920–1970* (Toronto: University of Toronto Press, 1994).
17. H.B. Hawthorn, ed., *A Survey of the Contemporary Indians of Canada: A Report on Economic, Political, Educational Needs and Policies in Two Volumes*, Volume I (Ottawa: Indian Affairs Branch, 1966), p. 5.
18. Arthur J. Ray, *I Have Lived Here Since the World Began: An Illustrated History of Canada's Native People* (Toronto: Lester Publishing & Key Porter Books, 1996), pp. 330–1.
19. Hugh Shewell, "'What Makes the Indian Tick?' The Influence of Social Sciences on Canada's Indian Policy, 1947–1964," *Histoire sociale/Social History*, 34, 67 (2001): 133–67.
20. Ian Mosby, "Administering Colonial Science: Nutrition Research and Human Biomedical Experimentation in Aboriginal Communities and Residential Schools, 1942–1952," *Histoire sociale/Social History*, 46, 91 (2013): 145–72.
21. Magda Fahrni, *Household Politics: Montreal Families and Postwar Reconstruction* (Toronto: University of Toronto Press, 2005), Chapter 5, "A Politics of Prices: Married Women and Economic Citizenship"; Joy Parr, *Domestic Goods: The Material, the Moral, and the Economic in the Postwar Years* (Toronto: University of Toronto Press, 1999), especially Chapter 8, "Domesticating Objects," pp. 165–95.
22. Jean-Pierre Charland et Mario Desautels, *Système technique et bonheur domestique : Rémunération, consommation et pauvreté au Québec, 1920–1960* (Québec: Institut québécois de recherche sur la culture, 1992); Stéphanie O'Neill, "L'argent ne fait pas le bonheur : les discours sur la société de consommation et les modes de vie à Montréal, 1945–1975" (PhD thesis, Université de Montréal, 2016).
23. Joy Parr, *Domestic Goods: The Material, the Moral, and the Economic in the Postwar Years* (Toronto: University of Toronto Press, 1999), p. 5.
24. Magda Fahrni, *Household Politics: Montreal Families and Postwar Reconstruction* (Toronto: University of Toronto Press, 2005), Chapter 5, "A Politics of Prices: Married Women and Economic Citizenship."
25. Joan Sangster, *Dreams of Equality: Women on the Canadian Left, 1920–1950* (Toronto: McClelland & Stewart, 1989); Julie Guard, *Radical Housewives: Price Wars and Food Politics in Mid-Twentieth Century Canada* (Toronto: University of Toronto Press, 2018); Brian Thorn, *From Left to Right: Maternalism and Women's Political Activism in Postwar Canada* (Vancouver: University of British Columbia Press, 2016), pp. 30–1, 27.

26. Brian Thorn, *From Left to Right: Maternalism and Women's Political Activism in Postwar Canada* (Vancouver: University of British Columbia Press, 2016), pp. 4–5. For previous arguments about women's mobilization and maternalist rhetoric, see Magda Fahrni, *Household Politics: Montreal Families and Postwar Reconstruction* (Toronto: University of Toronto Press, 2005), Chapter 5, "A Politics of Prices: Married Women and Economic Citizenship."
27. Franca Iacovetta, *Such Hardworking People: Italian Immigrants in Postwar Toronto* (Montreal; Kingston: McGill-Queen's University Press, 1992), p. 77. See also the discussion of living arrangements on pages 55–7.
28. Alvin Finkel, *Our Lives: Canada after 1945* (Toronto: James Lorimer, 1997), p. 54.
29. Magda Fahrni, *Household Politics: Montreal Families and Postwar Reconstruction* (Toronto: University of Toronto Press, 2005), especially pages 6–8, 146–7.
30. Doug Owram, *Born at the Right Time: A History of the Baby Boom Generation* (Toronto: University of Toronto Press, 1996), pp. xiii, 4.
31. Doug Owram, *Born at the Right Time: A History of the Baby Boom Generation* (Toronto: University of Toronto Press, 1996), pp. ix, 18.
32. Doug Owram, *Born at the Right Time: A History of the Baby Boom Generation* (Toronto: University of Toronto Press, 1996), pp. 4–5.
33. http://www.statcan.gc.ca/pub/11-630-x/11-630-x2014002-eng.htm.
34. François Ricard, *La génération lyrique. Essai sur la vie et l'œuvre des premiers-nés du baby-boom* (Montréal: Boréal, 1994); Doug Owram, *Born at the Right Time: A History of the Baby Boom Generation* (Toronto: University of Toronto Press, 1996), p. 4.
35. American historian Landon Jones has compared the demographic impact of the baby boom to "'the pig in the python,' distending society as it passes along." Quoted in Doug Owram, *Born at the Right Time: A History of the Baby Boom Generation* (Toronto: University of Toronto Press, 1996), p. 10.
36. Doug Owram, *Born at the Right Time: A History of the Baby Boom Generation* (Toronto: University of Toronto Press, 1996); François Ricard, *La génération lyrique. Essai sur la vie et l'œuvre des premiers-nés du baby-boom* (Montréal: Boréal, 1994); Bryan D. Palmer, *Canada's 1960s: The Ironies of Identity in a Rebellious Era* (Toronto: University of Toronto Press, 2009). Liz Millward argues that the women who worked to "build an enduring lesbian political and cultural scene" across Canada in the 1960s and 1970s "were baby boomers, part of the enormously influential generation born between 1946 and 1964." Liz Millward, *Making a Scene: Lesbians and Community Across Canada, 1964–84* (Vancouver: University of British Columbia Press, 2015), pp. 4–5.
37. Ruth Roach Pierson, *"They're Still Women After All": The Second World War and Canadian Womanhood* (Toronto: McClelland & Stewart, 1986); Gail Cuthbert Brandt *et al.*, *Canadian Women: A History*, 3rd edition (Toronto: Nelson, 2011).

38. Kristina Llewellyn, "Performing Post-War Citizenship: Women Teachers in Toronto Secondary Schools," *The Review of Education, Pedagogy, and Cultural Studies*, 28, 3–4 (2006), p. 319.
39. Ruth Roach Pierson, *"They're Still Women After All": The Second World War and Canadian Womanhood* (Toronto: McClelland & Stewart, 1986).
40. Jennifer A. Stephen, *Pick One Intelligent Girl: Employability, Domesticity and the Gendering of Canada's Welfare State, 1939–1947* (Toronto: University of Toronto Press, 2007), p. 6.
41. Betty Friedan, *The Feminine Mystique* (New York: W.W. Norton & Co., 1963); Daniel Horowitz, *Betty Friedan and the Making of* The Feminine Mystique: *The American Left, the Cold War, and Modern Feminism* (Amherst: University of Massachusetts Press, 1998).
42. Stephanie Coontz, *A Strange Stirring:* The Feminine Mystique *and American Women at the Dawn of the 1960s* (New York: Basic Books, 2011).
43. Stephanie Coontz, *The Way We Never Were: American Families and the Nostalgia Trap* (New York: Basic Books, 1992); Joanne Meyerowitz, ed., *Not June Cleaver: Women and Gender in Postwar America, 1945–1960* (Philadelphia: Temple University Press, 1994).
44. Veronica Strong-Boag, "Home Dreams: Women and the Suburban Experiment in Canada, 1945–60," *Canadian Historical Review*, 72, 4 (December 1991), p. 496; Valerie J. Korinek, *Roughing it in the Suburbs: Reading* Chatelaine *Magazine in the Fifties and Sixties* (Toronto: University of Toronto Press, 2000).
45. Tarah Brookfield, *Cold War Comforts: Canadian Women, Child Safety, and Global Insecurity* (Waterloo: Wilfrid Laurier University Press, 2012).
46. Wendy Mitchinson, *Giving Birth in Canada, 1900–1950* (Toronto: University of Toronto Press, 2002), p. 299.
47. Doug Owram, *Born at the Right Time: A History of the Baby Boom Generation* (Toronto: University of Toronto Press, 1996), p. 31.
48. Andrée Rivard, *Histoire de l'accouchement dans un Québec moderne* (Montréal: Les Éditions du remue-ménage, 2014).
49. Mona Gleason, *Normalizing the Ideal: Psychology, Schooling, and the Family in Postwar Canada* (Toronto: University of Toronto Press, 1999); Mary Louise Adams, *The Trouble with Normal: Postwar Youth and the Making of Heterosexuality* (Toronto: University of Toronto Press, 1997).
50. Adrienne Rich, "Compulsory Heterosexuality and Lesbian Existence," *Signs*, 5, 4 (Summer 1980): 631–60.
51. Mary Louise Adams, "Margin Notes: Reading Lesbianism as Obscenity in a Cold War Courtroom," especially pages 136–9, in *Love, Hate, and Fear in Canada's Cold War*, ed. Richard Cavell (Toronto: University of Toronto Press, 2004).
52. Gary Kinsman, "The Canadian Cold War on Queers: Sexual Regulation and Resistance," p. 109, in *Love, Hate, and Fear in Canada's Cold War*, ed. Richard Cavell (Toronto: University of Toronto Press, 2004). See also Gary Kinsman

and Patrizia Gentile, *The Canadian War on Queers: National Security as Sexual Regulation* (Vancouver: University of British Columbia Press, 2010).

53. Joyce Hibbert, *War Brides* (Scarborough, Ontario: Signet Books, 1978); Magda Fahrni, *Household Politics: Montreal Families and Postwar Reconstruction* (Toronto: University of Toronto Press, 2005), pp. 71–3. For an extreme example of an unhappy war bride, see Joan Sangster, "The Meanings of Mercy: Wife Assault and Spousal Murder in Post–Second World War Canada," *Canadian Historical Review*, 97, 4 (December 2016): 513–45.

54. Veronica Strong-Boag, "Home Dreams: Women and the Suburban Experiment in Canada, 1945–60," *Canadian Historical Review*, 72, 4 (December 1991), p. 475.

55. Ninette Kelley and Michael Trebilcock, *Making the Mosaic: A History of Canadian Immigration Policy* (Toronto: University of Toronto Press, 1998), p. 313.

56. Antoine Burgard, "'Une nouvelle vie dans un nouveau pays.' Trajectoires d'orphelins de la Shoah vers le Canada (1947–1952)" (PhD thesis, Université du Québec à Montréal and Université Lumière Lyon 2, 2017).

57. Anna Sheftel and Stacey Zembrzycki, "'We Started Over Again, We Were Young': Postwar Social Worlds of Child Holocaust Survivors in Montreal," *Urban History Review/Revue d'histoire urbaine*, 39, 1 (2010): 20–30. The quotations are from pages 21 and 22.

58. Franca Iacovetta, "Defending Honour, Demanding Respect: Manly Discourse and Gendered Practice in Two Construction Strikes, Toronto, 1960–1961," in *Gendered Pasts: Historical Essays in Femininity and Masculinity in Canada*, ed. Kathryn McPherson, Cecilia Morgan, and Nancy M. Forestell (Toronto: University of Toronto Press, 1999), p. 205.

59. Ninette Kelley and Michael Trebilcock, *Making the Mosaic: A History of Canadian Immigration Policy* (Toronto: University of Toronto Press, 1998), p. 312.

60. Ninette Kelley and Michael Trebilcock, *Making the Mosaic: A History of Canadian Immigration Policy* (Toronto: University of Toronto Press, 1998), p. 313.

61. See, for instance, the Vancouver Heritage Foundation's history of Benny's Market:http://www.vancouverheritagefoundation.org/place-that-matters/bennys-market/.

62. Freda Hawkins, *Critical Years in Immigration: Canada and Australia Compared* (Kingston; Montreal: McGill-Queen's University Press, 1989), pp. 38–9.

63. Ninette Kelley and Michael Trebilcock, *Making the Mosaic: A History of Canadian Immigration Policy* (Toronto: University of Toronto Press, 1998), p. 348.

64. Quoted in Veronica Strong-Boag, "Living," in *Working Lives: Vancouver, 1886–1986*, ed. The Working Lives Collective (Vancouver: New Star Books, 1985), p. 91.

65. Sasha Mullally and David Wright, *Foreign Practices: Immigrant Doctors and the History of Canadian Medicare* (Montreal; Kingston: McGill-Queen's University Press, 2020).

66. Ninette Kelley and Michael Trebilcock, *Making the Mosaic: A History of Canadian Immigration Policy* (Toronto: University of Toronto Press, 1998), p. 313;

Karen Flynn, "Experience and Identity: Black Immigrant Nurses to Canada, 1950–1980," pp. 381–98, in *Sisters or Strangers? Immigrant, Ethnic, and Racialized Women in Canadian History*, ed. Marlene Epp, Franca Iacovetta, and Frances Swyripa (Toronto: University of Toronto Press, 2004).

67. Micheline Labelle, Geneviève Turcotte, Marianne Kempeneers, and Deirdre Meintel, *Histoires d'immigrées. Itinéraire d'ouvrières colombiennes, grecques, haïtiennes et portugaises de Montréal* (Montréal: Boréal, 1987); Franca Iacovetta, "Defending Honour, Demanding Respect: Manly Discourse and Gendered Practice in Two Construction Strikes, Toronto, 1960–1961," in *Gendered Pasts: Historical Essays in Femininity and Masculinity in Canada*, ed. Kathryn McPherson, Cecilia Morgan, and Nancy M. Forestell (Toronto: University of Toronto Press, 1999), p. 210.

68. Franca Iacovetta, "Defending Honour, Demanding Respect: Manly Discourse and Gendered Practice in Two Construction Strikes, Toronto, 1960–1961," in *Gendered Pasts: Historical Essays in Femininity and Masculinity in Canada*, ed. Kathryn McPherson, Cecilia Morgan, and Nancy M. Forestell (Toronto: University of Toronto Press, 1999), pp. 202, 200.

69. Charmaine Crawford, "African-Caribbean Women, Diaspora and Transnationality," *Canadian Woman Studies*, 23, 2 (2004), p. 98.

70. Veronica Strong-Boag, "Home Dreams: Women and the Suburban Experiment in Canada, 1945–60," *Canadian Historical Review*, 72, 4 (December 1991), pp. 487–8.

71. Richard Harris, *Unplanned Suburbs: Toronto's American Tragedy 1900 to 1950* (Baltimore; London: The Johns Hopkins University Press, 1996).

72. Richard Harris, *Creeping Conformity: How Canada Became Suburban, 1900–1960* (Toronto: University of Toronto Press, 2004).

73. Veronica Strong-Boag, "Home Dreams: Women and the Suburban Experiment in Canada, 1945–60," *Canadian Historical Review*, 72, 4 (December 1991), p. 501.

74. John R. Seeley, R. Alexander Sim, and E.W. Loosley, *Crestwood Heights: A Study of the Culture of Suburban Life* (Toronto: University of Toronto Press, 1956), p. 11.

75. Historian Craig Heron, for example, recounts the story of his own working-class parents, who settled in eastern Scarborough in the immediate postwar years. Craig Heron, "Harold, Marg, and the Boys: The Relevance of Class in Canadian History," *Journal of the Canadian Historical Association*, 20, 1 (2009), pp. 3–4, 18. See also James Onusko, "Childhood in Calgary's Postwar Suburbs: Kids, Bullets, and Boom, 1950–1965," *Urban History Review/Revue d'histoire urbaine*, 43, 2 (Spring 2015), p. 32.

76. Pierre Vallières, *White N---- of America*, translated by Joan Pinkham (Toronto: McClelland & Stewart, 1971 [1968]), pp. 99–100.

77. Harold Bérubé, "Vendre la banlieue aux Montréalais: discours et stratégies publicitaires, 1950–1970," *Revue d'histoire de l'Amérique française*, 71, 1–2 (été – automne 2017): 83–112.

78. Evelyn Peters, Matthew Stock, and Adrian Werner, *Rooster Town: The History of an Urban Métis Community, 1901–1961* (Winnipeg: University of Manitoba Press, 2018).
79. As historian Veronica Strong-Boag notes, "An increase in the production of oil, gas, and hydroelectric power was available to power both new cars and the central heating characteristic of new homes." Strong-Boag, "Home Dreams: Women and the Suburban Experiment in Canada, 1945–60," *Canadian Historical Review*, 72, 4 (December 1991), p. 474.
80. Steve Penfold, "Selling by the Carload: The Early Years of Fast Food in Canada," pp. 162–89, in *Creating Postwar Canada: Community, Diversity, and Dissent, 1945–1975*, ed. Magda Fahrni and Robert Rutherdale (Vancouver: University of British Columbia Press, 2008); Steve Penfold, *The Donut: A Canadian History* (Toronto: University of Toronto Press, 2008).
81. Peter A. Stevens, "Cars and Cottages: The Automotive Transformation of Ontario's Summer Home Tradition," *Ontario History*, 100, 1 (2008): 26–56.
82. James Onusko, "Childhood in Calgary's Postwar Suburbs: Kids, Bullets, and Boom, 1950–1965," *Urban History Review/Revue d'histoire urbaine*, 43, 2 (Spring 2015), p. 32.
83. Simon-Pierre Lacasse, "À la croisée de la Révolution tranquille et du judaïsme orthodoxe: L'implantation de la communauté hassidique des Tasher au cœur du Québec francophone et catholique (1962–1967)," *Histoire sociale/Social History*, 50, 102 (November 2017): 399–422.
84. Richard Harris, *Unplanned Suburbs: Toronto's American Tragedy 1900 to 1950* (Baltimore; London: The Johns Hopkins University Press, 1996); Richard Harris, *Creeping Conformity: How Canada Became Suburban, 1900–1960* (Toronto: University of Toronto Press, 2004); Annick Germain, Damaris Rose, and Myriam Richard, Chapter 29, "Building and Reshaping the Suburban Landscape: The Role of Immigrant Communities," pp. 313–52, in *Montreal: The History of a North American City*, Volume 2, ed. Dany Fougères and Roderick MacLeod (Montreal; Kingston: McGill-Queen's University Press, 2018).
85. Craig Heron, "Harold, Marg, and the Boys: The Relevance of Class in Canadian History," *Journal of the Canadian Historical Association*, 20, 1 (2009), p. 3, note 4.
86. Veronica Strong-Boag, "Home Dreams: Women and the Suburban Experiment in Canada, 1945–60," *Canadian Historical Review*, 72, 4 (December 1991), p. 479.
87. Joan Sangster, *Transforming Labour: Women and Work in Post-War Canada* (Toronto: University of Toronto Press, 2010), p. 19.
88. Joan Sangster, *Earning Respect: The Lives of Working Women in Small-Town Ontario, 1920–1960* (Toronto: University of Toronto Press, 1995), Chapter 8, "Doing Two Jobs: The Wage-Earning Mother in the Postwar Years," pp. 221–47. See also Veronica Strong-Boag, "Home Dreams: Women and the Suburban Experiment in Canada, 1945–60," *Canadian Historical Review*, 72, 4 (December 1991),

p. 480; Arlie Russell Hochschild and Anne Machung, *The Second Shift: Working Parents and the Revolution at Home* (New York: Viking, 1989).

89. Madeleine Morgan, *La colère des douces: la grève des infirmières de l'hôpital Sainte-Justine en 1963: un momentum des relations de travail dans le secteur hospitalier* (Montréal: Confédération des syndicats nationaux, 2003); Linda Kealey, "No More 'Yes Girls': Labour Activism among New Brunswick Nurses, 1964–1981," *Acadiensis*, 37, 2 (2008), p. 3.

90. Joan Sangster, *Earning Respect: The Lives of Working Women in Small-Town Ontario, 1920–1960* (Toronto: University of Toronto Press, 1995).

91. Susana Miranda, "'An Unlikely Collection of Union Militants': Portuguese Immigrant Cleaning Women Become Political Subjects in Postwar Toronto," *Atlantis*, 32, 1 (2007): 114–24.

92. Karen Flynn, *Moving Beyond Borders: A History of Black Canadian and Caribbean Women in the Diaspora* (Toronto: University of Toronto Press, 2011); Flynn, "'I'm Glad That Someone is Telling the Nursing Story': Writing Black Canadian Women's History," *Journal of Black Studies*, 38, 3 (January 2008), p. 453.

93. Mary Jane Logan McCallum, *Indigenous Women, Work, and History, 1940–1980* (Winnipeg: University of Manitoba Press, 2014), pp. 127–30. The quotation is on page 128.

94. Mary Jane Logan McCallum, *Indigenous Women, Work, and History, 1940–1980* (Winnipeg: University of Manitoba Press, 2014), p. 130.

95. Joan Sangster, *Earning Respect: The Lives of Working Women in Small-Town Ontario, 1920–1960* (Toronto: University of Toronto Press, 1995), pp. 240–2.

96. Lisa Pasolli, *Working Mothers and the Child Care Dilemma: A History of British Columbia's Social Policy* (Vancouver: UBC Press, 2015), p. 110.

97. Lisa Pasolli, *Working Mothers and the Child Care Dilemma: A History of British Columbia's Social Policy* (Vancouver: UBC Press, 2015), especially Chapter 4, "'The working mother is here to stay': The Making of Provincial Child Care Policy in the 1960s."

98. Gregory P. Marchildon and Nicole C. O'Byrne, "Last Province Aboard: New Brunswick and National Medicare," *Acadiensis*, 42, 1 (2013): 150–67; Gregory Marchildon, "Douglas versus Manning: The Ideological Battle over Medicare in Postwar Canada," *Journal of Canadian Studies*, 50, 1 (2016): 129–49.

99. Kenneth Bryden, *Old Age Pensions and Policy-Making in Canada* (Montreal; London: McGill-Queen's University Press and The Institute of Public Administration of Canada, 1974), especially Chapters 6 and 7.

100. James Snell, "The Family and the Working-Class Elderly in the First Half of the Twentieth Century," p. 501, in *Family Matters: Papers in Post-Confederation Canadian Family History*, ed. Lori Chambers and Edgar-André Montigny (Toronto: Canadian Scholars' Press, 1998).

101. Aline Charles, *Quand devient-on vieille? Femmes, âge et travail au Québec, 1940–1980* (Québec: Presses de l'Université Laval, 2007).

102. James Struthers, *The Limits of Affluence: Welfare in Ontario, 1920–1970* (Toronto: University of Toronto Press, 1994), pp. 4–5.
103. James Struthers, *The Limits of Affluence: Welfare in Ontario, 1920–1970* (Toronto: University of Toronto Press, 1994), p. 250.
104. John Richards and Larry Pratt, *Prairie Capitalism: Power and Influence in the New West* (Toronto: McClelland & Stewart, 1979).
105. Maureen K. Lux, *Separate Beds: A History of Indian Hospitals in Canada, 1920s–1980s* (Toronto: University of Toronto Press, 2016), pp. 15–17.
106. Maureen K. Lux, *Separate Beds: A History of Indian Hospitals in Canada, 1920s–1980s* (Toronto: University of Toronto Press, 2016), p. 13.
107. Pat Sandiford Grygier, *A Long Way from Home: The Tuberculosis Epidemic among the Inuit* (Montreal; Kingston: McGill-Queen's University Press, 1994), p. 71.
108. Arthur J. Ray, *I Have Lived Here Since the World Began: An Illustrated History of Canada's Native People* (Toronto: Lester Publishing & Key Porter Books, 1996), pp. 343–5; Pat Sandiford Grygier, *A Long Way From Home: The Tuberculosis Epidemic among the Inuit* (Montreal; Kingston: McGill-Queen's University Press, 1994), Chapter 9, "After the Hospital: Going Home, or a Southern Grave," pp. 117–32.
109. Arthur J. Ray, *I Have Lived Here Since the World Began: An Illustrated History of Canada's Native People* (Toronto: Lester Publishing & Key Porter Books, 1996), pp. 345–6.
110. Frank Tester and Peter Kulchyski, *Tammarniit (Mistakes): Inuit Relocation in the Eastern Arctic, 1939–63* (Vancouver: UBC Press, 1994), p. 44.
111. A. Barry Roberts, "Eskimo Identification and Disc Numbers," report prepared for the Social Development Division, Department of Indian and Northern Affairs, June 1975, pp. 24–5.
112. Arthur J. Ray, *I Have Lived Here Since the World Began: An Illustrated History of Canada's Native People* (Toronto: Lester Publishing & Key Porter Books, 1996), pp. 344–5; A. Barry Roberts, "Eskimo Identification and Disc Numbers," report prepared for the Social Development Division, Department of Indian and Northern Affairs, June 1975, p. 30.
113. Quoted in Frank Tester and Peter Kulchyski, *Tammarniit (Mistakes): Inuit Relocation in the Eastern Arctic, 1939–63* (Vancouver: UBC Press, 1994), p. 94.
114. Chelsea Vowel, *Indigenous Writes: A Guide to First Nations, Métis and Inuit Issues in Canada* (Winnipeg: HighWater Press, 2016), p. 183.
115. Karen Dubinsky, *Babies Without Borders: Adoption and Migration across the Americas* (Toronto: University of Toronto Press, 2010), especially pp. 80–8.
116. Ian Milligan, *Rebel Youth: 1960s Labour Unrest, Young Workers, and New Leftists in English Canada* (Vancouver: UBC Press, 2014), p. 6.
117. Ian Milligan, *Rebel Youth: 1960s Labour Unrest, Young Workers, and New Leftists in English Canada* (Vancouver: UBC Press, 2014), p. 15.

118. Ian Milligan, *Rebel Youth: 1960s Labour Unrest, Young Workers, and New Leftists in English Canada* (Vancouver: UBC Press, 2014), pp. 4, 18.
119. Ian Milligan, *Rebel Youth: 1960s Labour Unrest, Young Workers, and New Leftists in English Canada* (Vancouver: UBC Press, 2014), p. 18.
120. James Onusko, "Childhood in Calgary's Postwar Suburbs: Kids, Bullets, and Boom, 1950–1965," *Urban History Review/Revue d'histoire urbaine*, 43, 2 (Spring 2015), pp. 31–2; Kristine Alexander, *Guiding Modern Girls: Girlhood, Empire, and Internationalism in the 1920s and 1930s* (Vancouver: UBC Press, 2018).
121. Doug Owram, *Born at the Right Time: A History of the Baby Boom Generation* (Toronto: University of Toronto Press, 1996).
122. Quoted in Veronica Strong-Boag, "Living," in *Working Lives: Vancouver, 1886–1986*, ed. The Working Lives Collective (Vancouver: New Star Books, 1985), p. 94.
123. Mary Louise Adams, *The Trouble with Normal: Postwar Youth and the Making of Heterosexuality* (Toronto: University of Toronto Press, 1997).
124. Sharon Wall, "'Some thought they were 'in Love'": Sex, White Teenagehood, and Unmarried Pregnancy in Early Postwar Canada," *Journal of the Canadian Historical Association*, 25, 1 (2014): 207–41.
125. Sharon Wall, "'Not ... the Same Damaging Effects'?: Unmarried Pregnancy, the State, and First Nations Communities in Early Postwar British Columbia," *Histoire sociale/Social History*, 50, 102 (November 2017): 371–98.
126. Stuart Henderson, *Making The Scene: Yorkville and Hip Toronto in the 1960s* (Toronto: University of Toronto Press, 2011); Marcel Martel, "'They smell bad, have diseases, and are lazy': RCMP Officers Reporting on Hippies in the Late Sixties," *The Canadian Historical Review*, 90, 2 (2009): 215–45. On the generation gap, see the quotation from the president of the Ontario Federation of Labour in Ian Milligan, *Rebel Youth: 1960s Labour Unrest, Young Workers, and New Leftists in English Canada* (Vancouver: UBC Press, 2014), p. 13.
127. Ian Milligan, *Rebel Youth: 1960s Labour Unrest, Young Workers, and New Leftists in English Canada* (Vancouver: UBC Press, 2014).
128. Joel Belliveau, *Le "moment 68" et la réinvention de l'Acadie* (Ottawa: Les Presses de l'Université d'Ottawa, 2014).
129. Caroline Durand, "Entre exportation et importation: La création de la chanson québécoise selon la presse artistique, 1960 – 1980," *Revue d'histoire de l'Amérique française*, 60, 3 (2007): 295–324.
130. Linda Mahood, "Hitchin' a Ride in the 1970s: Canadian Youth Culture and the Romance with Mobility," *Histoire sociale/Social History*, 47, 93 (May 2014), p. 217.
131. Ben Bradley, " 'Undesirables Entering the Town to Look for Good Times': Banff Confronts Its Counterculture Youth Scene, 1965–1971," *Urban History Review/Revue d'histoire urbaine*, 47, 1–2 (2018–2019): 71–87; Linda Mahood, "Hitchin' a Ride in the 1970s: Canadian Youth Culture and the Romance with Mobility," *Histoire sociale/Social History*, 47, 93 (May 2014): 205–27.

132. Andréanne Lebrun et Louise Bienvenue, "Pour 'un gouvernement jeune et dynamique': L'abaissement du droit de vote à 18 ans au Québec en 1964," *Revue d'histoire de l'Amérique française*, 71, 1–2 (2017): 113–35.

133. Liz Millward, *Making a Scene: Lesbians and Community Across Canada, 1964–84* (Vancouver: University of British Columbia Press, 2015), p. 7.

134. Karen Dubinsky, Catherine Krull, Susan Lord, Sean Mills and Scott Rutherford, eds, *New World Coming: The Sixties and the Shaping of Global Consciousness* (Toronto: Between the Lines, 2009).

135. On the Royal Commission on the Status of Women in Canada, see Barbara M. Freeman, *The Satellite Sex: The Media and Women's Issues in English Canada, 1966–1971* (Waterloo: Wilfrid Laurier University Press, 2001); and Joan Sangster, *Transforming Labour: Women and Work in Post-war Canada* (Toronto: University of Toronto Press, 2010), Chapter 7, "Tackling the 'Problem' of the Woman Worker: The Labour Movement, Working Women, and the Royal Commission on the Status of Women."

136. Christina Burr, "Letters to Mike: Personal Narrative and Divorce Reform in Canada in the 1960s," p. 400, in *Family Matters: Papers in Post-Confederation Canadian Family History*, ed. Lori Chambers and Edgar-André Montigny (Toronto: Canadian Scholars' Press, 1998).

137. Christina Burr, "Letters to Mike: Personal Narrative and Divorce Reform in Canada in the 1960s," pp. 401–2, in *Family Matters: Papers in Post-Confederation Canadian Family History*, ed. Lori Chambers and Edgar-André Montigny (Toronto: Canadian Scholars' Press, 1998).

138. Angus McLaren and Arlene Tigar McLaren, *The Bedroom and the State: The Changing Practices and Politics of Contraception and Abortion in Canada, 1880–1980* (Toronto: McClelland & Stewart, 1986).

139. Andrea Tone, "Medicalizing Reproduction: The Pill and Home Pregnancy Tests," *Journal of Sex Research*, 49, 4 (2012), p. 320.

140. Christabelle Sethna, "The Evolution of the Birth Control Handbook: From Student Peer-Education Manual to Feminist Self-empowerment Text, 1968–1975," *Canadian Bulletin of Medical History*, 23, 1 (2006): 89–118.

141. Christabelle Sethna and Steve Hewitt, *Just Watch Us: RCMP Surveillance of the Women's Liberation Movement in Cold War Canada* (Montreal; Kingston: McGill-Queen's University Press, 2018); Gary Kinsman, "The Canadian Cold War on Queers: Sexual Regulation and Resistance," pp. 121–3, in *Love, Hate, and Fear in Canada's Cold War*, ed. Richard Cavell (Toronto: University of Toronto Press, 2004).

CHAPTER 7

1. For the United States context, see Natasha Zaretsky, *No Direction Home: The American Family and the Fear of National Decline, 1968–1980* (Chapel Hill: University of North Carolina Press, 2007).

2. Catalogue no. 98-311-X2011003, Census in Brief, *Generations in Canada, Age and Sex, 2011 Census.*
3. Gary Kinsman writes, for instance, of "a mass 'sexual migration' of gays and lesbians from rural areas to the larger cities, where our lifestyles are more acceptable and family ties weaker." Gary Kinsman, *The Regulation of Desire: Sexuality in Canada* (Montreal: Black Rose Books, 1987), p. 183.
4. On queer communities in small-town and rural Canada, see Valerie Korinek, *Prairie Fairies: A History of Queer Communities and People in Western Canada, 1930–1985* (Toronto: University of Toronto Press, 2018); Liz Millward, *Making a Scene: Lesbians and Community across Canada, 1964–84* (Vancouver: UBC Press, 2016), especially Chapter 6.
5. Doug Owram, *Born at the Right Time: A History of the Baby Boom Generation* (Toronto: University of Toronto Press, 1996), p. 159.
6. Myrna Kostash, *Long Way from Home: The Story of the Sixties Generation in Canada* (Toronto: James Lorimer & Company, 1980), p. xv; see also Bryan D. Palmer, *Canada's 1960s: The Ironies of Identity in a Rebellious Era* (Toronto: University of Toronto Press, 2009), Chapter 6, "Riotous Victorianism: From Youth Hooliganism to a Counterculture of Challenge," pp. 181–209.
7. Owram, *Born at the Right Time*, Chapter 10; François Ricard, *La génération lyrique. Essai sur la vie et l'œuvre des premiers-nés du baby-boom* (Montréal: Boréal, 1992).
8. Christabelle Sethna, "The Evolution of the *Birth Control Handbook*: From Student Peer-Education Manual to Feminist Self-empowerment Text, 1968–1975," *Canadian Bulletin of Medical History*, Volume 23, number 1 (2006): 89–118.
9. Arthur Marwick, "The Cultural Revolution of the Long Sixties: Voices of Reaction, Protest, and Permeation," *International History Review*, 27, 4 (December 2005): 780–806. For a discussion of the "Long Sixties" terminology, see Lara Campbell and Dominique Clément, "Time, Age, Myth: Towards a History of the Sixties," in Lara Campbell, Dominique Clément, and Greg Kealey, eds, *Debating Dissent: Canada and the 1960s* (Toronto: University of Toronto Press, 2012).
10. Myrna Kostash, *Long Way from Home*, pp. 112–13.
11. Meg Luxton and Leah F. Vosko, "Where Women's Efforts Count: The 1996 Census Campaign and 'Family Politics' in Canada," *Studies in Political Economy*, 56, 1 (1998): 49–81; Camille Robert, *Toutes les femmes sont d'abord ménagères: histoire d'un combat féministe pour la reconnaissance du travail ménager* (Montréal: Somme toute, 2017).
12. Kostash, *Long Way from Home*, p. 174.
13. *Rapport de la Commission royale d'enquête sur la Situation de la Femme au Canada* (1970), pp. 297–310.
14. Kostash, *Long Way from Home*, pp. 176–8.
15. Katrina R. Ackerman, "'Not in the Atlantic Provinces': The Abortion Debate in New Brunswick, 1980–1987," *Acadiensis*, 41, 1 (Winter/Spring 2012): 75–101;

Katrina Ackerman, "In Defence of Reason: Religion, Science, and the Prince Edward Island Anti-Abortion Movement, 1969–1988," *Canadian Bulletin of Medical History*, 31, 2 (2014): 117–38. Shannon Stettner and Bruce Douville have demonstrated that religion occupied a considerable place in the public debate around abortion in the Toronto *Globe and Mail* in the 1960s: see Stettner and Douville, "'In the Image and Likeness of God': Christianity and Public Opinion on Abortion in *The Globe and Mail* during the 1960s," *Journal of Canadian Studies*, 50, 1 (Winter 2016): 179–213.

16. Christabelle Sethna, Beth Palmer, Katrina Ackerman, and Nancy Janovicek, "Choice, Interrupted: Travel and Inequality of Access to Abortion Services since the 1960s," *Labour/Le Travail*, 71 (Spring 2013), pp. 41–4.
17. Christabelle Sethna, Beth Palmer, Katrina Ackerman, and Nancy Janovicek, "Choice, Interrupted: Travel and Inequality of Access to Abortion Services since the 1960s," *Labour/Le Travail*, 71 (Spring 2013): 29–48.
18. Heather Murray, *Not in This Family: Gays and the Meanings of Kinship in Postwar North America* (Philadelphia: University of Pennsylvania Press, 2010), pp. viii, x–xi, xvii.
19. Kinsman, *The Regulation of Desire*, p. 180–1, 186. United States feminist Betty Friedan was notorious for having evoked the presence of a "lavender menace" within organized feminism.
20. For an overview of the reforms associated with the Quiet Revolution, see Y. Bélanger, R. Comeau and C. Métivier, eds, *La révolution tranquille: 40 ans plus tard: un bilan* (Montréal: VLB, 2000).
21. Diane Lamoureux, *L'amère patrie. Féminisme et nationalisme dans le Québec contemporain* (Montréal: Éditions du remue-ménage, 2001); Micheline Dumont, "L'histoire nationale peut-elle intégrer la réflexion féministe sur l'histoire?", pp. 19–36, in Robert Comeau and Bernard Dionne, eds, *À propos de l'histoire nationale* (Sillery: Septentrion, 1998).
22. Danielle Gauvreau, Diane Gervais, and Peter Gossage, *La fécondité des Québécoises 1870–1970: d'une exception à l'autre* (Montréal: Boréal, 2007); Collectif Clio, *L'Histoire des femmes au Québec depuis quatre siècles*, 2e édition (Montréal: Le Jour, 1992); Denyse Baillargeon, *Brève histoire des femmes au Québec* (Montréal: Boréal, 2012).
23. Employment and Social Development Canada, Canadians in Context—Population Size and Growth, Table: Fertility Rate, Canada, 1921–2011, consulted at http://www4.hrsdc.gc.ca/.3ndic.1t.4r@-eng.jsp?iid=35
24. Gauvreau, Gervais, and Gossage, *La fécondité des Québécoises 1870–1970*.
25. Marc Termote, "La dynamique démolinguistique du Québec et de ses régions," pp. 281–84, in Victor Piché and Céline Le Bourdais, eds, *La démographie québécoise. Enjeux du 21e siècle* (Montréal: Presses de l'Université de Montréal, 2003).
26. Anne Milan, Statistics Canada Catalogue no. 91-209-X, Report on the Demographic Situation in Canada, *Fertility: Overview, 2009 to 2011* (July 2013).

27. *Aboriginal Women in Canada: A Statistical Profile from the 2006 Census* (Ministry of Aboriginal Affairs and Northern Development, 2012), Figure 6, Total Fertility Rate among Registered Indian Women, Canada, 1976–2021.
28. Employment and Social Development Canada, Indicators of Well-being in Canada, Family Life—Marriage, Table: Average Age at First Marriage, by gender, 1921–2008 (years).
29. Lesley Andres and Johanna Wyn, *The Making of a Generation: The Children of the 1970s in Adulthood* (Toronto: University of Toronto Press, 2010), pp. 178, 186.
30. Collectif Clio, *Histoire des femmes au Québec*, pp. 352–54; Baillargeon, *Brève histoire*, pp. 148–9.
31. Divorce Act (R.S.C., 1985, c. 3 (2nd Supp.)), consulted at http://laws-lois.justice.gc.ca/eng/acts/d-3.4/.
32. Gail Cuthbert Brandt, Naomi Black, Paula Bourne, and Magda Fahrni, *Canadian Women: A History*, 3rd edition (Toronto: Nelson, 2011), p. 485.
33. Renée B. Dandurand, *Le mariage en question: essai sociohistorique* (Québec: Institut québécois de recherche sur la culture, 1988).
34. Brandt, Black, Bourne, and Fahrni, *Canadian Women: A History*, pp. 559–60; Law Reform Commission of Nova Scotia, *Division of Family Property: A Discussion Paper* (Halifax: The Law Reform Commission of Nova Scotia, 2016), p. 34.
35. Leslie Paris, "'The Strange Way We Lived': Divorce and American Childhood in the 1970s," pp. 175–91, in Mona Gleason, Tamara Myers, Leslie Paris, and Veronica Strong-Boag, eds, *Lost Kids: Vulnerable Children and Youth in Twentieth-Century Canada and the United States* (Vancouver: University of British Columbia Press, 2010).
36. Lizette Peterson, "Teaching Home Safety and Survival Skills to Latch-Key Children: A Comparison of Two Manuals and Methods," *Journal of Applied Behavior Analysis*, 17, 3 (Fall 1984): 279–93. The 1982 study is quoted on page 279.
37. Yves Péron, "Du mariage obligatoire au mariage facultatif," pp. 110–43, in Piché and Le Bourdais, eds, *La démographie québécoise*.
38. For one journalist's analysis of this situation, see Stéphanie Grammond, "Lola et le Conseil du statut de la femme, même combat," *La Presse*, 7 juin 2014, p. 4.
39. Institut de la Statistique du Québec, *Coup d'œil sociodémographique*, Numéro 18 (Juin 2012), "Les mariages au Québec en 2011: l'âge au premier mariage continue d'augmenter," p. 5.
40. George Chauncey, *Why Marriage? The History Shaping Today's Debate over Gay Equality* (New York: Basic Books, 2004), p. 3.
41. George Chauncey, *Why Marriage?* especially Chapter 4, "Why Marriage Became a Goal," pp. 87–136.
42. Elise Chenier, "Liberating Marriage: Gay Liberation and Same-Sex Marriage in Early 1970s Canada," in *We Still Demand! Redefining Resistance in Sex and Gender Struggles*, ed. Patrizia Gentile, Gary Kinsman, and L. Pauline Rankin (Vancouver: UBC Press, 2016).

43. *Un portrait statistique des familles au Québec* (Québec: Ministère de la Famille, des Aînés et de la Condition féminine, 2005), p. 12.
44. *Portrait of Families and Living Arrangements in Canada: Families, households and marital status*, 2011 Census of Population (2012), Table 1, *Distribution (number and percentage) and percentage change of census families by family structure, Canada, 2001 to 2011*, p. 5.
45. *Women in Canada: A Gender-based Statistical Report*, 5th edition (Ottawa: Statistics Canada, 2006), p. 144.
46. Enza Gucciardi, Nalan Celasun, and Donna E. Stewart, "Single-Mother Families in Canada," *Canadian Journal of Public Health*, Volume 95, Number 1 (2004), p. 70.
47. Karen C. Kranz and Judith C. Daniluk, "We've Come a Long Way Baby... Or Have We? Contextualizing Lesbian Motherhood in North America," *Journal of the Association for Research on Mothering*, Volume 4, Number 1 (2002), p. 59.
48. *Family Portrait: Continuity and Change in Canadian Families and Households in 2006*, 2006 Census Families and Households, 2006 Census, Census year 2006, p. 13.
49. Kranz and Daniluk, "We've Come a Long Way Baby... Or Have We?", p. 61.
50. Chantale Quesney, "'Un foyer pour chaque enfant!' Le rôle de la Société d'adoption et de protection de l'enfance à Montréal dans la désinstitutionalisation des enfants sans famille, 1937–1972," *Revue d'histoire de l'Amérique française*, Volume 65, Numéros 2–3 (automne 2011 – hiver 2012): 257–82.
51. Karen Dubinsky, "'We Adopted a Negro': Interracial Adoption and the Hybrid Baby in 1960s Canada," in Magda Fahrni and Robert Rutherdale, eds, *Creating Postwar Canada: Community, Diversity, and Dissent 1945–75* (Vancouver: University of British Columbia Press, 2008); Karen Dubinsky, "A Haven from Racism? Canadians Imagine Interracial Adoption," in Mona Gleason, Tamara Myers, Leslie Paris, and Veronica Strong-Boag, eds, *Lost Kids: Vulnerable Children and Youth in Twentieth-Century Canada and the United States* (Vancouver: University of British Columbia Press, 2010); Karen Dubinsky, *Babies Without Borders: Adoption and Migration across the Americas* (Toronto: University of Toronto Press, 2010), Chapter 3, "The Hybrid Baby: Domestic Interracial Adoption since the 1950s," pp. 57–92.
52. Dubinsky, "A Haven from Racism?", pp. 16, 21. On the "Adopt Indian Métis" (AIM) programme in Saskatchewan at the end of the 1960s, see Karen A. Balcom, *The Traffic in Babies: Cross-Border Adoption and Baby-Selling between the United States and Canada 1930–1972* (Toronto: University of Toronto Press, 2011), p. 199.
53. Lori Chambers, "Indigenous Children and Provincial Child Welfare: The Sixties Scoop," p. 199, in *Aboriginal History: A Reader*, 2nd edition, ed. Kristin Burnett and Geoff Read (Don Mills: Oxford University Press Canada, 2016).

54. Christine Smith (McFarlane), "A Legacy of Canadian Child Care: Surviving the Sixties Scoop," *Briarpatch Magazine*, 1 September 2013, consulted online at https://briarpatchmagazine.com/articles/view/a-legacy-of-canadian-child-care; Raven Sinclair, "Identity Lost and Found: Lessons From the Sixties Scoop," *First Peoples Child & Family Review*, 3, 1 (2007): 65–82; Lori Chambers, "Indigenous Children and Provincial Child Welfare: The Sixties Scoop," pp. 199–209, in *Aboriginal History: A Reader*, 2nd edition, ed. Kristin Burnett and Geoff Read (Don Mills: Oxford University Press Canada, 2016) ; Veronica Strong-Boag, *Fostering Nation? Canada Confronts Its History of Childhood Disadvantage* (Waterloo: Wilfrid Laurier University Press, 2011), pp. 100–5.

55. Suzanne Fournier and Ernie Crey, *Stolen from Our Embrace: The Abduction of First Nations Children and the Restoration of Aboriginal Communities* (Vancouver: Douglas & McIntyre, 1997).

56. Quoted on the welcome page of the website of the First Nations Child and Family Caring Society, consulted at https://fncaringsociety.com/welcome

57. *Canada Year Book* 2012, 11-402-X, "International Adoptions," consulted at http://www.statcan.gc.ca/pub/11-402-x/2012000/chap/c-e/c-e02-eng.htm

58. Dubinsky, *Babies without Borders*.

59. Lysiane Gagnon, "La dérive," *La Presse*, 29 avril 2014; Christine Overall, *Human Reproduction: Principles, Practices, Policies* (Toronto: Oxford University Press, 1993).

60. Overall, *Human Reproduction*; Gwynne Basen, Margrit Eichler, and Abby Lippman, eds, *Misconceptions: The Social Construction of Choice and the New Reproductive Technologies*, Volumes 1 and 2 (Hull: Voyageur Publishing, 1993 and 1994).

61. "Recensement: la famille nucléaire de moins en moins la norme, surtout au Québec," *Le Devoir*, 19 septembre 2012.

CONCLUSION

1. CTV News, "Pressure Mounts to Curtail Surgery on Intersex Children," 25 July 2017 (https://www.ctvnews.ca/health/pressure-mounts-to-curtail-surgery-on-intersex-children-1.3517548); "Egale Canada Urges the Federal Government to Meet Domestic and International Human Rights Requirements of Intersex People on International Intersex Awareness Day," 26 October 2018 (https://egale.ca/egale-canada-urges-the-federal-government-to-meet-domestic-and-international-human-rights-requirements-of-intersex-people-on-international-intersex-awareness-day/).

2. Canada, *Population Trends by Age and Sex, 2016 Census of Population* (https://www150.statcan.gc.ca/n1/pub/11-627-m/11-627-m2017016-eng.htm). In Ontario, the number of persons aged 15 or under is roughly equal to the number of persons aged 65 or older.

3. Historian Megan J. Davies has found that by the 1940s, "Prairie retirees" were already present in British Columbia in large numbers. Davies, *Into the House of Old: A History of Residential Care in British Columbia* (Montreal: McGill-Queen's University Press, 2003), p. 171.
4. Marc Termote, "La dynamique démolinguistique du Québec et de ses régions," p. 282, in *La démographie québécoise. Enjeux du XXIe siècle*, ed. Victor Piché and Céline Le Bourdais (Montréal: Les Presses de l'Université de Montréal, 2003).
5. Megan J. Davies, *Into the House of Old: A History of Residential Care in British Columbia* (Montreal: McGill-Queen's University Press, 2003), p. 6.
6. http://www12.statcan.gc.ca/census-recensement/2016/as-sa/98-200-x/2016004/98-200-x2016004-eng.cfm.
7. https://www.reuters.com/article/us-canada-crime-nurse/canadian-nurse-pleads-guilty-to-killing-eight-in-old-age-homes-idUSKBN18S5SD
8. Elizabeth Podnieks, "National Survey on Abuse of the Elderly in Canada," *Journal of Elder Abuse & Neglect*, 4, 1–2 (1993), pp. 5–58; Lynn McDonald, "Elder Abuse and Neglect in Canada: The Glass Is Still Half Full," *Canadian Journal on Aging*, 30, 3 (2011), pp. 437–65.
9. Megan J. Davies, *Into the House of Old: A History of Residential Care in British Columbia* (Montreal: McGill-Queen's University Press, 2003), pp. 168–9.
10. Megan J. Davies, *Into the House of Old: A History of Residential Care in British Columbia* (Montreal: McGill-Queen's University Press, 2003), p. 6.
11. Jean-Pierre Lavoie, Nancy Guberman, and Ignace Olazabal, "Une vieillesse en transition. Les solidarités intergénérationnelles en 2020," pp. 279–83, in *La famille à l'horizon 2020*, ed. Gilles Pronovost et al. (Quebec City: Les Presses de l'Université du Québec, 2008).
12. "Une hécatombe hors norme dans les CHSLD du Québec," *Le Devoir*, 25 April 2020; "Long-term care is now the front line of Ontario's COVID-19 battle," *National Observer*, 17 April 2020; Francine Pelletier, "La solitude tue," *Le Devoir*, 6 May 2020.
13. Census of Population, 2016, "Working Seniors in Canada," Released 29 November 2017 (http://www12.statcan.gc.ca/census-recensement/2016/as-sa/98-200-x/2016027/98-200-x2016027-eng.pdf).
14. *The Globe and Mail*, "Federal budget to restore Old Age Security eligibility to 65," 17 March 2016.
15. Jean-Pierre Lavoie, Nancy Guberman, and Ignace Olazabal, "Une vieillesse en transition. Les solidarités intergénérationnelles en 2020," pp. 273–7, in *La famille à l'horizon 2020*, ed. Gilles Pronovost et al. (Quebec City: Les Presses de l'Université du Québec, 2008).
16. *Tanguy* (Étienne Chatiliez, 2001).
17. Lesley Andres and Johanna Wyn, *The Making of a Generation: The Children of the 1970s in Adulthood* (Toronto: University of Toronto Press, 2010), p. 160.

18. Jeffrey Jensen Arnett, "Emerging Adulthood: What Is It, and What Is It Good For?", *Child Development Perspectives*, 1, 2 (2007): 68–73.
19. Karen L. Fingerman et al., "Helicopter Parents and Landing Pad Kids: Intense Parental Support of Grown Children," *Journal of Marriage and Family*, 74, 4 (August 2012), pp. 880, 892.
20. https://www.theguardian.com/us-news/2018/may/22/new-york-judge-court-man-30-parents-home
21. Lesley Andres and Johanna Wyn, *The Making of a Generation: The Children of the 1970s in Adulthood* (Toronto: University of Toronto Press, 2010), p. 161.
22. *Generation Boomerang*, Ann-Marie MacDonald (Narrator), Sharon Bartlett (Director), Maria Lerose (Director), Sue Ridout (Producer), Helen Slinger (Writer), CBC, 2011.
23. Pascale Beaupré, Pierre Turcotte, and Anne Milan, "Junior Comes Back Home: Trends and Predictors of Returning to the Parental Home," *Canadian Social Trends*, Statistics Canada — Catalogue No. 11-008, pp. 28–34; CBC News, "Boomerang kids trend returns in latest Canadian census," 19 September 2012 (https://www.cbc.ca/news/canada/boomerang-kids-trend-returns-in-latest-canadian-census-1.1162383).
24. Lesley Andres and Johanna Wyn, *The Making of a Generation: The Children of the 1970s in Adulthood* (Toronto: University of Toronto Press, 2010), p. 167.
25. Lesley Andres and Johanna Wyn, *The Making of a Generation: The Children of the 1970s in Adulthood* (Toronto: University of Toronto Press, 2010), pp. 171, 188.
26. Karen L. Fingerman et al., "Helicopter Parents and Landing Pad Kids: Intense Parental Support of Grown Children," *Journal of Marriage and Family*, 74, 4 (August 2012), pp. 882, 893; *Generation Boomerang*, Ann-Marie MacDonald (Narrator), Sharon Bartlett (Director), Maria Lerose (Director), Sue Ridout (Producer), Helen Slinger (Writer), CBC, 2011.
27. Madeleine Gauthier, "Quels scenarios entrevoir lorsqu'il est question de l'avenir des jeunes?" pp. 247–8, in *La famille à l'horizon 2020*, ed. Gilles Pronovost et al. (Quebec City: Les Presses de l'Université du Québec, 2008).
28. Madeleine Gauthier, "Quels scenarios entrevoir lorsqu'il est question de l'avenir des jeunes?" pp. 249, 251–2, in *La famille à l'horizon 2020*, ed. Gilles Pronovost et al. (Quebec City: Les Presses de l'Université du Québec, 2008).
29. Lesley Andres and Johanna Wyn, *The Making of a Generation: The Children of the 1970s in Adulthood* (Toronto: University of Toronto Press, 2010), pp. 175, 178, 186.
30. Statistics Canada, "The Daily—Immigration and Ethnocultural Diversity: Key Results from the 2016 Census" (25 October 2017): https://www150.statcan.gc.ca/n1/daily-quotidien/171025/t002b-eng.htm
31. Anne Bourgeois and Solène Lardoux, "La fécondité des unions conjugales mixtes au Québec," p. 100, in *L'intégration des familles d'origine immigrante. Les enjeux*

sociosanitaires et scolaires, ed. Fasal Kanouté and Gina Lafortune (Montréal: Les Presses de l'Université de Montréal, 2014).

32. Ministère de l'Immigration, de la Diversité et de l'Inclusion, "Présence et portraits régionaux des personnes immigrantes admises au Québec de 2006 à 2015" (Gouvernement du Québec, 2017), Tableau 5, "Population immigrante admise au Québec de 2006 à 2015 et présence en 2017 selon les 30 principaux pays de naissance, par catégorie d'immigration," p. 29 (http://www.midi.gouv.qc.ca/publications/fr/recherches-statistiques/PUB_Presence2017_admisQc.pdf).

33. Sean Mills, *A Place in the Sun: Haiti, Haitians, and the Remaking of Quebec* (Montréal: McGill-Queen's University Press, 2016), especially Chapter 3, "The Poetics of Exile," pp. 77–108, and Chapter 5, "Migrants and Borders," pp. 133–65.

34. Gina Lafortune, "Trajectoires sociomigratoires de familles d'origine haïtienne à Montréal," pp. 11–28, in *L'intégration des familles d'origine immigrante. Les enjeux sociosanitaires et scolaires*, ed. Fasal Kanouté and Gina Lafortune (Montreal: Les Presses de l'Université de Montréal, 2014).

35. Gina Lafortune, "Trajectoires sociomigratoires de familles d'origine haïtienne à Montréal," pp. 15, 20–2, in *L'intégration des familles d'origine immigrante. Les enjeux sociosanitaires et scolaires*, ed. Fasal Kanouté and Gina Lafortune (Montreal: Les Presses de l'Université de Montréal, 2014).

36. Elizabeth Jane Errington, *Emigrant Worlds and Transatlantic Communities: Migration to Upper Canada in the First Half of the Nineteenth Century* (Montreal; Kingston: McGill-Queen's University Press, 2007); Mario Mimeault, *L'exode québécois, 1852–1925. Correspondance d'une famille dispersée en Amérique* (Sillery: Septentrion, 2013).

37. Charmaine Crawford, "Sending Love in a Barrel: The Making of Transnational Families in Canada," *Canadian Woman Studies*, 22, 3–4 (2003): 104–9.

38. Charmaine Crawford, "African-Caribbean Women, Diaspora and Transnationality," *Canadian Woman Studies*, 23, 2 (2004), p. 101.

39. https://www.canada.ca/en/immigration-refugees-citizenship/services/work-canada/permit/caregiver-program.html.

40. Charmaine Crawford, "African-Caribbean Women, Diaspora and Transnationality," *Canadian Woman Studies*, 23, 2 (2004), p. 101.

41. Kwok B. Chan and Lawrence Lam, "Resettlement of Vietnamese-Chinese Refugees in Montreal, Canada: Some Socio-psychological Problems and Dilemmas," *Canadian Ethnic Studies*, XV, 1 (1983), especially pp. 8, 13.

42. Louise Bérubé, *Parents d'ailleurs, enfants d'ici. Dynamique d'adaptation du rôle parental chez les immigrants* (Sainte-Foy: Les Presses de l'Université du Québec, 2004), pp. 59, 103.

43. Justine Gosselin-Gagné, "Les élèves allophones récemment immigrés et la resilience scolaire," p. 130, in *L'intégration des familles d'origine immigrante. Les*

enjeux sociosanitaires et scolaires, ed. Fasal Kanouté and Gina Lafortune (Montreal: Les Presses de l'Université de Montréal, 2014).

44. Quoted in Louis-Jacques Dorais and Éric Richard, *Les Vietnamiens de Montréal* (Montréal: Les Presses de l'Université de Montréal, 2007), p. 117.

45. Kwok B. Chan and Lawrence Lam, "Resettlement of Vietnamese-Chinese Refugees in Montreal, Canada: Some Socio-psychological Problems and Dilemmas," *Canadian Ethnic Studies*, XV, 1 (1983), especially pp. 11–14.

46. Gertrude Mianda, "Sisterhood versus Discrimination: Being a Black African Francophone Immigrant Woman in Montreal and Toronto," pp. 266–84, in *Sisters or Strangers? Immigrant, Ethnic, and Racialized Women in Canadian History*, ed. Marlene Epp, Franca Iacovetta, and Frances Swyripa (Toronto: University of Toronto Press, 2004).

47. Gertrude Mianda, "Sisterhood versus Discrimination: Being a Black African Francophone Immigrant Woman in Montreal and Toronto," p. 278, in *Sisters or Strangers? Immigrant, Ethnic, and Racialized Women in Canadian History*, ed. Marlene Epp, Franca Iacovetta, and Frances Swyripa (Toronto: University of Toronto Press, 2004).

48. Louise Bérubé, *Parents d'ailleurs, enfants d'ici. Dynamique d'adaptation du rôle parental chez les immigrants* (Sainte-Foy: Les Presses de l'Université du Québec, 2004), pp. 58–9.

49. Michèle Vatz Laaroussi and Lilyane Rachédi, "Prospectives familles immigrantes 2007–2020. Les familles immigrantes au Québec en 2020: une excroissance des familles québécoises ou une trame du tissu social?" in *La famille à l'horizon 2020*, ed. Gilles Pronovost et al. (Quebec City: Les Presses de l'Université du Québec, 2008), especially pp. 354–6.

50. Michèle Vatz Laaroussi and Lilyane Rachédi, "Prospectives familles immigrantes 2007–2020. Les familles immigrantes au Québec en 2020: une excroissance des familles québécoises ou une trame du tissu social?" in *La famille à l'horizon 2020*, ed. Gilles Pronovost et al. (Quebec City: Les Presses de l'Université du Québec, 2008), p. 365.

51. Statistics Canada, "Aboriginal Peoples in Canada: Key Results from the 2016 Census," 25 October 2017 (https://www150.statcan.gc.ca/n1/daily-quotidien/171025/dq171025a-eng.htm).

52. Truth and Reconciliation Commission of Canada, *The Final Report of the Truth and Reconciliation Commission of Canada*, Volume 5, *Canada's Residential Schools: The Legacy* (Montreal; Kingston: McGill-Queen's University Press, 2015), p. 29.

53. Truth and Reconciliation Commission of Canada, *The Final Report of the Truth and Reconciliation Commission of Canada*, Volume 5, *Canada's Residential Schools: The Legacy* (Montreal; Kingston: McGill-Queen's University Press, 2015), p. 53.

54. Truth and Reconciliation Commission of Canada, *The Final Report of the Truth and Reconciliation Commission of Canada*, Volume 5, *Canada's Residential Schools: The Legacy* (Montreal; Kingston: McGill-Queen's University Press, 2015), p. 31.
55. Truth and Reconciliation Commission of Canada, *The Final Report of the Truth and Reconciliation Commission of Canada*, Volume 5, *Canada's Residential Schools: The Legacy* (Montreal; Kingston: McGill-Queen's University Press, 2015), pp. 11–12.
56. Truth and Reconciliation Commission of Canada, *The Final Report of the Truth and Reconciliation Commission of Canada*, Volume 5, *Canada's Residential Schools: The Legacy* (Montreal; Kingston: McGill-Queen's University Press, 2015), pp. 34–6.
57. Truth and Reconciliation Commission of Canada, *The Final Report of the Truth and Reconciliation Commission of Canada*, Volume 5, *Canada's Residential Schools: The Legacy* (Montreal; Kingston: McGill-Queen's University Press, 2015), pp. 49–50.
58. Truth and Reconciliation Commission of Canada, *The Final Report of the Truth and Reconciliation Commission of Canada*, Volume 5, *Canada's Residential Schools: The Legacy* (Montreal; Kingston: McGill-Queen's University Press, 2015), p. 17.
59. Truth and Reconciliation Commission of Canada, *The Final Report of the Truth and Reconciliation Commission of Canada*, Volume 5, *Canada's Residential Schools: The Legacy* (Montreal; Kingston: McGill-Queen's University Press, 2015), pp. 150–8; M. Patterson, S. Flinn, and K. Barker, "Addressing tuberculosis among Inuit in Canada," *Canada Communicable Disease Report Monthly*, 44, 3–4 (March 2018): https://www.canada.ca/en/public-health/services/reports-publications/canada-communicable-disease-report-ccdr/monthly-issue/2018-44/issue-3-4-march-1-2018/article-3-tuberculosis-among-inuit.html; Lori Chambers and Kristin Burnett, "Jordan's Principle: The Struggle to Access On-Reserve Health Care for High-Needs Indigenous Children in Canada," *The American Indian Quarterly*, 41, 2 (Spring 2017), pp. 103–4.
60. Lori Chambers and Kristin Burnett, "Jordan's Principle: The Struggle to Access On-Reserve Health Care for High-Needs Indigenous Children in Canada," *The American Indian Quarterly*, 41, 2 (Spring 2017): 101–24.
61. Cindy Blackstock, "The Canadian Human Rights Tribunal on First Nations Child Welfare: Why if Canada Wins, Equality and Justice Lose," *Children and Youth Services Review*, 33 (2011): 187–94; Lori Chambers and Kristin Burnett, "Jordan's Principle: The Struggle to Access On-Reserve Health Care for High-Needs Indigenous Children in Canada," *The American Indian Quarterly*, 41, 2 (Spring 2017), pp. 110–14; CBC News, "Ottawa ordered to compensate First Nations children impacted by on-reserve child welfare system," 6 September 2019 (https://www.cbc.ca/news/indigenous/child-welfare-on-reserve-compensation-1.5272667).

62. Leanne Betasamosake Simpson, *As We Have Always Done: Indigenous Freedom Through Radical Resistance* (Minneapolis: University of Minnesota Press, 2017), pp. 238–41. See also Leanne Betasamosake Simpson, Rinaldo Walcott, and Glen Coulthard, "Idle No More and Black Lives Matter: An Exchange," *Studies in Social Justice*, 12, 1 (2018), especially pp. 81–2.
63. Leanne Betasamosake Simpson, *As We Have Always Done: Indigenous Freedom Through Radical Resistance* (Minneapolis: University of Minnesota Press, 2017), p. 6.
64. Statistics Canada, "Aboriginal Peoples in Canada: Key Results from the 2016 Census," 25 October 2017 (https://www150.statcan.gc.ca/n1/daily-quotidien/171025/dq171025a-eng.htm); CBC News, "Indigenous population growing rapidly, languages surging: census," 25 October 2017 (https://www.cbc.ca/news/indigenous/indigenous-census-rapid-growth-1.4370727); *The Globe and Mail*, 25 October 2017, "Canada getting more diverse as immigration, Indigenous population increase" (https://www.theglobeandmail.com/news/national/census-2016-highlights-diversity-housing-indigenous/article36711216/).
65. Kath Weston, *Families We Choose: Lesbians, Gays, Kinship* (New York: Columbia University Press, 1991). For a fascinating discussion of the distinction between caring for and caring about, see Katie Barclay, "Love, Care, and the Illegitimate Child in Eighteenth-Century Scotland," *Transactions of the Royal Historical Society*, 29 (2019): 105–25.
66. Robert Frost, "The Death of the Hired Man," pp. 14–23, in Robert Frost, *North of Boston*, 2nd edition (New York: Henry Holt, 1915 [1914]).
67. Quoted in "A Conversation with Stuart Hall," *The Journal of the International Institute*, 7, 1 (Fall 1999), consulted online at http://hdl.handle.net/2027/spo.4750978.0007.107

Selected Works

The following are a selection of the works consulted in order to write this overview of the history of families in what is now Canada. The notes for each chapter give additional references. Although many of the works listed below could fit in more than one category, each title is listed only once.

EDITED COLLECTIONS AND SYNTHESES

Bradbury, Bettina, ed., *Canadian Family History: Selected Readings*. Toronto: Copp Clark Pitman, 1992.

Comacchio, Cynthia, *The Infinite Bonds of Family: Domesticity in Canada, 1850–1940*. Toronto: University of Toronto Press, 1999.

Gleason, Mona and Tamara Myers, eds, *Bringing Children and Youth into Canadian History: The Difference Kids Make*. Don Mills: Oxford University Press, 2017.

Gleason, Mona, Tamara Myers, Leslie Paris, and Veronica Strong-Boag, eds, *Lost Kids: Vulnerable Children and Youth in Twentieth-Century Canada and the United States*. Vancouver: University of British Columbia Press, 2010.

Janovicek, Nancy and Joy Parr, eds, *Histories of Canadian Children and Youth*. Don Mills: Oxford University Press, 2003.

Montigny, E.-A. and Lori Chambers, eds, *Family Matters: Papers in Post-Confederation Canadian Family History*. Toronto: Scholars Press, 1998.

Parr, Joy, ed. *Childhood and Family in Canadian History*. Toronto: McClelland & Stewart, 1982.

INDIGENOUS FAMILIES AND KINSHIP NETWORKS

Beaulieu, Alain, Stéphanie Béreau and Jean Tanguay, *Les Wendats du Québec. Territoire, économie et identité, 1650–1930*. Quebec City: Les Éditions GID, 2013.

Bohaker, Heidi, "'Nindoodemag': The Significance of Algonquian Kinship Networks in the *Eastern Great Lakes Region, 1600–1701*," *The William and Mary Quarterly*, Third Series, 63, 1 (January 2006): 23–52.

Carter, Sarah, *Aboriginal People and Colonizers of Western Canada to 1900*. Toronto: University of Toronto Press, 1999.

Carter, Sarah, *The Importance of Being Monogamous: Marriage and Nation Building in Western Canada to 1915*. Edmonton: University of Alberta Press, 2008.

Clermont, Norman, "La place de la femme dans les sociétés iroquoiennes de la période du contact," *Recherches amérindiennes au Québec*, 13, 4 (1983): 286–90.

Dickason, Olive Patricia, *Canada's First Nations: A History of Founding Peoples from Earliest Times*. Toronto: McClelland & Stewart, 1992.

Elbourne, Elizabeth, "Broken Alliance: Debating Six Nations' Land Claims in 1822," *Cultural and Social History*, 9, 4 (2012): 497–525.

Green, Gretchen, "Molly Brant, Catharine Brant, and Their Daughters: A Study in Colonial Acculturation," *Ontario History*, 81, 3 (September 1989): 235–50.

Havard, Gilles, *Empire et métissages. Indiens et Français dans le Pays d'en Haut, 1660–1715*. Paris: Presses de l'Université Paris-Sorbonne; Sillery: Septentrion, 2003.

Hill, Susan M., *The Clay We Are Made Of: Haudenosaunee Land Tenure on the Grand River*. Winnipeg: University of Manitoba Press, 2017.

Jackson, Victoria, "Silent Diplomacy: Wendat Boys' 'Adoptions' at the Jesuit Seminary, 1636–1642," *Journal of the Canadian Historical Association*, 27, 1 (2016): 139–68.

Jaenen, Cornelius J., "Amerindian Views of French Culture in the Seventeenth Century," *Canadian Historical Review*, 55, 3 (1974): 261–91.

Labelle, Kathryn Magee, *Dispersed but Not Destroyed: A History of the Seventeenth-Century Wendat People*. Vancouver: UBC Press, 2013.

Leacock, Eleanor, "Montagnais Women and the Jesuit Program for Colonization," pp. 43–62, in Leacock, *Myths of Male Dominance: Collected Articles on Women Cross-Culturally*. Chicago: Haymarket Books, 2008 [1981].

Leacock, Eleanor and Jacqueline Goodman, "Montagnais Marriage and the Jesuits in the Seventeenth Century; Incidents from the Relations of Paul Le Jeune," *The Western Canadian Journal of Anthropology*, VI, 3 (1976): 77–91.

Lozier, Jean-François, *Flesh Reborn: The Saint Lawrence Valley Mission Settlements through the Seventeenth Century*. Montreal; Kingston: McGill-Queen's University Press, 2018.

Ray, Arthur J., *I Have Lived Here Since the World Began: An Illustrated History of Canada's Native People*. Toronto: Lester Publishing & Key Porter Books, 1996.

Simpson, Audra, *Mohawk Interruptus: Political Life Across the Borders of Settler States*. Durham: Duke University Press, 2014.

Sioui, Georges E., *Histoires de Kanatha vues et contées. Essais et discours, 1991–2008/ Histories of Kanatha Seen and Told. Essays and Discourses, 1991–2008*. Ottawa: University of Ottawa Press, 2008.

Sioui, Georges E., *For an Amerindian Autohistory: An Essay on the Foundations of a Social Ethic*. Montreal; Kingston: McGill-Queen's University Press, 1992.

Trigger, Bruce G., *The Children of Aataentsic: A History of the Huron People to 1660*. Montreal: McGill-Queen's University Press, 1987.

Truth And Reconciliation Commission of Canada, *Honouring the Truth, Reconciling for the Future: Summary of the Final Report of the Truth and Reconciliation Commission of Canada*. Toronto: James Lorimer, 2015.

Viau, Roland, *Femmes de personne. Sexes, genres et pouvoirs en Iroquoisie ancienne*. Montreal: Boréal, 2005.

Vowel, Chelsea, *Indigenous Writes: A Guide to First Nations, Métis & Inuit Issues in Canada*. Winnipeg: HighWater Press, 2016.

White, Richard, *The Middle Ground. Indians, Empires and Republics in the Great Lakes Region, 1650–1815*. Cambridge: Cambridge University Press, 1991.

Witgen, Michael, *An Infinity of Nations: How the Native New World Shaped Early North America*. Philadelphia: University of Pennsylvania Press, 2012.

FAMILIES AND HOUSEHOLDS IN NEW FRANCE

Bates, Réal, "Les conceptions prénuptiales dans la vallée du Saint-Laurent avant 1725," *Revue d'histoire de l'Amérique française*, 40, 2 (1986): 253–72.

Beaugrand-Champagne, Denyse, *Le procès de Marie-Josèphe-Angélique*. Outremont: Libre Expression, 2004.

Bessière, Arnaud. "'Faire une bonne et fidèle servante' au Canada sous le Régime français," *Histoire sociale/Social History* 50, 102 (2017): 233–57.

Brun, Josette, *Vie et mort du couple en Nouvelle-France. Québec et Louisbourg au XVIIIe siècle*. Montreal; Kingston: McGill-Queen's University Press, 2006.

Choquette, Leslie, *Frenchmen into Peasants: Modernity and Tradition in the Peopling of French Canada*. Cambridge, MA: Harvard University Press, 1997.

Cliche, Marie-Aimée, "Filles-mères, familles et société sous le Régime français," *Histoire Sociale/Social History*, 21, 41 (1988): 39–69.

Cooper, Afua, *The Hanging of Angélique: The Untold Story of Canadian Slavery and the Burning of Old Montréal*. Toronto: HarperCollins, 2006.

Dépatie, Sylvie, "La transmission du patrimoine au Canada (XVIIe–XVIIIe siècle): Qui sont les défavorisés?", *Revue d'histoire de l'Amérique française*, 54, 4 (2001): 557–70.

Deslandres, Dominique, *Croire et faire croire: Les missions françaises au XVIIe siècle*. Paris: Fayard, 2003.

Dillon, Lisa, "Parental and Sibling Influences on the Timing of Marriage, XVIIth and XVIIIth Century Québec," *Annales de démographie historique*, 2010/1, 119: 139–80.

Donovan, Kenneth, "Slaves and Their Owners in Ile Royale, 1713–1760," *Acadiensis*, 25, 1 (Autumn 1995): 3–32.

Dumont, Micheline, "Les femmes de la Nouvelle-France étaient-elles favorisées?", *Atlantis*, 8, 1 (1982): 118–24.

Fournier, Marcel, "L'apport démographique des soldats de Montcalm au cours de la guerre de Sept Ans et ses répercussions sur la population canadienne," pp. 184–6, in *1763. Le traité de Paris bouleverse l'Amérique*, ed. Sophie Imbeault, Denis Vaugeois and Laurent Veyssière. Quebec: Septentrion, 2013.

Gauvreau, Danielle, "À propos de la mise en nourrice à Québec pendant le régime français," *Revue d'histoire de l'Amérique française*, XLI, 1 (été 1987): 53–62.

Greer, Allan, *Mohawk Saint: Catherine Tekakwitha and the Jesuits*. New York: Oxford University Press, 2005.

Greer, Allan, *Peasant, Lord, and Merchant: Rural Society in Three Quebec Parishes, 1740–1840*. Toronto: University of Toronto Press, 1985.

Greer, Allan, *The People of New France*. Toronto: University of Toronto Press, 1997.

Greer, Allan, *Property and Dispossession: Natives, Empires and Land in Early Modern North America*. Cambridge: Cambridge University Press, 2018.

Grenier, Benoît, *Brève histoire du régime seigneurial*. Montréal: Boréal, 2012.

Grenier, Benoît, *Marie-Catherine Peuvret. Veuve et seigneuresse en Nouvelle-France, 1667–1739*. Sillery: Septentrion, 2005.

Griffiths, Naomi E.S., *From Migrant to Acadian: A North American Border People, 1604–1755*. Montreal; Kingston: McGill-Queen's University Press, 2004.

Griffiths, Naomi, "The Golden Age: Acadian Life, 1713–1748," *Histoire sociale/Social History*, 17, 33 (May 1984): 21–34.

Kennedy, Gregory, "Marshland Colonization in Acadia and Poitou during the 17th Century," *Acadiensis*, XLII, 1 (2013): 37–66.

Kennedy, Gregory M.W., *Something of a Peasant Paradise? Comparing Rural Societies in Acadie and the Loudunais, 1604–1755*. Montreal; Kingston: McGill-Queen's University Press, 2014.

Landry, Yves, "Fécondité et habitat des immigrantes françaises en Nouvelle-France," *Annales de démographie historique* (1988): 259–76.

Landry, Yves, *Orphelines en France, pionnières au Canada: les Filles du roi au XVIIe siècle*. Montréal: Leméac, 1992.

Larin, Robert, *Brève histoire du peuplement européen en Nouvelle-France*. Sillery: Septentrion, 2000.

Lemieux, Denise, *Les petits innocents: L'enfance en Nouvelle-France*. Québec: Institut québécois de recherche sur la culture, 1985.

Moogk, Peter N., "Les Petits Sauvages: The Children of Eighteenth-Century New France," pp. 17–43, in *Childhood and Family in Canadian History*, ed. Joy Parr. Toronto: McClelland & Stewart, 1982.

Noel, Jan, *Along a River: The First French-Canadian Women*. Toronto: University of Toronto Press, 2013.

Podruchny, Carolyn and Kathryn Magee Labelle, "Jean de Brébeuf and the Wendat Voices of Seventeenth-Century New France," *Renaissance and Reformation/Renaissance et Réforme*, 34, 1–2 (Winter–Spring 2011): 97–126.

Rushforth, Brett, *Bonds of Alliance: Indigenous and Atlantic Slaveries in New France*. Chapel Hill: University of North Carolina Press, 2013.

Rushforth, Brett, "'A Little Flesh We Offer You': The Origins of Indian Slavery in New France," *William and Mary Quarterly*, 3rd series, 60, 4 (October 2003): 777–808.

Savoie, Sylvie, "La rupture du couple en Nouvelle-France: Les demandes de séparation aux XVIIe et XVIIIe siècles," *Canadian Woman Studies*, VII, 4 (hiver 1986): 58–63.

MÉTIS AND FUR-TRADE FAMILIES

Andersen, Chris, *"Métis": Race, Recognition, and the Struggle for Indigenous Peoplehood*. Vancouver: UBC Press, 2014.

Barman, Jean, *French Canadians, Furs, and Indigenous Women in the Making of the Pacific Northwest*. Vancouver: UBC Press, 2014.

Brown, Jennifer S.H., *Strangers in Blood: Fur Trade Company Families in Indian Country*. Vancouver: University of British Columbia Press, 1980.

Brownlie, Jarvis and Valerie J. Korinek, eds, *Finding a Way to the Heart: Feminist Writings on Aboriginal and Women's History in Canada*. Winnipeg: University of Manitoba Press, 2012.

Devine, Heather, *The People Who Own Themselves: Aboriginal Ethnogenesis in a Canadian Family, 1660–1900*. Calgary: University of Calgary Press, 2004.

Ens, Gerhard J. and Joe Sawchuk, *From New Peoples to New Nations: Aspects of Métis History and Identity from the Eighteenth to the Twenty-first Centuries*. Toronto: University of Toronto Press, 2015.

Gaudry, Adam, "Respecting Métis Nationhood and Self-Determination in Matters of Métis Identity," pp. 152–63, in *Aboriginal History: A Reader*, 2nd edition, ed. Kristin Burnett and Geoff Read. Don Mills: Oxford University Press Canada, 2016.

Gorham, Harriet, "Families of Mixed Descent in the Western Great Lakes Region," pp. 37–55, in *Native People, Native Lands: Canadian Indians, Inuit and Metis*, ed. Bruce Alden Cox. Montreal; Kingston: McGill-Queen's University Press, 2002.

Macdougall, Brenda, *One of the Family: Metis Culture in Nineteenth-Century Northwestern Saskatchewan*. Vancouver: University of British Columbia Press, 2010.

Millions, Erin, "Portraits and Gravestones: Documenting the Transnational Lives of Nineteenth-Century British-Métis Students," *Journal of the Canadian Historical Association*, 29, 1 (2018): 1–38.

Perry, Adele, "'Is your Garden in England, Sir': James Douglas's Archive and the Politics of Home," *History Workshop Journal*, 70 (2010): 67–85.

Peters, Evelyn, Matthew Stock, and Adrian Werner, *Rooster Town: The History of an Urban Métis Community, 1901–1961*. Winnipeg: University of Manitoba Press, 2018.

Peterson, Jacqueline and Jennifer S.H. Brown, eds, *The New Peoples: Being and Becoming Métis in North America*. Winnipeg: University of Manitoba Press, 1985.

Podruchny, Carolyn, *Making the Voyageur World: Travelers and Traders in the North American Fur Trade*. Toronto: University of Toronto Press, 2006.

St-Onge, Nicole, Carolyn Podruchny, and Brenda Macdougall, eds, *Contours of a People: Metis Family, Mobility, and History*. Norman: University of Oklahoma Press, 2012.

Van Kirk, Sylvia, *"Many Tender Ties": Women in Fur-Trade Society in Western Canada, 1670–1870*. Winnipeg: Watson & Dwyer Publishing, 1980.

Vibert, Elizabeth, "Real Men Hunt Buffalo: Masculinity, Race and Class in British Fur Traders' Narratives," *Gender & History*, 8, 1 (1996): 4–21.

MARRIAGE, HOUSEHOLDS, MIGRATION, AND KIN NETWORKS IN PREINDUSTRIAL CANADA, 18TH–19TH CENTURIES

Brownlie, Jarvis, "'Our fathers fought for the British': Racial Discourses and Indigenous Allies in Upper Canada," *Histoire sociale/Social History*, 50, 102 (November 2017): 259–84.

Cameron, Wendy, Sheila Haines, and Mary McDougall Maude, *English Immigrant Voices: Labourers' Letters from Upper Canada in the 1830s*. Montreal; Kingston: McGill-Queen's University Press, 2000.

Campbell, Gail G., *"I wish to keep a record": Nineteenth-Century New Brunswick Women Diarists and Their World*. Toronto: University of Toronto Press, 2017.

Coates, Colin M. and Cecilia Morgan, *Heroines and History: Representations of Madeleine de Verchères and Laura Secord*. Toronto: University of Toronto Press, 2002.

Conrad, Margaret, Toni Laidlaw, and Donna Smyth, eds, *No Place Like Home: Diaries and Letters of Nova Scotia Women, 1771–1938*. Halifax: Formac Publishing Company, 1988.

Conrad, Margaret, *Recording Angels: The Private Chronicles of Women from the Maritime Provinces of Canada, 1750–1850*. Ottawa: CRIAW, 1982.

Craig, Béatrice, Judith RYGIEL, and Elizabeth Turcotte, "The Homespun Paradox: Market-Oriented Production of Cloth in Eastern Canada in the Nineteenth Century," *Agricultural History*, 76, 1 (2002): 28–57.

Darroch, Gordon and Michael Ornstein, "Family and Household in Nineteenth-Century Canada: Regional Patterns and Regional Economics," *Journal of Family History*, 9, 2 (1984): 158–77.

Dépatie, Sylvie, "Maîtres et domestiques dans les campagnes montréalaises au XVIIIe siècle: bilan préliminaire," *Histoire, économie et société*, 27, 4 (2008): 51–65.

Errington, Elizabeth Jane, *Wives and Mothers, School Mistresses and Scullery Maids: Working Women in Upper Canada, 1790–1840*. Montreal; Kingston: McGill-Queen's University Press, 1995.

Errington, Elizabeth Jane, *Emigrant Worlds and Transatlantic Communities: Migration to Upper Canada in the First Half of the Nineteenth Century*. Montreal; Kingston: McGill-Queen's University Press, 2007.

Gagan, David, *Hopeful Travellers: Families, Land, and Social Change in Mid-Victorian Peel County, Canada West*. Toronto: University of Toronto Press, 1981.

Gagnon, Serge, *Plaisir d'amour et crainte de Dieu. Sexualité et confession au Bas-Canada*. Québec: Les Presses de l'Université Laval, 1990.

Gagnon, Serge, *Mariage et famille au temps de Papineau*. Sainte-Foy: Les Presses de l'Université Laval, 1993.

Gagnon, Serge, "Tu n'épouseras pas la cousine de ta défunte: La proche endogamie au Bas-Canada," pp. 249–66, in Yves Roby and Nine Voisine, eds, *Érudition, humanisme et savoir, Actes du colloque en l'honneur de Jean Hamelin*. Sainte-Foy: Les Presses de l'Université Laval, 1996.

Greer, Allan, *The Patriots and the People: The Rebellion of 1837 in Rural Lower Canada*. Toronto: University of Toronto Press, 1993.

Heaman, Elsbeth, "Constructing Innocence: Representations of Sexual Violence in Upper Canada's War of 1812," *Journal of the Canadian Historical Association*, 24, 2 (2013): 114–55.

Hudon, Christine, *Prêtres et fidèles dans le diocèse de Saint-Hyacinthe, 1820–1875*. Sillery: Septentrion, 1996.

Imbeault, Sophie, *Les Tarieu de Lanaudière. Une famille noble après la Conquête 1760–1791*. Quebec: Septentrion, 2004.

Ishiguro, Laura, "'A Dreadful Little Glutton Always Telling You about Food': The Epistolary Everyday and the Making of Settler Colonial British Columbia," *Canadian Historical Review*, 99, 2 (June 2018): 258–83.

Ishiguro, Laura, "'Growing Up and Grown Up . . . in our Future City': Discourses of Childhood and Settler Futurity in Colonial British Columbia," *BC Studies*, 190 (Summer 2016): 15–38.

Ishiguro, Laura, *Nothing to Write Home About: British Family Correspondence and the Settler Colonial Everyday in British Columbia*. Vancouver: UBC Press, 2019.

Johnson, J.K. and Bruce G. Wilson, eds, *Historical Essays on Upper Canada: New Perspectives*. Ottawa: Carleton University Press, 1989.

Little, J.I., ed., *Love Strong as Death: Lucy Peel's Canadian Journal, 1833–1836*. Waterloo: Wilfrid Laurier University Press, 2001.

Mckenna, Katherine M.J., *A Life of Propriety: Anne Murray Powell and Her Family, 1755–1849*. Montreal; Kingston: McGill-Queen's University Press, 1994.

Mackey, Frank, *Done with Slavery: The Black Fact in Montreal, 1760–1840*. Montreal; Kingston: McGill-Queen's University Press, 2010.

Mckinnon, Janice Potter, *While the Women Only Wept: Loyalist Refugee Women*. Montreal; Kingston: McGill-Queen's University Press, 1993.

Morgan, Cecilia, *Public Men and Virtuous Women: The Gendered Languages of Religion and Politics in Upper Canada, 1791–1850*. Toronto: University of Toronto Press, 1996.

Noël, Françoise, *Family Life and Sociability in Upper and Lower Canada, 1780–1870: A View from Diaries and Family Correspondence*. Montréal: McGill-Queen's University Press, 2003.

Oyeniran, Channon, "Black Loyalists in British North America," *The Canadian Encyclopedia*, Historica Canada, Article published 25 March 2019; Last Edited 25 March 2019. https://www.thecanadianencyclopedia.ca/en/article/black-loyalists-in-british-north-america

Perry, Adele, *On the Edge of Empire: Gender, Race and the Making of British Columbia, 1849–1871*. Toronto: University of Toronto Press, 2001.

Poutanen, Mary Anne, *Beyond Brutal Passions: Prostitution in Early Nineteenth-Century Montreal*. Montreal; Kingston: McGill-Queen's University Press, 2015.

Roberts, Julia, "'A Mixed Assemblage of Persons': Race and Tavern Space in Upper Canada," *Canadian Historical Review* 83, 1 (March 2002): 1–28.

Ward, Peter, *Courtship, Love, and Marriage in Nineteenth-Century English Canada*. Montreal; Kingston: McGill-Queen's University Press, 1990.

Young, Brian, "Getting around Legal Incapacity: The Legal Status of Married Women in Trade in Mid-Nineteenth-Century Lower Canada," pp. 1–16, in *Canadian Papers in Business History*, Volume 1, ed. Peter Baskerville. Victoria: University of Victoria Press, 1989.

Young, Brian, *Patrician Families and the Making of Quebec: The Taschereaus and McCords*. Montreal; Kingston: McGill-Queen's University Press, 2014.

CHARITY, INSTITUTIONS, AND THE HELPING PROFESSIONS

Arnup, Katherine, *Education for Motherhood: Advice for Mothers in Twentieth-Century Canada*. Toronto: University of Toronto Press, 1994.

Arnup, Katherine, "Raising the Dionne Quintuplets: Lessons for Modern Mothers," *Journal of Canadian Studies*, 29, 4 (Winter 1994–1995): 65–85.

Baillargeon, Denyse, *Naître, vivre, grandir. Sainte-Justine, 1907–2007*. Montréal: Boréal, 2007.

Fecteau, Jean-Marie et al., "Une politique de l'enfance délinquante et en danger: la mise en place des écoles de réforme et d'industrie au Québec (1840–1873)," *Crime, Histoire & Sociétés/Crime, History & Societies* 2, 1 (1998): 75–110.

Gilbert, Dale, "Assister les familles de Québec: l'école de réforme et l'école d'industrie de l'Hospice Saint-Charles, 1870–1950," *Revue d'histoire de l'Amérique française*, 61, 3–4 (2008): 469–500.

Gossage, Peter, "Les enfants abandonnés à Montréal au 19e siècle: la crèche d'Youville des Sœurs Grises, 1829–1871," *Revue d'histoire de l'Amérique française*, XL, 4 (printemps 1987): 537–59.

Lafferty, Renée N., *The Guardianship of Best Interests: Institutional Care for the Children of the Poor in Halifax, 1850–1960*. Montreal; Kingston: McGill-Queen's University Press, 2013.

Lapointe-Roy, Huguette, *Charité bien ordonnée: Le premier réseau de lutte contre la pauvreté à Montréal au 19e siècle*. Montreal: Boréal, 1987.

Ménard, Sylvie, *Des enfants sous surveillance. La rééducation des jeunes délinquants au Québec (1840–1950)*. Montréal: VLB Éditeur, 2003.

Morton, Suzanne, *Wisdom, Justice, and Charity: Canadian Social Welfare Through the Life of Jane B. Wisdom, 1884–1975*. Toronto: University of Toronto Press, 2014.

Myers, Sharon, "'Suffering from a sense of injustice': Children's Activism in Liberal State Formation at the Saint John Boys Industrial Home, 1927–1932," *Histoire sociale/Social History*, 52, 105 (May 2019): 1–30.

Myers, Tamara and Joan Sangster, "Retorts, Runaways, and Riots: Patterns of Resistance in Canadian Reform Schools for Girls," *Journal of Social History*, 34, 3 (Spring 2001): 669–97.

Neff, Charlotte, "Ontario Government Funding and Supervision of Infants' Homes 1875–1893," *Journal of Family History*, 38, 1 (2012): 17–54.

Nielson, Carmen J., *Private Women and the Public Good: Charity and State Formation in Hamilton, Ontario, 1846–93*. Vancouver: UBC Press, 2014.

Rooke, Patricia and R.L. Schnell, *Discarding the Asylum: From Child Rescue to the Welfare State in English Canada*. Lanham, MD: University Press of America, 1983.

Simmons, Christina, "'Helping the Poorer Sisters': The Women of the Jost Mission, Halifax, 1905–1945," *Acadiensis*, 14, 1 (Autumn 1984): 3–27.

Strong-Boag, Veronica, "Intruders in the Nursery: Childcare Professionals Reshape the Years One to Five, 1920–1940," pp. 160–78, in *Childhood and Family in Canadian History*, ed. Joy Parr. Toronto: McClelland & Stewart, 1982.

Valverde, Mariana, "The Mixed Social Economy as a Canadian Tradition," *Studies in Political Economy*, 14 (1995): 33–60.

Wright, David, *SickKids: The History of The Hospital for Sick Children*. Toronto: University of Toronto Press, 2016.

FAMILIES AND INDUSTRIALIZATION

Barman, Jean, "Beyond Chinatown: Chinese Men and Indigenous Women in Early British Columbia," *BC Studies*, 177 (Spring 2013): 39–64.

Beattie, Betsy, "'Going Up to Lynn': Single, Maritime-Born Women in Lynn, Massachusetts, 1879–1930," *Acadiensis*, 22, 1 (Autumn 1992): 65–86.

Bouchard, Gérard, *Quelques arpents d'Amérique: Population, économie, famille au Saguenay, 1838–1971*. Montréal: Boréal, 1996.

Bradbury, Bettina, *Working Families: Age, Gender, and Daily Survival in Industrializing Montreal*. Toronto: McClelland & Stewart, 1993.

Bullen, John, "Hidden Workers: Child Labour and the Family Economy in Late Nineteenth-Century Urban Ontario," *Labour/Le Travail*, vol. 18 (Fall 1986): 163–87.

Copp, Terry, *The Anatomy of Poverty: The Condition of the Working Class in Montreal, 1897–1929*. Toronto: McClelland & Stewart, 1974.

Desloges, Yvon and Alain Gelly, *Le canal de Lachine: Du tumulte des flots à l'essor industriel et urbain, 1860–1950*. Sillery: Septentrion, 2002.

Fahrni, Magda, "'Ruffled' Mistresses and 'Discontented' Maids: Respectability and the Case of Domestic Service, 1880–1914," *Labour/Le Travail*, 39 (Spring 1997): 69–97.

Ferretti, Lucia, "Mariage et cadre de vie familiale dans une paroisse ouvrière montréalaise: Sainte-Brigide, 1900–1914," *Revue d'histoire de l'Amérique française*, 39, 2 (1985): 233–51.

Forster, Ben and Kris Inwood, "The Diversity of Industrial Experience: Cabinet and Furniture Manufacture in Late Nineteenth-Century Ontario," *Enterprise & Society*, 4 (June 2003): 326–71.

Gagnon, France, "Parenté et migration: le cas des Canadiens français à Montréal entre 1845 et 1875," *Communications historiques*, 23, 1 (1988): 63–85.

Gossage, Peter, *Families in Transition: Industry and Population in Nineteenth-Century Saint-Hyacinthe*. Montréal: McGill-Queen's University Press, 1999.

Hareven, Tamara K., *Family Time and Industrial Time*. New York: Cambridge University Press, 1983.

Harton, Marie-Ève, "Veuvage et remariage à Québec à la fin du XIXe siècle: Une analyse différentielle selon le genre," *Cahiers québécois de démographie*, 37, 1 (2008): 13–34.

Kealey, Greg, ed., *Canada Investigates Industrialism: The Royal Commission on the Relations of Labor and Capital 1889*. Toronto: University of Toronto Press, 1973.

Kealey, Greg, *Toronto Workers Respond to Industrial Capitalism, 1867–1892*. Toronto: University of Toronto Press, 1980.

Kenny, Nicolas, *The Feel of the City: Experiences of Urban Transformation*. Toronto: University of Toronto Press, 2014.

Lacelle, Claudette, *Urban Domestic Servants in Nineteenth-Century Canada*. Ottawa: 1987.

Laflamme, Valérie, "Vivre en famille ou en pension: Stratégies résidentielles et réseaux d'accueil," *Cahiers québécois de démographie*, 37, 1, (2008): 61–96.

Lauzon, Gilles, "Cohabitation et déménagements en milieu ouvrier montréalais: Essai de réinterprétation à partir du cas du village Saint-Augustin (1871–1881)," *Revue d'histoire de l'Amérique française*, 46, 1 (été 1992): 115–42.

Lutz, John, "After the Fur Trade: The Aboriginal Labouring Class of British Columbia, 1849–1890," *Journal of the Canadian Historical Association, New Series*, 3 (1992): 69–94.

Lutz, John, "Gender and Work in Lekwammen Families, 1843–1970," in Kathryn McPherson, Cecilia Morgan, and Nancy M. Forestell, eds, *Gendered Pasts: Historical Essays in Femininity and Masculinity in Canada*. Don Mills: Oxford University Press, 1999.

Macleod, Roderick, "The Road to Terrace Bank: Land Capitalization, Public Space, and the Redpath Family Home, 1837–1861," *Journal of the Canadian Historical Association*, 14, 1 (2003): 165–92.

Mckay, Ian, "Capital and Labour in the Halifax Baking and Confectionery Industry during the Last Half of the Nineteenth Century," *Labour/Le Travail*, 3 (1978): 63–108.

Olson, Sherry and Patricia Thornton, *Peopling the North American City: Montreal, 1840–1900*. Montreal; Kingston: McGill-Queen's University Press, 2011.

Olson, Sherry, "Pour se créer un avenir: Stratégies de couples montréalais au XIXe siècle," *Revue d'histoire de l'Amérique française*, 51, 3 (hiver 1998): 357–90.

Olson, Sherry and Patricia Thornton, "Familles montréalaises du XIXe siècle: trois cultures, trois trajectoires," *Cahiers québécois de démographie*, 21, 2 (1991): 51–75.

Parnaby, Andrew, "'The best men that ever worked the lumber': Aboriginal Longshoremen on Burrard Inlet, B.C., 1863–1939," *Canadian Historical Review*, 87 (March 2006): 53–78.

Parr, Joy, *The Gender of Breadwinners: Women, Men, and Change in Two Industrial Towns, 1880–1950*. Toronto: University of Toronto Press, 1990.

Raibmon, Paige, "The Practice of Everyday Colonialism: Indigenous Women at Work in the Hop Fields and Tourist Industry of Puget Sound," *Labor: Studies in Working-Class Histories of the Americas*, 3, 3 (2006): 23–56.

Sager, Eric W. and Peter Baskerville, eds, *Household Counts: Canadian Households and Families in 1901*. Toronto: University of Toronto Press, 2007.

Strange, Carolyn, "Wounded Womanhood and Dead Men: Chivalry and the Trials of Clara Ford and Carrie Davies," in Franca Iacovetta and Mariana Valverde, eds, *Gender Conflicts: New Essays in Women's History*. Toronto: University of Toronto Press, 1992.

Sweeny, Robert C.H., *Why Did We Choose to Industrialize? Montreal 1819–1849*. Montreal; Kingston: McGill-Queen's University Press, 2015.

FAMILIES, THE STATE, AND THE LAW

Backhouse, Constance, *Petticoats and Prejudice: Women and Law in Nineteenth-Century Canada*. Toronto: The Osgoode Society and Women's Press, 1991.

Backhouse, Constance, "'Pure Patriarchy': Nineteenth-Century Canadian Marriage," *McGill Law Journal*, 31 (1986): 264–312.

Baskerville, Peter, *A Silent Revolution? Gender and Wealth in English Canada, 1860–1930*. Montreal; Kingston: McGill-Queen's University Press, 2008.

Baskerville, Peter, "Women and Investment in Late-Nineteenth-Century Urban Canada: Victoria and Hamilton, 1880–1901," *Canadian Historical Review*, 80, 2 (1999): 191–218.

Blake, Raymond, *From Rights to Needs: A History of Family Allowances in Canada, 1929–1992*. Vancouver: UBC Press, 2008.

Bradbury, Bettina, *Wife to Widow. Lives, Laws, and Politics in Nineteenth-Century Montreal*. Vancouver: UBC Press, 2011.

Bryden, Kenneth, *Old Age Pensions and Policy-Making in Canada*. Montreal; London: McGill-Queen's University Press and The Institute of Public Administration of Canada, 1974.

Burr, Christina, "Letters to Mike: Personal Narrative and Divorce Reform in Canada in the 1960s," pp. 401–2, in *Family Matters: Papers in Post-Confederation Canadian Family History*, ed. Lori Chambers and Edgar-André Montigny. Toronto: Canadian Scholars' Press, 1998.

Carter, Sarah, *Imperial Plots: Women, Land, and the Spadework of British Colonialism on the Canadian Prairies*. Winnipeg: University of Manitoba Press, 2016.

Carter, Sarah, *Lost Harvests: Prairie Indian Reserve Farmers and Government Policy*. Montreal and Kingston: McGill-Queen's University Press, 1990.

Chambers, Lori, "Women's Labour, Relationship Breakdown, and Ownership of the Family Farm," *Canadian Journal of Law and Society*, 25 (2010): 75–95.

Christie, Nancy, *Engendering the State: Family, Work, and Welfare in Canada*. Toronto: University of Toronto Press, 2000.

Clarkson, Christopher A., "Property Law and Family Regulation in Pacific British North America, 1862–1873," *Histoire sociale/Social History*, 30, 60 (1997): 386–416.

Clarkson, Chris, *Domestic Reforms: Political Visions and Family Regulation in British Columbia, 1862–1940*. Vancouver: University of British Columbia Press, 2007.

Cliche, Marie-Aimée, "Du péché au traumatisme: l'Inceste, vu de la Cour des jeunes délinquants et de la Cour du bien-être social de Montréal, 1912–1965," *Canadian Historical Review*, 87, 2 (June 2006): 199–222.

Couturier, Jacques Paul and Wendy Johnston, "L'État, les familles et l'obligation scolaire au Nouveau-Brunswick dans les années 1940," *Histoire sociale/Social History*, 35, 69 (2002): 1–34.

Curtis, Bruce, *The Politics of Population: State Formation, Statistics, and the Census of Canada, 1840–1875*. Toronto: University of Toronto Press, 2001.

Daschuk, James, *Clearing the Plains: Disease, Politics of Starvation, and Loss of Aboriginal Life*. Regina: University of Regina Press, 2013.

Deleury, Edith, "L'union homosexuelle et le droit de la famille," *Cahiers du droit*, XXV (décembre 1984): 751–75.

Emery, George, *Facts of Life: The Social Construction of Vital Statistics, Ontario, 1869–1952*. Montreal; Kingston: McGill-Queen's University Press, 1993.

Fish, Cynthia S., "La puissance paternelle et les cas de garde d'enfants au Québec, 1866–1928," *Revue d'histoire de l'Amérique française*, 57, 4 (2004): 509–33.

Girard, Philip, "'If two ride a horse, one must ride in front': Married Women's Nationality and the Law in Canada, 1880–1950," *Canadian Historical Review*, 94, 1 (March 2013): 28–54.

Guay, Hélène, "Abus et maltraitance envers les aînés: Quel est l'apport du droit?", *Revue du Barreau*, 73 (2014): 263–317.

Hamel, Thérèse, "Obligation scolaire et travail des enfants au Québec: 1900–1950," *Revue d'histoire de l'Amérique française*, 38, 1 (1984): 39–58.

Harvey, Kathryn, "To Love, Honour and Obey: Wife-Battering in Working-Class Montreal, 1869–1879," *Urban History Review*, XIX, 2 (October 1990): 128–40.

Harvey, Kathryn, "Amazons and Victims: Resisting Wife Abuse in Working-Class Montreal, 1869–1879," *Journal of the Canadian Historical Association*, 2 (1991): 131–48.

Jean, Dominique, "Les parents québécois et l'État canadien au début du programme des allocations familiales: 1944–1955," *Revue d'histoire de l'Amérique française*, 40, 1 (1986): 73–95.

Little, Margaret Jane Hillyard, *"No Car, No Radio, No Liquor Permit": The Moral Regulation of Single Mothers in Ontario, 1920–1997*. Toronto: Oxford University Press, 1998.

Lux, Maureen K., *Separate Beds: A History of Indian Hospitals in Canada, 1920s–1980s*. Toronto: University of Toronto Press, 2016.

Marchildon, Gregory, "Douglas versus Manning: The Ideological Battle over Medicare in Postwar Canada," *Journal of Canadian Studies*, 50, 1 (2016): 129–49.

Marshall, Dominique, "Nationalisme et politiques sociales au Québec depuis 1867: Un siècle de rendez-vous manqués entre l'État, l'Église et les familles," *British Journal of Canadian Studies*, 9, 2 (1994): 301–47.

Marshall, Dominique, *Aux origines sociales de l'État providence*. Montréal: Les Presses de l'Université de Montréal, 1998.

Mosby, Ian, "Administering Colonial Science: Nutrition Research and Human Biomedical Experimentation in Aboriginal Communities and Residential Schools, 1942–1952," *Histoire sociale/Social History*, 46, 91 (2013): 145–72.

Myers, Tamara, *Caught. Montreal's Modern Girls and the Law, 1869–1945*. Toronto: University of Toronto Press, 2006.

Myers, Tamara. "The Voluntary Delinquent: Parents, Daughters, and the Montreal Juvenile Delinquents' Court in 1918," *Canadian Historical Review*, 80, 2 (June 1999): 242–68.

Niget, David, *La naissance du tribunal pour enfants. Une comparaison France-Québec (1912–1945)*. Rennes: Presses universitaires de Rennes, 2009.

Nootens, Thierry, *Fous, prodigues et ivrognes. Familles et déviance à Montréal au XIXe siècle*. Montreal; Kingston: McGill-Queen's University Press, 2007.

Nootens, Thierry, *Genre, patrimoine et droit civil. Les femmes mariées de la bourgeoisie québécoise en procès, 1900–1930*. Montreal; Kingston: McGill-Queen's University Press, 2019.

Pasolli, Lisa, *Working Mothers and the Child Care Dilemma: A History of British Columbia's Social Policy*. Vancouver: UBC Press, 2015.

Roy, Alain, "Les couples de même sexe en droit québécois ou la quête d'une égalité sans compromis," *Annales de Droit de Louvain*, 65, 1–2 (2005): 29–48.

Sangster, Joan, *One Hundred Years of Struggle: The History of Women and the Vote in Canada*. Vancouver: UBC Press, 2018.

Shewell, Hugh, "'What Makes the Indian Tick?' The Influence of Social Sciences on Canada's Indian Policy, 1947–1964," *Histoire sociale/Social History*, 34, 67 (2001): 133–67.

Snell, James, "Marital Cruelty: Women and the Nova Scotia Divorce Court, 1900–1939," *Acadiensis*, 18 (Autumn 1988): 3–32.

Stephen, Jennifer A., *Pick One Intelligent Girl: Employability, Domesticity and the Gendering of Canada's Welfare State, 1939–1947*. Toronto: University of Toronto Press, 2007.

Strong-Boag, Veronica, "'Wages for Housework': Mothers' Allowances and the Beginnings of Social Security in Canada," *Journal of Canadian Studies*, 14, 1 (Spring 1979): 24–34.

Struthers, James, *The Limits of Affluence: Welfare in Ontario, 1920–1970*. Toronto: University of Toronto Press, 1994.

Struthers, James, *No Fault of their Own: Unemployment and the Canadian Welfare State 1914–1941*. Toronto: University of Toronto Press, 1983.

Tester, Frank and Peter Kulchyski, *Tammarniit (Mistakes): Inuit Relocation in the Eastern Arctic, 1939–63*. Vancouver: UBC Press, 1994.

FERTILITY, CHILDBIRTH, CONTRACEPTION, AND ABORTION

Ackerman, Katrina R., "'Not in the Atlantic Provinces': The Abortion Debate in New Brunswick, 1980–1987," *Acadiensis*, 41, 1 (Winter/Spring 2012): 75–101.

Ackerman, Katrina, "In Defence of Reason: Religion, Science, and the Prince Edward Island Anti-Abortion Movement, 1969–1988," *Canadian Bulletin of Medical History*, 31, 2 (2014): 117–38.

Baillargeon, Denyse, *Un Québec en mal d'enfants: La médicalisation de la maternité, 1910–1970*. Montréal: Éditions du Remue-Ménage, 2004.

Cliche, Marie-Aimée, "L'infanticide dans la région de Québec (1660–1969)," *Revue d'histoire de l'Amérique française*, 44, 1 (été 1990): 31–59.

Comacchio, Cynthia R., *Nations Are Built of Babies: Saving Ontario's Mothers and Children 1900–1940*. Montreal; Kingston: McGill-Queen's University Press, 1993.

Dodd, Diane, "The Canadian Birth Control Movement on Trial, 1936–1937," *Histoire sociale/Social History*, 16, 32 (November 1983): 411–28.

Gauvreau, Danielle, Peter Gossage, and Diane Gervais, *La fécondité des Québécoises 1870–1970: D'une exception à l'autre*. Montréal: Boréal, 2007.

Gervais, Diane and Danielle Gauvreau, "Women, Priests, and Physicians: Family Limitation in Quebec 1940–1970," *Journal of Interdisciplinary History*, 34, 2 (Fall 2003): 293–315.

Gervais, Diane, "Morale catholique et détresse conjugale au Québec: La réponse du service de régulation des naissances SERENA, 1955–1970," *Revue d'histoire de l'Amérique française*, 55, 2 (2001): 185–215.

Langford, Nanci, "Childbirth on the Canadian Prairies, 1880–1930," *Journal of Historical Sociology*, 8, 3 (September 1995): 278–302.

Lemieux, Denise and Lucie Mercier, *Les femmes au tournant du siècle 1880–1940: Ages de la vie, maternité et quotidien*. Québec: Institut québécois de la recherche sur la culture, 1989.

Mclaren, Angus and Arlene Tigar Mclaren, *The Bedroom and the State: The Changing Practices and Politics of Contraception and Abortion in Canada, 1880–1980*. Toronto: McClelland & Stewart, 1986.

Mitchinson, Wendy, *Giving Birth in Canada, 1900–1950*. Toronto: University of Toronto Press, 2002.

Nathoo, Tasnim and Aleck Ostry, *The One Best Way? Breastfeeding, History, Politics, and Policy in Canada*. Waterloo: Wilfrid Laurier University Press, 2009.

Rivard, Andrée (with Francine De Montigny), *De la naissance et des pères*. Montréal: Éditions du Remue-Ménage, 2016.

Rivard, Andrée, *Histoire de l'accouchement dans un Québec modern*. Montréal: Éditions du Remue-Ménage, 2014.

Sethna, Christabelle, "The Evolution of the Birth Control Handbook: From Student Peer-Education Manual to Feminist Self-empowerment Text, 1968–1975," *Canadian Bulletin of Medical History*, 23, 1 (2006): 89–118.

Sethna, Christabelle, Beth Palmer, Katrina Ackerman, and Nancy Janovicek, "Choice, Interrupted: Travel and Inequality of Access to Abortion Services since the 1960s," *Labour/Le Travail*, 71 (Spring 2013): 29–48.

Stettner, Shannon and Bruce Douville, "'In the Image and Likeness of God': Christianity and Public Opinion on Abortion in *The Globe and Mail* during the 1960s," *Journal of Canadian Studies*, 50, 1 (Winter 2016): 179–213.

Tone, Andrea, "Medicalizing Reproduction: The Pill and Home Pregnancy Tests," *Journal of Sex Research*, 49, 4 (2012): 319–27.

BABIES, CHILDREN, AND YOUTH

Adams, Annmarie and Peter Gossage, "Chez Fadette: Girlhood, Family, and Private Space in Late Nineteenth-Century Saint-Hyacinthe," *Urban History Review*, 26, 2 (1998): 56–68.

Alexander, Kristine, *Guiding Modern Girls: Girlhood, Empire, and Internationalism in the 1920s and 1930s*. Vancouver: UBC Press, 2017.

Archambault, Jacinthe, "'Pour la personne la plus précieuse de votre vie': Représentation des enfants dans la publicité et construction d'une norme sociale concernant la famille et l'enfance à Montréal (1944–1954)," *Revue d'histoire de l'Amérique française* 65, 1 (2011): 5–27.

Baillargeon, Denyse, "Éduquer les enfants, discipliner les parents: les rapports famille-école à Montréal, 1910–1960," *Revue d'histoire de l'éducation*, 21, 2 (2009): 46–64.

Balcom, Karen, *The Traffic in Babies: Cross-border Adoption and Baby-selling Between the United States and Canada, 1930–1972*. Toronto: University of Toronto Press, 2011.

Barman, Jean, "Separate and Unequal: Indian and White Girls at All Hallows School, 1884–1920," pp. 215–33, in Veronica Strong-Boag and Anita Clair Fellman, eds, *Rethinking Canada: The Promise of Women's History*, 2nd edition. Toronto: Copp Clark Pitman, 1991.

Bienvenue, Louise, *Quand la jeunesse entre en scène*. Montréal: Boréal, 2003.

Bienvenue, Louise and Christine Hudon, "Les prêtres, les parents et la sexualité des collégiens dans les années 1940," pp. 99–107, in V. Blanchard, R. Revenin and J.-J. Yvorel, eds, *Les jeunes et la sexualité*. Paris: Éditions Autrement, 2010.

Chambers, Lori, "Indigenous Children and Provincial Child Welfare: The Sixties Scoop," pp. 199–209, in *Aboriginal History: A Reader*, 2nd edition, ed. Kristin Burnett and Geoff Read. Don Mills: Oxford University Press Canada, 2016.

Cliche, Marie-Aimée, "Un secret bien gardé: l'inceste dans la société traditionnelle québécoise 1858–1938," *Revue d'histoire de l'Amérique française*, 50, 2 (1996): 201–26.

Cliche, Marie-Aimée, *Maltraiter ou punir? La violence envers les enfants dans les familles québécoises, 1850–1969*. Montréal: Boréal, 2007.

Comacchio, Cynthia, *The Dominion of Youth: Adolescence and the Making of a Modern Canada, 1920–1950*. Waterloo: Wilfrid Laurier University Press, 2006.

De Leeuw, Sarah, "'If Anything Is to Be Done with the Indian, We Must Catch Him Very Young': Colonial Constructions of Aboriginal Children and the Geographies of Indian Residential Schooling in British Columbia, Canada," pp. 329–47, in *Bringing Children and Youth into Canadian History: The Difference Kids Make*, ed. Mona Gleason and Tamara Myers. Don Mills: Oxford University Press, 2017.

Dubinsky, Karen, *Babies without Borders: Adoption and Migration across the Americas*. Toronto: University of Toronto Press, 2010.

Fahmy-Eid, Nadia, "Vivre au pensionnat: le cadre de vie des couventines," pp. 47–66, in *Les Couventines. L'éducation des filles au Québec dans les congrégations religieuses enseignantes 1840–1960*, ed. Micheline Dumont and Nadia Fahmy-Eid. Montréal: Boréal Express, 1986.

Fahrni, Magda, "Glimpsing Working-Class Childhood through the Laurier Palace Fire of 1927: The Ordinary, the Tragic, and the Historian's Gaze," *Journal of the History of Childhood and Youth*, 8, 3 (Fall 2015): 426–50.

Fontaine, Phil, Aimée Craft, and the TRUTH AND RECONCILIATION COMMISSION OF CANADA, *A Knock on the Door: The Essential History of Residential Schools from the Truth and Reconciliation Commission of Canada*. Winnipeg: University of Manitoba Press, 2015.

Gaffield, Chad, "Schooling, the Economy, and Rural Society in Nineteenth-Century Ontario," in Joy Parr, ed., *Childhood and Family in Canadian History*. Toronto: McClelland & Stewart, 1982.

Gleason, Mona, *Small Matters: Canadian Children in Sickness and Health, 1900–1940*. Montreal; Kingston: McGill-Queen's University Press, 2013.

Gossage, Peter, "*La Marâtre*: Marie-Anne Houde and the Myth of the Wicked Stepmother in Quebec," *Canadian Historical Review*, 76, 4 (1995): 563–97.

Gossage, Peter, "On Dads and Damages: Looking for the 'Priceless Child' and the 'Manly Modern' in Quebec's Civil Courts, 1921–1960," *Histoire sociale/Social History*, 49, 100 (November 2016): 603–23.

Haig-Brown, Celia, "Always Remembering: Indian Residential Schools in Canada," in *Aboriginal History: A Reader*, 2nd edition, eds Kristin Burnett and Geoff Read. Don Mills: Oxford University Press, 2016.

Houston, Susan E. and Alison Prentice, *Schooling and Scholars in Nineteenth-Century Ontario*. Toronto: University of Toronto Press, 1988.

Houston, Susan E., "The 'Waifs and Strays' of a Late Victorian City: Juvenile Delinquents in Toronto," p. 134, in Joy Parr, ed., *Childhood and Family in Canadian History*. Toronto: McClelland & Stewart, 1982.

Hudon, Christine, "L'éducation sentimentale et sexuelle dans les collèges pour garçons, du milieu du XIXe siècle à la Révolution tranquille," p. 32–53, *dans Une histoire des sexualités au Québec au XXe siècle*, ed. Jean-Philippe Warren. Montréal: VLB Éditeur, 2012.

Jean, Dominique, "Le recul du travail des enfants au Québec entre 1940 et 1960: Une explication des conflits entre les familles pauvres et l'État providence," *Labour/Le Travail*, 24 (1989): 91–129.

Joyal, Renée, ed., *L'évolution de la protection de l'enfance au Québec: entre surveillance et compassion: des origines à nos jours*. Sainte-Foy: Presses de l'Université du Québec, 2000.

Macdonald, Heidi, "Singleness and Choice: The Impact of Age, Time, and Class on Three Female Youth Diarists in 1930s Canada," in Catherine Carstairs and Nancy Janovicek, eds, *Feminist History in Canada: New Essays on Women, Gender, Work, and Nation*. Vancouver: University of British Columbia Press, 2013.

Mennill, Sally and Veronica Strong-Boag, "Identifying Victims: Child Abuse and Death in Canadian Families," *Canadian Bulletin of Medical History*, 25, 1 (2008): 311–33.

Milloy, John S., *A National Crime: The Canadian Government and the Residential School System, 1879 to 1986*, 2nd edition. Winnipeg: University of Manitoba Press, 2017.

Moss, Mark, *Manliness and Militarism: Educating Young Boys in Ontario for War*. Don Mills: Oxford University Press, 2001.

Parr, Joy, *Labouring Children: British Immigrant Apprentices to Canada*. Toronto: University of Toronto Press, 1980.

Poirier, Valérie, "'Polio Hysteria': La rentrée scolaire montréalaise de 1946 et l'épidémie de poliomyélite," *Bulletin canadien d'histoire de la médecine*, 30, 1 (2013): 123–42.

Prentice, Alison, *The School Promoters: Education and Social Class in Mid-Nineteenth-Century Upper Canada*. Toronto: McClelland and Stewart, 1977.

Quesney, Chantale, "'Un foyer pour chaque enfant!' Le rôle de la Société d'adoption et de protection de l'enfance à Montréal dans la désinstitutionalisation des enfants sans famille, 1937–1972," *Revue d'histoire de l'Amérique française*, 65, 2–3 (automne 2011–hiver 2012): 257–82.

Rollings-Magnusson, Sandra, *Heavy Burdens on Small Shoulders: The Labour of Pioneer Children on the Canadian Prairies*. Edmonton: University of Alberta Press, 2009.

Sinclair, Raven, "Identity Lost and Found: Lessons from the Sixties Scoop," *First Peoples Child & Family Review*, 3, 1 (2007): 65–82.

Smith (McFarlane), Christine, "A Legacy of Canadian Child Care: Surviving the Sixties Scoop," pp. 209–12, in *Aboriginal History: A Reader*, 2nd edition, eds Kristin Burnett and Geoff Read. Don Mills: Oxford University Press, 2016.

Strong-Boag, Veronica, *Finding Families, Finding Ourselves: English Canada Encounters Adoption from the Nineteenth Century to the 1990s*. Don Mills: Oxford University Press, 2006.

Strong-Boag, Veronica, *Fostering Nation? Canada Confronts its History of Childhood Disadvantage*. Waterloo: Wilfrid Laurier University Press, 2011.

Strong-Boag, Veronica, "Interrupted Relations: The Adoption of Children in Twentieth-Century British Columbia," *BC Studies*, 144 (Winter 2004/2005): 5–30.

Strong-Boag Veronica, *The New Day Recalled: Lives of Girls and Women in English Canada, 1919–1939*. Toronto: Copp Clark Pitman, 1988.

Sutherland, Neil, *Growing Up: Childhood in English Canada from the Great War to the Age of Television*. Toronto: University of Toronto Press, 1997.

Truth and Reconciliation Commission of Canada, *The Final Report of the Truth and Reconciliation Commission of Canada, Volume 5, Canada's Residential Schools: The Legacy*. Montreal; Kingston: McGill-Queen's University Press, 2015.

Wall, Sharon, *The Nurture of Nature: Childhood, Antimodernism, and Ontario Summer Camps, 1920–55*. Vancouver: University of British Columbia Press, 2009.

Zembrzycki, Stacey, "'There Were Always Men in Our House': Gender and the Childhood Memories of Working-Class Ukrainians in Depression-Era Canada," *Labour/Le Travail* 60 (Fall 2007): 77–105.

OLD AGE AND THE ELDERLY

Charles, Aline, "Femmes âgées, pauvres et sans droit de vote, mais . . . citoyennes? Lettres au premier ministre du Québec, 1935–1936," *Recherches féministes*, 26, 2 (2013): 51–70.

Charles, Aline, *Quand devient-on vieille? Femmes, âge et travail au Québec, 1940–1980*. Québec: Presses de l'Université Laval, 2007.

Davies, Megan J., *Into the House of Old: A History of Residential Care in British Columbia*. Montreal; Kingston: McGill-Queen's University Press, 2003.

Dillon, Lisa, *The Shady Side of Fifty: Age and Old Age in Late Victorian Canada and the United States*. Montreal; Kingston: McGill-Queen's University Press, 2008.

Snell, James G., *The Citizen's Wage: The State and the Elderly in Canada, 1900–1951*. Toronto: University of Toronto Press, 1996.

Snell, James G., "The Family and the Working-Class Elderly in the First Half of the Twentieth Century," pp. 499–510, in *Family Matters: Papers in Post-Confederation Canadian Family History*, ed. Lori Chambers and Edgar-André Montigny. Toronto: Canadian Scholars' Press, 1998.

Struthers, James, "'A Nice Homelike Atmosphere': State Alternatives to Family Care for the Aged in Post–World War II Ontario," pp. 335–54, in Lori Chambers and Edgar-André Montigny, eds, *Family Matters: Papers in Post-Confederation Canadian Family History*. Toronto: Canadian Scholars Press, 1998.

MIGRATION, 19TH–21ST CENTURIES

Anctil, Pierre, *Histoire des Juifs du Québec*. Montreal: Boréal, 2017.

Bérubé, Louise, *Parents d'ailleurs, enfants d'ici: Dynamiques d'adaptation du rôle parental chez des immigrants*. Sainte-Foy: Presses de l'Université du Québec, 2003.

Burgard, Antoine, "Retranscrire la violence et le traumatisme: mises en récit administratives de la persécution dans l'immédiate après-Shoah," *Vingtième Siècle. Revue d'histoire* 139, 3 (2018): 165–76.

Cancian, Sonia, *Families, Lovers, and their Letters: Italian Postwar Migration to Canada*. Winnipeg: University of Manitoba Press, 2010.

Chan, Anthony B., *Gold Mountain: the Chinese in the New World*. Vancouver: New Star Books, 1983.

Crawford, Charmaine, "African-Caribbean Women, Diaspora and Transnationality," *Canadian Woman Studies*, 23, 2 (2004): 97–103.

Crawford, Charmaine, "Sending Love in a Barrel: The Making of Transnational Families in Canada," *Canadian Woman Studies*, 22, 3–4 (2003): 104–9.

Dorais, Louis-Jacques and Éric Richard, *Les Vietnamiens de Montréal*. Montréal: Les Presses de l'Université de Montréal, 2007.

Dua, Enakshi, "Exclusion through Inclusion: Female Asian Migration in the Making of Canada as a White Settler Nation," *Gender, Place and Culture*, 14, 4 (2007): 445–66.

Eyford, Ryan, *White Settler Reserve: New Iceland and the Colonization of the Canadian West*. Vancouver: UBC Press, 2016.

Eyford, Ryan C., "Quarantined Within a New Colonial Order: The 1876–1877 Lake Winnipeg Smallpox Epidemic," *Journal of the Canadian Historical Association*, 17, 1 (2006): 55–78.

Fahrni, Magda and Yves Frenette, "'Don't I long for Montréal': l'identité hybride d'une jeune migrante franco-americaine pendant la Première Guerre mondiale," *Histoire sociale/Social History*, XLI, 81 (May 2008): 75–98.

Flynn, Karen, "Experience and Identity: Black Immigrant Nurses to Canada, 1950–1980," pp. 381–98, in *Sisters or Strangers? Immigrant, Ethnic, and Racialized Women in Canadian History*, ed. Marlene Epp, Franca Iacovetta, and Frances Swyripa. Toronto: University of Toronto Press, 2004.

Flynn, Karen, *Moving Beyond Borders: A History of Black Canadian and Caribbean Women in the Diaspora*. Toronto: University of Toronto Press, 2011.

Frenette, Yves, Étienne Rivard, and Marc St-Hilaire, eds, *La francophonie nord-américaine*. Québec: Presses de l'Université Laval, 2012.

Hibbert, Joyce, *War Brides*. Scarborough, Ontario: Signet Books, 1978.

Iacovetta, Franca, *Gatekeepers: Reshaping Immigrant Lives in Cold War Canada*. Toronto: Between the Lines, 2006.

Iacovetta, Franca, *Such Hardworking People: Italian Immigrants in Postwar Toronto*. Montreal; Kingston: McGill-Queen's University Press, 1992.

Labelle, Micheline, Geneviève Turcotte, Marianne Kempeneers, and Deirdre Meintel, *Histoires d'immigrées. Itinéraire d'ouvrières colombiennes, grecques, haïtiennes et portugaises de Montréal*. Montréal: Boréal, 1987.

Lafortune, Gina, "Trajectoires sociomigratoires de familles d'origine haïtienne à Montréal," pp. 11–28, dans *L'intégration des familles d'origine immigrante. Les enjeux sociosanitaires et scolaires*, ed. Fasal Kanouté and Gina Lafortune. Montréal: Presses de l'Université de Montréal, 2014.

Mianda, Gertrude, "Sisterhood versus Discrimination: Being a Black African Francophone Immigrant Woman in Montreal and Toronto," pp. 266–84, in *Sisters or Strangers? Immigrant, Ethnic, and Racialized Women in Canadian History*, ed. Marlene Epp, Franca Iacovetta, and Frances Swyripa. Toronto: University of Toronto Press, 2004.

Mimeault, Mario, *L'exode québécois, 1852–1925. Correspondance d'une famille dispersée en mérique*. Sillery: Septentrion, 2013.

Ramirez, Bruno (with Yves Otis), *Crossing the 49th Parallel: Emigration from Canada to the USA, 1900–1930*. Ithaca: Cornell University Press, 2001.

Ramirez, Bruno, *On the Move: French-Canadian and Italian Migrants in the North Atlantic Economy, 1861–1914*. Toronto: Oxford University Press, 1991.

Ramirez, Bruno, *Les premiers Italiens de Montréal: l'origine de la Petite Italie du Québec*. Montréal: Boréal Express, 1984.

Ross, Arthur, *Communal Solidarity: Immigration, Settlement, and Social Welfare in Winnipeg's Jewish Community, 1882–1930*. Winnipeg: University of Manitoba Press, 2019.

Sheftel, Anna and Stacey Zembrzycki, "'We Started Over Again, We Were Young': Postwar Social Worlds of Child Holocaust Survivors in Montreal," *Urban History Review/Revue d'histoire urbaine*, 39, 1 (2010): 20–30.

FAMILIES IN DEPRESSION AND WAR

Adachi, Ken, *The Enemy That Never Was: A History of the Japanese Canadians*. Toronto: McClelland & Stewart, 1991.

Alexander, Kristine, "An Honour and a Burden: Canadian Girls and the Great War," pp. 173–94, in *A Sisterhood of Suffering and Service: Women and Girls of Canada and Newfoundland During the First World War*, ed. Sarah Glassford and Amy Shaw. Vancouver: UBC Press, 2012.

Baillargeon, Denyse, *Ménagères au temps de la Crise*. Montréal: Éditions du remue-ménage, 1991.

Campbell, Lara, *Respectable Citizens: Gender, Family, and Unemployment in Ontario's Great Depression*. Toronto: University of Toronto Press, 2009.

Campbell, Lara, "'We Who Have Wallowed in the Mud of Flanders': First World War Veterans, Unemployment and the Development of Social Welfare in Canada, 1929–1939," *Journal of the Canadian Historical Association*, New Series, 11 (2000): 125–49.

Clarke, Nic, *Unwanted Warriors: Rejected Volunteers of the Canadian Expeditionary Force*. Vancouver: UBC Press, 2015.

Cook, Tim. "'He was determined to go': Underage Soldiers in the Canadian Expeditionary Force," *Histoire sociale/Social History*, 41, 81 (May 2008): 41–74.

Djebabla-Brun, Mourad, *Combattre avec les vivres. L'effort de guerre alimentaire canadien en 1914–1918*. Québec: Septentrion, 2015.

Duley, Margot I., "The Unquiet Knitters of Newfoundland: From Mothers of the Regiment to Mothers of the Nation," pp. 51–74, in *A Sisterhood of Suffering and Service: Women and Girls of Canada and Newfoundland During the First World War*, ed. Sarah Glassford and Amy Shaw. Vancouver: UBC Press, 2012.

Durflinger, Serge Marc, *Fighting from Home: The Second World War in Verdun, Quebec*. Vancouver: UBC Press, 2006.

Fahrni, Magda, "'Elles sont partout': les femmes et la ville en temps d'épidémie, Montréal, 1918–1920," *Revue d'histoire de l'Amérique française*, 58, 1 (2004): 67–85.

Fahrni, Magda and Esyllt W. Jones, eds, *Epidemic Encounters: Influenza, Society, and Culture in Canada, 1918–20*. Vancouver: UBC Press, 2012.

Fahrni, Magda, *Household Politics: Montreal Families and Postwar Reconstruction*. Toronto: University of Toronto Press, 2005.

Fahrni, Magda, "'Victimes de la tâche journalière': La gestion des accidents du travail au Québec pendant la Grande Guerre," in *Mains-d'œuvre en guerre, 1914–1918*, ed. Laure Machu, Isabelle Lespinet-Moret, and Vincent Viet. Paris: La Documentation française, 2018.

Girard, Denise, *Mariage et classes sociales: les Montréalais francophones entre les deux Guerres*. Québec, IQRC; Sainte-Foy: Presses de l'Université Laval, 2000.

Halstead, Claire L., "From Lion to Leaf: The Evacuation of British Children to Canada during the Second World War." PhD dissertation, University of Western Ontario, 2015.

Humphries, Mark Osborne, *The Last Plague: Spanish Influenza and the Politics of Public Health in Canada*. Toronto: University of Toronto Press, 2013.

Jones, Esyllt W., *Influenza 1918: Disease, Death, and Struggle in Winnipeg*. Toronto: University of Toronto Press, 2007.

Kelm, Mary-Ellen, "British Columbia First Nations and the Influenza Pandemic of 1918–1919," *BC Studies*, 122 (Summer 1999): 23–48.

Keshen, Jeffrey A., *Saints, Sinners, and Soldiers: Canada's Second World War*. Vancouver: UBC Press, 2004.

Lorenzkowski, Barbara, "The Children's War," pp. 113–50, in Steven High, ed., *Occupied St John's: A Social History of a City at War, 1939–1945*. Montreal; Kingston: McGill-Queen's University Press, 2010.

Lux, Maureen, "'The Bitter Flats': The 1918 Influenza Epidemic in Saskatchewan," *Saskatchewan History*, 49, 1 (Spring 1997): 3–13.

Macdonald, Heidi, "'Being in Your Twenties, in the Thirties': Liminality and Masculinity during the Great Depression," pp. 156–67, in *Bringing Children & Youth into Canadian History: The Difference Kids Make*, ed. Mona Gleason and Tamara Myers. Don Mills: Oxford University Press, 2017.

Maroney, Paul, "'The Great Adventure': The Context and Ideology of Recruiting in Ontario, 1914–17," *Canadian Historical Review*, 77, 1 (March 1996): 62–98.

Morin-Pelletier, Mélanie, "'The Anxious Waiting Ones at Home': Deux familles canadiennes plongées dans le tourment de la Grande Guerre," *Histoire sociale/Social History*, 47, 94 (2014): 353–68.

Morton, Desmond, *Fight or Pay: Soldiers' Families in the Great War*. Vancouver: UBC Press, 2004.

Morton, Desmond, *When Your Number's Up: The Canadian Soldier in the First World War*. Toronto: Vintage Canada, 1994.

Morton, Desmond and Glenn Wright, *Winning the Second Battle: Canadian Veterans and the Return to Civilian Life, 1915–1930*. Toronto: University of Toronto Press, 1987.

Morton, Suzanne, *Ideal Surroundings: Domestic Life in a Working-Class Suburb in the 1920s*. Toronto: University of Toronto Press, 1995.

Neary, Peter and J.L. Granatstein, eds, *The Veterans' Charter and Post–World War II Canada*. Montreal; Kingston: McGill-Queen's University Press, 1998.

Norman, Alison, "'In Defense of the Empire': The Six Nations of the Grand River and the Great War," pp. 29–50, in *A Sisterhood of Suffering and Service: Women and Girls of Canada and Newfoundland During the First World War*, ed. Sarah Glassford and Amy Shaw. Vancouver: UBC Press, 2012.

Pierson, Ruth Roach, *"They're Still Women After All": The Second World War and Canadian Womanhood*. Toronto: McClelland & Stewart, 1986.

Sangster, Joan, "Mobilizing Women for War," in *Canada and the First World War: Essays in Honour of Robert Craig Brown*, ed. David Mackenzie. Toronto: University of Toronto Press, 2005.

Srigley, Katrina, *Breadwinning Daughters: Young Working Women in a Depression-Era City, 1929–1939*. Toronto: University of Toronto Press, 2010.

Srigley, Katrina, "Clothing Stories: Consumption, Identity, and Desire in Depression-era Toronto," *Journal of Women's History* 19, 1 (2007): 82–104.

Sugiman, Pamela H., "Memories of Internment: Narrating Japanese Canadian Women's Life Stories," *Canadian Journal of Sociology*, 29, 3 (Summer 2004): 359–88.

Sugiman, Pamela, "Passing Time, Moving Memories: Interpreting Wartime Narratives of Japanese Canadian Women," *Histoire sociale/Social History*, 36, 73 (2004): 51–79.

Thompson, John, *The Harvests of War: The Prairie West, 1914–1918*. Toronto: McClelland and Stewart, 1978.

Toman, Cynthia, *Sister Soldiers of the Great War: The Nurses of the Canadian Army Medical Corps*. Vancouver: UBC Press, 2016.

Young, W.R., "Conscription, Rural Depopulation, and the Farmers of Ontario, 1917–19," *Canadian Historical Review*, 53, 3 (1972): 289–20.

SEX AND SEXUALITY

Adams, Mary Louise, *The Trouble with Normal: Postwar Youth and the Making of Heterosexuality*. Toronto: University of Toronto Press, 1997.

Chamberland, Line, *Mémoires lesbiennes: le lesbianisme à Montréal entre 1950 et 1972*. Montréal: Éditions du remue-ménage, 1996.

Charton, Laurence, "Le mariage homosexuel à la lumière des dispositifs d'alliance et de sexualité," *Bulletin d'histoire politique*, 15, 1 (automne 2006): 55–62.

Chauncey, George, *Why Marriage? The History Shaping Today's Debate over Gay Equality*. New York: Basic Books, 2004.

Chenier, Elise, "Liberating Marriage: Gay Liberation and Same-Sex Marriage in Early 1970s Canada," in *We Still Demand! Redefining Resistance in Sex and Gender*

Struggles, ed. Patrizia Gentile, Gary Kinsman, and L. Pauline Rankin. Vancouver: UBC Press, 2016.

Chenier, Elise, "Love-Politics: Lesbian Wedding Practices in Canada and the United States from the 1920s to the 1970s," *Journal of the History of Sexuality* 27, 2 (2018): 294–321.

Chenier, Elise, "Rethinking Class in Lesbian Bar Culture: Living 'The Gay Life' in Toronto, 1955–1965," *Left History*, 9, 2 (2004): 85–118.

Chenier, Elise, *Strangers in our Midst: Sexual Deviancy in Postwar Ontario*. Toronto: University of Toronto Press, 2008.

Cliche, Marie-Aimée, "Morale chrétienne et 'double standard sexuel': Les filles-mères à l'hôpital de la Miséricorde à Québec, 1874–1972," *Histoire sociale/Social History*, XXIV, 47 (May 1991): 85–125.

Dagenais, Dominic, *Grossières indécences. Pratiques et identités homosexuelles à Montréal, 1880–1929*. Montreal; Kingston: McGill-Queen's University Press, 2020.

Dubinsky, Karen, *Improper Advances: Rape and Heterosexual Conflict in Ontario, 1880–1929*. Chicago: University of Chicago Press, 1993.

Dubinsky, Karen, *The Second Greatest Disappointment: Honeymooning and Tourism at Niagara Falls*. New Brunswick, New Jersey: Rutgers University Press, 1999.

Duder, Cameron, *Awfully Devoted Women: Lesbian Lives in Canada, 1900–65*. Vancouver: UBC Press, 2010.

Kinsman, Gary, *The Regulation of Desire: Sexuality in Canada*. Montreal: Black Rose Books, 1987.

Korinek, Valerie J., *Prairie Fairies: A History of Queer Communities and People in Western Canada, 1930–1985*. Toronto: University of Toronto Press, 2018.

Lévesque, Andrée, *La norme et les déviantes: les femmes au Québec pendant l'entre-deux-guerres*. Montréal: Éditions du remue-ménage, 1989.

Maynard, Steven, "'Horrible temptations': Sex, Men, and Working-Class Male Youth in Urban Ontario, 1890–1935," *Canadian Historical Review*, 78 (June 1997): 191–235.

Murray, Heather, *Not in This Family: Gays and the Meaning of Kinship in Postwar North America*. Philadelphia: University of Pennsylvania Press, 2010.

Myers, Tamara, "Qui t'a débauchée?: Family, Adolescent Sexuality and the Juvenile Delinquents' Court in Early-Twentieth-Century Montreal," pp. 377–94, in *Family Matters: Papers in Post-Confederation Canadian Family History*, ed. Lori Chambers and Edgar-André Montigny. Toronto: Canadian Scholars' Press, 1998.

Myers, Tamara, "Embodying Delinquency: Boys' Bodies, Sexuality, and Juvenile Justice History in Early Twentieth-Century Quebec," *Journal of the History of Sexuality*, 14, 4 (2005): 383–414.

Perreault, Isabelle, "Morale catholique et genre féminin: la sexualité dissertée dans les manuels de sexualité maritale au Québec, 1930–1960," *Revue d'histoire de L'Amérique française*, 57, 4 (2004): 567–91.

Thomas, Wesley and Sue-Ellen Jacobs, "'... And We Are Still Here': From *Berdache* to Two-Spirit People," *American Indian Culture and Research Journal*, 23, 2 (1999): 91–107.

Wall, Sharon, "'Not . . . the Same Damaging Effects'?: Unmarried Pregnancy, the State, and First Nations Communities in Early Postwar British Columbia," *Histoire sociale/Social History*, 50, 102 (November 2017): 371–98.

Wall, Sharon, "'Some thought they were "in Love"'": Sex, White Teenagehood, and Unmarried Pregnancy in Early Postwar Canada," *Journal of the Canadian Historical Association*, 25, 1 (2014): 207–41.

Weston, Kath, *Families We Choose: Lesbians, Gays, Kinship*. New York: Columbia University Press, 1991.

BABY BOOM, COLD WAR, SOCIAL MOVEMENTS
OF THE LONG SIXTIES

Adams, Mary Louise, "Margin Notes: Reading Lesbianism as Obscenity in a Cold War Courtroom," pp. 135–58, in *Love, Hate, and Fear in Canada's Cold War*, ed. Richard Cavell. Toronto: University of Toronto Press, 2004.

Belliveau, Joel, *Le 'moment 68' et la réinvention de l'Acadie*. Ottawa: Les Presses de l'Université d'Ottawa, 2014.

Bérubé, Harold, "Vendre la banlieue aux Montréalais: discours et stratégies publicitaires, 1950–1970," *Revue d'histoire de l'Amérique française*, 71, 1–2 (été—automne 2017): 83–112.

Bradley, Ben, "'Undesirables Entering the Town to Look for Good Times': Banff Confronts Its Counterculture Youth Scene, 1965–1971," *Urban History Review/Revue d'histoire urbaine*, 47, 1–2 (2018–2019): 71–87.

Brookfield, Tarah, *Cold War Comforts: Canadian Women, Child Safety, and Global Insecurity*. Waterloo: Wilfrid Laurier University Press, 2012.

Campbell, Lara, Dominique Clement, and Greg Kealey, eds, *Debating Dissent: Canada and the 1960s*. Toronto: University of Toronto Press, 2012.

Charland, Jean-Pierre and Mario Desautels, *Système technique et bonheur domestique: Rémunération, consommation et pauvreté au Québec, 1920–1960*. Québec: Institut québécois de recherche sur la culture, 1992.

Dubinsky, Karen, "'We Adopted a Negro': Interracial Adoption and the Hybrid Baby in 1960s Canada," in Magda Fahrni and Robert Rutherdale, eds, *Creating Postwar Canada: Community, Diversity, and Dissent 1945–75*. Vancouver: UBC Press, 2008.

Duhaime, Vincent, "'Les pères ont ici leur devoir': le discours du mouvement familial québécois et la construction de la paternité dans l'après-guerre, 1945–1960," *Revue d'histoire de l'Amérique française*, 57, 4 (printemps 2004): 535–66.

Dummitt, Christopher, "Finding a Place for Father: Selling the Barbecue in Postwar Canada," *Journal of the Canadian Historical Association*, 9, 1 (1998): 209–23.

Finkel, Alvin, *Our Lives: Canada after 1945*. Toronto: James Lorimer, 1997.

Freeman, Barbara M., *The Satellite Sex: The Media and Women's Issues in English Canada, 1966–1971*. Waterloo: Wilfrid Laurier University Press, 2001.

Germain, Annick, Damaris Rose, and Myriam Richard, "Building and Reshaping the Suburban Landscape: The Role of Immigrant Communities," pp. 313–52, in *Montreal: The History of a North American City*, Volume 2, ed. Dany Fougères and Roderick MacLeod. Montreal; Kingston: McGill-Queen's University Press, 2018.

Gleason, Mona, *Normalizing the Ideal: Psychology, Schooling, and the Family in Postwar Canada*. Toronto: University of Toronto Press, 1999.

Harris, Richard, *Creeping Conformity: How Canada Became Suburban, 1900–1960*. Toronto: University of Toronto Press, 2004.

Henderson, Stuart, *Making the Scene: Yorkville and Hip Toronto in the 1960s*. Toronto: University of Toronto Press, 2011.

Heron, Craig, "Harold, Marg, and the Boys: The Relevance of Class in Canadian History," *Journal of the Canadian Historical Association*, 20, 1 (2009): 1–56.

Kealey, Linda, "No More 'Yes Girls': Labour Activism among New Brunswick Nurses, 1964–1981," *Acadiensis*, 37, 2 (2008): 3–17.

Keightley, Keir, "'Turn it down!' She Shrieked: Gender, Domestic Space, and High Fidelity, 1948–59," *Popular Music*, 15, 2 (May 1996): 149–77.

Kinsman, Gary and Patrizia Gentile, *The Canadian War on Queers: National Security as Sexual Regulation*. Vancouver: UBC Press, 2010.

Korinek Valerie J., *Roughing it in the Suburbs: Reading Chatelaine Magazine in the Fifties and Sixties*. Toronto: University of Toronto Press, 2000.

Kostash, Myrna, *Long Way from Home: The Story of the Sixties Generation in Canada*. Toronto: James Lorimer & Company, 1980.

Lacasse, Simon-Pierre, "À la croisée de la Révolution tranquille et du judaïsme orthodoxe: L'implantation de la communauté hassidique des Tasher au cœur du Québec francophone et catholique (1962–1967)," *Histoire sociale/Social History*, 50, 102 (November 2017): 399–422.

Langlois, Simon, "L'univers des aspirations des familles québécoises: 1959, 1977," *Recherches sociographiques*, 23, 3 (1982): 227–52.

Langlois, Simon, "Budgets de famille et genres de vie au Québec dans la seconde moitié du XXe siècle," *Les Cahiers des dix*, 62 (2008): 195–231.

Lebrun, Andréanne and Louise Bienvenue, "Pour 'un gouvernement jeune et dynamique': L'abaissement du droit de vote à 18 ans au Québec en 1964," *Revue d'histoire de l'Amérique française*, 71, 1–2 (2017): 113–35.

Llewellyn, Kristina, "Performing Post-War Citizenship: Women Teachers in Toronto Secondary Schools," *The Review of Education, Pedagogy, and Cultural Studies*, 28, 3–4 (2006): 309–24.

Mccallum, Mary Jane Logan, *Indigenous Women, Work, and History, 1940–1980*. Winnipeg: University of Manitoba Press, 2014.

Mcinnis, Peter S., *Harnessing Labour Confrontation: Shaping the Postwar Settlement in Canada, 1943–1950*. Toronto: University of Toronto Press, 2002.

Mahood, Linda, "Hitchin' a Ride in the 1970s: Canadian Youth Culture and the Romance with Mobility," *Histoire sociale/Social History*, 47, 93 (May 2014): 205–27.

Martel, Marcel, "'They smell bad, have diseases, and are lazy': RCMP Officers Reporting on Hippies in the Late Sixties," *The Canadian Historical Review*, 90, 2 (2009): 215–45.

Milligan, Ian, *Rebel Youth: 1960s Labour Unrest, Young Workers, and New Leftists in English Canada*. Vancouver: UBC Press, 2014.

Millward, Liz, *Making a Scene: Lesbians and Community Across Canada, 1964–84*. Vancouver: University of British Columbia Press, 2015.

Miranda, Susana, "'An Unlikely Collection of Union Militants': Portuguese Immigrant Cleaning Women Become Political Subjects in Postwar Toronto," *Atlantis*, 32, 1 (2007): 114–24.

Morgan, Madeleine, *La colère des douces: la grève des infirmières de l'hôpital Sainte-Justine en 1963: un momentum des relations de travail dans le secteur hospitalier*. Montréal: Confédération des syndicats nationaux, 2003.

O'neill, Stéphanie, "Anticiper 'la rançon d'une trop grande prospérité': perceptions québécoises de l'économie, 1945–1975." *Histoire sociale/Social History*, 51, 104 (2018): 375–400.

Onusko, James, "Childhood in Calgary's Postwar Suburbs: Kids, Bullets, and Boom, 1950–1965," *Urban History Review/Revue d'histoire urbaine*, 43, 2 (Spring 2015): 26–37.

Owram, Doug, *Born at the Right Time: A History of the Baby Boom Generation*. Toronto: University of Toronto Press, 1996.

Palmer, Bryan D., *Canada's 1960s: The Ironies of Identity in a Rebellious Era*. Toronto: University of Toronto Press, 2009.

Parr, Joy, *Domestic Goods: The Material, the Moral, and the Economic in the Postwar Years*. Toronto: University of Toronto Press, 1999.

Penfold, Steve, "Selling by the Carload: The Early Years of Fast Food in Canada," pp. 162–89, in *Creating Postwar Canada: Community, Diversity, and Dissent, 1945–1975*, ed. Magda Fahrni and Robert Rutherdale. Vancouver: UBC Press, 2008.

Ricard, Francois, *La génération lyrique. Essai sur la vie et l'œuvre des premiers-nés du baby-boom*. Montréal: Boréal, 1994.

Rutherdale, Robert, "New 'Faces' for Fathers: Memory, Life-Writing, and Fathers as Providers in the Postwar Consumer Era," in Magda Fahrni and Robert Rutherdale, eds, *Creating Postwar Canada: Community, Diversity, and Dissent*. Vancouver: UBC Press, 2008.

Rutherford, Paul, *When Television Was Young: Primetime Canada, 1952–1957*. Toronto: University of Toronto Press, 1990.

Sangster, Joan, *Earning Respect: The Lives of Working Women in Small-Town Ontario, 1920–1960*. Toronto: University of Toronto Press, 1995.

Sangster, Joan, *Transforming Labour: Women and Work in Post-War Canada*. Toronto: University of Toronto Press, 2010.

Sethna, Christabelle and Steve Hewitt, *Just Watch Us: RCMP Surveillance of the Women's Liberation Movement in Cold War Canada*. Montreal; Kingston: McGill-Queen's University Press, 2018.

Stevens, Peter A., "Cars and Cottages: The Automotive Transformation of Ontario's Summer Home Tradition," *Ontario History*, 100, 1 (2008): 26–56.

Strong-Boag, Veronica, "Home Dreams: Women and the Suburban Experiment in Canada, 1945–60," *Canadian Historical Review*, 72, 4 (December 1991): 471–504.

Thorn, Brian, *From Left to Right: Maternalism and Women's Political Activism in Postwar Canada*. Vancouver: UBC Press, 2016.

FAMILIES RECONFIGURED AT THE TURN OF THE TWENTY-FIRST CENTURY

Andres, Lesley and Johanna Wyn, *The Making of a Generation: The Children of the 1970s in Adulthood*. Toronto: University of Toronto Press, 2010.

Barker, Joanne, "Gender, Sovereignty, Rights: Native Women's Activism against Social Inequality and Violence in Canada," *American Quarterly*, 60, 2 (June 2008): 259–66.

Basen, Gwynne, Margrit Eichler, and Abby Lippman, eds, *Misconceptions: The Social Construction of Choice and the New Reproductive Technologies*, Volumes 1 and 2. Hull: Voyageur Publishing, 1993 and 1994.

Blackstock, Cindy, "The Canadian Human Rights Tribunal on First Nations Child Welfare: Why if Canada Wins, Equality and Justice Lose," *Children and Youth Services Review*, 33 (2011): 187–94.

Chambers, Lori and Kristin Burnett, "Jordan's Principle: The Struggle to Access On-Reserve Health Care for High-Needs Indigenous Children in Canada," *The American Indian Quarterly*, 41, 2 (Spring 2017): 101–24.

Côté, Christian et Marie-Christine Saint-Jacques, *Familles recomposées après divorce*. Sainte-Foy: Presses de l'Université Laval, 1990.

Dandurand, Renée B. et Lise Saint-Jean, *Des mères sans alliances. Monoparentalité et désunions conjugales*. Québec: Institut québécois de la recherche sur la culture, 1988.

Dandurand, Renée B., *Couples et parents des années quatre-vingt: un aperçu des nouvelles tendances familiales*. Québec: Institut québécois de recherche sur la culture, 1987.

Dandurand, Renée B., *Le mariage en question. Essai sociohistorique*. Québec: Institut québécois de recherche sur la culture, 1991.

Foster, Deborah, "The Formation and Continuance of Lesbian Families in Canada," *Canadian Bulletin of Medical History*, 22, 2 (2005): 281–97.

Fournier, Suzanne and Ernie Crey, *Stolen from Our Embrace: The Abduction of First Nations Children and the Restoration of Aboriginal Communities*. Vancouver: Douglas & McIntyre, 1997.

Kranz, Karen C. and Judith C. Daniluk, "We've Come a Long Way, Baby... Or Have We? Contextualizing Lesbian Motherhood in North America," *Journal of the Association for Research on Mothering*, Volume 4, Number 1 (2002): 58–69.

Luxton, Meg and Leah F. Vosko, "Where Women's Efforts Count: The 1996 Census Campaign and 'Family Politics' in Canada," *Studies in Political Economy*, 56, 1 (1998): 49–81.

Mcdonald, Lynn, "Elder Abuse and Neglect in Canada: The Glass Is Still Half Full," *Canadian Journal on Aging*, 30, 3 (2011): 437–65.

Piché, Victor and Céline Le Bourdais, eds, *La démographie québécoise. Enjeux du 21e siècle*. Montréal: Les Presses de l'Université de Montréal, 2003.

Pronovost, Gilles et al., *La famille à l'horizon 2020*. Quebec City: Les Presses de l'Université du Québec, 2008.

Robert, Camille, *Toutes les femmes sont d'abord ménagères: histoire d'un combat féministe pour la reconnaissance du travail ménager*. Montréal: Somme toute, 2017.

Saint-Jacques, Marie-Christine, *Séparation, monoparentalité et recomposition familiale: bilan d'une réalité complexe et pistes d'action*. Québec: Les Presses de l'Université Laval, 2004.

Simpson, Leanne Betasamosake, *As We Have Always Done: Indigenous Freedom Through Radical Resistance*. Minneapolis: University of Minnesota Press, 2017.

Index

abortion, 100, 101, 186, 189, 191
Abortion Caravan, 191
Acadia, 27, 36–7, 50–1
adolescents. *See* teenagers
Adonwentishon (Catharine Brant), 53, 54–5
adoption: Indigenous children, 181, 188, 203–4; international adoptions, 188, 204; interwar period, 145–6; in late 20th century, 202, 203; in 19th century, 202–3; research on, 11; transracial adoptions, 181, 203; *See also* Sixties Scoop
adultery, in British North America, 61–2
advertising, rise, 158–9
African Canadians, 40, 53, 54, 58, 141, 146, 169, 175, 203, 217–18
age, 121, 184, 195
aging population in 21st century, 207, 208–12
agriculture. *See* farms and farming
alimony, 98
American War of Independence, 51, 53, 55
Anderson, Jordan Rivers, 222
Anglican Church, and marriage, 59
animals, in cities, 90
Anishinaabe peoples, 17–18, 24, 25–6
Annales school of history, 4–5
apprenticeships, 75
Asian immigration, 77, 119–20, 169, 216
automobiles, 172
baby boom, 162–5, 213
Backhouse, Constance, 97
backwoods, settlement in, 63–5
banns in marriage, 59–60

Beatty, John, 121
bees, 67–8
Bennett, R.B., 138
birth. *See* childbirth
birth control, 142, 186, 189–90
Birth Control Committee of the McGill Students' Council, 189–90
Birth Control Handbook, 189–90
birth rates, 31, 48, 162
Blackstock, Cindy, 222
Blatz, William, 144, 145
"blended" families, 198
"blue-collar" jobs, 174
boomerang phenomenon, 207–8, 212–14
Borden, Robert, 126–7, 128
Bouat, Madeleine, 43
boys, 83–4, 126; *See also* children
Bradbury, Bettina, 91
Brant, Catharine (Adonwentishon), 53, 54–5
Brant, Joseph (Thayendanegea), 53, 54
Brant, Mary or "Molly" (Konwatsi'tsiaiénni), 53, 54–5
breadwinner ideology, 86, 162–3, 218
Britain: children to Canada in Second World War, 149; conquest of New France, 44–9; emigration schemes, 56; and Great War, 123–4; logic with Indigenous peoples, 49–50; migration to North America, 55–8, 149
British Columbia, 77–9, 120, 150–1, 155–6, 175–6
British North America Act (1867), 97, 100, 104, 185, 200; and social welfare, 134, 135, 177

British North America families: arrival of settlers in NS and QC, 44, 51–3, 55; arrivals from Britain, 55–8; childbirth, 62–3; economy, 65–6, 68, 72, 73; health and illness, 63; and Indigenous families, 53–5, 72; and Industrial Revolution, 73–4, 75, 79; labour, 67–8, 71; marriage, 60–2; population, 71–2; settlement, 63–6, 69–70, 71–2; and sexuality, 59–60; and social status, 68–9; support to families, 62, 70; and war, 69–70
Broadfoot, Barry, 137
Brook, Sidney and Isabelle, 129
Brown, Alan, 144, 145
Bruneau, Julie and family, 70
buffalo hunt, 113
Burgess, Daniel, 83
Burr, Christina, 185
Byles, Rebecca, 55
Callihoo, Doreen, 178–9
Campbell, Maria, 113
Canada Assistance Plan (1966), 177
Canada East, Civil Code (1866), 96
Canada Pension Plan (CPP), 177
Canadian Army Medical Corps (CMAC), 128
Canadian Council on Child Welfare (CCCW), 146
Canadian Food Bulletin, 131–2
Canadian Jewish Congress (CJC), 167
Canadian Pacific Railway completion, 77
Canadian Patriotic Fund, 128–9
canals, construction, 79
Cardinal, Richard, 221
caregivers, 216
Carignan-Salières Regiment, 27, 28, 30
Cartier, Jacques, 18–19
Catholic Church, 59–60, 93–4, 196; *See also* missionaries
censuses, 12, 121
census family, definition, 3–4
chain migration, 6, 80–2
Charbonneau, Hubert, 5
charity, 69, 93–4, 104, 108–9, 143
charivaris, 61
Chauncey, George, 201
Cherniak, Donna, 189–90
childbirth, 31–2, 62–3, 101, 165, 195
childcare, 175–6

childcare experts, 143–5, 164–5
child-protection system, and Indigenous children, 220, 221
children: in baby boom, 165; and biological parents, 198; corporal punishment at work, 84–5; custody of, 98–9; and delinquency, 105, 106–8; and divorce, 197–8; in family history, 7–8; and grandparents, 212; health and illness, 63; and "helping professions," 145–7; immigration and schooling, 216–17; infanticide legislation, 101–2; inheritance, 38; and legislation, 95, 101–2, 104–8; numbers in French settler period, 31; private institutions, 108–9, 146–7; protection of, 105–6; Second World War's impact, 148–9; work, 83–5, 88; *See also* boys; girls; Indigenous children; youth
Children's Aid Societies, 106
Children's Overseas Reception Board (CORB), 149
chosen families, 10–11
Chrétien, Jean, 200
cities: expansion, 74; immigration to, 168, 169–73; industry types, 76; internal migration, 165–6; life in Industrial Revolution, 89–92; and military bases, 148; population, 74; and public health, 91–2; and social class, 91, 92; street life, 91
Civil Code (1866) in Canada East, 96
Civil Code (1964) in Quebec, 192–3, 195, 196, 199
civil law, 37–9, 46, 61, 71, 96
civil registration systems, 121
civil union (*union civile*), 199–200
"clan segments," 17
Clark, Claire, 141
class. *See* social class
cleaning work, 174
Colbert, Jean-Baptiste, 27, 28
Colby, Martin, 125
Cold War thinking, 158
Collins, Louisa, 67
colonialism, and Indigenous families, 9–10, 111–12; *See also* Indigenous children; Indigenous families; Indigenous peoples; Indigenous women

Comacchio, Cynthia, 11
common law, 97, 99, 198
common-law relationships, 198–9, 206
community, and marriage, 61
community of property regime, 38, 60
Compagnie des Cent-Associés (Company of the One Hundred Associates), 27
conclusions of book, 223–5
Confederation (1867), 97, 100, 114
conjugal unions, 187–8, 198–201, 205–6
Connolly, William and Susanne, 112
Connolly case, 112
conquest of New France: and economy, 46–7; impact on families, 44–6; and Indigenous peoples, 49–50; and institutions, 46–8; land tenure, 47–8; in Maritime colonies, 50–1; and population, 48–9
conscription, 126–7
Constitutional Act (1791), 71
consumption and consumer society, 158–60, 182
contraception, 62, 100, 142, 186, 189, 193
correspondence, as sources, 12
Couagne, Thérèse de, 40
countercultures, 183–4
courts: delinquent youth, 107–8; for divorce, 195–6
Coutume de Paris (Custom of Paris), 37–9, 46, 61, 96
COVID-19 pandemic, 211
Crawford, Charmaine, 169, 215, 216
Criminal Code (1892), 100–2
criminal law, 100
Criminal Law Amendment Act (1968–1969), 186
Crotty, Hannah, 75
custody of children, 98–9
Dafoe, Allan Roy, 144
Daly, T. Mayne, 119
Davidson, George, 147
Davin, Nicolas Flood, 116
daycare, 175–6, 190
day nurseries, 149–50, 175
Dazemard de Lusignan, Paul-Louis, 43
death rates, in French settler period, 31
Deganne, Elisabeth, 68
"delinquent" children, 105, 106–8
demography, sources for, 12
Department of Health, establishment, 134

Department of Indian Affairs (DIA), 110, 115
Deportation, 50–1
deserted wives, 100
diaries, as sources, 12
Dionne, Oliva and Elzire, 144
Dionne quintuplets, 144–5
Displaced Persons, and migration, 167
division of labour: in apprenticeships, 75; in British North America, 67–8, 71; French settler period, 32–3, 47; in Great Depression, 139; Indigenous families, 23–4, 78; in Industrial Revolution, 78, 83, 86–7
divorce: in British North America, 61–2; among Indigenous peoples, 20; in late 20th century, 195–8; rates, 196; and state, 97–9, 185–6, 195–6; in thirty glorious years, 185–6
Divorce Act (1968), 186, 196
Divorce Act (1985), 196
domestic servants, 88–9
domestic violence, 8, 98, 102–3
domestic work: in Great Depression, 139; and immigrants, 216, 218; in Industrial Revolution, 75–6, 86–9; in thirty glorious years, 173
Dominion Lands Act (1872), 119
Douglas, Tommy, 176
dower rights, 38
dowries, 30
Dr. Spock's Baby and Child Care (Spock), 164–5
Duvernay, Ludger, 70
Eastern Townships (QC), 63, 66, 68
economy: in British North America, 65–6, 68, 72, 73; and cash, 86; and Great War, 129–30; and Indigenous peoples, 160; and Industrial Revolution, 72, 73, 86; and Métis peoples, 113–14; post-British Conquest, 46–7; in Second World War, 151–2; in thirty glorious years, 158–61; *See also* Great Depression
education: compulsory schooling, 105, 154; and delinquent children, 106–7; in French settler period, 34; and immigration, 216–17; Indigenous children, 20–2, 34; legislation, 105; as provincial responsibility, 104; resistance by

Indigenous peoples, 21–2; in thirty glorious years, 181–2; and universal family allowance, 153–4
elder abuse and neglect, 210
elderly: in couples, 206; female/male ratio, 210; pensions, 176–7; population and projections, 208, 209; research on, 8; and state, 210–11; and work, 211–12; *See also* aging population
elite and wealthy in British North America, 61, 68, 69
Ellesmere Island, 180
Emery, George, 121
emigration. *See* migration
engagés (indentured servants), 30
English Canadians, and Great War, 124
ethnicity, 103, 128, 172–3, 175; *See also* non-whites
eugenics, 142
factories, in Industrial Revolution, 75, 76, 83–5, 89
Family Allowances, 153–54; and Indigenous peoples, 154–55, 180–1
Family Compact, 68
family experts, in family history, 9
family history: agency in, 225; concepts of analysis, 13; development as field, 4–5; importance and purpose, 11–12; roots and routes, 224–5; sources and records, 12–13, 17, 23; topics of research, 5–12
family in Canada: definition, 3–4, 224–5; diversity of experiences, 2, 3–4, 223–5; role, 1; *See also* specific topic
family "sentiments," as approach, 5
family size, 187, 193–5, 205
Famine Migration (Great Famine), 57–8, 79
farms and farming: in British North America, 65–6; in French settler period, 36, 37; and Great War, 127, 131–2; Indigenous peoples, 114; *See also* labour on land
fathers, research on, 7
federal government: and criminal law, 100; day nurseries, 150; and divorce, 98, 185–6; health system for Indigenous families, 178; hospital insurance, 176; immigration policy, 118–21; and Indigenous families, 9, 10, 109–15, 178; land grants in western Canada, 119; legislation (*see* legislation); Métis and Indigenous peoples on Prairies, 114–15, 119; old-age pension, 135, 177; "points system" for immigration, 168; reconciliation initiatives, 222–3; relocation of Inuit, 180; and residential schools, 115–16; responsibility for Indigenous peoples, 109–11; and Second World War intervention, 151–5; sexuality decriminalization, 186; universal family allowance, 153; war veterans, 132, 153
Feingold, Allan, 190
"feminine mystique," 163
feminism, 6–7, 102, 134, 190–1, 192
fertility rates, 31, 187, 193–5, 205
Filles du Roi, 28–31, 33
Finkel, Alvin, 162
First Nations. *See* Indigenous families; Indigenous peoples
first-wave feminists, 102, 134
First World War. *See* Great War
fishers in pre-settlement contact, 17
food prices, 161
Fordism, 158
Forest Hill suburb (ON), 170
forms of family, transformations in, 187–9, 191–2, 193
Fortier, J.M., 84–5
foster homes, 106, 145–6, 149, 220, 221
France: migration to New France, 27–8; return from New France, 27, 44–5, 51
French Canadians and families, 80, 81–2, 92, 124, 127
French settler families: and British conquest, 44–9; changes over time, 41; and civil law, 37–9, 46; colony settlement, 27–9, 41; economy post-Conquest, 46–7; family houses and farms, 36; and *Filles du Roi,* 28–31, 33; food and health, 33; institutions establishment, 33–6, 37–8; and labour, 32–3, 47; land tenure system, 35–7; marriage and childbirth, 29–32, 38; parishes, 35; population distribution, 30; slavery, 39–41; and state, 37; women in, 38–9, 40–1
French settler families and Indigenous peoples: description, 18–19; description of families, 19–20, 22–3; and education, 20–2, 34; impact on, 24–7, 41; marriage, 28, 72, 111

Friedan, Betty, 163
fur trade and traders, 17–18, 72, 111
gay liberation and rights, 191–2, 201
gay parenthood, 202
gender, 71, 81, 86; *See also* division of labour
genealogy, *vs.* family history, 11
generational cohabitation, 213–14
generational relationships, 212
"generation gap," 183, 189
girls: and delinquency, 107; Indigenous children education, 21; in Industrial Revolution, 87–8; marriage and sexuality, 182–3, 184; *See also* children
government of Canada. *See* federal government
Gradual Enfranchisement Act (1869), 110
grandparents and grandchildren, 212
Great Depression: impact on family in Canada, 137–8, 142; men on the move, 140; representation of, 136; state support, 141–2; unemployment for men, 137–40; work for women, 140–1
Great Famine (Famine Migration), 57–8, 79
Great War (First World War): Canada as ally, 123–4; conscription, 126–7; food production, 131–2; and health, 125, 133; impact on family, 126, 129; and Indigenous peoples, 130–1; parents' concerns, 126; pensions, 132; recruitment and enrolment, 124–6, 129; returned soldiers, 132–3; and rural families, 127, 131; salary and allowances, 128–9; state intervention, 132; underage soldiers, 126; unpaid labour, 130–1; and women, 128, 129, 130–1; work and economy, 129–31, 132
Grey Nuns (Sisters of Charity), 94
Grierson, Charles, 138–9
Guyart, Marie. *See* Marie de l'Incarnation
Guyon, Louis, 130
Haiti, as immigration source, 215
Haldimand, Frederick, 53
Hall, Stuart, 224–5
Harmon, Daniel, 112
Harnois, Reine, 70
Harvey, Kathryn, 102
Haudenosaunee peoples: alliance with British, 49, 53; contact with settlers, 17; division of labour, 23–4; kinship and mobility, 17; land encroachment, 64, 70; migration, 53–5; and military "usefulness," 70

Hawthorn Report (*A Survey of the Contemporary Indians of Canada: A Report on Economic, Political, Educational Needs and Policies*), 160
Head Tax on migrants, 120
health: in British North America, 63; in French settler period, 33; and Great War, 125, 133; and Indigenous peoples, 178, 222; in Industrial Revolution, 79–80, 91–2
health insurance ("Medicare"), 176
"helping professions," 143–7
Heron, Craig, 158, 173
heterosexual family model, 187–9, 191–2, 193
heterosexuality, 10, 165
high-fidelity stereos, 159–60
Hill, Susan M., 17, 23
Hinds, Marjorie, 180–1
hippies, 183–4
historical documents, as sources, 12–13
history of family. *See* family history
hitchhiking, 183–4
home: in others' homes, 88–9; as workplace, 75–6, 86–9
homestead grants (land grants), 119
homosexuality, 165
hop picking work, 78
Hospital for Sick Children ("SickKids"), 109
hospital insurance, 176
hospitals, 34–5, 109, 165, 178–80
household appliances, 159–60
houses (family houses), 36, 90
housing, in thirty glorious years, 161–2
Houston, Susan, 106
Ideal Maternity Home, 146
identification discs for Inuit, 180
Île Royale (Cape Breton), and slavery, 40
illness, 63, 79–80, 116
immigration and immigrants: children and schooling, 216–17; conflicts within families, 217–19; and domestic work, 216, 218; family reunification, 216, 218–19; and federal policy, 118–21; need for *vs.* fear of, 219; new sources in 21st century, 208, 214–19; non-whites,

119–20, 168–9; "points system," 168–9; and suburbs, 173; and typhus, 80; to western Canada, 118–19; whites and Europeans, 118, 120–1, 166–9; and women, 120–1, 174–5; and work, 169, 174–5, 218; *See also* migration
indentured servants (*engagés*), 30
Indian Act (1876), 110–11
Indian Hospitals, 178–9
"Indian" status, 110
Indigenous children: adoption, 181, 188, 203–4; in care and child-protection system, 220, 221; education in French settler period, 20–2, 34; practices of parents, 20; and residential schools (*see also* residential schools); service gap on reserves, 222–3; in state care, 188
Indigenous families (First Nations, Inuit, and Métis): in British North America, 53–5, 72; description by Europeans, 15–16, 19–20, 22–3; division of labour, 23–4, 78; and first settlers, 15–17, 19–26; health system and social welfare, 178–81, 222; impact of colonialism, 9–10, 111–12; impact of French settler period, 24–7, 41; and industrial work in BC, 77–9; "intergenerational cycle of neglect and abuse," 219–23; land encroachment, 64, 69–70; as Loyalists, 53, 54–5; and malnutrition, 160; parenting practices, 20; resettlement, 53–5; "Sixties Scoop" adoptions, 10, 180–1, 188, 203; sources on, 17, 23; and state, 9, 10, 109–15, 178
Indigenous peoples: from allies to wards of state, 70; deprivations of 19th century, 114–15; description by settlers, 15–16, 18–19, 22; early contact, 15, 17–18; epidemics, 25, 133; farming, 114; as federal responsibility, 109–11; health and hospitals, 178–80, 222; and immigration policy, 119; kinship and mobility, 16–17; and legislation, 110–11; matrilineality, 23, 110; population growth in 21st century, 208, 219, 223; post-Conquest, 49–50; on Prairies, 114–15, 119; presence in Canada, 15; reconciliation initiatives, 222–3; residential schools (*see* residential schools); resistance to education, 21–2; service gap on reserves, 222–3; slavery, 40; status and rights, 110; and thirty glorious years, 160; and treaties, 49, 50, 110, 114; tuberculosis, 178–80, 222; universal family allowance, 154–5; in war, 70, 130–1
Indigenous women: fertility rates, 194–5; in fur trade, 72; role and power, 23–4; status and rights, 110; transracial relationships, 28, 72, 77, 111; and work, 175
Industrial Revolution: in Canada, 74–9; charity and social assistance, 93–4; city life, 89–92; description, 74–5; and economy, 72, 73, 86; hours of work, 83, 84; impact on British North America, 73–4, 75, 79; impact on family, 5, 73, 80–2, 94; industry types, 76–7; legislation on workplaces, 85; and migration, 79–82; population, 74, 82; and work, 75–6, 77–9, 83–5, 87–8; workplaces, 75–7, 83, 85, 86–9
industrial schools for Indigenous peoples, 115
infanticide legislation, 101–2
infant mortality, 31, 92
influenza pandemic of 1918–1919 ("Spanish flu"), 133–4
inheritance, 38
Innu peoples, description and contact, 17
institutionalization of children, 145–7
institutions: and agency of family, 225; and children, 108–9, 146–7; and conquest of New France, 46–8; establishment in French settler period, 33–6, 37–8; research on, 8–9; *See also* religious institutions
intergenerational relationships, 212
internal migration, 5–6, 80–1, 165–6
Inuit, 179–80, 222; *See also* Indigenous families; Indigenous peoples
Irish, 57–8, 79–80
Ishiguro, Laura, 120
Japanese Canadians, 155–6
Jesuit Relations accounts, 19, 21
Jewish immigrants, 118, 167
Johnson, William, 53, 54
Jones, Effie, 161
Jordan's Principle, 222
Julian, Peter, 117
juvenile delinquency, 105, 106–8
Juvenile Delinquents Act (1908), 107

Kaufman, Alvin R., 142
Kelso, John Joseph, 105–6
Kennedy, Dan, 117
Kenny, Nicolas, 89–90
"Keynesian" moment, 158
kinship, 16–17, 113–14
Konwatsi'tsiaiénni (Mary or "Molly" Brant), 53, 54–5
Koodlooalook, Jimmy, 180–1
labour from Industrial Revolution onwards. *See* work
labour on land: and bees, 67–8; in British North America, 64–5, 67; in French settler period, 30, 32–3, 36; in Industrial Revolution, 75
labour unions, 158, 174
Lacoste-Beaubien, Justine, 109
Lafortune, Gina, 215
land and territory: encroachment on Indigenous lands, 64, 69–70; and immigration in western Canada, 119; and kinship, 17; post-Conquest, 49
land clearing, 64–5
land grants (homestead grants), 119
land holding/land tenure system, 35–7, 47–8, 63; *See also* seigneuries
Laslett, Peter, 4
"latch-key" children, 198
Laurentian Iroquoians, description and contact, 17, 18–19
law. *See* civil law; common law
legislation: abortion and contraception, 100–1; on adoption, 145, 202; adoption and impact in 19th century, 95–6, 122; and childhood, 95, 101–2, 104–8; on divorce, 97–9, 185–6, 196; on education, 105; on family violence, 102–3; and Indigenous peoples, 110–11; industrial workplaces, 85; infanticide, 101–2; juvenile delinquents, 107; marriage, 96–7; and property for women, 38, 60, 99–100, 197; on religious symbols at work, 219; same-sex marriage, 200
Le Jeune, Paul, 20
Lekwammen families, and industrial work, 78–9
"lesbian baby boom," 201, 202
lesbians and rights, 191–2

LGBTQ+ and Two-Spirit peoples, research on, 10–11
life expectancy, in French settler period, 33
Little Canadas neighbourhoods, 82
Live-in Caregiver Program, 216
logging bees, 64–5
Loiselle, Georgiana, 84–5
Loi sur la laïcité de l'État (Bill 21, Quebec), 219
lone parenthood, 201–2
"Long Sixties," 190
long-term care homes, 210–11
Louis XIV, 27, 28, 30
Lower Canada: creation, 46; parish and curé, 48; *Patriotes,* 69–70; population, 48–9; sexuality and marriage, 59–62; slavery, 58; social status, 68; *See also* British North America families
Loyalist refugees and Loyalism, 51–3, 54–5, 68
Lux, Maureen, 178–9
Macdougall, Brenda, 113–14
McKenna, Katherine M.J., 69
McMaster, Elizabeth, 109
McNeil, Tim, 220
Mailloux, Gabriel Edouard, 75
male breadwinner ideology, 86, 162–3, 218
malnutrition, and Indigenous families, 160
Manitoba Act (1870), 114
manufactories in Industrial Revolution, 75, 76, 83–5, 89
manufacturing work, and women, 174
Marie de l'Incarnation (Marie Guyart): description, 21–2; on *Filles du Roi,* men, and marriage, 29, 30, 31; on Indigenous children education, 21, 22; on institutions, 35; on labour in colony, 32–3
Marie-Josèphe-Angélique, 40–1
Maritime colonies: arrival of settlers, 44, 51–2, 55; and divorce, 97–8; Indigenous peoples in, 50; migration for work, 80; poor and charity, 93; population in cities, 74; post-Conquest, 50–1
Maroney, Paul, 125–6
marriage: and age, 195; benefits, 59; changes in late 20th century, 187–8, 192–3, 198–201, 205–6; debates about, 11; dowries, 30; *à la façon du pays* and Métis, 111–13; and family, 60–1; and French settler

period, 29–30, 31–2, 38; legal definition, 200; and legislation, 96–7; in Lower Canada, 59–62; numbers in late 20th century, 206; remarriage, 62; same-sex marriage, 200–1; and state, 61, 96–100, 198; in thirty glorious years, 182–3, 184; transracial with Indigenous women, 28, 72, 77, 111
Married Women's Property Acts, 99
maternalist arguments, 161, 164
maternal mortality, in Industrial Revolution, 92
maternity homes, 146–7
Medical Care Act (1966), 176
Medical Services Branch (MSB), hiring of married women, 175
"Medicare" (health insurance), 176
men: and household appliances, 159–60; unemployment, 137–40; See also gender
Métis families: as dual-heritage, 111–12; kinship and networks, 113–14; and marriage, 111–13; research on, 9; and suburbs, 171–2; See also Indigenous families
Métis peoples and state, 111–15; See also Indigenous peoples
Mianda, Gertrude, 217
midwifery, 207
migration (immigration and emigration): chain migration, 6, 80–2; impact on family, 5–6; internal, 5–6, 80–1, 165–6; ties to worlds left behind, 6; transnational, 11, 80; and work, 80–2; See also immigration and immigrants
Mi'kmaq peoples, description and contact, 17, 18
military bases, 148
military nurses, 128
Military Service Act (1917), 126–7
Military Voters Act (1917), 128
Millward, Liz, 184
mining, 77
missionaries, 19–20, 21, 22–3, 34
mobility, and kinship, 16–17
Mohawk, resettlement, 53–5
Montgomery, Lucy Maud, 89
Montreal, 76, 92
Moodie, Susanna, 57, 64–5

mothers: age at childbirth, 128; allowances, 134–5; and childcare experts, 143–4; concerns for sons in Great War, 126; feminist lens on, 6–7; maternity homes, 146–7; single mothers, 201–2; and work, 149–51, 163
multiple parents on birth certificates, 207
munitions work, 129, 130
Munro, Mary and John, 52–3
Murdoch, Irene, 197
Murdoch v Murdoch, 197
Murphy, Emily, 99
Naturalization Act (1881 and 1914), 120–1
neighbourhoods, 82, 91, 92
New England, migration and work, 80, 81–2
New England Planters, 51
Newfoundland: and Indigenous contact, 17; and the two World Wars, 130, 148, 151
New France: British conquest, 44–9; institutions, 33–8; map, 34; and returns to France, 27, 44–5, 51; settlement, 27–8; slavery, 39–41; See also French settler families
"New Iceland" colony, 119
new reproductive technologies, 204–5
the North, tuberculosis and social welfare, 179–81
Northwest Resistance (1885), 115
Northwest Territories, surnames for Inuit, 180
notarial records, as sources, 12–13
Nova Scotia, 50–2, 53, 55, 146–7
Nova Scotia Home for Colored Children, 146
nuclear family model, transformation, 187–9, 191–2, 193
nurses, 128, 174, 175
old-age homes, 210–11
old-age pension, 135–6, 176–7
Old Age Security (OAS), 177, 211
older people. *See* elderly
Omnibus bill (1969), 186, 189, 191
Ontario, 105–6, 127, 131, 137–8, 177
oral history, as source, 13
orphanages, 93–4, 106, 109
orphans of war, 167
outdoor privies, 90
Pacific Northwest, 72, 77, 112–13
Palmer, Dorothea, 142
Papineau, Louis-Joseph and family, 70

parenthood, changes in late 20th century, 188, 201–4
parenting practices, Indigenous *vs.* French settler families, 20
parishes, 35, 48
parish priest (*curé*), 35, 48
Pasolli, Lisa, 150, 176
pass system, 110
Patriotes, 69–70
Pearson, Lester B., 185
Peel, Edmund and Lucy, 62, 63, 66
pensions, 132, 135–6, 176–7
Phillips, William, 56–7
the Pill, 186, 190
"pink-collar" jobs, 174
Podruchny, Carolyn, 113–14
poor and poverty, 69, 93–4, 108, 202
"postwar settlement" (or "compromise"), 158
Powell family daughters, 69
Prairies, 77, 111–15, 118–19
pregnancy, medicalization of, 165
prices of goods, 152, 161
private sphere, and gender, 86
Programme de recherche en démographie historique, 5
property: and common law, 99; rights and legislation for women, 38, 60, 99–100, 197
prostitution, 68
provinces: abortions, 191; adoption and foster homes, 145–6, 220; aging population, 208–10; changes in 21st century, 207; and charity, 104; civil registration systems, 121; compulsory schooling, 105, 154; day nurseries, 150, 175; divorce, 97–9, 195–6; education as responsibility, 104; family allowances, 153–4; farm work and food, 131, 132; fertility rates, 194–5; hospital insurance, 176; Indigenous children in care, 220; industrial legislation, 85; industry types, 76–7; influenza pandemic (1918–1919), 133; mothers' allowances, 134–5; old-age pension, 135–6; property rights for women, 99–100; same-sex marriage, 200; social assistance programmes, 177–8; social welfare in interwar period, 134–5; women and marriage, 97; women's vote, 96; *See also* specific province
public health, in cities, 91–2

public hospital insurance, 176
public sphere, and gender, 86, 96
"putting-out" work system, 87
Quebec Act (1774), 46, 60
Quebec family history, data sets, 5
Quebec Pension Plan (*Régime des rentes du Québec*), 177
Quebec province: aging population, 208–9; arrival of British North America settlers, 51–3; Civil Code (1866), 99; Civil Code (1964), 192–3, 195, 196, 199; common-law relationships, 198, 199, 206; and conscription, 127; COVID-19 pandemic, 211; day nurseries, 150; delinquent children, 106–7; divorce, 98–9, 195–6; establishment, 45; family size and fertility, 187, 193; gay liberation and feminism, 192–3; immigration sources in 21st century, 214–15; map after Conquest, 47; migration for work, 80, 81–2; old-age pension, 135–6; poor and charity, 93–4; reforms from 1960s, 192–3; religious symbols at work, 219; social welfare, 177–8; suburbs, 171; *union civile,* 199–200; youth culture, 183, 184; *See also* French Canadians and families
Quiet Revolution in Quebec, 192
race, 103, 128, 172–3, 175
racism, 141, 155–6
RCMP (Royal Canadian Mounted Police), and social changes, 186
Rebellions (1837–1838), 43–4, 70
reconstituted families, 198
records and sources, 12–13, 17, 23, 58
Red River Resistance (1869–1870), 111
reform schools, 106–7
refugees, 216
religious communities, 115, 116, 191
religious institutions: and charity, 93–4; establishment in French settler period, 34, 35, 39; and orphanages, 109; post-British Conquest, 46, 48
religious symbols at work, 219
remarriage, 62
Report of the Royal Commission on the Relations of Labor and Capital in Canada (1889), 94
republican ideologies of public sphere, 71, 86

reserves, 110, 222–3
residential schools: description and purpose, 115–16; impact and treatment of children, 10, 116–17, 208, 219–22; and malnutrition, 160; TRC report, 117, 118, 208
retirement, 177, 211–12
"Roaring Twenties" years, 136
Rolston, Tilly, 150–1
Rooster Town (MB), 171–2
Royal Commission on the Relations of Labor and Capital, 84, 94
Royal Commission on the Status of Women in Canada (1967) and report (1970), 185, 190
Royal Proclamation (1763), 45, 49
Rupert's Land, 114
rural areas: in British North America, 65–6, 71–2; consumer goods, 159; families and Great War, 127, 131; in French settler period, 46–7; population, 30
rural-urban migration, 80–1
Russell, Peter, 56
Ryerson, Egerton, 105
Sagard, Gabriel, 19–20
Saint Lawrence Valley/River, seigneuries and family houses, 35–6
salary and wages: in Great War, 128, 129; men, 86, 87; women, 174–5; youth, 83, 84, 88
salmon-canning industry, 77–8
same-sex marriage, 200–1
same-sex parenting, 202
sanatoria and Inuit, 179
Sangster, Joan, 173
Saskatchewan, and hospital insurance, 176
school attendance, 104–5
schooling. *See* education
Scots, migration to Upper Canada, 56
second-wave feminism, 190–1, 192
Second World War: children from Britain, 149; and economy, 151–2; impact on family, 147–9; and Japanese Canadians, 155–6; military bases, 148; recruitment and enrolment, 147–8; returned soldiers, 153; state intervention in daily life, 151–5; and women, 149–51; and work, 149, 150–1
Secord, Laura, 69

seduction law, 100
Seeley, John R., 170
seigneuries, 35–7, 47, 63, 71, 96
senior citizens. *See* elderly
"sentiments," as approach, 5
"separate spheres" ideology, 71, 86
separation, in common-law relationships, 199
"separation of bed and board," 61–2, 98
separation of property regime, 38
settlement and settlers: arrival in NS and QC, 44, 51–3, 55; in British North America, 63–6, 69–70, 71–2; first settlers in 16–17th centuries, 15–17, 19–26; in French settler period, 27–9, 41; impact on Indigenous peoples, 24–6; and migration from US, 51–3; on Prairies, 118–19; pre-settlement contact, 15, 17–18
sexuality: in baby boom, 165; changes in thirty glorious years, 186, 189–90; in juvenile delinquents, 107; in Lower Canada, 59–60; research on, 10; sources on, 58; and youth, 182–3, 189–90
Sexual Revolution, 190, 191
Sifton, Clifford, 118, 119
Simpson, Leanne Betasamosake, 223
single parent families, 201–2
Sioui, Georges, 20, 24–5
Sixties Scoop, 10, 180–1, 188, 203
size of family, 187, 193–5, 205
slavery, 39–41, 58
social assistance, 93–4, 122, 177–8; *See also* social welfare
social class, 91, 92, 133
social movements, 183, 184–5, 190–3
social status, in British North America, 68–9
social welfare: in Great Depression, 141; mothers' allowances, 134–5; old-age pension, 135–6, 176–7; in Second World War era, 152–5; in thirty glorious years, 177; *See also* welfare state
social workers. *See* "helping professions"
"Soldiers of the Soil" (S.O.S. programme), 132
Somerville, Richard, 83
sources and records, 12–13, 17, 23, 58
"Spanish flu," 133–4

spouses, and civil law, 37–8
state: and charities, 108–9; childhood and legislation, 95, 104–8; in daily life of Second World War, 151–5; and divorce, 97–9, 185–6, 195–6; and elderly, 210–11; and French settler period, 37; and immigration, 118–21; impact on family, 95; incentives for families, 37; and Indigenous families, 9, 10, 109–15; intervention in Great War, 132; in interwar period, 134–6; and marriage, 61, 96–100, 198; social assistance, 122; support in Great Depression, 141–2; and thirty glorious years, 158; and women's reforms and rights, 95; and women's suffrage, 103–4
state assistance. *See* social welfare
"stay-at-home generation," 207–8, 212–14
St-Onge, Nicole, 113–14
Stranger, Dorothy, 175
street life, 91
Strickland, Catharine and Susanna, 57
subcultures, 182–3
suburbanization, 170–2
suburbs, and diversity, 172–3
suffrage. *See* vote
support to families, 62, 70
Supreme Court of Canada, on common-law unions, 199
surnames, of Inuit, 180
Sweeny, Robert, 76
"Tanguy" phenomenon, 207–8, 212–14
Tarieu de Lanaudière family, 45
Taschereau, Louis-Alexandre, 135
The Tasher community (QC), 172–3
taverns, 66
teenagers: apprenticeships, 75; babies of, 183; in baby boom, 165; education, 181–2; research on, 7–8; Second World War's impact, 148, 149; work for Great War, 130; *See also* youth
Tekakwitha, Kateri, 20
television, 158–9
territories (Yukon, Northwest Territories, Nunavut and Nunavik), 179–81, 194–5, 208
territory. *See* land and territory
Thayendanegea (Joseph Brant), 53, 54

thirty glorious years (1945–1975): baby boom, 162–5; and consumption, 158–60, 182; description and overview, 157; economy and prices, 160–1; and housing, 161–2; immigration and cities, 165–73; and Indigenous peoples, 160; social movements and reforms, 183, 184–6, 1990–1; and state, 158; suburbanization, 170–3; welfare state, 176–81; and work, 158; work by married women, 173–6; and youth culture, 181–4, 189–90
"thirty-six-monthers," 30
Thompson, Abel, 75
Thompson, John Herd, 118
timber industry, 46
towns, in British North America, 66, 68, 71; *See also* cities
Traill, Catharine Parr, 57, 66, 67–8
transformation of family in 21st century: about, 207–8, 223–5; aging population, 207, 208–12; boomerang phenomenon, 207–8, 212–14; immigration sources, 208, 214–19; Indigenous population growth, 208, 219, 223
transformation of family in late 20th century: about, 187–9, 193, 205–6; and divorce, 195–8; family size and fertility, 187, 193–5, 205; and marriage, 198–201, 205–6; new reproductive technologies, 204–5; parenthood, 188, 201–4; and social movements, 190–3
transnational families, 215
transnational migration, 11, 80
treaties with Indigenous peoples, 49, 50, 110, 114
Treaty of Paris (1783), 53
Treaty of Utrecht (1713), 50
Truth and Reconciliation Commission (TRC) of Canada and report, 117, 118, 208, 219–21
tuberculosis (TB), 178–80, 222
typhus, 79–80
unemployment in Great Depression, 137–40, 141
Unemployment Insurance Act (1940), 141
union civile (civil union), 199–200
United Farmers of Ontario, 127
United States: industrialization, 81; migration impact, 6; migration of

settlers to NS and QC, 51–3; migration to for work, 80, 81–2; population of Canadians, 82; same-sex marriage, 201
Universal Declaration of Human Rights (1948), 157
universal family allowance, 153–5
university, 182, 190, 214
Upper Canada: creation, 46; Indigenous lands encroachment, 64, 69–70; migration of to, 56–8; settlement, 63–6; slavery, 58; social status, 68–9; *See also* British North America families
upside-down pyramid, 208
urbanization, 74, 80–1, 165–6
urban settlements, in British North America, 66, 68, 71
Ursuline nuns, education of Indigenous children, 21–2
Vallières, Pierre, 170–1
Vancouver Island, 77–9, 99–100
veterans of war, 132–3, 153
violence in family, 8, 98, 102–3
vote: and age, 184; and ethnicity, 103, 128; and women, 71, 96, 103–4, 128
Vowel, Chelsea, 181
wages. *See* salary and wages
war, in Upper Canada, 69–70; *See also* Great War; Second World War
war brides, 166–7
War of 1812, 69
War Orphans Project, 167
Wartime Day Nurseries Agreement, 150
Wartime Elections Act (1917), 128
weddings, in Lower Canada, 60
welfare state: and consumption, 158–9; emergence, 152–3; health insurance, 176; Indigenous and Inuit families, 178–81, 222; old-age pensions, 135–6, 176–7; social assistance programmes, 177–8; in thirty glorious years, 176–81; *See also* social welfare
Wendat peoples, 17, 19–20, 22, 23–5, 49
wet-nursing, 31
whalers and pre-settlement contact, 17
Whitton, Charlotte, 146
widows, 37–9, 61; rights, 71, 96, 99–100
women: in baby boom period, 162–3; in British North America, 68, 69; and food prices, 161; in French settler period, 38–9, 40–1; in Great War, 128, 129, 130–1; and homesteading, 119; and household appliances, 159; and immigration policy, 120–1, 174–5; impact of divorce, 197–8; in marriage, 61; maternalist arguments, 161, 164; migration, 28–31, 33; postwar militancy, 161; property legislation, 38, 60, 99–100, 197; as single parent, 201–2; and social movements, 190–1; and vote, 71, 96, 103–4, 128; *See also* gender; Indigenous women
women and work: in baby boom, 163; in Great Depression, 140–1; Indigenous and racialized women, 175; in Industrial Revolution, 82, 86–7, 91; by married women and mothers, 149–51, 163, 173–6; migration for, 80; salary and wages, 174–5; in Second World War, 149–51; unionized work and strike, 174
Women's Liberation Movement (WLM), 190
work: breadwinner ideology, 86, 162–3, 218; children and youth, 75, 83–5, 87–8; corporal punishment of children, 84–5; domestic work, 75–6, 86–9, 139, 173, 216, 218; and elderly, 211–12; and Fordism, 158; in Great Depression, 137–40; in Great War, 129–31, 132; hours of work, 83, 84; and immigration, 169, 174–5, 218; and Indigenous peoples, 77–9, 175; in Industrial Revolution, 75–6, 77–9, 83–5, 87–8; labour force in 21st century, 209; and migration, 80–2; as process or routine, 76; and religious symbols, 219; in Second World War, 149, 151; by women (*see* women and work); *See also* division of labour; salary and wages
workplaces in Industrial Revolution, 75–6, 83, 85, 86–9
Young, William and Lila, 146–7
youth: activism and protest, 183; courts for, 107–8; culture in thirty glorious years, 181–4, 189–90; and delinquency, 105, 106–8; and education, 181–2; life with parents, 207–8, 212–14; subcultures and countercultures, 182–4; work in Industrial Revolution, 75, 83–5, 87–8; *See also* children; teenagers